From Nurturing the Nation to

WEIMAR AND NAZI FAMILY POLICY, 1918–1945

Fearing that the future of the nation was at stake following the First World War, German policymakers vastly expanded social welfare programs to shore up women and families. Just over a decade later, the Nazis seized control of the state and created a radically different, racially driven gender and family policy. This book explores Weimar and Nazi policy to highlight the fundamental, far-reaching change wrought by the Nazis and the disparity between national family policy design and its implementation at the local level. Relying on a broad range of sources – including court records, sterilization files, church accounts, and women's oral histories – it demonstrates how local officials balanced the benefits of marriage, divorce, and adoption against budgetary concerns, church influence, and their own personal beliefs. Throughout both eras, individual Germans collaborated with, rebelled against, and evaded state mandates, in the process fundamentally altering the impact of national policy.

Michelle Mouton is assistant professor of history at the University of Wisconsin, Oshkosh. She received her Ph.D. from the University of Minnesota in 1997. She is the recipient of the Fritz Stern Prize awarded by the German Historical Institute for the best dissertation in German History, on which this book is based. She has published articles in *Central European History Journal*, the *Journal of Women's History*, and the *History Workshop Journal*.

"Since the 1980s the history of the Third Reich has been entirely rewritten as the history of the Holocaust and the racial state. Less widely appreciated is the equally far-reaching impact of women's history. First during a time of recurring crisis, political polarization, and unbounded hopes, and then under a regime of unparalleled coerciveness and ideological ambition, biopolitical questions involving family, reproduction, and the placement of women in the imagined moral-political order moved to the centerground of politics in early twentieth-century Germany. In a salutary reminder of the radicalism of the right-wing assault on Weimar welfarism, Michelle Mouton delivers an excellent guide to the Nazi counter-ideal of a racially driven familial state."

– Geoff Eley, University of Michigan

"Mouton's fascinating book is path breaking along numerous dimensions. It offers the first comprehensive and comparative account of Weimar and National Socialist family policy. Its evidence and analysis move gracefully between the national level of policy, laws, and regulation and the regional one of implementation, looking in detail at developments in Westphalia. It is based on an extraordinary range of carefully analyzed sources that allow Mouton to illuminate not only the responses to state policy of social workers, physicians, and judges but also ordinary Westphalians. In documenting the myriad ways in which non-Jewish Germans, especially women, maneuvered within and around Nazi family policies, it provides an unusual window onto everyday lives and attitudes, while always setting these individual responses within the framework of National Socialism's racist ideology, politics, and war."

– Donna Harsch, Carnegie Mellon University

PUBLICATIONS OF THE GERMAN HISTORICAL INSTITUTE
WASHINGTON, D.C.

WEIMAR AND NAZI FAMILY POLICY, 1918–1945

Edited by Christof Mauch
with the assistance of David Lazar

The German Historical Institute is a center for advanced study and research whose purpose is to provide a permanent basis for scholarly cooperation among historians from the Federal Republic of Germany and the United States. The Institute conducts, promotes, and supports research into both American and German political, social, economic, and cultural history; into transatlantic migration, especially in the nineteenth and twentieth centuries; and into the history of international relations, with special emphasis on the roles played by the United States and Germany.

Recent books in the series:

Hubert Zimmermann, *Money and Security: Troops, Monetary Policy, and West Germany's Relations with the United States and Britain, 1950–1971*

Roger Chickering and Stig Förster, editors, *The Shadows of Total War: Europe, East Asia, and the United States, 1919–1939*

Richard J. Bessel and Dirk Schumann, editors, *Life after Death: Approaches to a Cultural and Social History of Europe During the 1940s and 1950s*

Marc Flandreau, Carl-Ludwig Holtfrerich, and Harold James, editors, *International Financial History in the Twentieth Century: System and Anarchy*

Andreas W. Daum, Lloyd C. Gardner, and Wilfried Mausbach, editors, *The Vietnam War and the World: International and Comparative Perspectives*

Detlef Junker, editor, *The United States and Germany in the Era of the Cold War: A Handbook*, 2 volumes

Roger Chickering, Stig Förster, and Bernd Greiner, editors, *A World at Total War: Global Conflict and the Politics of Destruction, 1937–1945*

Kiran Klaus Patel, *Soldiers of Labor: Labor Service in Nazi Germany and New Deal America, 1933–1945*

Peter Becker and Richard F. Wetzell, editors, *Criminals and Their Scientists: The History of Criminology in International Perspective*

From Nurturing the Nation to Purifying the Volk

WEIMAR AND NAZI FAMILY POLICY, 1918–1945

MICHELLE MOUTON
University of Wisconsin, Oshkosh

GERMAN HISTORICAL INSTITUTE
Washington, D.C.
and

CAMBRIDGE
UNIVERSITY PRESS

CAMBRIDGE UNIVERSITY PRESS
Cambridge, New York, Melbourne, Madrid, Cape Town, Singapore, São Paulo, Delhi

Cambridge University Press
32 Avenue of the Americas, New York, NY 10013-2473, USA

www.cambridge.org
Information on this title: www.cambridge.org/9780521145749

First published 2007
First paperback edition 2009

Printed in the United States of America

A catalog record for this publication is available from the British Library.

Library of Congress Cataloging in Publication Data

Mouton, Michelle
From nurturing the nation to purifying the Volk : Weimar and Nazi family policy,
1918–1945 / Michelle Mouton.
p. cm. – (Publications of the German Historical Institute)
Includes bibliographical references.
ISBN 0-521-86184-5 (hardback)
1. Family policy – Germany – History. 2. Family – Services for – Germany – History.
I. Title. II. Series.
HV700.G3M68   2007
306.850943–dc22   2006010325

ISBN 978-0-521-86184-7 hardback
ISBN 978-0-521-14574-9 paperback

This book is for my children,
Kirsten and Bjorn,
And for the memory of my father,
David Lynn Mouton (1932–1986)

Contents

Acknowledgments

Since I began working on this project, I have looked forward to thanking all the people whose time, energy, knowledge, and enthusiasm have helped to shape and sustain this endeavor. My graduate advisor, Mary Jo Maynes, has supported me as a mentor, friend, and colleague for more than a decade. Her decisive and insightful questions and advice from the beginning through to the final drafts have been invaluable. Eric Weitz was a forceful advocate for textual clarity, brevity, and historiography in my writing. His time, energy, and critiques during the (now many) writing stages were always generously offered.

In Germany I had the good fortune to find several people who helped in immeasurable ways to improve my research and make my life happier. Leopold Schütte at the Münster Staatsarchiv shared his house, his family, and his bountiful knowledge of the German archives. He also acted as my guardian angel in the face of arbitrary archival rules and closed files. Countless evenings were spent reframing my questions to broaden the possible angles for research. Not only did this make my stay in Germany a pleasure, but it enriched my archival base and sharpened my thinking. Brigitte Wieman, in Detmold, kept my spirits high and, with her connections to the local population, opened many doors for my interviews. My host family from my Fulbright year, the Aleffs, continue to provide stimulating conversation and tremendous hospitality whenever I am in Berlin. Eberhard, who consistently provided constructive criticism about this work, has also brought history to life through his unique and fascinating walking tours of Berlin. Katrin deserves special thanks for the many times she shared her apartment space with me. Christa Schütte housed me on a return visit and helped me celebrate the discovery of the doctors' files.

I am grateful for the generous financial support from the German Academic Exchange Service that enabled me to spend the necessary time in

Germany to complete this detailed local study. I am also thankful for travel money and time off from teaching provided by research grants from the University of Minnesota, the University of Northern Iowa, and the University of Wisconsin, Oshkosh. The German Historical Institute honored the dissertation and aided its revision into book form in myriad ways.

Many archivists in state, regional, and local archives assisted me in my research. I thank in particular the staff in the Bundesarchive branches in Potsdam and Koblenz and the Staatsarchive in Münster and Detmold (especially Herr Bucholtz). The staff in the city archives in Bielefield, Minden, Münster, and Paderborn, as well as the Landschaftsverbandarchiv, Bistumsarchiv Münster, and the Archiv Evangelische Frauenhilfe, were always helpful. Herr Schmale in the Dortmund Landgericht deserves special thanks for having saved the documents on which my analysis of divorce is based. I also thank the many German women who in interviews shared their life stories with me. Though they remain anonymous to the reader, each one opened a window onto her unique experiences and reflections and contributed in an essential way to the writing of this book.

Conversations with scholars on both sides of the Atlantic also helped me design and carry out this project. I would especially like to thank Gabrielle Czarnowski, Karen Hagemann, Christine Eifert, and Dagmar Reese for their time and advice. Donna Harsch's detailed and challenging questions sent me back to the archives to convert the dissertation into a book. I thank Ann Taylor Allen and Dorothee Wierling, my Cambridge readers, who each provided astute and helpful comments. Birgitte Søland's insightful reading and comments, together with her personal support, helped throughout the process. Beginning with my first research proposals, Helena Pohlandt-McCormick has been with me the entire way, providing intellectual and emotional support.

Many colleagues and friends provided enthusiasm, encouragement, and support along the way: Franca Barricelli, Anne Callahan, Nancy Isenberg, Ana Maria Kapelusz-Poppi, Lisa Heinemann, Ruth-Ellen Joeres, Barbara Laslett, J. Kim Munholland, Susannah Smith, Ann Waltner, and Leigh Ann Wheeler. Without their friendship and support my life would be less rich and this book would have been the poorer.

This book also received critical aid in the production stages. Above all my thanks go to Lewis Bateman for identifying this manuscript as worthy of publication and putting me in touch with Ruth Homrighaus, who copyedited the text. David Lazar and his staff at the German Historical Institute turned a keen eye to make the text better. Alexander Mouton and Randall Bytwerk assisted with the photographs.

Two other people deserve special thanks. My mother, Janice Mouton, has never wavered in her confidence in my abilities or her interest in the directions they take me. She has taken on extraordinary grandmotherly responsibilities, which enabled me to work both at home and abroad. Our conversations about German history have been enlivening and have been critical in shaping this book and in making me who I am. Finally, I owe Erik Schoff, my husband, the greatest thanks. He is a determined editor who is now frighteningly familiar with the text. He has lived with this project since its origin and has provided love, humor, support, and an endless supply of encouragement that made this project both possible and enjoyable.

Abbreviations

BGB	German Civil Code, *Bürgerliches Gesetzbuch*
BDF	Federation of German Women's Organizations, Bund Deutsche Frauenvereine
BDM	League of German Girls, Bund Deutscher Mädel
BfM	Federation for the Protection of Mothers, Bund Deutscher Mütterschutz
DDP	German Democratic Party, Deutsche Demokratische Partei
DNVP	German National People's Party, Deutschnationale Volkspartei
DVP	German People's Party, Deutsche Volkspartei
EFH	Protestant Women's Aid Society, Evangelische Frauenhilfe
GEG	Marriage Law for Greater Germany, *Groß Deutsches Ehegesetz*
HJ	Hitler Youth, Hitler-Jugend
KPD	Communist Party of Germany, Kommunistische Partei Deutschlands
NSDAP	National Socialist German Workers' Party, Nationalsozialistische Deutsche Arbeiterpartei
NSF	National Socialist Women's Organization, Nationalsozialistische Frauen Organization
NSV	National Socialist People's Welfare Organization, Nationalsozialistische Volkswohlfahrt
RBdKR	Reich League of Child Rich Families, Reichsbund der kinderreichen Familien
RJWG	Reich Youth Welfare Law, *Reichsjugendwohlfahrtsgesetz*
RMD	Reich Mother Service, Reichsmütterdienst
SA	Nazi "Storm Front," Sturmabteilung

SD	Security Service, Sicherheitsdienst
Sopade	Executive Committee of the Social Democratic Party in Exile
SPD	Social Democratic Party of Germany, Sozialdemokratische Partei Deutschlands
SS	Nazi Paramilitary Organization, Schatzstafel
USPD	Independent Socialist Party of Germany, Unabhängige Sozialdemokratische Partei Deutschlands
VFV	Patriotic Women's Association, Vaterländische Frauenverein

Introduction

When Lina E., a maid, gave birth to her daughter Martha in 1922, the man she identified as the father denied paternity, and Lina began motherhood without any financial support. When Langenholzhausen city authorities discovered that Lina was virtually penniless, Martha's guardian took the case to court, whereupon the court ordered August K., a bricklayer, to pay child support. For sixteen years, the court, together with the youth department and Martha's state-appointed guardian, ensured that August paid and that Lina and Martha received economic assistance.[1]

At a Mother's Day celebration in Detmold, Frau Brielmann received the bronze Honorary Cross for German Mothers. Her award, the highest honor given to women under National Socialism, came after a close investigation of her mothering skills, her racial background, and her family's "worthiness." During the meal that followed the distribution of the crosses, Frau Brielmann told the women at her table, "They should have given me the means to stop bearing children instead of the award." Local Nazi authorities, offended by this remark, began an investigation seeking grounds to revoke Frau Brielmann's Honorary Cross.[2]

Herr Neske, a soldier, returned from the Russian front to discover that his exhausted wife had been strained to the limits caring for their two young daughters in war-torn Detmold. He turned to the local National Socialist authorities for help. Not long thereafter, Frau Neske spent six weeks in a resort on the North Sea coast at the state's expense, while the local Nazi women's organization made sure her children were cared for.[3]

---

1 Staatsarchiv Detmold (StaD), D23 Hohenhausen, 523.
2 Applications for Mother Crosses, StaD, L80 IC, Gruppe 24, Fach 11, 40a.
3 Frau Neske, interview. All personal names of individuals not in public positions have been changed to protect the identity of the speakers.

1

These three women, each with a different story and a different social situation, all reaped the benefits of German state officials' desire to support families. Their distinct experiences reflect the ambiguity associated with the politically, economically, and ideologically driven transformation of the relationship between the German state and families as the Weimar era gave way to the National Socialist era between the years 1918 and 1945. The almost unanimous belief of state leaders and Germans from all walks of life that the German family faced profound troubles induced concern and action at the national and local levels. Only by reinvigorating the family, Germans believed, could they could restore their embattled nation. Heightened concern for the family prompted government officials to develop an array of programs that offered women and children education, financial support, and medical aid. At the same time, families felt their privacy threatened as state policy empowered ever more legal, medical, welfare, and educational authorities to intervene directly and indirectly into family life.

Lina E., the maid, entered the court system – and the youth department's jurisdiction – during the period of the Weimar Republic (1918–1932), Germany's first democracy, which was spawned by the revolution at the end of the First World War. In 1918, reeling from the war and the subsequent revolution, Germans faced not only high mortality rates but also hunger, the destruction of physical property, and a deep sense of loss. The cataclysmic demographic, political, economic, and cultural shifts associated with modernization altered people's understanding of the world in which they lived and exacerbated their feelings of insecurity. The "rationalization" and mechanization of industry restructured the labor force. Mass consumption and mass media drew Germans together across class lines as never before, even as income differences persisted and deepened. Gender roles were acutely disrupted by the so-called New Woman who stepped out of the confines of domesticity, rejecting patriarchal authority and prewar morality. In the face of these changes, German lawmakers made strengthening German families central to their project of rebuilding postwar Germany. Despite deep ideological divisions that influenced the way lawmakers understood the problems threatening families, they all shared a strong commitment to the provision of state services to families. Even through the cycles of inflation and depression that devastated the German economy between 1918 and 1932, legislators struggled to shore up families. For Lina and her daughter Martha, the state's interest in families took the form of a court-appointed guardian whose responsibility it was to ensure that she received child support from Martha's biological father.

Frau Brielmann received her Mother Cross at a time when the Nazi leadership had silenced the political cacophony of Weimar's parliamentary democracy and replaced it with an ideologically driven family policy that had race at its center. The racialist thinking intrinsic to Nazism had important implications for family policy. Nazi leaders believed that the "degeneration" of the German *Volk* had its roots in a deadly combination of foreign influences, including communism, feminism, modernism, and, above all, racial mixing. Consequently, Hitler sought to return Germany to its previous glory by instituting a forceful racial policy designed to strengthen the *Volk*. In contrast to Weimar lawmakers, who struggled to balance the liberal commitment to the privacy and sanctity of families with a countervailing willingness to deploy the state's interventionist potential, Nazi policymakers explicitly and unreservedly elevated the state's purported needs above those of the individual, profoundly altering the relationship between the state and families. Pronatalism assumed a new, more aggressive form as Nazi policy enrolled myriad professionals – including physicians, judges, social workers, teachers, welfare and youth department employees, mayors, and party members – in the project of policing families.

During the Second World War, Nazi family policy, like other aspects of the Nazi project, was altered to accommodate wartime exigencies. Nazi leaders found that wartime reality conflicted with their efforts to fulfill their racial and pronatalist aims. Their struggle to raise (or even sustain) the birthrate and to keep morale high conflicted with a daily reality in which more and more men were called away to serve in the military and domestic living conditions worsened. Frau Neske's resort vacation resulted from the wartime shift in policy. Although she had only two children (prior to the war, the prerequisite had been four), the local National Socialist authorities felt that the peace of mind of her soldier husband should take precedence over the strict enforcement of pronatalist and racial guidelines. They therefore granted Frau Neske a recuperative holiday despite her small family and without the requisite health examination. Throughout the war, policymakers explicitly revised programs in this way in order to counter flagging morale – or were forced to do so when the war made adaptation unavoidable.

Just as economic and political circumstances affected family policy in the Weimar and Nazi periods, local implementation, too, changed the character and effects of family policy in Germany. Examining the implementation of family policy at the local level reveals that during both the Weimar and Nazi eras, people at every level collaborated with, rebelled against, and maneuvered around the state's dictates regarding families. When women found state programs personally beneficial, they often served as willing allies in supporting and promoting them. When they perceived state policies to be against their interests, however, they were quite capable of challenging, evading, or otherwise manipulating them for their own personal benefit, and in so doing they frequently undermined policy aims. Women were often persistent in their demands that state officials accommodate their needs. Some, like Frau Brielmann, publicly challenged the fundamental goals of policy. Others, like Frau Neske, reaped the benefits of expanding state policy.

Moreover, families and bureaucrats at all levels engaged with each other. Even as science promulgated a clearer definition of good parenting, Weimar welfare and youth department authorities sometimes hesitated to use this definition to intervene in family matters. Whereas some doctors enthusiastically endorsed Nazi racial policy before it became codified in law, others failed to comply even after the law had been enacted. During both the Weimar and Nazi eras, the interplay among policymakers, local authorities, and German families had a moderating impact on family policy and in particular tempered the radical transformation of the family the National Socialists sought to effect after 1933.

WEIMAR GERMANY AND FAMILY UPHEAVAL

Founded amid the chaos of a lost war, Germany's first parliamentary government set out to reconstruct German society. Politicians on the Left and Right battled over the appropriate course for the future of the country. Because they did not agree on economic, foreign, or domestic policy, they fought over nearly every legislative issue. Yet beneath this disharmony lay a belief shared across the political spectrum that German national restoration depended on the government's supporting and encouraging family life. Wartime conditions had eroded the family as a site of economic provision, security, and stability. The deaths of more than 1.6 million men in the war, permanently disrupted the lives of many German families. The birthrate, which fell to an all-time low of 14 per 1,000 during 1916–1917, failed to return to prewar levels throughout the 1920s. Together with war casualties, the low birthrate induced fears among some Germans that they were dying out as a people (*Volkstod*). Furthermore, the war left in its wake close to 600,000 widows and almost 1.2 million war orphans, whose standard of living deteriorated sharply as they became dependent on limited widows' pensions and their single mothers' meager earnings from low-paid work.[4] Even more ominous for the future of the nation, 15 percent of men aged

4 Bessel, *Germany after the First World War*, 225–7.

twenty to forty had been killed, leaving a "surplus" of over 2 million women whose prospects of marriage were dim.[5] Even the dramatic upsurge in the marriage rate immediately after the war to 14.5 per thousand in 1920, up from 4.2 per 1,000 in 1915–1916 – a result of both the wartime postponement of marriages and the desire of many men and women to reestablish "home" after the war ended – did not quell widespread fears of societal crisis. This was in part because the divorce rate, which had averaged 24.6 per 100,000 between 1909 and 1913, rose to a record high of 62.9 in 1921. Illegitimacy rates, too, were on the rise, underscoring for many how far societal morality had strayed from prewar standards. As one Christian Conservative delegate to the Prussian *Landtag* (state parliament) put it, the most important task facing the new regime was to heal "the corrosive, nearly incurable ills" that had befallen the German people, which were those "predominantly caused by the fact that our *Volk* no longer has a healthy family life."[6]

In light of this, it is perhaps not surprising that many Germans, including politicians from all parties, feared that the German family, the only institution they deemed capable of stabilizing and restoring German society, might not be equal to the task without substantial help. In particular, paternal authority, widely viewed as the essential core of families, needed to be shored up. In some families, women had grown restless in their roles as traditional wives and mothers and thus resisted the reestablishment of paternal authority. In others, men fortunate enough to survive the war returned with physical and emotional wounds that prevented them from reasserting themselves as patriarchs. Many Germans associated the absence of paternal authority with rising juvenile crime rates and the proliferation of antisocial youth gangs. Although the claim that the war had destroyed patriarchy is exaggerated, there is no doubt that many families had been shaken to the core.[7] Reestablishing families and fathers' place in them thus assumed a position of primary importance in the postwar period. Chief among the perceived obstacles was the matter of women's work. Of the more than 2 million women who had entered the labor market to boost the war economy, many resisted returning to their domestic roles after 1918.[8] Returning soldiers complained that women's continued employment made it more difficult for them to find work and prevented a restoration of the prewar patriarchal family structure.

---

5 These figures come from the 1925 census and are cited in Grossmann, *Reforming Sex*, 6.
6 Bronisch, *Verhandlungen des Preussischen Landtags* 51, Sitzung 19 September 1919, cols. 4098–4100, quoted in Hong, *Welfare, Modernity*, 56.
7 Domansky, "Militarization and Reproduction."
8 Women's employment rose 17 percent between 1914 and 1918. Rouette, "Mothers and Citizens," 52.

As a result, politicians across the political spectrum envisioned a "peaceful and harmonious society" based on the "patriarchal principle": soldiers and "women of the war" (*Kriegerfrauen*) would become, respectively, "providers and mothers."[9] No one imagined that this process would be easy. As early as 1916, Gustav Stresemann, a delegate for the German People's Party (Deutsche Volkspartei, DVP) and future Reich chancellor, predicted that the crucial task of removing women from the labor force "could not be carried out without hardship, since the women who have grown accustomed to high wages and independent work [would] naturally not always return to the old circumstances smoothly and voluntarily." Rather than shy away from the problem, however, he emphasized the importance of tackling this "enormous task."[10] One year later, Catholic Center Party (Zentrum) member Hans Bell clarified the point by declaring that since returning soldiers could not be expected to tolerate unemployment, women's "dismissals" were "the law of the hour."[11] In March 1919, a demobilization bill was decreed that called for the removal of women from veterans' jobs. Even the Social Democrats (Sozialdemokratische Partei Deutschland, SPD), whose prewar program had touted employment as the road to women's emancipation, abandoned their platform in light of returning soldiers' need for jobs.[12] Only a small group of six female legislators from four different parties protested the hardship that demobilization would cause working women.[13]

While government-organized demobilization committees worked to reintegrate returning soldiers into the labor market and relegate women to the home, Reichstag politicians set out to create policy that would ameliorate the social chaos of postwar German society. They tried to shore up families by enshrining in the constitution the preservation of marriage and "the maintenance of the purity and health of family, and public support for the family" (Art. 119).[14] Despite unanimous agreement that the state had a responsibility to protect and strengthen families, great disparities existed in the way politicians conceptualized the family itself, the problems facing families, and the appropriate role for the state. At the heart of the matter lay a fundamental disagreement about what caused families' distress: theories ranged from women's rejection of domesticity and the war to industrialization, rising immorality, and the decreasing influence of the church.

---

9 Rouette, *Sozialpolitik als Geschlechterpolitik*, 41.
10 Zeller, "Demobilmachung und Geschlechtspezifische Arbeitsteilung," 282.
11 Ibid.
12 Sneeringer, *Winning Women's Votes*, 67.
13 The women came from the DNVP, Center, DVP, and SPD parties. Ibid., 28.
14 Quoted in Peukert, *Weimar Republic*, 131.

Nor did politicians hold a monopoly on explanations of what troubled families. Throughout the Weimar era, myriad interest groups, from feminists to morality leagues, entered the debates, sometimes siding with specific political parties and at other times straddling political lines in support of specific platforms. Because each interpretation of what troubled the family reflected a particular vision of Germany, debates over many legislative proposals were characterized by bitter conflict. Attempts to formulate and implement family policy during the Weimar era failed repeatedly for lack of consensus on what to do about benefits for large families, contraception, abortion, counseling for engaged couples, and a variety of other issues.

At the crux of many family policy disagreements lay the question of proper gender roles. Members of the right-wing German National People's Party (Deutschnationale Volkspartei, DNVP) believed that the high mortality rate during the war, the low birthrate, and what they saw as the spread of immorality at all levels of society undermined national rejuvenation and threatened the German race. They asserted that German women's refusal to fulfill their "biologically destined" role as mothers – in conjunction with men's failure to establish themselves as patriarchs – posed a dire threat to German society. The DNVP rejected arguments about the benefits of modernity and supported a return to more traditional gender roles.[15] Catholic Center Party delegates also attributed the modernist struggle for women's rights to pure egoism and called for women to "apply maternal self-sacrifice to the wounds of war and arrest the moral decline stemming from blockade and revolution."[16] Together, the DNVP and Center Party supported legislation to increase penalties for abortion and prostitution, forbid contraception, and restrict the accessibility of divorce.

This legislation was strongly opposed by the liberal parties. Following lines developed for the middle-class women's movement before the war, the German People's Party and the German Democratic Party (Deutsche Demokratische Partei, DDP) maintained that the stability of the nation depended on women's active political participation and called for equal wages for women. Members of these parties argued that although women and men had interests and needs that were fundamentally different, the sexes were nonetheless to be regarded as equal in value. Consistent with these views of gender complementarity, they argued that women should limit themselves "to female work" where their "motherly 'essence' could blossom." Employment in nursing, teaching, and social work, for example, enabled women to practice and teach motherliness and domesticity. A 1928

15 Usborne, *Politics of the Body*, 34.   16 Sneeringer, *Winning Women's Votes*, 37.

DVP flyer emphasized that "the model woman served *Volk* and fatherland by bringing the values she personified in the home – silent devotion and selfless love – to the public."[17] Liberal politicians agreed with their right-wing counterparts that not all modern influences on women were good. Although the DVP and DDP fought for sexual equality before the law and in education, they worried that divorce reform and legal abortion would discourage women from becoming mothers.

In their own legislative proposals, Social Democratic Party delegates rejected arguments about faltering morality, asserting instead that the disruption of families and the falling birthrate stemmed primarily from the social upheaval caused by war and the bitter hardships that industrialization caused the working classes. Although Socialists, too, believed that motherhood constituted women's highest calling, they championed women's equality, fought for better wages for women, and forced a women's suffrage bill through parliament. They believed that by supporting mothers and infants, providing adequate housing, and improving health care for all Germans, the state could ameliorate the stark class divisions that plagued German society, giving women the strength and confidence to choose motherhood. Though the SPD's pronatalist message resembled that of more conservative parties, its consistent support of women's equality and voluntary motherhood was fundamentally different.

On the far left, the Communist Party (Kommunistische Partei Deutschlands, KPD) was alone in rejecting the idea that a woman's natural role was that of wife and mother. Communist delegates consistently argued for women's right to work and to earn higher wages, both of which they considered essential to strengthening families. They scorned the traditional household, which they saw as a bourgeois institution, and advocated instead collective kitchens and day care to free women from domestic burdens. They also – in theory at least – opposed the double burden on many women to work both outside and inside the home, since it prevented women's active political participation as comrades. The KPD, more than any other party, championed the revision of the laws limiting access to contraception and banning abortion.

Working within these political parties, women shared their own opinions about gender roles. Beginning with their forceful protest of the extreme hardship caused by the Demobilization Acts, they asserted their presence on the political landscape. Though an increasing number of women were elected to the Reichstag, they did not always agree among themselves about

17 Ibid., 137.

what best reflected women's interests. Women on the right and center, who saw motherhood, not employment, as women's proper role, did not support the radical demands of their Socialist and Communist sisters for improved working conditions and equal pay. On some issues, however, especially those that dealt with maternal and child protection, female delegates did tend to work together across party lines.[18]

Women's organizations also actively organized to strengthen German families and society. On the right, members of the Federal Organization of Protestant Women's Groups (Vereinigung Evangelischer Frauenverbände) disapproved of all suspected modern influences on gender, scorned women's suffrage because it forced women into roles inappropriate to their "life calling," and even attacked the act of voting, which they believed exacerbated the blurring of women's and men's roles. These Protestant women also resisted any reform of divorce or liberalization of abortion that would sully "the dignity and honor of women" (*die Würde und Ehre der Frauen*).[19] In the Federation of German Women's Organizations (Bund Deutscher Frauenvereine, BDF), an umbrella organization of women's groups, women sought to unite across political parties in the name of "organized motherhood." Their 1919 program declared that "The purity of family life is . . . the basic condition of social health and national fitness."[20] The women of the BDF believed they could conquer the immoral influences within society – prostitution, pornography, abortion, and venereal disease – even as they resisted both the birth control movement and the eugenic movement that justified it.[21] By the 1920s, however, the BDF, whose membership primarily represented an older generation – and its conservative elements at that – spoke for an ever smaller number of women. While the BDF leadership decried the problems created by the New Woman, who supposedly shunned motherhood, many young bourgeois and Social Democratic women acknowledged and even applauded Weimar's independent young women.[22] This social, cultural, and generational division influenced women's support of legislative proposals. Whereas older women argued that married mothers should be banned from factory work so that they could care for their children, young women more often advocated the establishment of day care. The older generation opposed young women who sought support from the numerous other organizations that fought for women's education, access to birth control, and elective

18 See Stoehr, "Housework and Motherhood," 228.
19 Kaufmann, "Die Begründung und Politik," 384.
20 Evans, *Feminist Movement*, 236.
21 Ann Taylor Allen, "Feminism and Eugenics," 491–2.
22 See Usborne, "New Woman."

motherhood. Doctors, health experts, feminists, and members of the international birth control league, which was politically allied with the SPD and
KPD, brought new perspectives to bear on questions of reproduction and
motherhood. Sex reformers established birth control and sex advice counseling centers "that took as their motto 'better to prevent than to abort.'"[23]
The League for the Protection of Motherhood and Family Hygiene (Liga
für Mutterschutz und Familien Hygiene) worked to provide working-class
women with more control over motherhood and to improve health conditions for both mothers and children.

Policy formulation in the Weimar Republic was impeded not only by disagreements over appropriate gender roles but also by disagreements over the
state's right to intervene in families. As the application of science, medicine,
and technology to social policy expanded the potential for state intervention, Social Democrats and Communists eagerly advocated applying this
new knowledge. They envisioned a comprehensive social welfare program
that went well beyond providing material support and involved intervention
"in all aspects of family life including health, sexuality, child-rearing, and
education to help create an 'orderly family.'"[24] These politicians on the Left
believed that reviving German society depended on monitoring families in
their everyday lives, and they were willing to grant state agents from the
welfare and youth departments greater access to families even before clear
signs of trouble had developed. In contrast, many conservative politicians
and religious leaders worried that intensive intervention would ultimately
destroy the very families it sought to help. They feared that the generous
state benefits advocated by Socialists and Communists would make families
dependent on the state and erode the masculine independence so critical to
notions of citizenship. They contended that state intervention in the family, even in the name of child welfare, threatened a father's authority over
his children and diminished parental responsibility. The Christian welfare
organizations – the Catholic Caritas and the Protestant Inner Mission – also
opposed such "godless" and "worldly socialist influences" (*weltlich sozialistische Einflüsse*) in families, arguing that "civil society had the duty to protect and foster the family, but by no means [the right] to absorb it and the
individual, or to substitute itself for them."[25]

Because individual families tended to avoid state-sponsored efforts at
social discipline even when they were designed with an eye to social benefit,

23 Grossmann, *Reforming Sex*, 15.   24 Weitz, *Creating German Communism*, 110.
25 Crew, "Eine Elternschaft zu Dritt," 269; Hong, *Welfare, Modernity*, 82.

resistance to a policy of intervention was not limited to conservative politi-cians and the churches. To be sure, the burgeoning ranks of social workers increased individualized scrutiny of families. As they intervened more directly into households, their middle-class backgrounds not infrequently caused them to see working-class families in a negative light.[26] Through-out the Weimar era, the relationship between state agents and the families they sought to assist remained volatile, and many families found the state's increased supervision invasive. Families sometimes resented even educa-tion and preventive care when it occurred in combination with disciplinary efforts. As historian Eric Weitz has demonstrated, "Often, the 'clients' defi-antly rejected such interventions."[27]

A third powerful influence on family policy design – also based in the "new science" – was a eugenic orientation already apparent during the pre-war period and clearly influential in Weimar family policy.[28] In the context of postwar social chaos, a broad coalition of public administrators, health officials, welfare advocates, the Catholic and Protestant churches, Social Democrats, Communists, and ultra-right-wing nationalists joined together "to promote 'valuable' and discourage 'valueless' life." Before the war, gov-ernment officials had largely ignored the eugenics movement, but the social disruption associated with military defeat prompted many politicians to feel "they could no longer afford to exclude eugenics from official policy."[29] New organizations like the German League for Regeneration and Heredity (Deutscher Bund für Volksaufartung und Erbkunde) flourished and pro-moted public eugenic education. "Racial hygiene" even became a new and respected field of study at the universities.[30]

But whereas supporters of racial hygiene generally agreed that "there was a 'hierarchy of human worth'" and that restoring Germany "demanded the subordination of the individual to the community[,] or the *Volk*," they often vehemently disagreed about how to translate this belief into policy.[31] Some advocates of eugenics believed that by allowing people with weaker constitutions to live, medical progress had destroyed the natural Darwinian

26 See Christoph Sachße, *Mütterlichkeit als Sozialberuf*; and Crew, "Ambiguities of Moderity," 336–44.
27 Weitz, *Creating German Communism*, 114.
28 Whereas doctors and scientists on the political Right tended to favor the term "racial hygiene," those on the Left used "eugenics." According to Paul Weindling, the "racial hygiene movement split between state-supported eugenic research institutes and welfare schemes, and Nordic racism." *Health, Race and German Politics*, 319.
29 Usborne, *Politics of the Body*, 134.
30 Proctor, *Racial Hygiene*, 38.
31 Usborne, *Politics of the Body*, 134. See also Dickinson, "Biopolitics, Fascism, Democracy."

struggle for survival.[32] They also held that "inferior" people's faster reproduction rate underlay the genetic deterioration of the German population.[33]
They argued that eugenics, including compulsory sterilization, differential
medical care, and, in extreme cases, euthanasia, would purge "alien socialist,
democratic and racial elements" so that "a truly Germanic social order could
be realized."[34] But the advocates of such so-called negative eugenics met
stiff resistance from others who rejected compulsory eugenics programs as
contradictory to the democratic principles of the Weimar Republic. They
attributed social degeneration to deteriorating social conditions and advocated welfare-oriented measures, including improved public housing, state-
supported maternal and infant health care, and readily accessible contraception, to improve individual lives and national health. Because these divergent
views could not be reconciled, Weimar legislation remained focused on
health education rather than on more invasive eugenic policies.

As this array of perspectives suggests, concern about the German family was nearly universal during the Weimar Republic, but the divergent
voices both within and outside the government dramatically complicated
the legislative process. Richard Bessel has asserted that in the Weimar period,
"domestic politics could no longer be described as peacetime politics;
German domestic politics after 1918 became an expression of a latent civil
war."[35] Dirk Blasius points to social policy as one of Weimar lawmakers' most important battlefields "because differences of opinion in this area
most directly contributed to the downfall of the Weimar Republic."[36] As
this study demonstrates, although Weimar lawmakers did ultimately create
extensive family-directed legislation, the deep-seated disagreement at the
national and local levels meant that Weimar family policy never assumed a
uniform shape or overcame differences in emphasis.

The ultimate crisis for Weimar family policy occurred in 1929, when the
worldwide depression overwhelmed the government's fragile welfare system.
When unemployment skyrocketed to nearly 25 percent, the economic security of many German families was destroyed. Middle-class daughters joined
working-class women in the workforce, male heads of household lost their
jobs, and wives with unemployed husbands began working to sustain their
families. Ironically, in the face of such upheaval, many blamed women for
overstepping their domestic roles, and the antifeminist backlash fed into

---

32 Weindling, *Health, Race and German Politics*, 341.
33 Proctor, *Racial Hygiene*, 15 n 20.
34 Weindling, *Health, Race and German Politics*, 305.
35 Bessel, *Germany after the First World War*, 262.   36 Blasius, *Ehescheidung in Deutschland*, 164.

right-wing critiques of modernity.[37] The DVP sided with the DNVP and the Catholic Center Party against left-wing efforts to modernize marriage, make birth control more accessible, and expand abortion rights. Married women's employment fueled contentious debates about "double income earners" (*Doppelverdiener*) – women who simultaneously threatened their own husbands' status as breadwinners and relegated other men to unemployment. By 1932, faced with escalating male unemployment nationwide, even DDP delegates downplayed their prior equal rights rhetoric, instead calling homemaking a "career" (*Beruf*) and celebrating women's roles as mothers. And SPD delegates did not protest the attacks on married women's work out of fear that they might offend male party members.[38] The KPD, though it never retreated from defending women's right to work, increasingly shifted its focus from work to leading the campaign for women's right to reproductive freedom.[39] The BDF, for its part, voiced muffled protest, mostly because its member organizations worried that blocking women's work would encourage divorce.[40]

With the onset of the Depression in 1929, the National Socialist German Workers' Party (Nationalsozialistische Deutsche Arbeiterpartei, NSDAP or Nazi Party) became more vocal in criticizing parliamentary democracy for its failure to save German families from peril. Exploiting "the anxieties and resentments of those social groups in Germany that were adversely affected by the process of modernity," Adolf Hitler promised decisive solutions to all of Germany's problems.[41] Hitler located the crisis not only in the German economy but also in German society, and he insisted that only a racially based *Volksgemeinschaft* (national community) could restore Germany to its former greatness. Offering to replace the parliamentary system's confusion with his strong leadership, he proposed abolishing the diversity of opinion and active debate characteristic of the Weimar era in favor of a uniform, coherent, and far-reaching family policy. Nazi leaders "decried a 'perverse' society where healthy women resisted having children because of egoism or the need to work."[42] They promised women "emancipation from emancipation" and called for clear gender role differentiation. Their enthusiastic

---

37 That many observers pointed to women's employment as a sign that relations between the sexes – and families in general – were being undermined was the result of middle-class women's entrance into the labor market, since working-class women had a long history of paid employment. See Kramer, "Frankfurt's Working Women,"

38 Sneeringer, *Winning Women's Votes*, 203.

39 Grossmann, "German Communism and New Women," 144.

40 Sneeringer, *Winning Women's Votes*, 221.

41 Mommsen, *Rise and Fall of Weimar Democracy*, ix.

42 Sneeringer, *Winning Women's Votes*, 135.

endorsement of authoritarianism and their aversion to democracy, together with their call to revive traditional families, appealed to many Germans, including those who had earlier supported the DVP and DNVP, because their program linked the return to a traditional family and gender code to national renewal. Conservative Protestant women, who were "awash in *völkisch* thought" throughout the 1920s, also responded positively to Hitler's *Volksgemeinschaft.*[43]

As fiscal resources grew scarce after 1929, Weimar politicians, local government leaders, and welfare agents all sought ways to decrease state expenditure at exactly the moment when more German families were applying for help. With the rationing of social resources, pressure to apply eugenics to welfare and social policy decisions increased. Advocates of eugenics found it easier than their opponents to argue against the idea that everyone in need deserved state support. Instead, they pointed to "the declining standard of living of the general populace and the increasingly inadequate support provided to the able-bodied unemployed" as evidence that "excessive amounts were being spent on the care of those whom they regarded as unproductive, asocial, and otherwise parasitic groups."[44] Under these circumstances, Albert Grotjahn, a prominent Social Democratic doctor, advocated a "differential distribution" of state benefits that would save scarce resources for the most valued Germans. These early attempts at rationing led doctors and social workers to begin to judge the "caliber" of the people who requested their help.

It is within this context that some historians draw a connection between Weimar social policy during the Depression years and the Nazi policy that followed it. Detlev Peukert, for example, has argued that during the Weimar Republic's crisis years, when "social progress" seemed to stop and social welfare faced "insurmountable obstacles" on every level, "the optimistic, utopian vision of the *Volkskörper* [was] stripped of its universality and . . . instead defined in negative, restrictive terms."[45] Taking a broader view, Cornelia Usborne has emphasized that already during the 1920s the belief in progress had aided in the medicalization of birth control and marriage counseling. She asserts that this was the start of the elevation of the interests of the "race" above those of the individual.[46] The conservative, *völkisch* opinions frequently voiced in Weimar discussions of medicine, social welfare, and health have likewise led Paul Weindling to conclude that the precursors of Nazism were present in the Weimar era. In this study, however, I emphasize that what appears clearly in all analyses of Weimar family policy

---

43 Phayer, *Protestant and Catholic Women,* 47–52.   44 Hong, *Welfare, Modernity,* 241.
45 Peukert, "The Genesis of the Final Solution," 285. 46 Usborne, *Politics of the Body,* 212.

is its ongoing contestation – contestation that was ultimately suppressed only with the Nazi seizure of power in 1933, which brought a new coherence and single-mindedness at the national level.

In shifting focus from national family policy decrees to their implementation at the local level, moreover, this study reveals the profound differences in the reception and impact of Weimar and Nazi policy design. Concurring with Atina Grossmann's study of sex reform, Edward Ross Dickinson's examination of eugenics, and Michael Burleigh's analysis of euthanasia, I argue that although Weimar-era efforts to "normalize" behavior did make it easier for Nazi authorities to intrude into the private sphere to evaluate the worth of individuals, Nazi policy represented a radical departure from anything that preceded it. At no point during the Weimar era was family policy conceived as a uniform top-down code in which the family was clearly state-defined or in which the guidelines for worthiness were delineated; the divergent voices that persisted throughout the Weimar era ensured that family policy issues were publicly contested. At no time did Weimar policymakers claim the right to dictate what the family did: women were encouraged to mother, but they were also granted the right to pursue university studies or employment outside the home. While improving family health did involve state monitoring of families to a greater degree than before, both conservative and liberal politicians maintained the importance of preserving the family. Although the vagaries of implementation sometimes diluted the sharp differences between Weimar and Nazi family policy, this study demonstrates that Nazi policy did not develop continuously or smoothly from that of its Weimar predecessor.

NATIONAL SOCIALISM'S BLUEPRINT FOR FAMILIES

From his first day in office, Hitler claimed that Germany's survival depended on the reversal of the devastating demographic decline, the elimination of class conflict, and the eradication of the contradictions of modern industrial life. At the center of his plan for the restoration of German society was the creation of a *Volksgemeinschaft*, a monolithic, racially pure, and socially cohesive community, which he saw as the antidote to the social ills of the Weimar era. Nazi leaders found widespread support for the creation of a *Volksgemeinschaft* because it "tapped into German traditions that lauded social harmony over conflict and . . . valued hard work, clean living, and law and order."[47] The revolution Hitler launched to create the *Volksgemeinschaft*

---

47 Gellately and Stolzfus, *Social Outsiders*, 4.

dramatically transformed civic, political, and private life as the state assumed a greater presence in every realm.

Upon assuming power, the Nazis initiated a program of *Gleichschaltung* (synchronization or coordination) that aimed to bring all social, political, economic, and cultural institutions under the control of the Nazi Party. Using a three-pronged strategy, the Nazis eliminated, infiltrated, and usurped the membership of organizations that might have served as bases of resistance to the state. During their first six months in power, they destroyed trade unions and banned all political parties except the National Socialist Party. At all other levels of society, they outlawed established organizations and incorporated the members into corresponding National Socialist groups. To bring the civil service into line with the new political leaders, the Law on the Professional Civil Service (7 April 1933) called for the dismissal of all "undesirables," in particular Jews and outspoken Communists, from the ranks of the civil service. By centralizing all authority into a hierarchical party-based system emanating from the Führer (*Führerprinzip*), Hitler planned to create a unified and monolithic society that conformed to National Socialist ideology.[48]

Within the *Volksgemeinschaft*, Hitler believed the state's interests took precedence over the individual's at all levels. Using a blend of medicine, technology, scientific knowledge, and racial policy, the Nazis established the contours of the *Volksgemeinschaft* upon which the new Germany would be based. For members of the *Volksgemeinschaft*, Hitler and his followers initiated a pronatalist and racially based population policy. Hitler, "lauded as the great doctor of the German people,"[49] claimed that "the only genuine 'culture-creating' race, the Aryans, had permitted themselves to be weakened to the point of endangered survival by the 'destroyers of culture,' characterized as the Jew."[50] Geneticists, anthropologists, racial theorists, and members of the medical profession joined forces in the project of rejuvenating the Aryan race. Informed by a lethal combination of social Darwinism and scientific racism, they applied modern technology to separate the worthy from the unworthy. Members of the worthy Aryan race were eligible for membership in the party and specific state-sponsored programs, including state welfare. In sharp contrast, those people who were labeled unworthy found themselves excluded from the *Volksgemeinschaft* and denied all benefits. These included Jews and Gypsies for racial reasons, Communists for political reasons, and the

---

48 The degree to which Nazi policy was monolithic has been widely debated by historians. See, for instance, Broszat, *Hitler State*.
49 Proctor, *Racial Hygiene*, 64.
50 Lifton, *Nazi Doctors*, 16.

"hereditarily ill" (*Erbkrank*) for health reasons. Hereditary illness was broadly defined to encompass physical features such as dwarfism, behaviors such as work-evasion, and medical illnesses such as epilepsy. In sum, any physical feature, activity, or medical condition the Nazis found undesirable could be included in the definition of hereditary illness. Because the Nazis labeled those they deemed unworthy as "enemies of the *Volk*," these individuals became candidates for sterilization and euthanasia. The extent to which the Third Reich sought to prevent the reproduction of certain segments of the population qualified it as an antinatalist state that also supported some pronatalist policies for the "racially pure."[51] As the regime strengthened its grip on power, many of those who were first denied benefits for reasons of race became the victims of genocide.

In order to win support for their racial goals, the Nazis launched a general campaign to educate the German population about race. The National Socialist Office for Enlightenment on Population Policy and Racial Welfare "oversaw an ambitious public relations drive to heighten ethnic consciousness among the general population."[52] Using radio, schooling, posters, and magazines, the Nazis blanketed society with their ideological belief that the members of the *Volk* were a superior people whose very survival stood in jeopardy. The Office for Enlightenment on Population Policy and Racial Welfare, together with the Nuremberg Laws (1935) and other anti-Semitic legislation, helped to popularize the Nazi view that Aryans were fundamentally different from and better than Jews.

In addition to blaming racial illnesses for Germany's demographic decline, Hitler ascribed it to the decadence rampant in German society and the spread of immoral behavior (as evidenced, for example, by the alleged proliferation of homosexuality and the public appearance of the New Woman). Nazi family policy reflected Hitler's pledge to rejuvenate German families by eliminating immorality and restoring patriarchy and traditional familial and moral order. Harking back to an imagined pre-industrial era, Hitler insisted that family policy create jobs for men, restore the patriarchal family so that women could mother, and strengthen the Aryan race. He promised that in the Third Reich every worthy woman would be able to marry and answer her natural calling to bear children.

In Hitler's eyes, class conflict also sapped the German *Volk*'s strength. Nazi ideology maintained that the *Volksgemeinschaft* would eliminate class conflict, though in staking out its boundaries Nazi policymakers replaced class divisions with new social and racial boundaries. The rapid disconnection of

51 Bock, "Antinatalism, Maternity and Paternity."　52 Koonz, *Nazi Conscience*, 106.

status from wealth within many areas of Nazi society led many Germans to believe in the ability of the *Volksgemeinschaft* to eliminate class conflict.[53] But while working-class economic status did not inherently conflict with inclusion in the *Volksgemeinschaft*, the realities of working-class life frequently did. Economic hardship often precluded couples from producing the orderly households and immaculate children Nazi social workers considered ideal. Since employment was a necessity for working-class women, they were unable to attain the Nazi ideal of full-time motherhood. Conversely, unemployment suggested a poor work ethic and could mark an individual as "asocial." Moreover, Weimar labor conditions were bad enough to swell the ranks of the Communist Party, leaving many working-class men and women with a political record that automatically excluded them from the *Volksgemeinschaft*. In contrast, middle-class families, whether politically active or not, found it easier to conform to Nazi family ideals.

Nazi policymakers reinforced their general rhetoric about "healthy" families with specifically targeted propaganda, financial incentives, and honorary programs designed to encourage women to bear children. Their initiatives included an extra tax for bachelors, a tax break for large families, state-sponsored marriage loans contingent upon women leaving the workforce, health clinics to advise and support mothers, the revamping of Mother's Day, and the creation of the Mother Cross to publicly honor worthy German mothers. The new National Socialist People's Welfare Organization (Nationalsozialistisches Volkswohlfahrt, NSV) offered material, financial, and educational advice to "healthy" German women and their families. Along with these positive incentives, however, Nazi family policy contained brutal disincentives and asserted that "'anyone who attempts to curb artificially the natural fertility of the German people [through contraception]' [would] be punished by imprisonment for 'racial treason' [*Rassenverrat*]."[54] During the war, abortion was made a capital offense.

Even after Nazi policymakers had created national, racially based policy decrees, variable local implementation undermined the monolithic policy design intended to create model Aryan families. Individual judges, doctors, and social workers continued to tailor their decisions to reflect communal needs and their own personal bias, even after public discussion had been silenced. Moreover, individual Germans' responses, which were even more varied, also weakened state policy; they reveal that, at least in their personal lives, ordinary Germans were neither fully won over by National Socialism

53 Frei, "People's Community and War," 64; Schoenbaum, *Hitler's Social Revolution*.
54 Proctor, *Racial Hygiene*, 121.

nor thoroughly paralyzed by the Nazi state. Rather, on a mostly individual basis, they challenged policy decisions that threatened their families while demonstrating a great degree of complicity in the state's implementation of its brutal policies against those outside the *Volksgemeinschaft*.

METHODOLOGY

Westphalia

Understanding how national policy affected individual lives requires a microhistorical approach only possible in a local study. This study of family policy, which focuses on Westphalia, follows in the footsteps of other local and regional studies that have illuminated such dimensions of Weimar and Nazi history as how welfare was distributed,[55] how the Gestapo functioned,[56] and how small-town social and political life adapted to National Socialism.[57] It is based on the premise that examining areas outside Berlin, where archival collections are better preserved than they are in the capital, can tell us much about the impact of both Weimar democracy and National Socialism on German society.

During both the Weimar and National Socialist eras, Westphalia was dominated by heavy industry in the south, textile production in the north, and agriculture in the east, while the economy in its major city of Münster was based largely on civil service administration. The population of the state, 4.8 million in 1925, was divided almost equally between Catholics and Protestants, with a small, relatively stable Jewish population.[58] The regional boundaries of Westphalia, traditionally a Prussian state, varied between 1918 and 1945. The Nazis divided Westphalia into two "*Gaus*," north and south, and incorporated Lippe, previously a free state, into North Westphalia. This study includes Lippe in its definition of Westphalia.[59]

After the armistice in 1918, Westphalians, like other Germans, tried to rebuild their lives. Throughout the 1920s, however, many factors obstructed

---

55 Crew, *Germans on Welfare*.

56 Gellately, *Gestapo and German Society*; Johnson, *Nazi Terror*.

57 William Sheridan Allen, *Nazi Seizure of Power*; Koshar, *Social Life, Local Politics*.

58 *Statistisches Jahrbuch* 17 (1921): 261–4; *Statistisches Jahrbuch* 25 (1929): 18, 220–21. The Jewish population fell from 18,819 in 1933 to 7,384 in 1941, when emigration was outlawed. By the beginning of April 1943, when the deportations began, only 796 Jews remained. Borscheid, "Vom Ersten zum Zweiten," 336; Aschoff, "Zum jüdischen Vereinswesen," 133.

59 The heavier bombings experienced by the southern half of the Westphalian *Gau* during the Second World War, and possibly also more extensive destruction of files (*Vernichtung*), have resulted in less complete archival holdings.

a smooth return to normal life. The wartime mortality rates in Westphalia ranked among the highest in Germany and resulted in a significant postwar birth deficit. Population concerns were heightened by premature deaths due to malnutrition and disease within the civilian population and by the effects of modern family planning, which was already in widespread use before the war.[60] The difficult and only gradual conversion of Westphalia's heavy industry from wartime to peacetime production resulted in high unemployment. Although, in accordance with the Demobilization Decrees, women were dismissed from wartime positions to make jobs available for returning soldiers, the rationalization of industry reduced the number of skilled workers needed and elevated unemployment levels even further. Everyday life was made harder by the dramatic fluctuation in the prices and availability of many essential products, including milk, meat, and butter, during the early postwar years.[61] Strikes and political unrest also continued to destabilize life. In 1923, when the French occupied the industrial region to protest German violations of the reparations payments, local authorities enacted nighttime curfews and issued warnings about the "dangerous" French soldiers.[62] The inflation caused by the occupation–inspired strikes dramatically devalued the German currency and ensured that personal income for Westphalians did not return to its prewar level until 1927.[63] To combat the impact of inflation, teams of coal miners, who were paid daily in an attempt to keep up with the currency's rapid devaluation, in desperation foraged for food in nearby fields.[64] When the Depression struck in 1929, welfare rolls expanded dramatically, mirroring conditions elsewhere in Germany. Between October 1930 and April 1932, the number of Westphalian welfare recipients rose exponentially from 49,000 to 268,000.[65] So devastating were the economic crises of 1923 and 1929 that they temporarily reversed the historical trend of emigration from rural areas to cities; since food was more plentiful in rural areas, many people, especially those with family on the land, left urban areas.[66]

The political views of Westphalians during the Weimar Republic varied locally. While the SPD and KPD held sway in the southern industrial area (especially in Bochum and Dortmund), the strong Catholic majority in

---

60 Borscheid, "Vom Ersten zum Zweiten," 331–3. 61 Ibid., 337.
62 Frau Rott, interview.
63 Borscheid, "Vom Ersten zum Zweiten," 423–4.
64 Ibid., 422–4.
65 These figures include both unemployment insurance and crisis welfare. During the same period, the number of Westphalians registered as seeking work rose from 72,300 in October 1929 to 529,800 in April 1932. Ibid., 426.
66 See ibid., 335, 344.

Paderborn and Münster favored the Catholic Center Party.[67] In the east, Detmold and Bielefeld consistently supported the SPD, though not without challenges from the more conservative DNVP and DVP parties. Some towns experienced relative political stability: in Detmold, for example, Dr. Emil Peters served as mayor throughout the Weimar years.

Despite the uncertain economic times, Westphalia showed little early support for National Socialism. Though nationalism and anti-Semitism in the form of the *Schutz- und Trutzbund* organizations (fraternal associations) gained popularity after World War I, the fledgling local National Socialist organizations (*Ortsgruppen*) that began to appear in Westphalia in the early 1920s remained small.[68] Hitler supported the local NSDAP groups by visiting various Westphalian cities during the pre-1933 period (Münster in 1926, Bielefeld in 1930, and Lemgo in 1932) and by encouraging large-scale propaganda campaigns. In January 1932, the local National Socialist newspaper, *Westfalenstürmer*, began publication. Still, with the exception of the NSDAP's astonishingly good showing in Lippe in July 1932 – a victory that drew national attention to the region on the eve of the Nazi seizure of power – the Nazi party won only relatively weak electoral support in Westphalia.[69] Even in May 1933, in the last democratic election after Hitler had already been appointed chancellor, the Catholic Center Party received more votes than the National Socialists did in Münster.[70] Nazi leaders declared the people of Lippe "completely conquered" as of July 1932, but my evidence suggests a much less thoroughgoing Nazi takeover.[71] In Münster, for example, one local Nazi group had so few members that 70 percent of them had to maintain positions in the political leadership or the offices remained unfilled.[72]

Once in power, the Nazi leadership took immediate action to build a Westphalian government more sympathetic to their aims. In February 1933, for example, Hermann Göring abruptly fired *Oberpräsident* Gronowski, the highest political officer in Westphalia, for his refusal to strictly censor Catholic Party literature. His replacement, Ferdinand Freiherr von Lüninck, had resigned from public office in 1922 as a gesture of protest

67 In the 1928 elections in Münster, the Catholic Center Party received 60 percent of women's votes and 40 percent of men's. Kaufmann, *Katholisches Milieu im Münster*, 77.
68 Groups began in Münster 1922, in Lage 1923, and in Detmold and Bielefeld 1925. Klein, "Der Weg zur Macht," 15; Wehrmann, *Lippe im Dritten Reich*, 20.
69 The National Socialist Party won 41.1 percent of the vote in Lippe in July 1932. Wehrmann, *Lippe im Dritten Reich*, 21–22.
70 Stadt Museum Münster, *Bomben auf Münster*, 101–103.
71 Wehrmann, *Lippe im Dritten Reich*, 22.
72 Kuropka, "Münster in der nationalsozialistischen Zeit," 304.

against the Weimar Republic and later actively led the right-wing Stahlhelm before being appointed to the chamber of commerce (*Landwirtschaftskammer*) in 1931. Nazi leaders hoped that by appointing von Lüninck, himself a Catholic, they would simultaneously bring Westphalia into line politically and silence Catholic opposition.[73] Records reveal, however, that *Gleichschaltung* had an uneven impact on Westphalian towns and cities. In cases where the Nazi leadership did not replace local politicians, they often appointed a Nazi to work with them. In Bielefeld, for example, although the mayor had had no political affiliation and demonstrated loyalty to the new regime, Nazi authorities appointed a second mayor in 1933 to ensure that all decisions reflected party demands.[74] In other towns, including Bad Salzuflen and Lage, Nazi authorities allowed the Weimar mayor to remain in office. Although neither mayor had belonged to a political party before 1933, their willingness to join the NSDAP shortly thereafter undoubtedly contributed to their continued presence in political office.[75] And there were worse fates than being removed from office: Dr. Emil Peters, the *Oberbürgermeister* of Detmold – before 1933 a political independent described by contemporaries as a "bourgeois conservative" – protested when local Nazi leaders hung the swastika flag from the Detmold city hall. Before the government could even complete its disciplinary action against him for doing so, members of the National Socialist Motor Corps (Nationalsozialistisches Kraftfahrkorps) and SA (Sturmabteilung, or stormtroopers) attacked and beat him, releasing him only after he agreed to resign. They then blacklisted him, making it impossible for him to secure another job – a situation which in the end led to his suicide.[76] Using similar strategies elsewhere in Westphalia, the Nazi leadership threatened, physically abused, and blacklisted those officials they deemed obstructionists.

Yet despite the interventions and manipulations of Nazi leaders, the claim of the NSDAP Gau press that the Nazis had "completely conquered" the province of Westphalia was clearly exaggerated. Inexplicably, in some small towns like Bünde and Lemgo, mayors survived in office even though they were Freemasons. Moreover, in a situation that matches Martin Broszat's description of a "polycracy" at the upper levels of government, all manner of local conflicts persisted.[77] Rather than work together, the two Westphalian

73 Teppe, *Provinz, Partei, Staat*, 18–20.   74 Vogelsang, *Im Zeichen des Hakenkreuzes*, 63–64.

75 Hans Briemann was mayor in Bad Salzuflen from 1927 until 1945. Edmund Gierlichs was mayor in Lage from 1921 until his death in 1943. Bender, "Die 'NS-Machtergreifung' in Detmold."

76 In his autobiography, the co-mayor made the connection between Peters's death and his inability to find a job. Ibid., 240–42.

77 Broszat, *Hitler State*.

Gau leaders, Alfred Meyer in the north and Josef Wagner in the south, carried on a rivalry that dramatically compromised Nazi control. Lower-level party officials routinely contradicted provincial government decisions and court verdicts, creating extra work and inefficiency at all levels and undermining the public's trust in the National Socialist state.[78] Not until 1938, when Wagner was promoted to *Oberpräsident* of Silesia and Meyer became *Oberpräsident* in Westphalia, did their competition cease and the Westphalian government attain a significant degree of unity.

One reason for Westphalians' hesitance to embrace National Socialism was the strong presence of the Catholic Church in the region. Especially in areas such as Catholic charity and youth work, Nazi authorities encountered unrelenting friction. Bishop Clemens August Graf von Galen of Münster used his allegedly apolitical position to protest the arrest of church leaders and the Nazi attempt to dominate Catholic schools. More impressively, he succeeded in halting the euthanasia program initiated by the National Socialists. In his sermons, von Galen shared his objections to the new Nazi policies with his parishioners and received applause and cheers from the congregation.[79] Even new party members were steadfast in their loyalty to the Church. Though the Nazi leadership realized that the alternative worldview provided by the Catholic Church undermined National Socialism, their fear of creating martyrs stymied their efforts to eliminate the competition completely.[80] Not everything Nazi leaders did caused the Catholic community to raise objections, however. In fact, some Nazi rhetoric directed at families resonated with long-standing and familiar church doctrines. The celebration of large families, for instance, echoed traditional Catholic Church teachings. Likewise, the campaign against women's employment coincided with the traditional gender roles long advocated by the Catholic Church.

In some cases, the Nazis also found that Westphalians impeded anti-Semitic policy. Most people in Münster recognized and respected the rights of the approximately 7,000 Jewish citizens living there, and they therefore opposed anti-Semitic actions. Nazi leaders discovered that without exception boycotts and other anti-Semitic measures "met with a lack of understanding and rejection that burdened the relationship between the party and the population."[81] Non-Jews and even party members in uniform continued to shop in Jewish-owned stores.

---

78 Teppe, *Provinz, Partei, Staat*, 83.   79 Kuropka, *Meldungen aus Münster*, 422.
80 Schlögl, Schwartz, and Thamer, "Konsens, Konflikt und Repression," 18.
81 Kuropka, "Münster in der nationalsozialistischen Zeit," 306.

The Protestant Church had an equally troubled relationship with National Socialism in Westphalia. Despite the National Socialist effort to bring Protestants into line by creating the German Christian Church, not all Protestants accepted the new church leadership.[82] When the newly Nazified German Christians dissolved the provincial synod immediately after winning the provincial synodal elections in March 1934, many Westphalian Protestants saw it as their calling to break away and independently represent "the Protestant Christians in Westphalia."[83] In some towns, Protestant pastors who were enthusiastic about National Socialism swayed their congregations to join them in supporting the new regime. But the residents of Schale, to cite just one example, were so offended by the German Christian pastor's intrusive recruitment efforts that they left the Nazi Party as a protest against state intervention in the church.[84] In the end, 90 percent of Protestant churches in Westphalia rejected the German Christian Church, supporting instead the Confessing Church (Bekennende Kirche).[85]

Protestant women's organizations were similarly divided in their loyalties. Initially, the leadership of the Protestant Women's Aid Society (Evangelische Frauenhilfe, EFH) looked favorably on Nazi nationalist and *völkisch* goals, which they believed would strengthen Germany. But some Westphalian women in the EFH found the intrusion of politics into religion impossible to accept and, following Agnes von Harnack's leadership, split from the group allied with the German Christian Church and struggled to maintain organizational independence from National Socialism.

The prominent role of the Westphalian Catholic and Protestant churches and their rejection of some Nazi aims was especially evident in the realm of charity. Both before and after 1933, Westphalian residents received support from a variety of charities – both church-affiliated and secular – including Caritas, Inner Mission, the Protestant Women's Aid Society, the Patriotic Women's Association (Vaterländischer Frauenverein), and the Worker's Welfare Organization (Arbeiterwohlfahrt). During the Weimar era, this range of organizations offered a more extensive support network for the needy than the state alone could provide. After 1933, it hampered Nazi efforts to monopolize welfare through the NSV in Westphalia. Throughout the 1930s, the *Landeshauptmann*, Karl Friedrich Kolbow, worked steadfastly to prevent the NSV's exclusive control of welfare. Though he was a member of the NSDAP, he firmly maintained the position that "the

---

82 See Bergen, *Twisted Cross*.   83 Vogelsang, *Im Zeichen des Hakenkreuzes*, 131.
84 In Schale, the German Christian Church pastor was removed after people began to resign from the party. Trütken-Kirsch, "Die Landgemeinde Schale," 357–60.
85 Reese, *Straff aber nicht Stramm*, 126 n 18.

entire public welfare [system] must be looked after by the community and run in cooperation with the mayor... in a uniform manner and without cutbacks."[86] In his view, only local administrators could accurately assess local needs. He felt certain that the NSV's monopoly of welfare would inevitably lead to "duplicate work, friction, and competence conflicts." Not surprisingly, Erich Hilgenfeldt, director of the NSV, lambasted Kolbow for undermining the NSV's work. When the two men finally met in April 1939, Hilgenfeldt flatly "declared the community incapable of organizing the welfare delivery system in the National Socialist spirit."[87] The struggle continued, and despite Kolbow's efforts the NSV gradually usurped control of many welfare-oriented programs in Westphalia, though the churches continued to run kindergartens, provide welfare, and care for children.

Alltagsgeschichte

This study is driven by a belief that understanding the past requires historians to look beyond the public, political, and national narrative to the local, everyday, and even individual level. As such, it situates itself at the intersection of *Alltagsgeschichte* (the history of everyday life) and women's history. *Alltagsgeschichte* pushes the historian to investigate the layers of life that otherwise lie hidden below the official record. As historian Alf Lüdtke has emphasized, at the center of *Alltagsgeschichte* are the "actions and sufferings of those who are frequently labeled everyday, ordinary people."[88] Where traditional studies of German family policy have examined national policy as it was written and designed,[89] this study enters the maze of implementation and asks how family policy played out in everyday life. Because family policy in any era reflects accepted notions of appropriate gender roles, this study provides a window into how gender roles were understood and contested in the democratic Weimar state and under the totalitarian Nazi regime. In investigating the inner workings of policy, it demonstrates that during the Weimar era – but also under the terror that characterized the Third Reich – men and women still found resources to challenge state assumptions about their lives.

The new state interest in the health of families after World War I prompted the creation of a welfare state and brought German state policy into

86 Teppe, *Provinz, Partei, Staat*, 99.   87 Ibid., 100.
88 Lüdtke, "Introduction," 3.
89 Usborne, *Politics of the Body*; Weindling, *Health, Race and German Politics*; Pine, *Nazi Family Policy*; Klinksiek, *Die Frau im NS-Staat*.

greater contact with women's lives. Though many historians have examined German women, with the exception of Atina Grossmann's study of the sex reform movement, very few studies examine policy across the divide between Weimar and National Socialism.[90] This study, by examining women's experiences across the two eras, reveals both the tremendous change that took place in policy toward women as the Nazi regime replaced the Weimar regime and the great extent to which women found ways to exert their agency – to act in their own self-interest within the bureaucracy and on their own – even after the Nazis came to power and reinstituted patriarchy as the rule of the day.[91] This reminds us of the important distinction between documenting women's agency and seeing women as "heroic" figures. In this account, women are brought into Nazi history not as victims but as historical actors who were arguably complicit in many of the same ways that men were.[92]

In focusing on women and state family policy, I only occasionally discuss the history of one group that might otherwise be expected to be an area of focus: German Jewish women. A short explanation is necessary. Under the Weimar regime, being Jewish was not a distinguishing factor in the creation or administration of family policy. In contrast, under the Nazis, Jewish Germans were explicitly excluded from the benefits of state family policy. As a result they rarely enter the scope of this study. In some cases, for example when the state advocated the dissolution of racially mixed marriages, the study does shed light on how dramatically conditions for marriage, divorce, and adoption changed for Jewish Germans after 1933. However, this study does not investigate the private Jewish organizations that supported – and played a fundamental role in sustaining – Jewish families, especially after 1933. In part, a more thorough discussion of Jewish Germans was hindered by a lack of sources in Westphalia. More importantly, I believe that given

---

90 Some historians have examined Weimar's New Women. See, for example, Grossmann, "The New Woman," and Bridenthal and Koonz, "Beyond Kinder, Küche, Kirche." Karen Hagemann provided a comprehensive study of working-class women during the Weimar era in *Frauenalltag und Männerpolitik*. Others have examined areas of state policy as they affected German women, including Weimar sexual advice centers, compulsory sterilization, and marriage policy under the Nazis. See von Soden, *Die Sexualberatungsstellen der Weimarer Republik*; Bock, *Zwangssterilisation im Nationalsozialismus*; and Czarnowski, *Das kontrollierte Paar*. Marion Kaplan has investigated the impact of anti-Semitic policy and German Jewish women in *Between Dignity and Despair*. Birthe Kundrus and Elizabeth Heinemann have each analyzed women and families during the Second World War. See Kundrus, *Kriegerfrauen*, and Heinemann, *What Difference*.
91 To borrow the term coined by Alf Ludtke, it asks how Germans expressed their *Eigensinn* (self-interest) in the realm of family policy.
92 Historians have long debated women's role in and responsibility for the National Socialist regime. See Koonz, *Mothers in the Fatherland*; Bock, *Zwangssterilisation im Nationalsozialismus*; and Ebbinghaus, *Opfer und Täterinnen*.

how dramatically policy toward Jewish Germans changed after 1933, the subject is worthy of its own study.[93]

The depth of the story historians can tell depends on the breadth and variability of the sources available to them. In addition to two state archives, Westphalia has an extremely rich local archival base. At the state level, archives in Münster and Detmold house court and government records. Court records of illegitimacy, divorce, adoption, and sterilization allowed me to evaluate how changing state definitions of family and motherhood were reflected in decisions to construct and dissolve families. Extensive collections of Nazi Party documents also made clear some of the difficulties the Nazis had in implementing their family policy. I combed the city archives in Münster, Paderborn, Minden, Lemgo, Dortmund, and Bielefeld, as well as a regional archive (*Landschaftsverbandarchiv*) for information detailing state–family interactions. It is here that I was able to trace Weimar efforts to finance and increase access to kindergartens and later Nazi attempts to centralize and apply racial standards to all child care. Social work case histories – including records of child neglect, child support, war support, and welfare – also provided an important and varied source.

Because the Catholic and Protestant churches played an important role in supporting and aiding families during both the Weimar and National Socialist eras, I used records from church archives to augment my research. Two diocesan archives in Münster and Paderborn, the pastoral archive in Detmold, and the Protestant Women's Aid archive offered details of how churches negotiated the Nazi intrusion into what they considered their realm. To better understand the background and motivations of the people entrusted to carry out family policy, I examined personnel files for judges and doctors housed in the state archives. Although social workers also played a crucial role in the implementation of family policy, I could locate no individual personnel files for them. For material on the mayors who play a large role in this study, especially after the Nazis came to power, I have relied on the rich secondary literature available for many local towns in Westphalia.

The individual "ordinary Germans" who were the targets and recipients of family policy strongly influenced its ultimate shape. Some individual stories can be found in social workers' case histories; others appear as they argue their cases before the courts. Still other stories come to light in the reports of the exiled Social Democratic Party and the Nazis' own spy organization,

---

93 *Between Dignity and Despair*, Marion Kaplan's examination of Jewish everyday life in Nazi Germany, begins to provide this.

the Security Service (Sicherheitsdienst, SD). But the view we gain from such sources reflects the specific setting in which the record was created. To gain a fuller sense of how women interpreted family policy and the way the state influenced their everyday lives, I supplemented an array of personal narratives, published and unpublished,[94] with oral history interviews I conducted with forty-eight women who were born between 1902 and 1933. These women, almost equally divided between Protestants and Catholics, lived primarily in Münster and the villages around Lippe. Two migrated to Westphalia during the war, and two lived in bigger cities, Dortmund and Duisburg. Most were young women during the Nazi era. Although the majority were housewives, several of them worked outside the home: one was a nurse, one was a social worker, three were teachers, two were nuns, and one was a lawyer. Many (thirteen) were youth whose adolescence or early adulthood was tied to the League of German Girls (Bund Deutscher Mädel, BDM). These women had a wide range of life experiences during the Weimar and Nazi eras, but none were Jewish, nor did any belong to the other groups targeted for persecution under National Socialism. Because most of the women would have been considered Aryan, their potential for motherhood was of prime value to the Nazi state, and it put them at the epicenter of family policy. As a result, these women's memories and explanations of their lives provide an important perspective into what it meant to be female during such a tumultuous political and social era.[95]

All narrators speak through the filter of their past and present experiences. Memory reflects not only what actually happened but also what people think or wish had happened. Especially among the elderly, the process of forgetting, whether voluntary or not, can play an increasingly prominent role. Indeed, history itself can be seen as both a recorded past and a living memory; as F. J. Brüggemeier has rightly argued, "History is always constructed in the process of remembering."[96] Since 1945, the collective national memory of Nazi Germany has been repeatedly revised, challenging individuals to revise their private memories to fit the collective memory. In addition, as historian Luisa Passerini has argued, people feel the challenge of "justifying themselves, and at the same time of establishing some sort of continuity in their life stories."[97] The women I spoke to clearly used their

---

94 Unpublished personal narratives include twenty-one found at the Institut für Biographie und Gedächtnis Forschung in Hagen as well as a diary and a set of letters written during the war given to me by two of my interviewees, Frau Frandsen and Frau Löhr.
95 Personal Narratives Group, *Interpreting Women's Lives*, 4.
96 Brüggemeier, "Sounds of Silents," 9.
97 Passerini, "Introduction," 12.

memories to explain, justify, and rationalize their own histories.[98] One of them, Frau Schumacher (b. 1903), explained that as an early supporter of National Socialism, she rose to a position of relative power supervising young people. She left this position only under duress because her sister – who, she pointed out to me, was more aware of the "other side" of Nazism – insisted that she distance herself before it was too late. Even today, Frau Schumacher resolves the disjuncture between her positive recollections and the reality of the Third Reich by seeing Hitler as "an innocent and good man" who had bad advisors.[99] In other cases, women who initially down-played their support of the regime altered these preliminary accounts either during the course of the interview or afterward. While making coffee after our interview, Frau Kemper (b. 1919) came back into the living room to tell me she thought she "had not told her story exactly correctly." I turned my tape recorder back on, and she emphasized that she had loved the League of German Girls and had actively sought out a position of leadership. Three days later, she called me to reemphasize this.[100]

It is important to note the varied motives these women gave for speaking to me. Some said they wanted to record their stories before they died; others sought to make me understand what life under the Nazis had "really" been like. Still others said they simply wanted to contribute to my research. I believe loneliness in old age also motivated some to agree to spend an afternoon discussing their lives. My status as a non-German, my promise to give everyone anonymity, and the time I spent sitting with each woman over coffee and cake helped to build a relationship that made some degree of honesty possible.[101] Only one woman asked me to turn my tape recorder off so she could talk off the record.[102] No one who was not prepared to probe their experiences under National Socialism volunteered to be interviewed. Whatever their motives, the effort most women put into telling their stories and in getting the details "right" was moving. Their individual descriptions of how policy intersected with, bypassed, or benefited their lives provide invaluable insight into everyday life in Nazi Germany.[103] Because oral history is complicated by issues of personal interpretation and memory, I have

---

98 For more on women's oral history, see Gluck, Berger, and Patai, eds., *Women's Words*.
99 Frau Schumacher, interview.
100 Frau Kemper, interview.
101 In contrast to one researcher I encountered in the Detmold archive, who claimed that all her interview partners told her stories of their active resistance to the Nazis, I never heard any resistance stories. My interviews lasted up to four hours; in some cases, I returned to do follow-up interviews.
102 Frau Schmitt, interview.
103 For further discussion about memory and history, see Mouton and Pohlandt-McCormick, "Boundary Crossings," and Mouton, "Sports, Song, and Socialization," esp. 63–5.

always interpreted what I learned from interviews in conjunction with other sources; the interviews enrich the analysis of family policy, but my argument never rests solely on oral sources.

Focusing on the everyday life of Germans not directly involved in the murder and genocide can cause the horror of the Nazi regime to recede into the background. My intention is not to normalize the Third Reich. I am also not suggesting that ordinary Germans were innocent or entirely ignorant of the Holocaust. Instead, my study seeks to understand how the Germans not directly targeted in the Holocaust experienced Nazi efforts to shape the family. Detlev Peukert has argued that many people saw in Hitler a chance to "return to normality, to regular work, to secure planning of their lives and certainty about their own place within the social scheme."[104] Moreover, many women looked on the Nazi regime positively because they believed it would finally treat motherhood with the proper level of respect and allow them to run their families with dignity.[105] There are historians who see Nazi family policy as having had exactly the opposite effect on private life – as having removed from it any resemblance of normalcy. Adelheid von Saldern has claimed that the "division between the private and the public spheres actually dissolved under the Third Reich."[106] Lisa Pine asserts that "the legacy of the National Socialist era for the German family was the ultimate destruction of the private sphere, in physical and practical terms, as well as morally and spiritually."[107] This study reveals that although the Nazis did try to infiltrate all aspects of private life, the outcome was very uneven. Clearly, for Jews, Gypsies, and other people targeted as "enemies of the state" (*Staatsfeinde*), Nazi policy went even beyond destroying families to attempting to exterminate so-called races. For the many families with members defined as "hereditarily ill" or "asocial," Nazi family policy had far-reaching, often devastating effects as the regime deprived them of resources, excluded them from state benefits, forbade them to marry, and ultimately in many cases sterilized them. As Gisela Bock has correctly argued, "with respect to the 'inferior,' National Socialism pursued a policy not of family welfare, but of family destruction."[108] But for Germans, especially women, whom the state viewed as worthy and who were the intended beneficiaries of Nazi family policy, the impact was much less consistent. For them, daily life became a series of "multiple and conflicting events and experiences, private

---

104 Peukert, *Inside Nazi Germany*, 236. Robert Gellately has further argued that many Germans supported the Nazi regime simply because they "liked what they heard and became instrumentally and emotionally invested in the Nazi dictatorship." *Backing Hitler*, 256.
105 Bridenthal and Koonz, "Beyond Kinder, Küche, Kirche," 56.
106 Von Saldern, "Victims or Perpetrators?" 146.   107 Pine, *Nazi Family Policy*, 183.
108 Bock, "Antinatalism, Maternity and Paternity," 129.

and public, in which people were involved, willingly or not."[109] This book reveals that German women collaborated with, accommodated, evaded, and sometimes challenged National Socialist family policy, even in the face of a totalitarian regime that tried to deny them political agency. In the process, many women succeeded relatively well in preserving their families – and private sphere – from the most intrusive state intervention.

German women and their families attempted to ward off unwanted state attention and to tailor policy to their personal needs. When state authorities tried to impose ideologically driven policies on families, some Germans felt they had the right and ability to challenge authorities. Others manipulated ideology to try to convince authorities of the legitimacy of their cases, even when their actual intentions ran exactly counter to Nazi priorities. Sometimes, they capitulated and followed the Nazis' demands out of fear, lack of courage, or perhaps sheer lack of energy. As one woman (b. 1916), the mother of two children, noted with some regret, "We were not all heroes."[110] The evasion and manipulation by the women I describe did not constitute resistance comparable to the actions of Hans and Sophie Scholl, the Kreisau Circle, and the July 20th Uprising. That such resistance was so rare can be attributed in part to the "drastic atomisation of social relations" that "impeded the communal effort" necessary for resistance and to the terror that the Gestapo inspired.[111] Even if historians are correct in arguing that the Gestapo's image of "omnipotence, omniscience and ubiquity" grossly overestimates its actual capacity to control German society, its ability to lash out arbitrarily at individuals assured a low rate of overt opposition.[112]

Organization

To better demonstrate how Germans experienced state policy, this study is organized thematically rather than strictly chronologically. Each chapter examines the interactions between national policy and local implementation – between state authorities and individual Germans – in a different context. Chapters 1 and 2 highlight the conflicts between modernity and tradition that arose when Weimar and Nazi policymakers perceived marriage as the panacea for declining birthrates and societal immorality. Chapter 1 investigates the compromise Weimar authorities sought to strike between the state's desire to reestablish traditional marriages and individual Germans'

---

109 Nolan, "Rationalization, Racism, and *Resistenz*," 148.
110 Frau Müller, interview.
111 Peukert, *Inside Nazi Germany*, 63.
112 Mallmann and Paul, "Omniscient, Omnipotent, Omnipresent?"; Gellately, *Gestapo and German Society*; Gellately, *Backing Hitler*.

efforts to accommodate "modern" marriages. It shows how the Nazis attempted to create unlimited rights for the state to control marriage in the name of racial interests but found that local authorities, individual Germans, and ultimately the war itself confounded their efforts. This debate played out even more starkly when couples went to court to end their marriages. Chapter 2 explores how, even as Weimar policymakers battled over the reform of divorce law, couples brought more liberal understandings of marriage into the courtroom, forcing judicial reform. Under the cloak of modernity, the Nazis then enacted a new racially based divorce law that had at its core a blend of pronatalism and racial discrimination.

The conflict between traditional and modern gender roles plagued both Weimar and National Socialist policymakers. Chapters 3 and 4 show how both regimes used modern notions of genetics and hygiene to create guidelines for what constituted a good mother. Chapter 3 examines how both regimes made raising the birthrate a state priority, sponsored training programs for prospective mothers, supported those who already had children, and honored prolific mothers. Despite these similarities, however, Weimar policymakers championed motherhood as only one of many acceptable roles for women. In contrast, Nazi officials encouraged a backlash against the New Woman, closed off alternate roles for women, and publicly celebrated traditional motherhood. Furthermore, Nazi family policy, which established centralized, state-controlled, and racially based programs to help mothers and children, had a much more menacing antinatalist side as it removed children from the homes of "bad" mothers and sterilized those deemed "racially ill." Chapter 4 examines how both regimes tried to train mothers and help them to raise healthier families by making it easier for them to do so. During the Weimar era, state authorities worked side by side with churches to maximize the support available for mothers and children. Nazi authorities, on the other hand, tried to impose their racially based criteria on all mother-directed programs by excluding those deemed unworthy from the expanded state programs and by monopolizing church programs. In both eras, women limited their participation in mother-directed programs to their own self-defined needs, which did not always agree with state definitions.

The disruptive effects of the First World War and the turmoil of the 1920s meant that German state authorities were forced to recognize and support alternative family forms. In this context, unmarried mothers posed an especially intractable problem. The children they bore clearly proved that these women had breached the line of traditional moral respectability, and yet ostracizing these women exacerbated their precarious economic status and had devastating effects on their children. The contention that surrounded policy toward unmarried mothers reflects this dilemma and individual Germans' reluctance to eliminate entirely the stigma attached to out-of-wedlock birth. Chapter 5 examines attempts by the Weimar and Nazi regimes to create pronatalist policies that would support illegitimate children without condoning their mothers' behavior. How could the state ensure illegitimate children's welfare without subverting its claim to uphold high morals? Unmarried mothers framed the question differently: How could they gain benefits for their children without sacrificing their autonomy and without bringing their households under state scrutiny?

Some children had no parental home, and the state was forced to assume a much greater role in the creation of their families. Chapter 6 examines foster care and adoption as alternative family forms made more frequent by the First and Second World Wars and by changing economic and personal circumstances. For Weimar officials, establishing physically and morally safe homes sometimes pitted children's interests against their parents'. Nazi authorities tried to force foster and adoptive families to conform to their racial ideology but encountered trouble when these racial goals conflicted with the successful creation of families.

Throughout the period 1918 to 1945, German family policy represented a balancing act between the state's shifting aims, its changing claim to intervene in families, and individuals' compliance, negotiation, and opposition to state policies. When Weimar officials at the national level disagreed about the shape family policy should take, they left local authorities to sort out their confused directives. In contrast, Nazi policymakers designed a monolithic, racially based policy that gave the state far-reaching rights to intervene in the family. But local bureaucrats modified this policy as well, as they accommodated local conditions, their personal beliefs, and individual circumstances. As we explore the dynamics between national policy decrees, state authorities, and individual Germans, we discover that although national policy changed dramatically after 1933, the changes in implementation at the local level were less thorough – and above all less consistent – than either regime intended. The conservatism of local institutions, the attitudes of individuals charged with policy implementation, and the actions of the Germans targeted by policy together obstructed the smooth implementation of national policy. Individual German women, a primary focus of state family policy, demonstrated their ability to maintain their agency under both regimes as they held positions that ranged from collaborator to victim.

1

Marriage Policy in Turmoil

Stabilizing Society, Reordering Gender Roles, and Guaranteeing the Future

During the summer of 1932, Frau Dewald, a twenty-two-year-old university student, served as a volunteer in the Labor Service on the island of Soest. When she received her first marriage proposal from a co-worker, she remembers thinking: "Me, marry?! Now, when I have just begun to live? No. No. . . . Impossible." Instead, she "wanted to live," she says: "Life stood before me. I wanted to earn money – not always be dependent on my father." Many Germans would have seen Frau Dewald's postponement of marriage and her search for independence as symptomatic of what was wrong with gender relations after the First World War. If young women balked at marriage, the possibility of rebuilding and repopulating the nation after years of war and turmoil could never be realized.

Women like Frau Dewald seemed to exacerbate the demographic disruption caused by the war and prompted Weimar authorities to get involved in marriage. But beyond a general desire to influence marriage, no consensus existed about what form this influence should assume. While racial theory and eugenics offered the possibility of creating a stronger, healthier race, Weimar politicians did not agree that the state had the right to intervene in marriage. While left-wing politicians advocated strengthening the health of marriage by providing birth control and material support, their more conservative colleagues argued that the state should intervene to prevent "undesirable" marriages. Feminists believed women should have more rights inside marriage, while sex reformers argued that the fear of pregnancy placed a burden on couples and threatened marital health. Faced with this diversity of opinion, consecutive Weimar governments weighed the benefits of marriage counseling, birth control, and education as means to shore up marriage.

The Nazis read far more dire consequences into Frau Dewald's refusal to marry. Not only was hers a selfish gesture that threatened gender relations, but it also struck at the heart of the German nation. That such behavior was not expressly condemned provided the Nazis with clear proof that Weimar policymakers' openness to women's pursuit of nondomestic roles and their hesitance to ban marriages not in the state's interest were weak and far too tentative. Following Adolf Hitler's admonition that "marriage cannot be an end in itself, but must serve the one higher goal, the increase and preservation of the species and the race,"[1] Nazi policymakers sought ever more effective ways to control marriage. It was this greater resolve to prevent unhealthy marriages that Frau Dewald confronted in 1938 when she accepted another proposal to marry. This time the state forbade the marriage because her fiancé, the son of an unmarried Czechoslovakian woman and an unknown father, could not prove his Aryan heritage.[2] Basing marriage policy on explicit racial principles that fostered considerable state intrusion into marriage, the Nazis called on doctors, civil registry authorities, and judges to determine the worthiness of potential marriages.

In both the Weimar and National Socialist eras, the promotion and regulation of marriage struck many policymakers as the key to increasing the birthrate and rejuvenating German society. As a result, both Weimar and Nazi policymakers enacted new legislation to boost marriage figures and strengthen families. Looking at the form Weimar marriage policy finally took has caused some historians to question the uniqueness of Nazi policy. Others disagree, arguing not only that Nazi policy was unique but that the Nazis destroyed marriage as a private sphere. Through an exploration of Weimar and Nazi marriage policy, this chapter reveals that Nazi policy did not develop continuously from Weimar policy and that individual Germans blocked the Nazi effort to destroy the private sphere.

REGULATING FAMILIES UNDER WEIMAR

With the grim realities of the First World War behind them, Weimar politicians eagerly looked to a future in which marriage constituted a central foundation upon which German society would be rebuilt. As an institution, marriage created a bond not only between two individuals but also between two socially stabilizing forces: church and state. Lawmakers believed that the promotion of marriage would help German society return to the status quo ante by limiting the gender confusion caused by the war and by reestablishing more traditional gender roles. In addition, a rise in the marriage

---

1 Hitler, *Mein Kampf*, 252.
2 Not until 1940 did her fiancé finally receive permission to marry her. Frau Dewald, interview.

rate promised to provide greater family economic security and to reduce welfare dependence. This optimistic view of the power of marriage led politicians to write a constitution that proclaimed that "marriage is the basis of family life and the preservation and reproduction of the nation, and as such stands under the protection of the Constitution."[3]

Under the Weimar Republic, the German Civil Code (*Bürgerliches Gesetz Buch*, BGB) legally defined every aspect of marriage.[4] Beginning with a couple's engagement, the state prescribed the process by which a couple could marry. Men were prohibited from marrying before their nineteenth birthdays, women before their seventeenth, and both parties needed their father's permission to marry.[5] The state encouraged couples to obtain marriage certificates from physicians that guaranteed the health of both partners, but these were not obligatory. After a couple announced their intent to marry, the state posted public notices of couples' engagements in plain view on the court house. These postings were intended to enable other Germans to raise concerns about the potential marriages before they took place and thus to increase the likelihood that a marriage would contribute to the "public good" and not just private interests (BGB §1316). If no one came forth to protest and the couple was old enough, the state assumed no prior conflict of interest existed and permitted the marriage.

Once a couple had married, the German Civil Code established further guidelines for proper marital behavior. Beginning with BGB §1353, which stated that "Spouses are obligated [to share] a marital household," it dictated very traditional roles for each partner in marriage. The man and woman were obligated to fulfill their respective marital duties, to remain faithful (*treu*), and to care for one another in case of illness. Following middle-class gender expectations, the code carefully detailed asymmetrical financial obligations, mandating that husbands had to support their wives at their standard of living and that wives had to turn over their financial possessions and leave all financial matters to their husbands (§§1363–1409). The law named the husband the "head of household" (*Vorstand des Haushalts*) with the right to decide "in all matters pertaining to the common marital life," including where the couple lived. The woman's corresponding role lay in her right and duty "to manage the common household" (*gemeinschaftliches Hauswesen*). She was obligated to work in the family business "insofar as such activity [was] part of the normal conditions in which the couple lives"

---

3 BGB §1588, art. 119.
4 The German Civil Code was written after German unification in 1871 and revised in 1900.
5 BGB §1303 and §1305. For illegitimate children, the mother had to give permission.

(BGB §1356). She could only work outside the home if it did not interfere with her household responsibilities.

But despite the law's clear codification of the traditional bourgeois marriage, attitudes toward marriage remained in flux during the Weimar era at both the legislative and the popular level. The same Weimar constitution that supported traditional marriage also declared women's equality. Throughout the 1920s, more German women than ever before appeared to reject an exclusively domestic role in favor of gainful employment outside the home, study at university, and the postponement of marriage. Simultaneously, consumerism, leisure, and mass entertainment significantly reshaped unmarried women's lives. The New Woman, according to her contemporaries, discarded traditional values in favor of self-indulgence and luxury. Fashion and cosmetics sales skyrocketed; young women cut their hair and wore their skirts shorter. Some even rebelled actively against marriage. It seems to have been in this spirit that Frau Dewald (b. 1910), whose story began this chapter, decided not to marry at twenty-two. She emphasized that when she received her first marriage proposal, marriage itself held no appeal for her. At the time, she was working with a group of unemployed Communist and Nazi men and women in the Labor Service program building a children's home. As she worked, she recalled, she felt invigorated by political debate that introduced her to the ideas of both Friedrich Engels and Adolf Hitler. She enjoyed interacting collegially with both men and women and took pleasure in a previously unknown level of personal freedom. In her eyes, marriage would have brought everything she was enjoying to an end.[6] Many young working-class women, familiar with the burdens of married life and the loss of freedom it brought, similarly put off marriage as long as possible.[7] In the Weimar period, then, young women symbolized both Germany's chance to return to "normalcy" and the improbability of such a return. As future wives, mothers, and workers, women were, in the eyes of one historian, at once "modernity's agents, victims, and mediators."[8]

Yet closer examination reveals that, far from disappearing, a belief in patriarchal marriage and traditional gender relations remained largely intact in Weimar Germany. Although more women worked outside the home than ever before, demobilization policy ensured that most were employed at "women's jobs." That most young women considered work to be a temporary stage preceding marriage suggests their ambivalence toward traditional gender roles. Even women in white-collar jobs "longed to marry, give up

6 Frau Dewald, interview.   7 Hagemann, *Frauenalltag und Männerpolitik*, 162.
8 Grossmann, *Reforming Sex*, 5.

their job and at last be their 'own master.'"[9] As this quotation suggests, although marriage caused women to lose some of their civil rights, it also considerably increased their social standing. Political rhetoric, church teachings, and popular culture all continued to instruct young women that they belonged at home bearing and raising children. The courts, too, persisted in supporting traditional marriage. If a woman's husband abused his powers, her only recourse lay in her right to refuse to obey. It was "only progressive lawyers [who] considered it inherently an 'abuse' if the man made important decisions about the common marital affairs without consulting with his wife."[10] And while the New Woman created antagonism by raising the specter of women's "boundless egoism," the image of women's freedom at work "turned out to be a projection of the men of the time who, either from fear or from an exaggerated sense of progress, painted a distorted picture of female modernity and ignored traditional structures in the world of work."[11] In middle-class families, sons' educations continued to be given a higher priority than daughters' because it was assumed that daughters would marry. As Frau Krämer (b. 1918) recalled, "It was usual that the boys had career training, but for the girls, well . . . they learned to sew and cook and then they married."[12] Finally, even though the New Woman rejected early marriage proposals, Germany nonetheless experienced a veritable "flood of marriages" (*Heiratsflut*). The married proportion of the population increased to 40.1 percent in 1925 as compared to 36.1 percent in 1910.

The continued popularity of traditional marriage did not dispel the fear of marriage's uncertain future. The "surplus" of women created by wartime mortality ensured that large numbers of women would remain unmarried despite high marriage rates. By 1926, one-third fewer women between the ages of twenty and twenty-five were married than in 1910. Many people believed that traditional bourgeois marriage, founded as it was on female fidelity and male financial stability, was being upended by new sexual mores and inflation. Furthermore, low birthrates magnified fears that even women who did marry were failing to fulfill their "natural" roles. As information about contraception spread, many German adults sought to limit their family size, and the two-child family became the norm. While condoms and diaphragms were either unheard of or too expensive for most people, women used douching or insisted that their partners practice coitus interruptus. As Lisa Pine has asserted, "Birth control was part of the way of life of Weimar

9 Frevert, *Women in German History*, 183.
10 BGB §1354; Hagemann, *Frauenalltag und Männerpolitik*, 161.
11 Frevert, *Women in German History*, 179.
12 Ibid., 180; Frau Krämer, interview.

society."[13] Abortion, though illegal, was also prevalent, especially during hard economic times.[14]

While marriage and childbearing were seen as the antidote to population decline, they also promised to combat both the perceived loosening of morals and the imagined deterioration of national health. Debates about population policy quickly expanded to everything from marriage certificates to abortion, from contraception to euthanasia. As the debate broadened, it incorporated the voices of doctors, church leaders, welfare advocates, sex reformers, eugenicists, and racial hygienists. Though nearly everyone agreed that healthy marriages would yield healthy children, there was a widespread divergence of opinion on how to promote healthy marriage. Should the emphasis be on improving the health of those marrying, as the Socialists and Communists argued, or rather on preventing the unhealthy from marrying and bearing children, as those on the political Right asserted?

The belief that public health and well-being took precedence over the interests of the individual led to an increase in support for eugenics and racial hygiene on the political Right in the 1920s. Conservative nationalists advocated public eugenic education and mandatory marriage counseling to ensure that only healthy, well-matched couples married. For supporters of this view, the most attractive element of racial hygiene was that "it provided *ideological tools* for a *biological solution* to a *social problem.*"[15] A widely influential textbook on human heredity published in 1921 demonstrated that the rise and fall of civilizations could be attributed to the health of their people. The book also asserted that improving national health depended on parents, doctors, teachers, and priests working together to teach children that they "were a subordinate part of a great racial organism."[16] The DNVP petitioned the Prussian Assembly to have the science of heredity taught in medical schools.[17] Although racism and anti-Semitism began to appear in the right wing of the Weimar eugenic movement, the primary focus remained on personal and societal health. Most who advocated the application of eugenics to government policies emphasized that because negative characteristics could be inherited, genetically unhealthy people should be prevented from reproducing, and they advocated the compulsory sterilization of those who could not be trusted to behave responsibly. While discussion of eugenics became widespread in the Weimar period, the "number of

13 Pine, *Nazi Family Policy*, 90.
14 Frevert, *Women in German History*, 187; Grossmann, *Reforming Sex*, esp. ch. 4.
15 Pross, "Introduction," 1. Italics in original.
16 Weindling, *Health, Race and German Politics*, 330.
17 Ibid., 337.

eugenic measures actually passed through German parliaments in the 1920s was . . . zero," as Edward Dickinson has emphasized.[18]

Politicians on the Left also saw marriage as key to society's health, but their analysis led them to different conclusions about how to improve the institution. Left-wing politicians opposed the "conventional bourgeois forced marriage," believing that no healthy relationship could be so integrally bound to civil registration, economic connections, or financial dependence as it was. Instead, they advocated a companionate marriage grounded in "love, respect and trust" between two people.[19] The Social Democrats believed that only expanding the grounds for divorce so that unhappy partners could separate would strengthen marriage. More broadly, they hoped that creating a more open and just society, making women equal to men, and allowing people a greater freedom of lifestyle would improve health. Albert Grotjahn, spokesman for the SPD, petitioned to create a Reich Ministry of Health in 1918 that would both oversee education and health care and teach about heredity. Although the ministry never came to be, the state did begin to employ more full-time medical officers and social workers to seek out and assist families in need.[20]

The Federation of German Women's Organizations, which also worried about the degradation of marriage, argued that marriage needed to become more advantageous to women. It pointed out that if women had to forfeit their rights and become imprisoned by marriage, they would inevitably avoid it. BDF members thus campaigned to enhance married women's legal status and establish their right to own property. Though they held no firm position on contraception and scorned "free love," they acknowledged that a "temporary and infertile union" outside of marriage "might sometimes be "a reasonable way out of the 'modern marriage crisis.'" They also agreed with the SPD that divorce reform was essential to strengthen marriage. But in the end, BDF women came down firmly in favor of the "undivided trinity [of] love, marriage and motherhood," which they believed was the only way to "guarantee women's self-realization, the protection of their children and the preservation of the national culture."[21]

In a context in which scientific expertise was deemed central to improving health, doctors also weighed in on the debate about marriage. The use of mandatory marriage certificates, proposed by lawmakers as a way to exercise

---

18 Dickinson, "Biopolitics, Fascism, Democracy," 1, 14.
19 Hagemann, *Frauenalltag und Männerpolitik*, 331.
20 Weindling, *Health, Race and German Politics*, 323.
21 Usborne, *Politics of the Body*, 92.

control over marriage, would in fact have depended on doctors' judgments. Such plans promised that "the healthy as well as the diseased... [would] become the responsibility of the doctor as a state official."[22] Many doctors actively supported eugenics and other interventional programs. Others favored the National League for Birth Control and Sexual Hygiene (RV), which saw limiting family size as a form of economic self-defense. Far from acting as a homogenous group, doctors represented a broad spectrum of opinion. While left-leaning doctors staffed birth control clinics and fought along with sex reformers to liberalize sexual mores, their more conservative colleagues rallied against such clinics and interpreted them as competition or as completely misguided in their goals.

Despite discord over state intervention, one point on which politicians could agree was that more education about health issues was essential. In 1920, the Reich government introduced a pamphlet to be distributed to all couples when they registered their engagements at the civil registry.[23] Couples were explicitly encouraged to notify their parents or guardians before they finalized their engagements, since "those who refuse [to notify their parents] commit a serious wrong, which can take bitter revenge."[24] Individual *Länder* (states) had the legal right to declare a marriage invalid if the bride's or groom's parents had not been informed about their child's future spouse (BGB §1333 and §1334).[25] Health was deemed "the cornerstone of marital happiness," and couples were encouraged to consult a physician before marriage, since "some people are sick without ever being aware of it." Couples were further advised that it was their "holy duty to themselves, their future partner and their desired children, as well as to the fatherland, which desperately needs healthy offspring," to avoid marriages that would create unhappy couples and children, and burden the state with inferior, even useless citizens.[26] Unhealthy partners or partners who abused alcohol or drugs endangered not only their marriages but also their future children – and, as a result, the *Volkskörper*. Though it lacked any legal

22 Weindling, *Health, Race and German Politics*, 346.
23 The Federation for the Protection of Mothers and the Monist League had petitioned the Reichstag to introduce marriage certificates already in 1912, and both the Society to Combat Venereal Disease and eugenicists had also previously campaigned for marriage certificates. Ibid., 293.
24 "Merkblatt für Eheschließende," "Familienstammbuch" (Gießen: Verlag Emil Roth, 1924), StaD, L 80 IA, Gruppe 26, Titel 6, 15.
25 Already during the Wilhelmine era, government officials had contemplated interfering in marriage for the "greater good" of the community. Usborne, *Politics of the Body*, 35.
26 "Merkblatt für Eheschließende," "Familienstammbuch" (Gießen: Verlag Emil Roth, 1924), StaD, L 80 IA, Gruppe 26, Titel 6, 15.

force, the pamphlet appealed to couples' common sense and their desire to gain the state's blessing to marry. By means of the marriage pamphlet, the Weimar state set new health-based guidelines for "proper" marriage and imbued marriage with national significance without directly embracing interventional eugenics.[27]

Perhaps unsurprisingly, the pamphlet had a decidedly modest impact on couples' behavior. The members of the German Society for Racial Hygiene (Deutsche Gesellschaft für Rassenhygiene) argued that the pamphlet's impact was limited because it was too little too late, "since when the permission [to marry] is applied for – approximately a month before the marriage – it is no longer possible for many couples to postpone or cancel their marriages." They asserted that marital health should be taught in school before young people began seriously considering marriage.[28] Others insisted that couples who failed to obtain pamphlets at the civil registry ought to be pursued. In December 1920, the Prussian minister of justice announced that because imposing further regulations to ensure that all couples received the pamphlet would have exceeded his jurisdiction, problems with the distribution of the pamphlets would be left to the discretion of the individual German *Länder*.[29]

State authorities expressed concern about couples who either did not receive the pamphlet or who ignored the pamphlet's advice and refused to see a doctor before marrying, even though the pamphlet emphasized that "the doctor alone can identify the existence of an illness, which makes marriage inadvisable." To reduce any fears of medical examinations, couples were assured that in most cases doctors would only confirm the desirability of their marriage and give them the state's blessing to marry. By 1921, however, state authorities were facing a new concern. How were doctors to maintain confidentiality – as the pamphlet promised – for women who had not yet reached adulthood? In contrast to men, who could not legally marry before they reached legal age, one-sixth of all brides were not yet legally adults. As a result, obtaining a young bride's health history involved questioning her father or guardian, thus violating her right to confidentiality and risking causing "exceptional complications" for girls who had a history

27 Germany was by no means the only country to regulate marriage. Between 1907 and 1913, twelve U.S. states introduced eugenic sterilization and marriage prohibitions. Laws to ban marriage were introduced in Sweden in 1915, in Norway in 1918, and in Denmark in 1922. Usborne, *Politics of the Body*, 143 n 129.
28 Deutsche Gesellschaft für Rassenhygiene to Lippische Regierung, Detmold, received 30 April 1923, StaD, L 80 IA, Gruppe 26, Titel 1, 1, Bd. 16.
29 Statement by the Reichsminister der Justiz, 13 December 1920, Bundesarchiv Potsdam (BaP), R 15.01, 9379.

of "delicate illness." Doctors also felt that for divorced women, a complete medical history should include the health records of former spouses and any children, though they did not feel the same way about divorced men.[30]

The question of how to make the marriage pamphlet more effective in improving the health of marriage persisted. In 1921, the Reich health department polled local governments about the effectiveness of the marriage pamphlets and whether they thought the benefits of making premarital exams compulsory would justify the level of state intervention. In Berlin, local authorities acknowledged the potential benefit of increasing state control over marriage by making the voluntary marriage exams mandatory. Their great concern was practical, however. They worried that the time between the date of engagement and the date of marriage was inadequate for them to complete exams on all couples. In Westphalia, none of the health departments polled believed the state had the right to divulge information about an individual's health to a future spouse, even for the so-called good of the fatherland. Moreover, officials in Schaumberg-Lippe opposed any effort to hinder marriage, arguing that doing so would encourage men to have more extramarital affairs and spread venereal disease. In a second letter, they added that a state ban on some marriages, rather than altering behavior, would be more likely to decrease the absolute number of marriages while increasing the number of illegitimate births.[31] As a result of the unequivocally negative consensus among local authorities – and the fundamental belief among Weimar lawmakers that the democratic nature of the republic itself precluded compulsory exams – the Reich minister of the interior never made premarital medical exams mandatory.

Many politicians recognized that the government-sponsored pamphlet was inadequate to improve the health of marriage. The Social Democrats and Communists favored legalizing contraception in order to free couples from the constant fear of unwanted pregnancy. In light of government inaction, members of the sex reform movement opened clinics to educate couples about contraception under the motto that sexuality was better regulated than repressed.[32] The staff of these clinics – doctors, feminists, and social workers – led the charge for inexpensive, safe, effective, and accessible contraception. The Federation for the Protection of Mothers (Bund Deutscher Mütterschutz) also opened clinics to provide advice about contraception,

---

30 Gesundheitsamt Charlottenburg to the Reichsministerium des Innern, 30 June 1921, BaP, R 15.01, 9379.
31 Schaumberg-Lippische Landesregierung to Reichsminister des Innern, 5 May, 27 December 1921, BaP R 15.01, 9379.
32 Grossmann, *Reforming Sex*, 15.

abortion, and sexuality. It skirted the anti-obscenity regulations of Article 184.3 of the BGB by referring women to doctors for the fitting of diaphragms.[33] In addition, an array of organizations provided contraception and evaded the requirements of the obscenity clause by collecting membership dues.[34] The emphasis in all these private organizations was on public education. They were all allied with the political Left, though the SPD's support was compromised by its efforts to appease its coalition partner, the Catholic Center. Because only the KPD consistently supported them, the clinics' existence was tenuous.[35]

Right-wing politicians, the churches, and much of the medical profession allied against the lay clinics, which they complained lacked any consistent attention to eugenics. Members of the DNVP and the Catholic Center opposed the clinics because they believed that contraception and abortion distracted women from their roles as mothers and permitted – even encouraged – a loosening of societal morals. August Mayer, a Catholic gynecologist, was not alone in feeling that the clinics were contributing to the "dissolution of the family [and] the state." He stated boldly, "I believe it is no exaggeration if we say, this is the beginning of the decline of the West."[36] Members of the Center party argued that preserving and shoring up traditional bourgeois marriage represented the only way to save Germany, and the Catholic Church established its own marriage clinics "to promote the Christian ideal of large families." Catholic clinic workers praised women for their roles as wives and mothers and taught them to accept their responsibility to civilize their husbands' carnal desires.[37] They also vehemently opposed the decriminalization of abortion and any reform of the obscenity clause that banned the advertisement, display, or publication of "obscene" material, including contraceptives (Art. 184.3).

In response to the ongoing political wrangling at the national level and the pleas of the medical profession, Prussian Minister of Welfare Hirtsiefer issued a decree on 19 February 1926, encouraging local authorities throughout

---

33 The federation's success with its first clinic led to the rapid establishment of others. It is difficult to say exactly how many clinics were established during the Weimar era, because many kept their existence secret to avoid police intervention. By 1927, another organization, the Association for Free Sexual Reform (Arbeitsgemeinschaft Freier Sexual Reform Verein), had opened 80 clinics, and by 1928 the League for the Protection of Mothers and Social Hygiene had 500 clinics. Von Soden, *Die Sexualberatungsstellen der Weimarer Republik*, 65.

34 Usborne, *Politics of the Body*, 123–6.

35 In 1930, the leaders of the League for the Protection of Mothers and Social Family Hygiene, which was founded "to explain family limitation and to show women the ways and means by which contraception was used," were arrested for violating article 184.3, even though they claimed to have discussed contraception exclusively among members. They were convicted but received only a light sentence. Staatsarchiv Münster (SaM), Rechtsanwaltschaft Bochum no. 5.

36 Grossmann, *Reforming Sex*, 60.

37 Usborne, *Politics of the Body*, 96.

Germany to establish marriage counseling clinics (*Eheberatungsstellen*). His decree caused a veritable boom of marriage clinics, and by the beginning of the 1930s, more than 200 new marriage clinics had opened in Prussia to provide eugenic and health advice – rather than contraceptive information – and to consolidate and control the lay movement for birth control information and advice that had grown up among the working classes.[38] The marriage clinics were staffed by state social workers and doctors, who collected general and social information, conducted detailed medical examinations, and issued health certificates to engaged couples. In many towns, marriage counseling took place in the office of the district doctor, who generally believed his primary responsibility was to educate the public about hereditary health.[39]

Far from making sex reformers' clinics obsolete, doctors in the state clinics largely obeyed their mandate and refused to distribute (or discuss) contraceptives, so many women preferred lay clinics that provided contraceptive information. In Westphalia, Social Democratic and workers' organizations, the Organization for Population Control (Bund für Geburtenregelung), and, after 1931, the League for the Protection of Motherhood and Social Family Hygiene, offered women contraceptive information. By 1930, this competition had forced many doctors in state-sponsored marriage advice clinics to provide contraceptive information in order to build a clientele. Practicing birth control inside marriage became a reality for many couples, but even in small towns like Herford, conflicts arose between doctors and private organizations over providing contraceptives.[40] Once government-sponsored marriage clinics began to discuss contraception, it fostered the sense among Germans that traditional rules were loosening their hold on the people.[41]

During the Depression, a renewed debate over abortion politicized both sex advice clinics and state marriage counseling centers even further. Already hard-pressed to feed the children they had, many working-class families were devastated by unwanted pregnancies; speaking for such families, the KPD declared Civil Code §218, which criminalized abortion, "a particularly brutal and immediately personal form of sex-specific class oppression."[42] At the same time, the right-wing Reich Health Education Council, the Protestant Union for Health, and the League for Child-Rich Families (Bund der Kinderreichen) preached against contraception.

---

38 Von Soden, *Die Sexualberatungsstellen der Weimarer Republik*, 68.
39 Jahresgesundheitsbericht, Siegen, 1931, SaM, Kreis Siegen Kreis Wohlfahrtsamt, 8, Bd. 3.
40 Blank, "Die Schutzmittel," 66–71.
41 Grossmann, *Reforming Sex*, 11.
42 Grossmann, "Abortion and Economic Crisis," 74.

"Don't enter into marriage blindly! Get advice before you marry." This 1927 poster, created for a marriage advice center in the Hygienic Institute of the Technical College in Dresden, publicly encouraged couples to consult with medical authorities to determine the suitability of their proposed marriage before it was too late. "Aufforderung zum Aufsuchen der Eheberatungsstellen," courtesy of the Staatsarchiv Detmold (Signatur D 81 Nr. 1737).

Instead, they held up moral duty and restraint as the solutions to the "catastrophe" that had befallen the German family.[43] The Catholic position was reinforced on New Year's Eve 1930, when Pope Pius XI issued an encyclical titled "On Christian Marriage" that denounced sexual intercourse without procreative intention and called on the state to protect the weak and unborn. The encyclical was viewed by the KPD as a sign of the "increasing fasc%ization of the bourgeoisie" and as reflective of the Reich government's willingness to forsake working-class women. On International Women's Day, 8 March 1931, demonstrations and rallies took place throughout Germany to protest §218, and by June a broad coalition had developed that included the Communist women's movement, sex reformers, independent feminists, and pacifist groups, all of whom called for the immediate revocation of §218.

With time, the debates over abortion reform faded, and the Weimar Republic became paralyzed by its own struggle for survival. The Depression necessitated cutbacks in social welfare programs and sparked discussions about the potential benefit of a "differentiated welfare" system that would distribute state aid only to those deemed genetically worthy. In this context, contraception was seen as weakening the nation when genetically healthy Germans used it, but as requisite for those deemed unhealthy. Differentiated care would require the participation of doctors, who would conduct genetic evaluations. Although few went so far as to defend euthanasia, many physicians believed the status and prestige of medicine had suffered and blamed their troubles on "Jews, socialists, [and] the increasing number of quacks."[44] Many were also convinced that applying eugenics to marriage would restore the prestige of the medical profession and fulfill their responsibility to help reverse the "degeneration" of the German racial stock. For some physicians, "the quest for professional advancement . . . obscured moral and political issues" and significantly altered the aim and impact of marriage advice clinics.[45]

German couples often resisted the application of eugenic criteria to reproduction in their private lives. This meant that "healthy" couples were as likely to limit family size as so-called unhealthy couples. Contrary to popular belief, the majority of requests for birth control came from married or engaged women who wanted to control their family size, not from

43 Weindling, *Health, Race and German Politics*, 422.
44 Proctor, *Racial Hygiene*, 69.
45 Usborne, *Politics of the Body*, 148. Paul Weindling argues that marriage advice clinics were "a crucial place in a transition which saw eugenics shift from being the concern of an educated elite to providing the rationale of expert planners supporting state-imposed population policy." See *Health, Race and German Politics*, 429.

"immoral" single women.[46] As Atina Grossmann has astutely pointed out, "In a context where the average working-class family size had shrunk to about four, and the 'two-child system' had become the norm, women were redefining the meaning of 'need' or 'hardship' requiring prevention or termination of pregnancy."[47] Especially during difficult economic times, women sought contraception, not genetic advice, and people across the political and social spectrum rallied together against §218. Throughout the Weimar era, official intervention into marriage was tentative and remained largely voluntary. Though state authorities considered a more interventional policy, they stopped short of making medical exams mandatory. For most Germans, marriage remained a private affair and responses to marriage policy varied widely.

REGULATING MARRIAGE, 1933–1945

When the National Socialists came to power in 1933, they imposed an ideology on Germans that defined marriage as a "long-term relationship . . . based on the mutual trust, love and respect between two genetically healthy and racially identical people, of opposite gender, for the purpose of preserving and promoting the common good through peaceable work together and with the aim of conceiving like-raced and genetically healthy children and raising them to be able-bodied national comrades."[48] To an unprecedented degree, marriage was endowed with a public importance, and the birthrate was seen as an indicator of Germany's economic and political future.[49] Moreover, the Nazi state appropriated the right to intervene in all marriages in order to control the quality (and quantity) of their ensuing children. Nazi policymakers reconceptualized the state's relation to family, marriage, and motherhood and firmly established race as the central factor guiding family policy. To control the racial quality of marriage, Nazi authorities intruded into the private sphere and, in the eyes of some historians, destroyed the division between it and the public sphere.[50] Many Germans found, however, that the disparity between the intent of Nazi programs and the actual implementation of those programs permitted them to preserve some degree of autonomy.

---

46 Grossmann, *Reforming Sex*, 55.   47 Ibid., 99.

48 Ludwig Nockher, "Vorschläge zur Gestaltung des deutschen Ehescheidungsrechts," quoted in Klinksiek, *Die Frau im NS-Staat*, 69.

49 Grossmann, *Reforming Sex*, 104.

50 Von Saldern, "Victims or Perpetrators?" 146; Pine, *Nazi Family Policy*, 183.

Upon taking power, Nazi leaders lashed out at the institutions they accused of undermining the German birthrate, especially the Weimar sex advice and marriage counseling centers. In May 1933, the Prussian minister of the interior called on the police to close the "organizations for contraception and sexual hygiene that served the Bolshevik cultural leanings."[51] The police responded by confiscating records; firing, arresting, and driving into exile personnel; and closing sex advice centers throughout Germany. It was not counseling itself that made the centers reprehensible in the eyes of the new government but rather the separation of sexuality and procreation and the absence of racial eugenics. In addition, both the female solidarity that had its roots in the clinic waiting rooms and the antifascist political perspective common among employees and clientele were anathema to the Nazi leadership.[52] Although marriage centers existed under both the Weimar and National Socialist regimes, then, their leadership, staff, and goals were not at all continuous.[53]

As early as March 1934, the Nazis began to replace the Weimar marriage counseling centers with National Socialist centers, which Reich Minister of the Interior Wilhelm Frick believed would help win the trust and confidence of the *Volk*.[54] The new centers, run by the National Socialist People's Welfare Organization (NSV), were responsible for providing "systematic, responsible education for future German fathers and mothers." In contrast to the Weimar clinics, which had been variously run by the state, the Catholic Church, and sex reform advocates, the NSV centers advertised extensively and were linked to the health department and civil registries to reach all Germans. Nazi authorities hoped the new centers would teach all young and "racially pure" people that as members of the *Volksgemeinschaft* they had a responsibility to marry and bear children but remain independent of government support.

Whereas Weimar marriage pamphlets reassured couples that most marriages would be approved upon examination, as the Nazis tightened racial and genetic requirements, they added a more menacing tone to the marriage pamphlets. Before an engagement was finalized, Nazi authorities encouraged both bride and groom to visit a doctor and become familiar with one another's family histories, since "you do not marry your partner alone, rather

---

51 Prussian Minister des Innern to the state police departments, 17 May 1933, in von Soden, *Die Sexualberatungsstellen der Weimarer Republik*, 148.
52 Von Soden, *Die Sexualberatungsstellen der Weimarer Republik*, 146.
53 Ibid., 8; Grossmann, *Reforming Sex*, ch. 6.
54 Reichsminister des Innern to Kreis Warburg, 29 November 1937, StaD, D 102 Warburg, 35.

To celebrate publicly the importance of healthy marriage, the Nazis encouraged mass weddings. These 122 couples married ca. 1938 with support from the Nazi authorities. Men were encouraged to wed in their NSDAP or army uniforms to show their support for the new regime. Courtesy of Getty Images.

to an extent you marry his ancestors [as well]."[55] Doctors were instructed to focus on the general well-being of the German *Volk*, even as their patients concentrated on their own future happiness and families.[56] The Nazis hoped that a reliable doctor would examine every German couple before marriage so that those deemed unfit could be forbidden to marry.

The Nazi marriage guidelines depended heavily on the involvement of the medical profession in policy implementation. In a speech before the National Socialist Physicians' League (Nationalsozialistischer Ärztebund), Hitler announced: "You, you National Socialist doctors, I cannot do without you for a single day, not a single hour. If not for you, if you fail me, then all is lost."[57] He succeeded in gaining the support of a substantial number of doctors, many of whom joined the Nazi Party even before 1933 and some of whom served as NSDAP representatives in parliament. The National Socialist Physicians' League was formed by physicians "to coordinate Nazi medical policy and 'to purify the German medical community of the influence of Jewish Bolshevism.'" Its members agreed with Hitler's aim of applying race to public policy and supported his goal of creating "a totality of the physicians' community, with physicians having total dedication to the *Volk*."[58] National Socialism's appeal to many physicians lay less in its ideology than in more practical professional considerations. The Nazi

---

55 Das Ehegesetz.   56 StaD, D 102 Warburg, 35.
57 Bartels, "Der Arzt als Gesundheitsführer des deutschen Volkes," supplement to *Deutsches Ärzteblatt* 68 (1938): 4–9, quoted in Proctor, *Racial Hygiene*, 64.
58 Lifton, *Nazi Doctors*, 33.

emphasis on racial health vastly expanded the scope of job opportunities for physicians to include positions in the party, SS (*Schutzstaffel*, or Protective Squadron), army, and industry and boosted physicians' professional status, prestige, and earning capacity. Many physicians believed that by driving Jewish doctors from the profession, furthermore, the Nazis would relieve the overcrowding that had come to characterize the medical field.

Even with the support of many doctors, tightening the health requirements for marriage proved difficult. The Reich minister of the interior readily acknowledged that denying marriage certificates to young people threatened to damage trust in the regime as a whole. To avoid devastating individuals who had invested time and money in planning their weddings, the minister argued that marriage certificates should be awarded with some flexibility – at least initially. Furthermore, in 1937, he recognized that doctors might find the task of informing their patients that they were unfit for marriage to be an unpleasant one. Since he could find no alternative, however, he merely stated, "I must leave it up to the personal tact of doctors and public health nurses, to select the way and time . . . [for informing people] so that a special mental agitation will be avoided."[59]

Only an obligatory marriage certificate program would have effectively reached all Germans before marriage. For practical reasons, the Nazi leadership never succeeded in establishing such a program. Nazi policymakers' hesitance to make the marriage certificates mandatory can be attributed, at least in part, to the fact that doctors were already overwhelmed by the other demands placed on them by National Socialist racial laws.[60] In addition, they feared protest from people who interpreted the marriage certificates as an unnecessary, undesirable intrusion into their private lives. As a 1935 article in the journal *Erbarzt* (Genetic Doctor) emphasized, "a forced exchange of health certificates before marriage is not foreseen."[61] Rather than making them mandatory, Nazi policy radically broadened the scope of the exams that did take place and expanded the reasons for denying couples permission to marry.

The Nazis' rigid guidelines often wreaked havoc at the local level. Even though no legislation was enacted, in January 1934, a rumor circulated in Detmold that as of 1 January 1934, all engaged couples had to obtain a marriage certificate, causing a flood of people to pour into the health

59 Reichsminister des Innern to Kreis Warburg, 29 November 1937, StaD, D 102 Warburg, 35.
60 Vossen, "Gesundheitsämter im Kreis Herford," 105.
61 *Der Erbarzt*, Beilage zum *Deutschen Ärzteblatt*, Eheberatung und erbbiologische Bestandaufnahme durch stadtlichen Gesundheitsämter, Berlin, 21 September 1935, StaD, D 102 Warburg, 35.

department.[62] In October 1935, the *Kreisarzt* in Bad Salzuflen, Dr. Augener, requested that the Lippe government publish a notice in the local newspaper warning people that they could not appear at the health department without an appointment. He wrote: "Already now some authorities send people to the health department to be examined without previous notification. This leads to the situation in which, possibly 40–50 people arrive at the three medical officers' office hours."[63] In their rush to determine marital health for the ever growing number of couples seeking certification, doctors were sometimes forced to perform only superficial exams. In 1938, the *Landrat* (district administrator) complained that the Herford Health Department and another doctor, Dr. A., worked at a pace so slow that it had "reached a degree that hindered and paralyzed."[64] Despite a file rife with complaints about work whose inefficiency prevented the smooth implementation of the state's racial policy, Dr. A. never suffered any negative professional sanction, probably because his political allegiance stood beyond question and there was no one to replace him.[65]

To reduce the number of "unhealthy" marriages without making medical certificates mandatory, nonphysician health department and civil registry authorities were also called upon to identify people for whom "reservations concerning marriage" (*Ehebedenken*) existed. Decisions regarding marriage certificates rested on physical appearance, rumor, and possibly even revenge as much as they did on "legitimate" reasons.[66] Thus, although the Nazi rhetoric stressed the importance of restricting marriage to healthy partners, the Nazis failed to create a comprehensive policy to evaluate all marriages. Instead, they compromised, requiring medical examinations only for some couples – a decision that decisively drew the state into some, but not all, marriages.

In addition to subjecting as many engaged couples as possible to state scrutiny, Nazi marriage policy broadened the definition of a bad marriage.

---

62 Letter Kreisarzt Detmold to Lippische Landesregierung, 17 January 1934, StaD, L 80 IC, Gruppe 26, Fach 6, 19b.

63 Kreisarzt Bad Salzfulen to Regierung Detmold, 24 October 1935, StaD L 80 IC, Gruppe 26, Fach 2, 2.

64 Letter Landrat to Regierungspräsident Minden, 1 September 1938, StaD, Personal Akten Ärtze, Dr. A.

65 Dr. A., a county doctor in Lübbecke and Herford, was promoted to *Obermedizinalrat* (head medical director) and appointed to the racial hygiene court despite complaints that his work suffered from a "superficiality, indifference, and carelessness that really know no bounds." NSDAP Kreisleiter to Regierungspräsident Minden, 21 May 1940, StaD, Personal Akten Ärtze, Dr. A. In July 1945, Dr. A. retired at the insistence of the occupation government at the age of sixty-eight.

66 Vossen, "Die Gesundheitsämter in Kreis Herford," 105. That personal revenge may have played a role is a speculation based on Klaus-Michael Mallmann and Gerhard Paul's analysis. "Omniscient, Omnipotent, Omnipresent?" 179–80. See also Gellately, *Gestapo and German Society*, 158.

Whereas marriages had previously been discouraged primarily for health-related reasons – tuberculosis, venereal disease, and schizophrenia were among the most common reasons to deny couples permission to marry – after 1933, the reasons increasingly involved personal behavior and family history. Nazi policymakers identified genetic roots for many social problems, from irregular employment to trouble in school, and tried to prevent people who had troubled personal histories from passing on inferior genes to their children. So-called deviant sexual histories also diminished many people's chances of being approved for marriage. Women suspected of leading a "bad lifestyle" were often denied permission to marry. When Frau Schreyer, a divorced woman, tried to remarry, all the residents in her apartment building testified against her, claiming that men visited her at home. Because genetic flaws, not social circumstances, were purported to cause undesirable behavior, the Nazis did not think marriage would end Frau Schreyer's allegedly bad lifestyle.[67] The Nazis appointed block leaders (*Blockwärter*) and individual Germans to watch one another and report inappropriate behavior to authorities, providing unprecedented access to private life. Nazi authorities also interpreted any attempt on the part of "healthy" Germans to marry an "inappropriate" person as a sign of mental weakness. When one young man announced his desire to marry a woman who was old enough to be his mother and clearly beyond childbearing age, authorities labeled him "weak" and forbade the marriage.[68]

Although Nazi policymakers never declared marriage certificates mandatory, they did fundamentally revise marriage law to accommodate their racial ideology. Even before they took power, the National Socialists had proposed adding an amendment titled "Betrayal of the Race" (*Rassenverat*) to the Law for the Protection of the Republic that would have sentenced to imprisonment or death anyone "who contribute[d] or threaten[ed] to contribute to the racial deterioration and dissolution of the German people through interbreeding with Jewish blood or the colored races."[69] After 1933, many judges did not wait for the law to change before refusing to perform marriage ceremonies between Jews and Gentiles on the ground of "general national principles." The propensity among judges to rewrite the law became so common that on 7 January 1934, Reich Minister of

---

67 NSDAP Kreisleitung Herne-Castrop-Rauxel to Ortsgruppe der NSDAP Herne-West, 23 June 1942, SaM, NS Kreis und Ortsgruppenleitung, 34.

68 After the war began, authorities tended to label women "feebleminded" rather than identify a problem with a soldier at the front, regardless of whether it was the potential bride or groom who was judged inappropriate for marriage. Reichsminister des Innern, 21 September 1942, StaD, D 102 Lemgo, 244.

69 Müller, *Hitler's Justice*, 91.

the Interior Frick sent a memorandum to all judicial officials "instructing them to respect the 'Aryan Laws' more carefully and to perform official acts, such as marriage ceremonies when the legal conditions were satisfied, even if such laws perhaps appear[ed] not to conform fully to National Socialist views."[70] Despite Frick's memorandum and the Supreme Court's confirmation of its legality, many civil registry officials continued to forbid marriage between Jews and Gentiles. When in the summer of 1935 several couples turned to the courts to protest, they found many judges backed the civil registry officials on the ground that "'although the letter of the law did not prohibit' mixed marriages, they violated 'the most important laws of the nation, which consist[ed] in cultivating German blood and maintaining its purity.'"[71] The county court in Königsberg added further that "No one can be in any doubt that marriage between a Jew and an Aryan woman is contrary to the German understanding of what is right."[72] In July 1935, Frick "postponed until further notice" all mixed marriages. Finally, on 15 September of that year, the Law to Protect German Blood and Honor (also known as the Nuremberg Laws) explicitly banned marriage between Jews and Gentiles. One month later, the law was expanded to prohibit marriage between the healthy and the hereditarily ill.[73] By outlawing mixed-race and "unhealthy" marriages, the Nazis established a legal basis for doctors and civil registry authorities to identify "suspicious" people. Subsequently, many Germans found their marriages forbidden because, from the standpoint of genetic history, the intended marriage did not lie in the state's interest.[74] Even after the passage of the Nuremberg Laws, however, the definitions of "Jewish" and of "unhealthy" remained ambiguous, giving doctors tremendous leeway in evaluating proposed marriages.

Nazi policymakers were themselves aware of this flexibility, and they used it as another means to advance their racial agenda. On 2 November 1936, the Reich minister of the interior issued a list of cases in which exemptions should be granted regardless of troubled genetic histories. For the most part, the cases involved couples who wanted to marry despite their inability to reproduce. Nazi authorities permitted these marriages if they believed that marriage would prevent the further spread of genetic diseases – for example, if a hereditarily ill person proposed to marry someone who had been

70 Ibid., 92.   71 Ibid.
72 Ibid.
73 Pressure for the Nuremberg Laws came from two groups: anti-Semites and the public health lobby. Weindling, *Health, Race and German Politics*, 531.
74 Doctors, mayors, and individuals actively negotiated marital eligibility. These negotiations reveal that the definitions of "hereditarily ill" and "genetically unworthy" were slippery when applied to marriage candidates. StaD, L 80 IC, Gruppe 24, Fach 2, 4.

sterilized – and if the marriage promised to increase social stability. In particular cases, they even encouraged marriage between sterilized Germans (Marriage Law for Greater Germany, §1, paragraph 2). In 1936, the National Meeting of Delegates from Local and Rural Committees (Deutscher Gemeindetag) and Provincial Governors (*Oberpräsidenten*) began to discuss arranging marriages between sterilized men and women. Directors of psychiatric institutions were optimistic that such marriages might decrease the number of people dependent on institutional care. They noted that in the past, many residents had applied to marry and been turned away.[75] Other provincial governors argued that these marriages would underscore the importance of marriage and might diminish the stigma attached to sterilization. If sterilized people married one another, they would also be less likely to marry – or block marriages between – "healthy" Germans. Some people opposed this effort because they thought trying to arrange marriages that would not produce healthy children was a waste of state resources.[76] Although no concrete legislation was passed, the fact that Nazi officials sought to encourage marriage even between sterilized women and men shows the tremendous value they placed on the institution of marriage as a stabilizing structure in society.

Exemptions were also granted when family formation was likely to decrease the state's welfare load. In 1940, Johannes, a factory worker and father of five children, applied to marry Susanna. Although Susanna had five illegitimate children of her own and had been sterilized, he was convinced that she would take good care of his household. The health department agreed that Susanna was "industrious and clean" and would probably be capable of running a good household. The Reich minister of the interior, who had requested that all such cases be presented to him for approval, deemed the marriage "desirable" because it would provide a home for the many children without producing more children. In another instance, Minna W. and Albert S. found a doctor who supported their marriage despite her sterilization. The physician believed the longevity of their relationship and their mutual child proved they would not part ways even if the marriage was prohibited. As he put it, "Refusing to permit the marriage would only encourage a concubine situation."[77]

---

75 Deutscher Gemeindetag to Oberpräsident Verwaltung des Provinzial bezw. Bezirksverbandes, 24 June 1936, Landschaftsverbandarchiv (LSVA), C60, 258.
76 Deutscher Gemeindetag to Oberpräsidenten der Provinzial Westfalens, 18 September 1936, LSVA, C60, 258.
77 SaM, Landgericht Arnsberg, 712.

Still, for Nazi policymakers, procreation remained the explicit goal of marriage among the racially healthy. With the introduction of the marriage loan program in 1935 as part of the Law to Reduce Unemployment (*Gesetz zur Verminderung der Arbeitslosigkeit*), the Nazis hoped to encourage couples to marry at a younger age, to lengthen couples' childbearing years, and to raise the birthrate. As further encouragement, they reduced the principal to be repaid by 25 percent for each child born to a participating couple.[78] To lower Germany's male unemployment rate, they also made the loans contingent upon the woman leaving the labor market. Women who had not worked before marriage were initially ineligible for the loans – testimony to the importance placed on women's yielding jobs to men.

Selection of marriage loan recipients followed strict racial guidelines, and doctors became integrally involved in the process. They rejected approximately 20 percent of the marriage loan applications they received, most often because the applicants did not meet health standards.[79] Denials were not limited to medical problems, however. Couples also failed to qualify for loans if they were labeled "asocial," "immoral," or "work-shy," or even if someone in their families exhibited such characteristics. The most incriminating evidence of 'unhealthy' genes was when another family member had been sterilized. Even being morally and physically healthy did not guarantee applicants a loan, because the Nazis did not want the marriage loans to be confused with welfare. Couples who did not appear capable of repaying a loan promptly were at a higher risk of disqualification. The Detmold City Council refused a loan to Alfred S., for example, stating, "He does not offer the certainty that he will follow through with the repayment of his loan."[80] Thus, a precarious balance existed between being too needy, in which case couples appeared a "bad risk," and not being needy enough, as in the case of nonworking women.

The implementation of marriage loans wreaked havoc at the local level. Before the loans could be awarded, all applicants had to be examined by the *Kreisarzt*, whom Minister Frick proclaimed "guardian of the genetically healthy family."[81] Local doctors gathered family histories and examined couples free of cost to ascertain that "neither partner suffered from genetically based mental or physical afflictions, infectious diseases, or other

---

78 StaD, L 80 IC, Gruppe 42, Fach 70, 1.   79 Czarnowski, *Das Kontrollierte Paar*, 123.
80 Beschwerde der Eheleute Alfred Setter to Lippische Regierung, 14 October 1933, StaD, L 80 IC, Gruppe 24, Fach 6, 19a.
81 *Der Erbarzt*, Beilage zum *Deutschen Ärzteblatt*, Berlin, 21 September 1935, StaD, D 102 Warburg, 35.

life-threatening illnesses."[82] But doctors quickly became overwhelmed by this new responsibility. Between 1933 and 1937, a total of 93,984 marriage loans were distributed in Westphalia. By 1937, almost half (42.6 percent) of all newlyweds received marriage loans.[83] Already in September 1933, the Bad Salzuflen county doctor complained that he could not deal with the "storm of people" who needed to be examined. He explained: "After returning from Reelkirchen yesterday, there were already sixty mothers and children in the Hofmannstift Advice Center, and when I went home at 6:00 at night, there were still thirty marriage loan applicants sitting and standing in my rooms.... After a long discussion, I succeeded in sending some of them away, but there were still approximately twenty-two present until around 10:00 at night." These people, he claimed, came not only from his district but also from Detmold and Lemgo, presumably because the doctors in these other cities were even busier.[84] Generally, doctors in large and medium-sized cities felt less overburdened because communal health departments were able to carry some of the cases. In rural areas, however, the county doctor was usually solely responsible for all examinations.[85] The racial laws that banned Jewish doctors from practicing medicine only worsened the situation.[86]

The examination of marriage loan applicants not only placed an undue demand on doctors' time, it was also a financial drain. Although the law required medical exams, it made no provision to pay for them, and applicants were explicitly not responsible for the cost of the exams. The Reich government denied any responsibility, and so the financial burden fell on doctors. Since all applicants were required to have both tuberculosis and syphilis exams, moreover, the cost was substantial. As a result, one adviser to the Prussian Medical Department proposed that the government pay doctors three marks per approved loan to cover the costs of exams. The Reich minister of finance worried that this would place too heavy a financial burden on the government. Instead, on 26 July 1933, the government announced that while it would be willing to pay, tuberculosis and syphilis tests were to be limited to "suspicious" cases in order to keep costs down. In

---

82 Letter from Lippische Landesregierung Detmold, 12 August 1933, StaD, L 80 IC, Gruppe 24, Fach 6, 19b.
83 *Statistisches Jahrbuch* 58 (1940): 52.
84 Kreisarzt Bad Salzuflen to Regierung/Fürsorgeabteilung, Detmold, 7 September 1933, StaD, L 80 IC, Gruppe 24, Fach 6, 19b. See also Amtsarzt Dr. Augener to Lippische Landesregierung, 24 October 1935, StaD, L 80 IC, Gruppe 24, Fach 2, 2.
85 Rural county doctors acted as district medical doctors (*Bezirksfürsorgearzt*) and state medical officers (*Staatliche Medizinalbeamte*) in addition to running private practices. Procter, *Racial Hygiene*, 89–90.
86 Ibid., 90.

addition, the Reich government appealed to the *Länder* and communities to relieve doctors financially, since the local community stood to benefit from healthy marriages.[87] In April 1936, a year after its introduction, the marriage loan program began to require couples themselves to pay for the examinations.

The medical exams were made more frustrating for doctors by the difficulty they had obtaining reliable medical information. Forced to depend on scanty records, their own memories, and information provided by their patients, they soon discovered that most applicants did not have reliable knowledge about their own families, nor did doctors trust patients to describe their families accurately. One doctor in Duisburg learned only after approving a couple's marriage loan that the woman's brother was mentally handicapped. He discovered this not through state channels but from his own young daughter, who met the boy while she was playing.[88] Even more discouraging to the many doctors interested in applying Nazi racial guidelines was "how few applicants...even tried to create a picture of the genetic health of their families." As one Paderborn county doctor complained, "Only the smallest number know the cause of death of their parents, to say nothing of their grandparents."[89] Thus, in a number of ways, medical evaluations for marriage loans proved to be extremely difficult, and even when it was supported by German doctors, the implementation of Nazi marriage policy was often inconsistent and unreliable.

Doctors did not hesitate to voice their concerns to the government.[90] In December 1933, the Detmold county doctor complained bitterly to the Lippe *Land* government authorities that the marriage loan program was destroying many doctors' medical practices. He claimed that "the examinations for marriage suitability overwhelm the county doctors so severely that they are forced to neglect many of the other duties of their jobs completely." Furthermore, he noted with outrage that all applicants for marriage loans were being sent directly to the doctor rather than only those who had passed a preliminary screening, thus unnecessarily compounding the doctors' burdens. The onslaught of complaints forced government officials to respond, but when they did so, they showed little sympathy for the plight of doctors. On 13 January 1934 the government officials declared,

---

87 Czarnowski, *Das kontrollierte Paar*, 108–9.   88 Frau Löhr, interview.
89 Letter from Staatlichen Gesundheitsamt des Kreises Paderborn to Kreis Warburg, 15 November 1935, StaD, D 102 Warburg, 36.
90 In 1933, the Detmold county doctor complained that he was unable to do the examinations for marriage loans because he had never received the correct forms. Letter from Kreisarzt Bad Salzuflen to Regierung/Fürsorgeabteilung, Detmold, 7 September 1933, StaD, L 80 IC, Gruppe 24, Fach 6, 19b.

"While we do not fail to recognize that the county doctors' work is in heavy demand as a result of the examinations for marriage loan recipients, and the processing of applications for sterilization according to the Law to Prevent Hereditarily Sick Offspring, we expect you to fulfill these obligations without requesting assistants."[91] The Nazis did, however, recommend that all other regulations for the marriage loan be met *before* applicants were referred to the doctors. Finally, in August 1934, government authorities began to require people to schedule an appointment with the doctor rather than just show up during office hours. Nevertheless, the practical difficulties of implementing the marriage loan program were never appreciated by the national government, which continued to complain that the medical examinations were taking far too long.[92]

Even after the first year, when the initial confusion over the marriage loans had subsided, the stress on doctors continued as ever more couples applied for the loans.[93] When, in August 1936, the National Socialist Women's Organization (Nationalsozialistische Frauen Organization, NSF) leadership asked Dr. Frenzel of Lemgo to send at least one of his nurse hygienists to an NSF workshop, he unequivocally refused, claiming that he could not spare anyone even for a few days due to the burden the marriage loans placed on him. The NSF complained to higher party officials, and Dr. Frenzel was compelled to let his nurses participate.[94] This struggle illustrates how ideological aims trumped practical considerations in the context of marriage.

Despite their dependence on doctors for medical examinations, the Nazis continued to push ideological agendas. Dr. Frenzel, not a Nazi Party member, was transferred against his wishes to a less prestigious post after 1933.[95] Even after his transfer to Lemgo, Dr. Frenzel continued to experience the state's intrusions into his practice. He found vexing his nurses' inclination to

---

91 Lippische Landesregierung Detmold to Kreisarzt, 31 January 1934, StaD, D 102 Lemgo, 240.

92 Präsident des Landesfinanzamts, Münster, to the Lippische Landesregierung, 25 November 1935, StaD, L 80 IC, Gruppe 24, Fach 10, 29. To save time, Hitler Youth and SS members were made exempt from extra doctors' examinations when they applied for marriage loans. StaD, D 102 Lemgo, 247.

93 In Westphalia in 1933–1935, 54,569 marriage loans were granted to 33.3 percent of marrying couples. In 1937, 21,069 loans were granted to 42.6 percent of marrying couples. In 1938, the program hit its high point at 51.4 percent of marriages, after which it declined slightly to 44.4 percent in 1939 and 48.0 percent in 1940. *Statistisches Jahrbuch* 57 (1939): 48.

94 Dr. Frenzel, Gesundheitsamt Kreis Lemgo, to Die Lippische Regierung, Abteilung Fürsorge, 18 August 1936; Der Reichsstatthalter Lippe und Schaumberg Lippe to NSF, Kreis Lemgo, Bad Salzuflen, 3 September 1936; Response, NSF, Kreis Lemgo, Bad Salzuflen, 5 September 1936, all in StaD, L 80 IC, Gruppe 27, Fach 20, 4.

95 He forcefully protested the demotion, citing his well-established tuberculosis clinic, his success at keeping Lippe free of the "poverty, misery and illness" common in other areas of the Reich, and his son's education as reasons for opposing the transfer. Dr. Frenzel to Oberregierungsrat, 28 April 1933, StaD, Personal Akten Ärzte, M. Frenzel.

overextend themselves in particular to approve marriage loans themselves. As he emphasized, "It is out of the question for a nurse to award marriage loans; if she does so, this must be labeled impertinent."[96] Dr. Frenzel's increasingly desperate effort to maintain a degree of autonomy and his distance from the regime may explain the NSF's insistence that his nurses participate in the NSF seminar.

Though Nazi authorities encouraged couples to apply for marriage loans, ultimately the decision whether to apply lay with the potential applicants. In many cases, it was quite a simple decision to make. With a value of up to 1,000 Reichsmark in store coupons – the average worker's annual wage was 1,520 Reichsmark – the marriage loans provided many couples with the money they needed to marry and start families.[97] As Frau Siebold (b. 1912) remembered, "It was 800 Reichsmark. We took advantage of that [to furnish our living room]. Everyone received one." Frau Siebold's comment suggests that not all Germans grasped the implications of the state's larger eugenic program; Frau Schmitt (b. 1910) also thought that the marriage loan "came automatically with marriage." Many loan applicants thus questioned the need for a health examination.[98] Frau Neske (b. 1917) remembered more accurately: "We had to be examined by a doctor first to prove that we were healthy and so forth, otherwise one did not receive [a marriage loan]."[99]

Not everyone saw the loans in a positive light. Some couples, especially those in secure financial situations, viewed the loans as welfare and rejected them as such. As Frau Kemper (b. 1919) assured me, "It was not necessary." When asked about the marriage loan program, Frau Ludwig (b. 1915) said she believed that accepting state money would have undermined her own parents' role in helping her establish a household. "My husband and I, we did not want that," she told me. "We received what we needed from our parents."[100]

Some Germans viewed the loans simply as an opportunity to reap personal benefit from state policy. Herr Steinke recalled that he and his wife applied for and received a loan because they saw no reason not to accept

---

96 Amtsarzt Dr. Frenzel to Lippische Regierung Detmold, 15 July 1937, StaD, L 80 IC, Gruppe 27, Fach 20, 4.

97 Frevert, *Women in German History*, 230. There is evidence that the average amount of marriage loans decreased over time from 1,000 RM in 1933 to 730 RM and then to 540 RM. Bock, *Zwangssterilisation im Nationalsozialismus*, 148.

98 *Berichte der Sozialistische Demokratische Partei Deutschlands* (hereafter *Sopade Berichte*) 5 Jahrgang (1938) no. 6, 643.

99 Frau Siebold, interview; Frau Schmitt, interview; Frau Neske, interview.

100 Frau Kemper, interview; Frau Ludwig, interview.

the "free money."[101] But authorities denied marriage loans to couples who obviously did not support the program's goals. When Herr Müller and his bride applied, their chance of receiving a loan was diminished because the groom allegedly supported Communist organizations. But their application was rejected definitively when it was discovered that the bride had called members of the SA "mustard pants" (an insult stemming from the color of their uniforms). Although Nazi Party membership was not mandatory for the recipients of the loans, "political reliability" was. The local NSDAP officials deemed the couple merely opportunistic, saying of them, "They feel their allegiance to the national Reich government suddenly now because they can expect money from the current state." The officials rejected such attempts to profit at the state's expense, arguing, "We have led the victorious party struggle to a triumphant conclusion, and will fight also against profiteers including Herr Müller."[102]

Some couples tried to increase their chances of approval by changing their circumstances. One couple in Brake resigned from their church in the hope that such a step would win state approval and result in a marriage loan. When their application was rejected, they immediately rejoined the church.[103] In another case, a woman took a job before applying for a loan since she knew that not having a job before marriage would make it appear that she and her fiancé did not need financial assistance to marry. Despite her employment, however, her marriage loan application was rejected.

Nazi authorities manipulated the marriage loan program to fit the regime's shifting needs. In 1937, as the country's labor demands increased, the Nazis dropped the requirement that women cease to work outside the home, a change that the populace generally welcomed. Far more troubling, they tried to use information gathered during marriage loan exams in other contexts, making the claim that state interests took precedence over individual interests. The doctor who examined Bertha S. and Hermann T. for a marriage license first denied their application, then turned to the state and recommended Bertha S. for sterilization.[104] As Germans learned of the potential risk involved in revealing information to doctors, many refused even to apply for marriage loans. Government authorities failed to recognize that laziness or fear might make individuals hesitant to apply. They even blamed other authorities for couples' refusal to apply.

---

101 Herr Steinke, interview.
102 Letter protesting marriage loan application signed by Gemeindevorsteher, Beiordneter, Ortsgruppenführer der NSDAP, StaD, L 80 IC, Gruppe 24, Fach 6, 19a.
103 Marriage loan applications, StaD, L 80 IC, Gruppe 24, Fach 6, 19a.
104 Case file, Tilke and Stein, 1939, StaD, L 80 IC, Gruppe 28, Fach 23, 10.

In 1942, the state health department criticized one nurse's alleged inefficiency, complaining that "It cannot continue, that [marriage loan] applications lie unattended for so long."[105] Nurse Paula denied any responsibility for people's failing to fill out their applications and claimed that "One cannot demand that we welfare workers constantly run after such applicants when it concerns looking after their own individual economic interests. I leave no application unattended, process – what I can – immediately, and do not need to be reminded of it."[106] Three months later, in response to a governmental inquiry about an incomplete file, Nurse Paula confirmed that though she pressured people to apply, she did not have time for hand-holding: "Ultimately the population believes we are servants, and in the present context [of war] – where everyone must manage their time to the utmost – that cannot be expected."[107] The discrepancy between the demands government officials made and social workers' experiences reveals not only a lack of communication but also a significant lack of official comprehension of the everyday realities of implementing the marriage loan program.

Despite encouragement from the state to waive their oath of confidentiality (*Schweigepflicht*) to further the state's racial aims, not all doctors did so. In fact, rather than use their power to speak out against couples, many political functionaries and doctors were able to shield individuals from the harsher consequences of state intervention. Nurse hygienists often defended couples they deemed worthy, even if they did not strictly meet racial criteria. If an extended family member was genetically "flawed" but the immediate family was "worthy," a nurse's report could make the difference for a couple. People whose families could not be traced posed a particular problem, but youth department officials sometimes spoke on behalf of the illegitimate children in their custody. When Ellie R. and her fiancé applied for a marriage loan, the Detmold Youth Department pointed out that Ellie "enjoyed a good reputation." Since she graduated from high school, she had consistently worked, and neither mother nor daughter could be considered an enemy of the state. Although Ellie and her fiancé did not have any money saved, she was employed at the post office and was saving money for her dowry. The youth department argued that a marriage loan would enable

105 Staatliches Gesundheitsamt Lemgo to Gesundheitspflegerin Schwester Paula T., 13 January 1942, StaD, D 102 Lemgo, 243.
106 Schwester Paula T. to Staatliches Gesundheitsamt Lemgo, 17 January 1942, StaD, D 102 Lemgo, 243.
107 Ibid., 4 April 1942, StaD, D 102 Lemgo, 243.

this desirable young couple to establish a household sooner than would otherwise be possible.[108]

Nazi marriage policy, already complicated by the difficulties of implementation and the differences of opinion between those who designed it, those who implemented it, and those who were its targets, grew enormously more complicated during the Second World War. Although during the first winter of the war couples married at an accelerated rate – a fact the Nazi SD attributed to successful state propaganda encouraging marriage[109] – the number of marriages dropped almost immediately thereafter. Almost half of the 20 million men who served in Germany's military had left civilian life by 1941, thus virtually eliminating the prospect of marriage. As the war progressed, moreover, existing marriages came under increasing pressure. The long-term separation of husbands and wives caused a "stark psychological burden" (*starke seelische Belastung*) on all concerned. Reunions were often fraught with conflict that caused even previously harmonious marriages to suffer irreparable damage.[110]

Marital conflict was further exacerbated by women's allegedly widespread involvement in adulterous relations during the war. As one Hamburg social worker noted in September 1940, it is "'frightening'" how many "'wives of military men do not adhere very precisely to marital fidelity.'"[111] While Nazi authorities believed that soldiers benefited from brothels, they did not extend the same freedom to women on the home front. Many soldiers blamed Germany's leaders for their perceived inability "to maintain order in the family while they fought at the front," which forced the Nazi leadership to hold women to a higher standard of virtue than men.[112] And indeed, some German wives established relationships with POWs or foreign workers, thus blatantly violating Nazi racial laws. As Otto Georg Thierack, the Reich minister of justice, wrote in 1943, "'Marital fidelity' was not a moral issue but rather, a racial imperative and in wartime a national obligation in service of the '*Volk* community.'"[113] To combat infidelity, courts meted out harsher sentences to married women – especially mothers, war wives, and war widows – than they did to unmarried women.[114] In doing so, they worked against the tide of public opinion, which did not uniformly condemn married women's

108 Ehestandsdarlehen Anträge, StaD, D 102 Warburg, 36.
109 Boberach, *Meldungen aus dem Reich*, 17 January 1940, 658–9.
110 Ibid., 18 November 1943, 6027.
111 Quoted in Heinemann, *What Difference*, 54.
112 Boberach, *Meldungen aus dem Reich*, 13 April 1944, 6485; Kundrus, "Forbidden Company," 207.
113 Thierack, *Richterbriefe*, 1943, quoted in Kundrus, "Forbidden Company," 213.
114 Kundrus, "Forbidden Company," 213; Heinemann, *What Difference*, 59.

adulterous relationships. Many people sympathized with the hardships war imposed on women and wondered why they should be punished more harshly for adultery than their soldier husbands.[115] Even husbands reacted inconsistently. Although many condemned their adulterous wives, others forgave them, forcing the state to retract its punishment (in most cases by restoration of family allowances) and restore the women's civic rights.[116]

Nazi authorities worried about couples' disinclination to marry in wartime, and they also worried that strict health requirements would exacerbate the declining marriage rate and demoralize the populace. In response, the Nazis selectively loosened the standards for permission to marry and eased the eligibility requirements for marriage loans, especially for members of the military. Although they worried about the consequences of compromising health standards, a far greater fear was that weakening soldiers' allegiance to the nation would affect the outcome of the war. Initially Lippe government officials rejected Bernard B.'s marriage loan application because his fiancé had a flawed family history. When it became known that he had participated in the attack on Poland, however, the medical officer wrote that "despite the considerable hesitation arising from the genetic defects in the woman's family history, because of social, economic, and above all ethical circumstances" the loan could be approved. The official worried that rejecting the soldier would cause hardship and damage his morale.[117] The November 1939 introduction of "war marriages," which enabled a man on the front lines and his fiancée at home to make their declarations of marriage at separate times and in separate places, further loosened the enforcement of health regulations. Though technically the health of each prospective spouse had to be evaluated to determine their suitability for marriage, in reality, the emphasis in war marriages was on allowing as many couples to marry as possible. For couples who had earlier been (or might have been) labeled "undesirable," the war marriage policy made it possible to evade both bureaucratic and racial restrictions.[118]

Maintaining soldiers' morale was the primary but not the sole factor in prompting changes in marriage policy. In 1940, SA member Schmidt and his fiancée's marriage loan was rejected because Schmidt had a goiter. Schmidt's membership in the SA clearly was not by itself sufficient to qualify them. Because the woman and their child were perfectly healthy,

---

115 Heinemann, *What Difference*, 55.
116 Boberach, *Meldungen aus dem Reich*, 13 December 1943, 6145; Kundrus "Forbidden Company," 213.
117 Medizinalrat to Lippische Regierung, 3 April 1940, StaD, L 80 IC, Gruppe 24, Fach 6, 17.
118 Heinemann, *What Difference*, 46.

however, the decision was reversed on appeal. This time, Schmidt's membership in the SA, in conjunction with his bride's health and the health of their child together, convinced authorities that the marriage loan would help to establish a desirable – and moral – home.[119] In another case, when a woman applied to marry, her pastor spoke on her behalf, arguing that although her husband-to-be had epilepsy, his illness was not visible. The woman had turned to Herr K., her fiancé, for advice and help raising her child after her husband died in combat. The pastor pointed out that "there will barely be a chance for the engaged T. to find another man under the bad marriage prospects for women during the war." Furthermore, if the marriage was not permitted, "the child would always have to do without a father." Under the circumstances, the Reich minister of the interior approved the marriage.[120]

So many exceptions were granted and problems overlooked that the marriage rate temporarily increased. As Elizabeth Heinemann has pointed out, this increase "suggests a backlog of couples who had previously been unable to marry."[121] In fact, many allegedly undesirable Germans whose applications to marry had earlier been rejected reapplied after the war began and found their requests granted.[122] The German population, which throughout the 1930s had been "virtually bombarded" with propaganda warning of the threat posed by unhealthy reproduction, scorned this state of affairs.[123] Noting that even soldiers with mental disabilities were being allowed to marry, some Germans wondered about whether the restrictions had any meaning any more.[124] Some Germans, who had only discovered their own spouses carried genes for hereditary illnesses when their marriage loan applications were rejected, protested the lenient marriage standards they felt were crucial to ensure the nation's health.[125]

Because the introduction of war marriages and the relaxation of marriage standards quickly proved insufficient to keep the marriage rate from falling, Nazi leaders devised even more radical wartime marriage policies. In November 1941, a Führer's decree made "postmortem marriages" possible. During the war, approximately 18,000 women (many of them mothers) availed themselves of this macabre option primarily to become eligible for widows' benefits and to legitimize their children. Though the Nazis

---

119 Marriage Loan Applications, 20 January 1940, StaD, L 80 IC, Gruppe 24, Fach 6, 17.
120 Case from 1944, StaD, L 80 IC, Gruppe 24, Fach 2, 4.
121 Heinemann, *What Difference*, 46.
122 Boberach, *Meldungen aus dem Reich*, 27 December 1939, 606.
123 Bock, "Antinatalism, Maternity and Paternity," 119.
124 Boberach, *Meldungen aus dem Reich*, 1 October 1942, 4270–71.
125 Ibid., 17 June 1940, 1269.

tried to keep the policy secret, news of it spread, and it came to be called "corpse marriage" in popular speech.[126] For the state, postmortem marriages promised to turn single mothers into soldiers' widows and legitimize children, both acts which authorities hoped would raise morale. For women, the prospect of receiving widows' benefits and avoiding societal scorn were sufficient to make news of the postmortem marriage option spread. The Nazis forbade postmortem marriages only when more than one woman claimed to have been a soldier's fiancée or when the bride was Jewish or a Gypsy. Postmortem marriages sometimes created turmoil when newly declared brides collected widows' benefits, causing soldiers' parents to lose their state aid as soldiers' dependents. Inheritance issues also caused considerable concern, as parents worried when a woman whom they could not be certain their son had intended to marry claimed a right to his inheritance.[127]

In 1943, a program was unveiled to facilitate marriage between "desirable" women and desirable but severely wounded soldiers. The inspiration behind this initiative was the belief that many severely wounded soldiers carried good genes but had a poor chance of finding a wife. The program met with little success, because most women lost interest when they learned the definition of "severely wounded."[128]

Another program introduced in 1944 by the Reich League of German Families (Reichsbund Deutscher Familien) established letter centers to help eligible women and men meet. They limited the letter writers to "racially pure" men and women in good health, as proven by both a doctor and a health department. Letter centers then paired men and women according to their backgrounds and professional status. Lisa Pine has claimed that the large number of letters received by the centers "corresponded to a genuine need," yet the letter centers appear to have had little impact.[129] The program began late in the war, and many German men and women (especially those in their twenties) were hesitant to marry when the future was so uncertain. In both programs, most women came from middle-class backgrounds and had worked in the female professions; the majority of male applicants were farmers, small-time artisans, and laborers. The men, especially those who were veterans, did not want to settle for women who were "older, physically imperfect, or uppity because of class background."[130] The letter centers

---

126 Heinemann, *What Difference*, 47; Kundrus, *Kriegerfrauen*, 362.
127 Boberach, *Meldungen aus dem Reich*, 2 March 1944, 6392–3.
128 Heinemann, *What Difference*, 48–9.
129 Pine, *Nazi Family Policy*, 97.
130 Boberach, *Meldungen aus dem Reich*, 27 March 1940, 934; Stephenson, "Reichsbund der Kinde-reichen"; Heinemann, *What Difference*, 48–9.

provide one more example of the desperate lengths to which the German
state went to create marriages during the war.

CONCLUSION

Both Weimar and National Socialist policymakers heralded patriarchal marriage as the one institution capable of restoring social stability and rejuvenating the German nation, but they envisioned the state's role in promoting
and regulating marriage very differently. Although the Reich government
had begun to explore the relationship between national health and private behavior as early as 1920, it was no accident that Weimar marriage
certificates remained voluntary. The very nature of the democratic republic
mitigated against the adoption of a single, all-encompassing marriage policy.
As a result, it was not Weimar marriage counseling centers that paved the
way for the Nazis' negative eugenics.[131] Rather, the Weimar government's
very inability to create a uniform policy of state intervention in families
enabled the Nazis to promise just that.

When the Nazis silenced objections to state intervention in the private
realm and introduced a racially based marriage policy, they took state regulation of marriage into a radically new realm. By banning marriage between
Jews and Aryans and between "healthy" and "unhealthy" Germans, the
Nazis dramatically changed the state's role in marriage. Moreover, the policies introduced during the war to facilitate marriages between women at
home and soldiers on the front reveal an interest in marriage that extended
well beyond traditional state interests.

Ideal gender roles stood at the center of marriage policy during both
the Weimar and National Socialist eras. In Weimar Germany, traditional
notions of marriage vied for space with more modern ideas of companionate marriage. While conservative forces discussed eugenics and fought
against birth control and abortion, the KPD rallied support against §218,
and New Women postponed marriage as they experimented with gender
roles. Though Frau Dewald's decision not to marry in 1932 may have raised
eyebrows and even predictions of doom in some circles, it did not result in
policy change. In contrast, Nazi policymakers came down firmly on the side
of traditional gender roles in marriage and shaped their marriage policy –
at least for "racially pure" women – around them. They rejected companionate marriage and the New Woman and rewarded women who gave up
their jobs with marriage loans.

131 Usborne, *The Politics of the Body*, 212.

Despite their clearly delineated and far-reaching policy intentions, however, the Nazis encountered serious obstacles at the level of implementation. Marriage certificates and loans created a workload so heavy that doctors could not follow strict guidelines for assessing genetic health.[132] The war posed further obstacles to collecting health documentation and forced a dramatic loosening of health requirements for marriage. As a result, Nazi policymakers never made marriage certificates mandatory, and many engaged couples encountered no state surveillance. Beyond that, German couples themselves hindered Nazi efforts to control marriage. Although the percentage of couples receiving marriage loans rose from 33.3 in 1933–1935 to reach a high of 51.4 in 1938,[133] this still meant that about half of all German couples married outside the purview of health inspectors. Although the percentage of children born to marriage loan recipients increased, it did so far less dramatically (from 22.9 percent in 1937 to 32 percent in 1940) than the percentage of couples accepting marriage loans.[134] Most couples who accepted marriage loans did not adhere to the expectation that they begin families immediately, and they did not have a higher birthrate on average than couples who did not receive marriage loans. Yet, although the Nazis failed to implement their policy as intended, and although this failure compromised the effectiveness of their racial policy, these facts should not detract from the enormity of their effort to control marriage – an effort vastly more invasive and far-reaching than anything undertaken under Weimar.

---

132 The number of doctors in Lemgo remained constant at twenty-seven between 1933 and 1938, despite the increased workload. In Detmold, the number of doctors climbed from twenty-one in 1925 to twenty-eight in 1937 and thirty-four in 1938. StaD, L 80 IC, Gruppe 24, Fach 2, 2.
133 *Statistisches Jahrbuch* 57 (1939): 48.
134 *Statistisches Jahrbuch* 59 (1941/42).

2

Divorce

Balancing Individual Freedom and the Public Good

In 1932, Frau R. petitioned the Dortmund Landgericht (regional court) for a divorce from her husband Otto, claiming that in his drunken stupors, he threatened her with statements such as: "You whore! You swine! I will beat you to death." Earlier that year, he had hit her in the face with his fists. Otto did not deny the charges against him but responded with the counterclaim that his wife was having an affair with another man.[1]

In 1939, Herr Voges, a photographer, filed a petition to divorce his wife, Beate, on the grounds that she neglected the household and refused to cook meals for him. He further asserted that her multiple criticisms of the Führer and defense of Jews made her an enemy of the state (*staatsfeindlich eingestellt*). In her rebuttal, Frau Voges flatly denied that she had neglected her household, portraying herself as a good wife and mother whose husband had so severely abused her that she had appealed to the Führer himself for advice. While she admitted that she thought some Jews were good Germans, she emphasized that overall she supported the Third Reich.[2]

The Dortmund Landgericht judges who heard these two cases bore responsibility for determining whether the legal conditions for divorce existed. In reaching their verdicts, the judges evaluated not just the facts presented to them in the courtroom but also their own ideas about gender and marriage and their perceptions of the "public good." Because the essential facts in every divorce case were to a large extent subjective, the outcome of divorce petitions often depended on how well husbands and wives could prove that their marriages had deteriorated. Unhappy spouses and the judges who decided their fates were strongly influenced by the political

---

1 All names have been changed to preserve anonymity. SaM, Landgericht Dortmund, 9.8.R.238/31.
2 SaM, Landgericht Dortmund, 10.R.4/39.

order of the day, and public debate about divorce reform was intense and highly polarized during both the Weimar and Nazi eras.

At the heart of the issue for Weimar lawmakers lay one question: Could a reformed divorce law increase individual happiness without undermining the state's effort to bolster families and shore up the German nation? In the Reichstag, left-wing advocates of divorce reform believed that freeing spouses from unhappy marriages would illustrate the state's commitment to democratic gender roles, ensure greater personal freedom, and make Germany a more just place for men, women, and families. They argued that many couples, like Herr and Frau R., suffered unnecessarily in socially worthless marriages while waiting for their relationships to deteriorate sufficiently to give them grounds to file for divorce. In contrast, opponents of divorce reform feared that any change in the divorce code would lower moral standards, overburden the state with unsupported wives and children, and discourage responsible male behavior. Moreover, they believed that any departure from traditional law would lead to the destruction of the family and the ruination of German civilization. As a result, divorce remained one of several intractable domestic issues in the struggle between maintaining traditional values and modernizing families and society at large.

From their first day in office, Nazi policymakers viewed divorce as they viewed marriage – as an institution that must serve the state. They considered all divorce reform proposals primarily in light of their contribution to the public good as it was defined by Nazi biological, social, and racial criteria. They sought to create a separate set of guidelines to govern divorce among "unworthy" spouses, whose potential contribution to the state they deemed as fundamentally different from that of "healthy" spouses. Still, the Nazis' reconceptualization of divorce did not eliminate the conflicts that had stymied earlier efforts at divorce reform. They worried that too great a liberalization of divorce laws might create the appearance that the National Socialist regime had failed to support the traditional family. In the courtroom, moreover, many judges who supported National Socialism hesitated to revise their notion of family completely or to waive their belief in the sanctity of the law. Judges were also forced to take into account the fact that many couples, like Herr Voges and his wife, understood Nazi ideology and tailored their stories accordingly.

This chapter probes the changing parameters of divorce policy both as it was created by Weimar and National Socialist lawmakers and as it was interpreted by judges. It argues that beyond Weimar politicians' wrangling and the Nazis' ideologically driven effort to reform divorce, judges and the people who stood before them in court strove on a case-by-case basis to define a healthy marriage, sometimes in line with current legal and political thought and at other times violating the spirit of that thought.

WEIMAR DIVORCE LAW, 1918–1932

Although the number of divorces in Germany fell during the First World War, by 1920 it had risen to a record high. The apparent impermanence of marriage shocked many Germans and reinforced the feeling that the German family was in a state of crisis. In Westphalia, the divorce rate averaged 17.6 per 1,000 marriages, and this figure was held down by the low divorce rate in predominantly Catholic Münster. Some people worried that Germany was experiencing a divorce epidemic: in Prussia, the number of divorces rose from 9,277 in 1910 to 6,409 in 1916 to 22,534 in 1920.[3] As a result, divorce law and the circumstances under which the state permitted families to dissolve became a matter of heated debate in the 1920s.

Not only was the number of divorces increasing, but the traditional factors that led to divorce had themselves changed. Rather than the typical circumstances (adultery, failure to provide, and abuse, for example) heralding the demise of marriage, new war-related conditions struck marriages. Hastily arranged wartime marriages dissolved once couples began to live together, and the discovery of wartime adultery strained marriages beyond repair. The financial independence many women had enjoyed during the war also posed significant challenges for some newly reunited couples. Other couples' marriages were in trouble before the war, and separation simply postponed the inevitable. Assessing postwar German society, historian Richard Bessel concluded that the high divorce rate was caused by the myriad new stresses placed on traditional marriages rather than by a dramatically new perspective on marriage itself.[4]

Legal and political authorities did not take the ending of marriage lightly. It had long been mandated by the German state that couples had to undergo a mandatory court "attempt at reconciliation" (*Sühneversuch*) before filing for divorce. During the early nineteenth century, attempts at reconciliation had "united state and church interests in preserving crumbling marriages," as priests, who had an extensive knowledge of family histories, listened to and

---

3 Georg Guggemoos, Director of the Stadtjugendamtes, Freising, "Schutz der Kinder aus zerrütteten Ehen," *Caritas* 10 (1927), Zeitschrift für Caritaswissenschaft und Caritasarbeit hrsg. Caritasverband Caritasverlag, Freiburg im Br. p. 307, StaD, L 80 IC, Gruppe 28, Fach 25, 5. The divorce rate was much higher among religiously mixed couples, in cities, and among the working class. Blasius, *Ehescheidung in Deutschland*, 156–7.
4 Bessel, *Germany after the First World War*, 232.

advised troubled couples.[5] With the adoption of the Civil Code of Procedure (*Zivilprozeßordnung*) of 30 January 1877, however, control over attempts at reconciliation reverted to the courts.[6] Because the courts lacked the intimate background knowledge that the priests possessed and the ability to exert intense pressure on couples, "the attempts at reconciliation increasingly became exactly what their opponents criticized most vociferously: namely, empty formalities which only delayed the trial."[7] Despite the shortcomings of attempts at reconciliation, however, they remained the state's primary means of discouraging divorce and so continued to be mandatory into the twentieth century.

The records of eighty-seven attempts at reconciliation I examined from the Recklinghausen Amtsgericht (local court), though a statistically small sample, help to make clear the goals and results of these proceedings.[8] Sixty-eight percent of the attempts at reconciliation I examined were filed by wives, while 32 percent were filed by husbands. Gender strongly influenced the reasons for filing. The most common complaint cited by women was abuse (46 percent), while adultery (23 percent) and lack of financial support (19 percent) were the second and third most common complaints. Among men, desertion and adultery were the most prevalent complaints. The frequency with which particular complaints were cited was comparable in the early and late 1920s. Many women had multiple complaints, often citing alcohol abuse in conjunction with adultery and physical abuse. Men less frequently cited multiple reasons, except those who accused their wives of both desertion and failing to run the household properly.

The stated causes of marital unhappiness generally reflected women's and men's different status inside marriage. Most men described a home life destroyed either by infidelity or desertion. In contrast, most women pointed to ongoing abuse rather than a marriage that had completely dissolved. Perhaps as a result, attempts at reconciliation succeeded more frequently

---

5 Blasius, *Ehescheidung in Deutschland*, 54.

6 As a rule, the Catholic and Protestant churches' attempts at reconciliation were biased toward keeping couples together and leaned especially heavily on women's sense of responsibility to their marriages to prevent them from escaping even abusive marriages. Ibid., 73.

7 Ibid., 80.

8 They can be divided by date: the first forty-four cases date from March 1921 to February 1924, while the second forty-three cases date from September 1928 through September 1930. The fact that all the cases for any given year fall close together suggests that they are representative of short time spans randomly saved rather than a selected group of cases. German law requires that records from civil court cases be stored in the courts for fifty years, after which time the state archives can add the records to their holdings. Records the state archives reject are destroyed. Until recently (and in many archives still), records pertaining to family matters outside of inheritance were discarded, and despite searching the records of more than twenty other *Amtsgerichte*, I never found any other records of attempts at reconciliation.

when women filed than when men did. Of the cases whose conclusion is known (fifty-five), 29 percent ended in reconciliation, and of these, 81.3 percent were filed by women. More striking, 69 percent of the women whose cases ended in reconciliation had filed due to abuse. Even the women who most graphically described the abuse they suffered at the hands of their husbands often remained married. Frau E. alleged that her husband "hit... and threatened [her] without giving a reason." Before her court date, however, she and her husband wrote a joint letter canceling their court appointment. Another woman who reported that her husband had abused her repeatedly and had even threatened to strangle her forgave her husband during the court meeting and dropped the charges.

No single explanation can account for women's greater likelihood to remain married after filing for an attempt at reconciliation, but a number of theories provide partial explanations. It is likely that women who had accepted more modern expectations of companionate marriage used the court meetings to get outside intervention to help reform their abusive spouses. Drawing attention to their troubled marriages and to their husbands' negative behavior may have increased women's risk of serious abuse or financial deprivation, forcing them to yield. It is also possible that once legal proceedings began and judges alerted husbands to the severity of their wives' complaints, the husbands changed their behavior. Judges and other court representatives present at the meetings may well have emphasized to the men that their behavior was inappropriate. Alternatively, the court experience itself may have made the consequences of divorce all too clear to the women, causing them to have a change of heart. As historian Karen Hagemann found in her Hamburg study, "Above all women seem to have pressed to maintain the marriage out of concern for the children, out of fear of an uncertain future and out of consideration of public opinion."[9] Finally, there is reason to believe that judges took women's complaints less seriously than men's. Judges who were inclined to link Germany's future to the fate of traditional marriages may have been unsympathetic to women's attempts to divorce. The records I examined do not settle this issue, but they do make clear that men and women used the attempts at reconciliation with different results.

The outcome of attempts at reconciliation was affected by the fact that they allowed the state a chance to protect children. The summons explicitly warned parents, "The meeting is also intended to discuss the personal circumstances of your marriage and the minor children stemming from

9 Hagemann, *Frauenalltag und Mannerpolitik*, 326.

your marriage." In December 1920, the chief magistrate of the high court (*Oberlandesgerichtspräsident*) in Hamm wrote the Bielefeld Landgericht president to express his concern that especially in cases in which parents had led a "dissolute way of life," their children were "alarmingly endangered morally and physically and that this danger often escalate[d] after the spouses separate[d]." He suggested that the state bypass parents to collect information about children in troubled marriages and alert the guardianship courts (*Vormundschaftsgerichten*) as soon as they found children in trouble. In November 1927, the Prussian minister of welfare recommended that other courts follow Hamburg's example and bring children to the youth departments' attention at the time of the attempts at reconciliation, or at the very latest during the divorce trial.[10]

Governmental attempts to intervene on behalf of children were often undermined in Westphalia by judges who viewed the attempts at reconciliation first and foremost as an opportunity to help couples repair their marriages. They often delayed notifying the youth departments because they believed that forcing couples to discuss their children increased the likelihood of reconciliation. Already in December 1927, the Prussian minister of justice reported his finding that *Amtsgericht* authorities believed that discussions "about the circumstances and future of mutual children can lead to securing an endangered marriage."[11] In Berleburg, court officials believed that discussing mutual children "serves as the most effective means to preserve the marriage."[12] The judge in Brilon reported that he did not want to involve the guardianship court, since "in most cases despite the fruitless conclusion of the meeting, a petition for divorce seem[ed] improbable." He also feared that additional "court intervention would only advance the deterioration of the marriage." Indeed, some couples may have used the attempts at reconciliation as a means to bring an ornery spouse to counseling rather than as a preliminary step toward divorce.

---

10 Preußisches Minister für Volkswohlfahrt to Oberpräsidium, 26 November 1927, SaM, Oberpräsidium Münster, 5916. See also Harvey, *Youth and the Welfare State*, 176. In 1929, the Justice Ministry newsletter (*Justizministerialblatt*) advocated that children under sixteen years of age should "promptly" be brought to the attention of "the current guardianship court or the youth department in the district." *Justizministerialblatt*, 1929, 133, StaD, D20A Zug 75/92, 83 (5-VI-73) Bd. 1.

11 Prussian Minister of Justice to Kammergerichtspräsidenten und Oberlandesgerichtspräsidenten, 23 December 1927, SaM, Amtsgericht Medebach, 4. In many small-town courts, the same judge bore responsibility for both guardianship decisions and attempts at reconciliation, so that no additional steps were necessary to alert the youth department.

12 Later, they admitted that when a couple had already decided to divorce, the meetings were of no avail. Amtsgericht Berleburg to Oberlandesgerichtspräsident Hamm, 15 February 1929, SaM, Landgericht Arnsberg, 342, Bd. 3.

During the 1920s, as attempts at reconciliation increasingly failed, the growing prevalence of divorce kept divorce reform at the center of debates about Weimar family policy. Just as the larger Weimar political process became mired in party strife, so too did debates over divorce reform break down over ideologically disparate philosophies. The five grounds for divorce established in the civil code continued to regulate divorce law during the Weimar Republic. They were, in the order of frequency of usage, adultery (§1565), culpable marital breakdown (*Schuldhafte Ehezerrüttung*, §1568), desertion (§1567), mental illness (§1569), and death threats (*Lebensnachstellung*, §1566). The law permitted couples to divorce only with proper grounds and in most cases only if guilt could be determined. Culpable marital breakdown was the only ground that acknowledged that some couples grew apart, but even it required a determination of guilt. At the crux of the debate over divorce reform lay the question of whether "irreconcilable differences" should replace the mandatory guilt clause. In April 1922, the liberal German Organization of Law (Deutscher Rechtsbund) advocated such a change to allow the "thousands in the Reich who still currently must remain in the deepest of mental anguish in socially utterly worthless marriages to become useful members of the state again."[13] Marie Elisabeth Lüders, a German Democratic Party delegate and an early champion of divorce reform, was the first to raise the issue in the Reichstag. Gustav Radbruch, the SPD justice minister from October 1921 through November 1923 and a strong proponent of reform, proposed adding a subclause (§1579a) that would separate guilt from alimony, making one spouse (usually the man) responsible for economic support regardless of guilt. He argued that this would eliminate the humiliating situation in which a spouse who wanted to divorce had to engage in adultery or abuse in order to create the grounds for divorce. According to Radbruch's proposal, guilt would be discussed only if the innocent spouse applied for alimony. Radbruch hoped his proposal would secure women's income after divorce while preserving their dignity.

Conservative lawmakers' passionate disagreement with the liberals' divorce reform proposals ensured that from the outset, divorce reform debates were hyperbolic. DNVP, DVP, and Center Party politicians who defended traditional divorce law claimed that nothing less than German civilization was at stake. They accused Radbruch and his SPD supporters of using the Soviet legal system as their model. The Catholic Church, which saw itself as the protector of tradition and Christian morality, stood firmly

---

13 Entschließung einer Versammlung des "Deutschen Rechtsbundes" vom 4 April 1922, Bundesarchiv Koblenz (BaK), R 431/1219, s. 50, quoted in Blasius, *Ehescheidung in Deutschland*, 165.

and unwaveringly against any divorce reform throughout the Weimar era. In January 1922, Adolf Cardinal Bertram, *Fürstbischof* (prince bishop) of Breslau, wrote the justice minister, the leader of the Catholic Center Party, and the Reichstag to oppose the reform of the "culpable marital break-down" clause (§1568). In his letter, he explained: "Marriage and the family are the basis of the whole of human society, the holy cell of the nation's life [*Volksleben*], and the nation's strength [*Volkskraft*]. . . . Making divorce easier is a concession to that kind of cowardice, which will not wait and suffer, will not make sacrifices, but rather allows itself to be guided by mood, passion, and fickleness."[14] Center Party delegates used this letter from the cardinal to bolster their refusal to discuss divorce reform.

Nonetheless, on 30 January 1922, three DDP delegates brought a divorce reform proposal to the floor of the Reichstag again. They emphasized that their intention was not to increase the number of divorces but rather to make the entire divorce process more just. They argued that deleting the guilt clause would enhance the position of the weaker partner (usually the woman), and they claimed that alimony should be firmly connected to equality and need, not marital circumstances or guilt. To this, Center Party politician Johannes Bell, the Reich minister of justice from July 1926 through January 1927, retorted, "From our religious and moral perspective we maintain the unshakable conviction that marriage is insoluble, and thus we will decisively resist all bills and all petitions that seek to expand the grounds for divorce."[15] Although in general support for and against divorce divided along party lines, some individuals, like Wilhelm Kahl (DVP), diverged from their parties to claim that divorce law should be secularized as Prussian law had been.[16] The debates came to a temporary halt in November 1922 when the new minister of justice, Rudolf Heinze (DVP), announced that because divorce reform was a question "lacking urgency," he would not discuss it.[17]

Between 1925 and 1928, the precarious nature of the governing coalition sidetracked divorce reform. The SPD, divorce reform's staunchest sponsor, increasingly found itself forced to scale back its demands in order to get along with its coalition partners. Its position on divorce was further threatened when the Communist Party entered the debates in 1925, when its presence in the Reichstag increased from four to sixty-four seats. Martha Arendsee, a bookseller from Berlin and KPD delegate, articulated the Communist viewpoint: "When we Communists approach this question

---

14 Blasius, *Ehescheidung in Deutschland*, 169.   15 Ibid., 170.
16 Ibid., 172–3.   17 Ibid., 171.

we do not labor under any illusions. We know that precisely in the matter of divorce and in questions of §218 and §219 [which deal with abortion] all the lies and hypocrisy of bourgeois society are made clearly manifest." In the Communist interpretation, all the laws governing marriage were "forced laws" created by the bourgeoisie and their "socialist" lackeys "to protect the outer appearance" and "to hold together outwardly, that which is destroyed inside."[18] But rather than criticize capitalist society's destructive influence on families or even the German Civil Code, KPD delegates focused their critique on the SPD. They labeled the SPD's effort to support both capitalism and families as hypocritical. Although ideologically the Social Democrats scorned the system that trapped people in loveless marriages, the overwhelming fear of Communism shared by the other bourgeois parties forced them to distance themselves from the Communists and thus compromised their support of divorce reform.[19] In a sense, the SPD was caught between "maintaining power and staying true to its beliefs."[20] The Weimar Republic's precarious political stability made the SPD's alliances with parties that rejected divorce legislation (especially the Center Party) too important to sacrifice for the sake of divorce reform. When the German National People's Party reentered the coalition in 1927, its delegates tried to end debates over divorce reform permanently. They viewed any liberalization of the divorce law as synonymous with treason. In February 1928, Alexander Freiherr von Freytagh-Lorinhoven, one of the most influential representatives of the DNVP, announced, "If marriage is bolshevized and disparaged as concubinage, the family will be destroyed," with the result that "a rebirth of Germany will be impossible."[21]

In 1928, the formation of the Great Coalition created an atmosphere that allowed the discussion to be reopened.[22] In an effort to broker a compromise on divorce reform, Minister of Justice Erich Koch-Weser (DDP) tried to leave the guilt clause intact but to add a "breakdown principle" to it. He explained: "Broken marriages, even when the guilt of one spouse cannot be established, cannot be maintained over time against the will of the participants. Today the dissolution of such a marriage is either impossible or it is the result of manipulation, which is humiliating for the parties involved and degrading for the legal authorities."[23] Koch-Weser proposed making

18 Ibid., 173–4.   19 Ibid., 167.
20 Ibid., 176.
21 Freiheer v. Freytagh-Loringhoven in a press release (*Presseerklärung*) from February 1928, quoted in ibid., 175.
22 The Grand Coalition included the SPD, DDP, Center, DVP, and BVP (Bayrische Volkspartei).
23 Blasius, *Ehescheidung in Deutschland*, 181.

it possible for the participants in such marriages to declare the irretrievable breakdown of the marriage and be granted a divorce. But Center Party delegates remained absolutely unwavering in their opposition, and Koch-Weser's attempt to calm the debate failed. When Karl Theodor V. Guevard, a staunch Center Party representative, replaced Koch-Weser as minister of justice, he halted the debates.

Thus, despite ongoing debates about the reform of the law in regard to divorce, no legislative changes were made during the Weimar period. However, the implementation of divorce law did not remain static in these years. Just as doctors played an increasingly important role in determining the suitability of potential marriages, responsibility for assessing the viability of existing marriages fell to judges. Although technically the judiciary was supposed to remain independent, during the Weimar era the courts themselves became political institutions, and the political context of the day strongly influenced judges' verdicts. As historian H. W. Koch has pointed out, "Weimar, quite simply, thrust the judiciary into a political position."[24]

During the Weimar era, judges constituted a conservative force and tended to identify with Wilhelminian Germany rather than lend their support to the republic. Most judges favored the DNVP and DVP political parties – a result, in part, of their lengthy and expensive education, which self-selected a group of wealthy, conservative men.[25] As Dr. Walter Simons, president of the Supreme Court, said in 1926: "In our country the judiciary of the monarchy entered the new state as a whole. The judges have placed themselves in the service of the new republic and sworn an oath to the republic. They have certainly striven to keep that oath, but they would not and could not change their spirit under the new regime."[26] The difficult economic situation in Weimar Germany, which lowered judicial salaries, exacerbated the judges' animosity toward the republic.[27] Furthermore, the working conditions for the judiciary worsened during the Weimar era. In Prussia, the number of judges and support staff shrank, while the number of civil cases grew, creating heavier workloads for individual judges.[28] Their sense of a loss of authority, moreover, convinced many judges that "the rule

---

24 Koch, *In the Name*, 7.
25 One Berlin Senate president estimated that only 5 percent of Prussian judges supported parties of the republic (SPD, Center, DDP) at the end of the republic, while the Republican Judges Organization (Republikanische Richterbund), an organization of pro-republic judges and lawyers, counted only 300 of the 10,000 judges as members. Angermund, *Deutsche Richterschaft*, 41.
26 Müller, *Hitler's Justice*, 10.
27 Angermund, *Deutsche Richterschaft*, 24.
28 The number of judges shrank from 7,044 in 1915 to 6,044 in the mid-1920s, while the number of cases increased from 235,000 in 1913 to 305,000 in 1930. For those in training, the situation was far worse, with waiting periods of eight years in 1921 and six years and ten months in 1927. Ibid., 25–9.

of parliament and the parties had nothing good to be said for it and hurt the people [*Volk*] and the state."[29]

As conservative, upper-class representatives of the state, Weimar judges viewed preserving marriage and sustaining families as beneficial to the public interest and as one of their most important responsibilities. Many judges felt it was their duty to use their positions on the bench to help stabilize postwar society. As the battle lines between liberal lawmakers – especially members of the SPD – and judges became entrenched, many judges explicitly sought to reestablish the status quo ante through their verdicts. They resisted all legislation that they believed eroded patriarchal authority or undermined women's roles as wives and mothers, as defined by the German Civil Code of 1900. In effect, judges contested all efforts to modernize family law.

Even as the divorce laws remained constant, many signs indicated that significant changes in their interpretation and application were underway. During the First World War, women had surpassed men for the first time in being declared guilty in divorce cases. This increase seemed to be clearly linked to women's adultery, which had risen from causing only 22.7 percent of all Prussian divorces in 1913 to causing 38.4 percent in 1918.[30] In his study of German divorce, historian Dirk Blasius argued that the increase in guilty verdicts for women after the war did not necessarily reflect women's greater emancipation or the courts' increased willingness to view men and women as equal before the law. He suggests instead that judges punished women who refused to play their traditional role as nurturers.[31] Another interpretation of this trend is that judges tried to compensate – even reward – men's war-related suffering at the expense of women. A third possibility is that judges' hostility toward the Weimar lawmakers' successive attempts to alter traditional gender roles bolstered their desire to uphold those very roles. Judges' own sense that they were suffering from the societal changes of the Weimar era may well have increased their lack of sympathy for those women they perceived as benefiting.[32]

Judges increasingly assigned guilt to women when men were clearly the guilty parties.[33] This had a profound impact on women's future well-being.

---

29 Ibid., 31.
30 Whereas before 1914 women were assigned guilt in just under 40 percent of cases, by 1917 they had surpassed men and were found guilty in 55.6 percent of cases. *Statistisches Jahrbuch* 18 (1922): 52–3.
31 Blasius, *Ehescheidung in Deutschland*, 162.   32 Angermund, *Deutsche Richterschaft*, 21.
33 All the individual divorce cases discussed in this chapter were found uncataloged in the records of the Landgericht Arnsberg in the Staatsarchiv Münster. For cases from 1932, the earliest year for which there are records, I read either every fifth or every tenth record. Most files contained only descriptions of the grounds for the decisions and the testimonies of the couple and the witnesses from the Landgericht Arnsberg. Occasionally, when the verdict was challenged, records of the Oberlandesgericht Hamm were included also.

Although nineteenth-century divorce law had been written in gender-neutral language, historically, men's greater earning potential had made them responsible for supporting their ex-wives financially. After Weimar lawmakers wrote sexual equality into the constitution, however, many judges assumed that women could support themselves and began to hand down decisions negating attempts to compensate for men's greater earnings. According to the civil code, the spouse declared solely guilty bore responsibility for paying alimony, but after 1918 judges increasingly declared the woman or both parties guilty.[34] Frau R. and her husband, with whom the chapter began, were both declared guilty even though the judges admitted that the evidence of Frau R.'s adultery was inconclusive.[35] For women, who earned an average of 20 to 40 percent less than men,[36] the loss of alimony was a strong economic disincentive, even when the divorce itself freed them from undesirable marriages. As Dirk Blasius has said, a guilty verdict "materially reduced [them] to the absolute meagerest level."[37]

In 1932, for example, Joachim P., a worker, sued Dorothea, his wife of thirteen years, alleging that she was having an affair with the man for whom she kept house. Dorothea disputed Joachim's allegation, claiming that because of her husband's desertion in 1925, his failure to support her or their child despite a court order, her inability to prevail on Joachim to establish a "respectable married life," and the inadequacy of the welfare payments she received, she had been forced to work as a housekeeper and to take a room in her employer's home. Witnesses confirmed Dorothea's allegations and even suggested that Joachim had not been faithful. After hearing all the evidence, the court permitted Joachim and Dorothea to divorce but declared them both guilty. Joachim's failure to support his family and his threats against Dorothea's life confirmed his guilt. Regarding Dorothea, the judges admitted that because the man with whom Dorothea was alleged to have had an affair was sixty-five years old, it was "very improbable" that the affair had occurred, but they nonetheless concluded that though "the defendant was forced by circumstances to live in one of [her client's] rooms, it was her duty to do everything in her control to avoid anything which might encourage a rumor that she was having an extramarital relationship."[38] Dorothea's failure

34 While in 1913, on the eve of World War I, only 20.2 percent of cases resulted in a husband and wife sharing the guilt, by 1923 this number had risen to 27.7 percent. *Statistisches Jahrbuch* 21 (1925): 27.
35 SaM, Landgericht Dortmund, 9.8.R.238/31.
36 Frevert, *Women in German History*, 184.
37 Blasius, *Ehescheidung in Deutschland*, 161.
38 SaM, Landgericht Dortmund, 3.3.R.209/32.

to guard against rumors effectively undermined her innocence in the judges' eyes. In declaring both Joachim and Dorothea guilty, the judges spared him the burden of providing for his wife and child after the divorce.

Judges also shifted the meaning and impact of divorce through their interpretation of the law. After the First World War, "culpable marital breakdown" surpassed adultery as the number one cause of divorce.[39] The law defined "culpable marital breakdown" as an instance in which one partner violated the marital duties through shameful, immoral, or abusive behavior to such a degree that the marriage was no longer sustainable. Judges heard testimony from both spouses and often from other witnesses before determining if a marriage had suffered from culpable marital breakdown. Divorce records reveal that judges considered each spouse's interests, the well-being of their children, the sanctity of marriage, and the public good in rendering their verdicts. Because determining the extent to which a marriage had broken down to render a judgment of culpable marital breakdown was so subjective, judges could loosen their standards to make them resemble irreconcilable differences even without changing the law.[40]

If some judges were inclined to stretch their culpable marital breakdown ruling to make it easier for unhappy spouses to divorce, other judges at the Dortmund Landgericht reacted to the rising divorce rate by trying to restore failed marriages even after the couples had given up. The law mandated that

39

	Adultery		Culpable Marital Breakdown	
	M	F	M	F
1917	21.4	36.2	21.2	13.7
1918	22.4	38.1	19.7	13.8
1919	27.8	38.4	17.1	12.5
1920	31.8	35.5	16.9	12.4
1921	31.8	29.1	21.5	13.6
1922	30.7	23.5	26.1	15.0
**				
1925	28.3	18.5	33.4	15.4
1926	28.2	18.8	34.0	14.6
1927	26.8	18.1	35.2	15.7
1928	23.5	16.5	37.7	17.9
1929	22.2	15.7	39.2	19.3

Sources: *Statistisches Jahrbuch* 21 (1925): 27; *Statistisches Jahrbuch* 27 (1931): 111.

40 In her study of German divorce verdicts during the nineteenth century, Lynn Abrams argues that "the courts constituted the last bastion in the state's effort to defend traditional stereotypes of masculinity and femininity." "Restabilisierung der Geschlechterverhältnisse," 11.

before they could file for divorce based on desertion, a spouse was required to obtain a court order demanding the absent spouse return to the marriage. Husbands more often than wives sought these court injunctions, perhaps because unhappy wives so frequently moved in with their parents. When judges deemed the grounds for divorce inadequate, they ordered the women to return to their husbands. In May 1932, Albert F., a metalworker, went to court to get a court order to force his wife, Gertrud, to bring their child and move back into his apartment. Gertrud answered the court order by filing for divorce, claiming that her husband had repeatedly abused her and even stalked her in the street (*auflauern*). Albert did not deny these allegations, but he did deny their validity as evidence by arguing that his wife had forgiven him in August 1931.[41] On the basis of these testimonies, the judge denied Gertrud a divorce and ordered her to reestablish her marriage.

Ample evidence exists that individuals routinely disregarded the courts' verdicts, severely limiting judges' influence. In 1930, when the judges denied Agnes P. a divorce, she set about creating just grounds. Two years later, her husband, the worker Wilhelm P., filed for divorce himself, claiming that because his wife had publicly mocked and slandered him, her behavior was not that of a married woman (*ehewidrig*). This time, the court had to recognize that Agnes's behavior was unbearable, and the judges declared her solely responsible for destroying the marriage.[42] Agnes may have lost the case in the sense that she was declared guilty, but she succeeded in legally escaping an unwanted marriage.

As the courts reinterpreted guilt and the grounds for ending marriage, they necessarily contended with issues of alimony and child support. Unfortunately, a paucity of evidence makes it difficult to assess how these decisions changed over time. After couples separated, most children stayed with their mothers and were supported by their fathers up to the time of the divorce trial. Following the trial, the "innocent" parent uniformly received child custody. When both parents shared the guilt, courts awarded mothers custody of all daughters and sons under the age of six, while they granted fathers custody of their older sons (§1635). Even when the courts granted the woman alimony and child support, this did not guarantee her income, since many men refused to cooperate and stalled in making payments. As Dr. Georg Guggemoos, director of the city youth department in Freising,

---

41 SaM, Landgericht Dortmund, 9.8.R.1/32. According to the BGB, continued life together and especially sexual intercourse constituted proof that "crimes," including adultery, had been forgiven and hence could not be used as evidence. The courts failed to recognize that a partner might try to rebuild a marriage after abuse – hence recreating a household and marital relations – only to decide in the end that the marriage was unsustainable.
42 SaM, Landgericht Dortmund, 9.8.R.266/31.

pointed out, "Anyone active in practical welfare work knows only too well that in the *majority* of cases in which marriages deteriorate, and especially if divorce follows and the children stay with their mothers, fathers neglect their obligation to support their children."[43] Youth departments, which often acted as mediators between mothers and fathers in cases of alimony and child support, also did not always receive or turn over the money to mothers punctually.[44] When fathers remarried, the likelihood that they would support their prior families declined precipitously. In many cases the burden of supporting the child fell to youth departments placing their interests in conflict with judges who tried to uphold moral standards by controlling remarriage.

To limit the number of unsupported families, German law controlled new family formation after divorce. The law forbade women from remarrying sooner than ten months after a divorce, since doing so might raise confusion about the paternity of a child born immediately after divorce, and it prohibited adulterous couples from marrying (BGB §§1313, 1312). Judges waived this prohibition only if a new marriage promised to be morally sound and economically viable, and if it reflected the best interests of the ex-spouse, the potential future spouse, any children involved, and German society itself. In one case from 1930, a woman applied to marry the man with whom she had had an adulterous relationship, and the court requested proof of their combined income. When the couple provided evidence that they earned an ample income in cash and in kind: the man earned 14 Pfennig per hour, 2 Pfd. rye, and 5 Pfd. potatoes per day while the woman earned 12 Pfennig an hour plus 19 Ztr. rye, 2 Ztr. wheat, 2 Ztr. barley, and 80 Ztr. potatoes yearly. She also had a free apartment and heat, daily milk, and oats. With this information, the judge became convinced that their household would be stable and issued the woman a waiver to marry.[45] In another case, the judge allowed a woman to marry because her continued contribution was "absolutely required" in the inn her fiancé owned. The fact that her adultery took place only after "her [ex-]husband's adultery had already been established" further strengthened her petition.[46] In both these cases, judges decided that the economic and moral desirability of the marriages outweighed the immoral nature of the relationships.

---

43 Guggemoos, "Schutz der Kinder," 308. Emphasis mine.
44 StaD, L 80 IC, Gruppe 42, Fach 70, 1. In 1934, Frau R. wrote the Staatsminister Rieke protesting that she and her three minor children, who depended on a combination of child support, alimony, and welfare to survive, never received the money on time. In response, in a letter heavily laden with complaints about Frau R., the welfare office (*Fürsorgestelle*) explained that for "technical reasons" the money had been paid on February 6, March 3, and April 10.
45 SaM, Landgericht Arnsberg, 712.
46 Ibid.

In 1921, when Cornelia R. applied to marry following a divorce, the judges decided in her favor because they believed it would raise the morality of her household. Cornelia and her ex-husband, Thomas R., had married just before he was drafted in the First World War, and Cornelia had given birth to their child in his absence. After the war ended, Thomas did not return to Cornelia, nor did she try to follow him, since both had lost interest in their brief marriage. When Cornelia petitioned the court for permission to marry Friedrich, they emphasized that their relationship and household already constituted a family, since Friedrich devoted his entire income to supporting Cornelia and the child. The Arnsberg *Landgericht* agreed that the marriage would create a moral household for the child and, on a practical and financial level, recognized that it would eliminate the state's financial responsibility to provide for the child.[47] From a judicial perspective, the fact that Cornelia and her husband had both been declared guilty and not that she had done her previous husband wrong (a circumstance that would have elicited less sympathy from the court) simplified her case.

Judges worried that ex-spouses might shun their responsibility to provide for their previous partners and families once they remarried. When Albert C., a divorced businessman, requested permission to marry his "common law" wife, Paula S., the court initially applauded his effort to make his household moral. Albert's lawyer assured the court that since Albert's ex-wife owned a piece of land, Albert's marriage did not jeopardize her livelihood. When the judge asked Albert's ex-wife, however, she unequivocally opposed the marriage. She denied owning property and emphasized that though she received very little from Albert, she depended on this income. This new information forced the judge to reconsider and Albert was allowed to remarry only after signing an oath (*vollstreckbare Urkunde*) guaranteeing his ex-wife a regular income.[48] In a similar case, when Horst S. wanted to marry his housekeeper, Eva T., the court found itself in a quandary. The judges agreed that Eva would run an orderly household, take care of him, and provide his two sons with a proper family. However, Horst and his ex-wife, Alwine S., had ten children during their marriage, eight of whom lived with their mother. Because Alwine S. was in weak physical condition and could not support eight children on her own, the judge deemed it absolutely crucial that Horst continue to support his ex-wife and family. Thus, the benefit of legalizing the immoral relationship and providing a family for the sons did not outweigh the potential danger of Horst's failure to support his ex-family. The court denied Horst's application

---

47 Ibid.   48 Ibid.

for remarriage until he agreed to sign an oath promising to pay 100 Reichs-mark per month to support his ex-wife and children. Only after his ex-family's income was guaranteed did the court permit him to create another family.[49] Despite the value accorded to marriage, then, judges did not always encourage remarriage. Instead, they held the responsibility of ex-spouses (especially men) for their previous families above their wishes for new family formation.

Not all couples felt compelled to have their new relationships sanctioned by the state. Many divorcees who were declared guilty of the breakup of their marriages ignored the state's censure of their relationships and contin-ued to live together without state sanction. Sometimes, this posed problems in the long term, since, as Karen Hagemann found, "wild marriages" (*wilde Ehen*) "represented not only a favorite research subject for snooping police, but... were also a beleaguered target of gossip, curiosity, and moral indig-nation among all the scandalmongers in the neighborhood."[50] In 1930, Gustav K. applied for an exemption to marry Elizabeth W., the mother of his child, with whom he had shared a household for three years. In his letter to the *Landgericht*, Gustav emphasized his desire to establish a religiously sound household and to legitimize his child. The judge granted Gustav permission to remarry on account of the child. Interestingly, however, he and Elisabeth only decided to marry after the police refused to tolerate their immoral household any longer.[51] Neighborhood gossip, not higher morals, doubtless played a significant role in many couples' decision to legitimize their relationships.

Other couples who feared that morality alone would not convince the court of the virtues of their relationships waited to apply until they had created circumstances more favorable to their cases. Bearing a child was an especially effective strategy, since both the state and many couples sought to avoid the stigma of illegitimacy. When Philip T., a nurse's assistant, applied for permission to marry Ulrike G., a factory worker, in 1924, the court assessed both the economic feasibility and the moral desirability of the mar-riage before reaching a decision. The fact that high inflation made the economic analysis almost comical did not deter the court. Since Ulrike and Philip together had earned 446 million marks in the previous week, the court determined that their household would be financially viable. More impor-tant from an economic standpoint was the discovery that since his divorce,

49 Ibid.
50 Hagemann, *Frauenalltag und Männerpolitik*, 173.
51 SaM, Landgericht Arnsberg, 712.

Philip had regularly supported his ex-wife. Finally, and most critical for the court's verdict, Ulrike was pregnant, giving the marriage a definite moral advantage. The fact that they had lived together for many years unmarried and only sought permission to marry once they were expecting a baby suggests that Ulrike and Philip themselves might also have wanted to avoid having an illegitimate child.[52]

Even in the absence of legislative change, then, the practical application of divorce law shifted during the 1920s. German men and women brought their heightened hopes for happiness together with their more modern understandings of marriage into the courtroom. Judges who worried that diminishing the sanctity of marriage would further undermine society rejected modern notions of marriage, delivering verdicts that reflected their unwillingness to support individuals' apparently frivolous desire to escape unwanted marriages. Even when they granted a divorce, judges often refused to give individuals total freedom. Instead, they continued to balance creating moral relationships and founding families against securing income for ex-spouses and children.

NAZI DIVORCE LAW, 1933–1945

Unlike Weimar lawmakers, whose efforts at divorce reform failed, the Nazis enacted the Marriage Law for Greater Germany in 1938, dramatically shifting the focus of divorce by making it permissible only if it coincided with the state's larger racial and population goals. As a result, two different sets of guidelines governed divorce: one for "healthy" partners and another for "unhealthy" partners. Nazi divorce policy also undermined Weimar efforts at promoting gender equity by subtly privileging male power.

Yet despite the Nazis' desire to make racial ideology the guiding philosophy in all marriage-related questions, divorce reform did not come easily for them. From the outset, Nazi policymakers favored allowing divorce and remarriage for "racially incompatible" couples and couples whose marriages failed to produce "racially healthy" children because they realized that unhappy marriages, even among the "racially pure," did not boost the size of the population. They considered replacing the culpable marital breakdown clause with the right to a no-fault divorce. The Committee for Family Law (*Familienrechtsausschuß*), one wing of the Academy of German Law, advocated the creation of a "principle of irretrievable breakdown" (*Ehezerrüttungs Prinzip*) and no-fault divorce, arguing that "in the future . . . divorce should

---

52 Ibid.

be available solely on account of the deterioration of the marital relationship."[53] It also argued that irretrievable breakdown should be redefined to make the state's interest a higher priority than individual interests and needs. In turn, the state's interests would take into account the sanctity of marriage as an institution, the morality it preserved, and Nazi racial ideology. The National Socialist Lawyers' Association supported a more radical divorce reform, emphasizing that "only a healthy marriage is a building block of the *Volk*." It stated: "A sick marriage loses its power to maintain order in society. The crumbling marriage is no longer a source of strength; rather the strength is bound up in small-scale bitter warfare. It is the right and duty of the state administration of justice to remove this sick – in any case useless, and often damaging – member of the *Volkskörper*."[54]

Like their predecessors, however, Nazi policymakers faced stiff opposition not only from the church but also from politicians who feared that broadening the legitimate grounds for divorce would impair the sanctity of marriage. In 1933, Reich Minister of Justice Franz Gürtner (a Catholic, non–Nazi Party member) argued that liberalizing divorce laws would cause people to believe that "because marriage [was] more easily dissolvable under the Third Reich, it [was] a weaker life commitment than in earlier times."[55] For a regime whose rhetoric extolled the virtues of marriage and the traditional family, a policy that appeared to undermine the family posed too great a risk. Furthermore, Nazi policymakers worried that too liberal a divorce law might make countless ex-wives and children dependent on the state's limited resources. But requiring divorced women to work would have run contrary to Nazi rhetoric that before 1937 praised married women and mothers who stayed at home. It would also have raised difficult questions about motherhood for Nazi policymakers. For the duration of the Nazi era, the party's wish to advocate a new, modern divorce policy that offered individuals (in particular men) greater freedom to leave unsatisfactory marriages when their desire to do so was compatible with state population and racial goals remained in conflict with the necessity to adhere to a set of very traditional values and concerns.

---

53 The Committee for Family Law, founded in 1933 by Hans Frank, was a vocal advocate of divorce reform during the Nazi era. F. Mößmer, Vorschlag zur Neugestaltung des deutschen Ehescheidungsrechtes, München, August 1935, quoted in Blasius, *Ehescheidung in Deutschland*, 196.

54 They, too, argued for a "principle of irretrievable breakdown," which would make all other grounds for divorce irrelevant. NS Rechtswahrerbundes zum Entwurf v.J., 1937, quoted in Blasius, *Ehescheidung in Deutschland*, 201.

55 Rundbrief Reichsminister der Justiz, 19 June 1936, quoted in Blasius, *Ehescheidung in Deutschland*, 199.

In the absence of a clear consensus on divorce reform, the Nazis passed other legislation that directly affected the parameters of marriage and divorce. Marriage certificates and marriage loans both served to further the state's overarching aim of increasing the number of genetically and racially healthy marriages. The Law to Prevent Hereditarily Sick Offspring (*Gesetz zur Verhütung erbkranken Nachwuchses*), passed in July 1933, took this process one step further and defined all marriages that did not promise healthy children as "worthless." Infertility thus became both grounds for being denied a marriage permit and a new reason for divorce. More importantly, anti-Semitism, actively promulgated by the state after 1933, inspired a divorce boom as Gentiles divorced their Jewish spouses in escalating numbers. Whereas in 1933, 29.7 mixed marriages per 10,000 ended in divorce, one year later, after the Nazis had begun implementing anti-Semitic measures and stripping German Jews of their political, civic, and economic rights, the divorce rate rose to 37 per 10,000 mixed marriages.[56] This trend gained explicit political support in September 1935 with the creation of the Nuremberg Laws "to Protect German Blood and Honor." By outlawing marriage and sexual intercourse between Jews and Gentiles, the Nuremberg Laws directly infringed upon individual freedom to marry and, in the eyes of many judges, also provided grounds for divorce. In October 1935, the Reichstag passed a law prohibiting all marriages between hereditarily ill and healthy Germans. While these laws were being enacted, policymakers continued to wrestle with the contradictory positions they held on divorce reform issues. Throughout 1936 and 1937, Ferdinand Mößmer, a Munich lawyer and director of the Committee for Family Law, debated the meaning of and guidelines for divorce with Minister of Justice Franz Gürtner. In 1936, Hitler recommended that Gürtner find a middle way rather than radically reconstituting divorce law. Instituting a waiting period prior to divorce – one possible compromise proposal – had long been advocated by authorities at the main office of the National Socialist People's Health Department (Hauptamt für Volksgesundheit NSDAP).[57]

Not until 1938 did the annexation of Austria bring divorce reform to the fore and make rewriting the law imperative. Austria had no uniform state divorce law; instead, each church set its own divorce policy. Since

---

56 Blasius, *Ehescheidung in Deutschland*, 190. One woman I interviewed knew a couple who had divorced for this reason. The Jewish woman emigrated to Israel in 1941, while the "Aryan" father moved with their children to another city in Germany, where they could erase any trace of Jewish blood. Frau Rohde, interview.

57 Stellungnahme des Hauptamtes für Volksgesundheit in der NSDAP zum Entwurf v.J., 1937, quoted in Blasius, *Ehescheidung in Deutschland*, 199.

the Catholic Church – in this heavily Catholic country – forbade divorce even when only one of the marriage partners was Catholic, Austrians rarely divorced. The Catholic Church's policy of "separation of bed and board" (*Trennung von Tisch und Bett*) directly conflicted with Nazi population policy because it simultaneously promised no children and prevented the creation of new potentially prolific families. Many Austrians looked to the Nazis to liberalize divorce law. In April 1938, Hitler ordered Gürtner to "fix" the Austrian divorce laws "immediately" by making infertility a ground for divorce and easing the restrictions on remarriage even in cases of adultery.[58] The Marriage Law for Greater Germany (*Großdeutsches Ehegesetz*, GEG) was enacted in August 1938, bringing years of debate to an abrupt close.

The new marriage laws transformed divorce by broadening the legitimate grounds for divorce – both with and without fault. The laws identified three guilt-based grounds for divorce: adultery, refusal to procreate, and "serious marital transgression" (*schwere Eheverfehlung*) (GEG §§47–9). Even under the new law, however, judges retained the right to make the final determination of when a marriage was irredeemably damaged and hence no longer of value to the state. In general, if the court believed a couple could recover and lead a productive (and prolific) marital life or if a couple had young children, judges shied away from ending the marriage. For example, when Dora F. filed for divorce from Christian, a railway employee, in 1939, the court[59] refused her request. Dora, eight months pregnant at the time of her court appearance, claimed that since their marriage, Christian had not given up his bachelor ways. He came home only to eat and regularly stayed out late at night playing cards with his friends. He was unfriendly to her, complained, and had hit her. Christian agreed that their relationship was troubled but blamed his mother-in-law for inciting Dora to fight. Since the fighting and hitting was mutual and insignificant, he did not think divorce was necessary. The court concurred, claiming that as young people, Dora and Christian had not yet mastered marriage. In a rather patronizing fashion, the judge concluded: "The court is convinced that the present crisis in the young marriage of the parties is only temporary. If both sides have solid intentions to get used to one another, to respect one another, to adapt to one another, and to be good parents to the expected children, the couple's marriage will, in the opinion of this court, proceed harmoniously." Clearly,

58 Die Aufzeichnung des Reichsminister der Justiz über seinen Vortrag beim "Führer und Reichskanzler," quoted in Blasius, *Ehescheidung in Deutschland*, 204–5.
59 Westphalia had 1 *Oberlandgericht* in Hamm, 9 *Landgerichte* (in Essen, Dortmund, Bochum, Münster, Hagen, Siegen, Paderborn, and Arnsberg), and 108 *Amtsgerichte*, at which 613 judges and 110 prosecuting attorneys were employed in 1933. Knobelsdorf, "Das Bielefelder Landgericht," 50–51.

in this case, permitting the couple to divorce would have destroyed a family at its origin and raised troubling long-term questions about Dora's and the child's economic livelihood.[60]

Judges who blocked divorces they deemed unnecessary were not the only obstacle to divorce in Nazi Germany. In some cases, the new laws themselves, far from facilitating easier divorce, prevented divorces that during the Weimar era would have been permitted. Adultery, for example, now only constituted grounds for divorce if the innocent party had not "facilitated or made the adultery easier through their behavior" (GEG §49). Judges denied divorce if the adulterer had been driven to have an affair by an unsupportive or unloving spouse. When both the husband and wife had committed adultery, judges sometimes ruled that they deserved one another and should stay married despite deep animosity. In one such case, Frau Schmidt accused her husband of adultery and alleged to have seen him in their bedroom with another woman. He denied her accusations and proceeded to accuse his wife of neglecting her household duties and discussing intimate details of their relationship in public. The judge remained unconvinced of the need for a divorce and denied their request. The fact that they disliked one another enough to level such caustic accusations did not constitute grounds for divorce.[61] Clearly, in such cases, judges based their decisions on social stability and the public good rather than the happiness of the individuals involved. In the eyes of many judges, marital stability did not depend on marital harmony.

Only after the war began did the Nazis change their attitudes toward adultery, and then only in some cases. In 1942, a new crime was introduced – "the insult of husbands at the front" – that allowed soldiers to sue their wives' lovers without bringing an end to their own marriages. In fact, the Justice Department tried to discourage the divorce of soldiers and their wives unless the damage to their marriages was irreparable, a determination left to judges. Only after the soldier husband had been killed – and hence the state stood to free itself from the burden of paying widow's benefits – did it censure adultery. In March 1943, the Reich introduced the "postmortem divorce"

---

60 SaM, Landgericht Dortmund, Ehescheidung 10.R.96/39. This examination is based on a survey of divorce cases from the Landgericht Dortmund taken from 1934, 1939, 1940, and 1941. I selected 1934 to examine the period after the Nazis came to power but before the law was changed. The first year the Nazi Marriage Laws were in effect before the war began was 1939. And 1940 and 1941 were chosen to assess the effects of war on divorce. For each year, I examined roughly seventy-five cases randomly selected from a set of 150.

61 SaM, Landgericht Dortmund, Ehescheidung 3.6.R.3/33.

to defend soldiers' reputations and to spare the state's coffers in cases in which a dead soldier's spouse could be shown to have been adulterous.[62]

Nazi pronatalist aims meant that spouses who willfully refused to reproduce posed a graver problem than those who were unfaithful. Whereas under the civil code the refusal to reproduce was termed a "marital transgression" and was weighed in the larger context of a dispute, Nazi divorce law deemed it a sufficient cause for divorce (GEG §48). As one legal commentator pointed out, "The fact that the new Marriage Law put it in its own separate paragraph was intended to emphasize that: Whoever refuses a child without justifiable grounds negates the marriage."[63] When Paul M. filed for divorce in October 1941, he cited his wife's persistent refusal to bear children as his chief complaint. Frau M. admitted her refusal but defended her position with the assertion "that the preparation for marriage had caused her to become very run down." Her complaint continued: "As a result she and the plaintiff had agreed to wait six months to a year before conceiving a child. Then she had to move her eighty-year-old mother.... Subsequently, caring for her own household had demanded all her attention. As a result she had absolutely not noticed that her behavior hurt the plaintiff and thwarted his most cherished wish to have children. [Moreover,] her over-inflated concerns about the household had completely repressed her own thoughts about a child. She feared that the birth of a child would make it impossible for her to cope with her work. Finally, her tremendous nervousness left her no other option." Despite this elaborate explanation and the defendant's expressed desire to bear children, the court[64] found her resistance to her husband's wishes "unfounded." Its judgment, in which Paul M. was granted a divorce, read: "In every marriage the birth of a child brings with it significantly more work. Only a tiny percent of the German *Volk* is in a position to pass on this extra work to hired help. Nevertheless we are talking about a completely normal problem, which cannot repress the desire for children. The couple's desire to bear children was not deferred by any exceptional circumstances. The defendant should have repressed her exaggerated idea about future work and given in to the plaintiff's natural desire for children.... She should have revised her ideas about household duties. Her husband's health and her own health should have been placed above these petty concerns." The judges' explanation revealed their belief in the

---

62 Heinemann, *What Difference*, 55–6.
63 Von Scanzoni, *Das Großdeutsche Ehegesetz*, 105. This point was further strengthened by the "Ten Commandments for Spousal Selection" published by the Reichsausschuss für Volksgesundheit.
64 Sometimes, this was a group of judges. The Landgericht Arnsberg, for example, generally had a body of three judges in divorce cases.

primacy of a wife's duty to mother.[65] Frau M.'s refusal to bear children rendered her marriage incapable of fulfilling its "function in terms of population policy: [namely,] to raise present children and bear further children."[66]

Though the Nazis' third guilt-based ground for divorce, "serious marital transgression," was open to interpretation, it did not simplify divorce. Because judges believed that only the innocent party could accurately assess the damage to a marriage, only the aggrieved spouse could file for divorce on the ground of serious marital transgression. When Peter R., a master carpenter, filed for divorce, he argued that his wife had destroyed the marital relationship by neglecting her household duties and pursing an extramarital relationship. His wife filed a countercharge (*Widerklage*) denying the truth of the accusation and requesting that the marriage be sustained. After evaluating the relationship and listening to testimony from witnesses, the court concluded that although Frau R. had not adequately fulfilled her household duties, Peter could not "base his reason for divorce on his wife's shortcomings in the marriage, because . . . he, the petitioner, brutally abused, insulted and threatened the defendant for reasons other than her neglect of the household." The court concluded, "In light of his own marital transgressions, his petition for divorce cannot be successful."[67] Since Peter's behavior had caused more damage to the marriage than his wife's had, her allegiance to the marriage outweighed his request for divorce. In another case, when a woman tried to divorce her husband on account of the violence she had endured, the judge discounted the violent nature of that marriage because "both parties [had] easily provoked natures."[68] Paradoxically, one result of the Nazi divorce reform was that many couples who in an earlier era would have won divorces found themselves compelled to remain in unhappy and childless marriages.

In the hope of using divorce to create more healthy, prolific marriages, Nazi divorce law identified four additional health-related grounds for divorce for which no fault was assigned: mental disorder, mental illness, contagious or repulsive illness, and early infertility in marriages without biological or adopted children (GEG §§50–53). The overarching goal of these clauses was to help free from childless marriages all racially pure and potentially reproductive members of the *Volk*. In such cases, judges based their

---

65 SaM, Landgericht Dortmund, Ehescheidung 3.R.41/725. The Nazis were not alone in their assumption that wives should also be mothers. Elaine Tyler May found that in Los Angeles during the 1920s, "very few wives admitted having no desire for children." See *Great Expectations*, 89.

66 Holzhauer, "Die Scheidungsgründe," 61.

67 SaM, Landgericht Dortmund, Ehescheidung 9.5.R.62/33.

68 Ibid., Ehescheidung 3.6.R.6/33.

decisions on the duration of the marriage, the age of the participants, and the existence of infertility or illness. Even these medical conditions, however, proved insufficient grounds for divorce if the "desire for divorce [was] not morally justified."[69] Moreover, infertility only constituted a legitimate basis for divorce if a judge believed that the fertile person intended to remarry and reproduce. Thus, although the Marriage Law for Greater Germany expanded the legal grounds for divorce and created means of obtaining no-fault divorce, judges continued to balance the sanctity of marriage against population concerns.

During the Nazi era, controlling divorce among "unhealthy" Germans was believed to be as critical as controlling it among "healthy" Germans. Judges evaluated divorces between two people identified as unhealthy in terms of the state's interests. When Frau S. tried to divorce her husband in 1934, she argued that he had beaten and insulted her and currently resided in jail. But since both she and her husband were unhealthy according to racial guidelines and a divorce would have permitted her to remarry, the judge denied her a divorce. Frau S. was incensed by this verdict and took her case to the high court in Hamm. The next judge who heard Frau S.'s story drew a different conclusion. He argued that "the public at large [did] not have an interest in preserving this kind of marriage." Although neither judge took the unhappy woman's own interests into consideration, they interpreted the public good differently. The first judge feared that Frau S.'s divorce would enable her to remarry and pass her unhealthy genes on to any potential children. The second judge saw no advantage for the state in preserving the current bad marriage.[70] Both these verdicts reflected the state's belief that in matters of population and race, the individual's interests had to be secondary to the interests of the *Volk*.

Germans wishing to divorce encountered the fewest obstructions if the state had deemed only one of the spouses unhealthy. When Anna M. went to court to divorce her husband, Martin, who had been sent to the concentration camp Sachsenhausen for theft, she met no resistance. Martin's imprisonment in Sachsenhausen not only made him an undesirable marriage partner but also reinforced his status as unworthy. Freeing Anna from her marriage had the potential benefit of enabling her to remarry and bear children.[71] Similarly, when Max S. went to court to divorce his wife, who had been sterilized on account of mental illness, the court permitted the

---

69 Von Scanzoni, *Das Großdeutsche Ehegesetz*, 49, 109.
70 SaM, Landgericht Dortmund, Ehescheidung 8.9.R.249/34.
71 Ibid., Ehescheidung 3.R.619/40.

divorce without any serious investigation. In its eyes, her sterilization inherently made her an unfit spouse.[72] By freeing Anna and Max from their "undesirable" marriages, the judges enabled them to enter new, healthy marriages and, they hoped, bear healthy children.

As early as 1933, when the first Aryans tried to divorce their Jewish spouses, judges began to discuss how to incorporate explicit racial policy into divorce law. Not all judges considered themselves Nazis, but many shared the antiparliamentary, antirepublican, and at least some of the anti-Semitic sentiments of the new leadership.[73] After an initial skepticism about Hitler's appointment as chancellor, the majority of German judges overcame their doubts, and even in the absence of any compulsion to join the Nazi Party, over 82 percent of judges became party members. The first concrete debate about the application of race to divorce law arose over the question whether to extend civil code §1333 to permit Aryan men to divorce their Jewish wives. Originally, §1333 permitted divorce if a "mistake" (*Irrtum*) had been made with regard to personal characteristics, including alcoholism and mental disabilities. The proposal to extend §1333, published in an article in the *Juristische Wochenschrift* (Judicial Weekly) in the summer of 1933, advocated adding Jewish blood to the list of qualifying "personal characteristics." The author, Gerichtsassessor (lawyer) Wöhrmann, argued that only after Hitler began to teach the population about "the interconnections of the race question" could Aryan men who married Jewish women have realized the error of their spousal choice. Only then did they learn that the children they bore in a mixed marriage would never be full German citizens.[74] Historians disagree about how willingly German justices incorporated race into their decisions. Ralph Angermund believes that most justices disagreed with Wöhrmann's article. He claims that while some preferred to wait until Hitler and his legal advisors rewrote the divorce laws rather than to reinterpret them selectively on their own, others rejected the argument because of the "obvious holes" in it.[75] Nonetheless, he notes that even though "only a minority" of judges agreed with Wöhrmann, court verdicts began to vary.

---

72 Ibid., Ehescheidung 3.R.675/40.
73 One sample found that before 1933, 60.4 percent of Westphalian judges had already joined the NSDAP. In 1937, another 28.4 percent joined, and after 1937, another 5.7 percent. Niermann, "Die Durchsetzung politischer," 66. Given these statistics, H. W. Koch's claim that "Staunch monarchists under Bismarck, loyal (if unenthusiastic) servants of the law under the Weimar Republic, these men [judges], known for their integrity and strict adherence to the letter of the law, continued their careers under the Third Reich with scarcely a murmur of protest" seems an understatement. *In the Name*, 7.
74 Angermund, *Deutsche Richterschaft*, 111.
75 Ibid., 118–19.

While Cologne judges quickly allowed the use of §1333 in mixed marriages, Berlin judges consistently disallowed its use. Judges in Münster permitted them but allowed the Jewish spouse a countercharge.[76] In contrast, Ingo Müller emphasizes the great degree to which judges stepped beyond the law and applied racial criteria in their verdicts. The "wave" of decisions that allowed race as a factor in §1333 was so great, Müller argues, that it prompted concern even among "leading Nazi jurists." In November 1934, Roland Freisler, the future president of the People's Court, even issued a public statement stressing that it was not the role of the judge "to alter the existing laws of the nation"; "if every judge were to deal with them as he saw fit and to 'decide questions which [can] be solved only from the superior vantage point of the Führer,'" he stated, "then 'chaos and anarchy would replace unified leadership.'"[77]

Judges did not receive the legal clarification they sought until 1938, when the Marriage Laws for Greater Germany legalized the annulment of racially mixed marriages. Thereafter, they generally dissolved such marriages. Even in the case of mixed marriages, however, judges continued to require at least verbal evidence that the marriages had dissolved. In 1940, when Frau H. sued her husband, a Jewish businessman, for divorce, she testified that he had beaten and slandered her and that they had last had intercourse two years prior. Her testimony provided both a legal ground for divorce (the fact that her husband was Jewish and she was not) and evidence that the marriage had dissolved (they had not had intercourse in more than a year). Her husband, who did not appear in court, wrote that he "did not contest the allegations in the charge or the additional legal documents." The judge terminated the marriage.[78] In another case from 1941, an Aryan woman, Christa L., claimed somewhat incredibly that her marriage had deteriorated because her Jewish husband, who had been sent to a concentration camp, no longer wrote to her. Because Peter himself could not appear in court, the Jewish representative (*Consultant*)[79] reported that while Peter "[did] not contest the plaintiff's statement," he wanted it understood that "the separation ha[d] occurred involuntarily." The judge, not surprisingly, noted: "It is true that the separation does not rest on P.'s free will. In the final analysis, however, this is not the relevant issue in the preceding case. An involuntary

---

76 Ibid., 117–18.　　　　　　　　　77 Müller, *Hitler's Justice*, 95.

78 Evidence in such cases often meant proving that the marriages had lost their intimacy for the requisite period of time (under the Nazis, one year). SaM, Landgericht Dortmund, Ehescheidung 3.R.614/40.

79 The Fifth Decree of the Reichsburgergesetzes said Jews could only be represented by one of 170 Jewish judicial consultants. Beginning on 12 June 1940, judges could legally exclude consultants from the courtroom under special circumstances, leaving Jews without legal representation. Angermund, *Deutsche Richterschaft*, 122–3.

separation suffices, if this takes place outside the usual or natural progression of things."[80] Whether Frau H. or the judge knew Peter's fate or understood that maintaining the correspondence would in all likelihood have been impossible cannot be known, but the marriage was dissolved. Both Christa L. and Frau H. also benefited from the Nazis' overriding propensity to hold Jewish men, not their Aryan wives or lovers, responsible for racially undesirable relationships.[81] Aryan men were similarly held responsible for their relationships with Jewish women, but judges frequently allowed them to plead mitigating circumstances and as a result gave them lesser sentences.[82]

Even after the marriage law had been enacted, not all judges strictly adhered to racial policy. As late as August 1940, one judge denied an Aryan woman the right to divorce her Jewish husband. When Gerda B. appeared in court, she claimed that "as an Aryan... [she] could no longer live with the defendant, a Jew." She complained that her husband, Paul Israel,[83] not only demanded that their only son be raised according to Jewish law but also sent him to a Jewish school. The late date of her complaint may reflect societal pressure rather than her own change of heart. The judge recognized that in the case of "a marriage which from a racial political perspective is as undesirable as the current one, one would certainly not have to hold a stringent standard." He nonetheless emphasized that "that cannot lead to an evasion of the law." The judge did not believe that the father alone had selected their son's school, and he recognized that the defendant had remained in Germany on account of his wife rather than emigrating with the rest of his family. Finally, he concluded that the petition for divorce was unjustified because he did not believe the marriage had deteriorated, since up until just prior to her appearance in court, Gerda still lived with her husband. "If the plaintiff ever found the defendant's behavior damaging to the marriage [ehefeindlich]," he asserted, she had since "[given] her will to reconciliation and forgiveness."[84] This judge's refusal to grant a divorce to a mixed couple in 1940 was an unusual exception, and it was probably also a risky decision for the judge to have made so late in the regime. Unfortunately, the personnel file for the judge who presided in Gerda's case has been lost (nor do we know the fate of Paul Israel), but the fact that he continued to preside over divorce cases until the end of the war makes clear

80 SaM, Landgericht Dortmund, Ehescheidung 3.R.695/40.
81 Müller, Hitler's Justice, 110.
82 Ibid., 104.
83 Law mandated that all Jews take either Israel or Sarah as a middle name.
84 SaM, Landgericht Dortmund, Ehescheidung 3.R.811/40. Jutta Scott has argued that many judges who believed in the integrity of marriage were reluctant to carry out the new sentences. See "Governmental Laws," 199.

that the Nazis did not force him out of the judiciary. The case clearly reveals that even in the face of the most fanatically held ideas – namely, Nazi anti-Semitic policy – judges still interpreted and applied the law as they saw fit.

Nazi leaders recognized that judges failed to apply the racial laws strictly. In 1936, Roland Freisler, state secretary of the Reich Justice Ministry, wrote the presidents of both the *Oberlandesgericht* and the *Landgericht* to pressure them to force their judges to issue harsher sentences in racial cases. But overall, the NSDAP and the Gestapo seldom intervened in judicial issues or took disciplinary action against individual judges who failed to issue racially appropriate verdicts.[85]

If the Nazi leadership's inability to bring all judges into line influenced the implementation of their policies, so too did the population's disregard of the aims of Nazi ideology. Because lawmakers feared popular protest, they stopped short of introducing unrestricted no-fault divorce. They partially compensated for their defeat in the no-fault debate by adding to the 1938 law additional grounds for divorce based on the "dissolution of the house-hold" (GEG §55). According to the law, if after three years of living separately a couple determined that their marriage had suffered "a far-reaching, incurable breakdown" that prevented the reestablishment of the relationship, they were permitted to file for divorce. Though this clause approximated the Nazis' desired principle of irretrievable breakdown, it differed in one significant way: judges, not individuals, defined the meaning of "far-reaching, incurable breakdown." Couples still had to prove to the court that their marriages had deteriorated beyond repair, a requirement that brought the most intimate details of marital life into the courtroom. Nevertheless, the law rapidly gained popularity, and in 1939 it accounted for roughly 20 percent of all divorces. In 1940, after the war had begun, the proportion of marriages that ended on the basis of Section 55 dropped to 15 percent, probably because so many couples were separated by the war.[86] Though requiring couples to live separately for three years before being granted a divorce in effect "wasted" potentially reproductive years, Nazi policymakers found no resolution to this contradiction.

Some men and women tried to manipulate National Socialist ideology to make their case for divorce even when race was not relevant. Herr Voges, with whom this chapter began, tried to strengthen his case against his wife by accusing her of being an enemy of the state. Not only did she fail as a wife and mother, he claimed, but she also criticized Hitler and defended the Jews. In her defense, Frau Voges claimed to have run a good household and

85 Angermund, *Deutsche Richterschaft*, 130–31.   86 Blasius, *Ehescheidung in Deutschland*, 211.

to have supported Hitler. She suggested that her effort to enlist Hitler's help in correcting her husband's abusive behavior was evidence of both her level of despair and her faith in Hitler. In their verdicts, the judges recognized that Herr Voges had been abusive to his wife but that no evidence had come to light that Frau Voges had neglected her household. As to her correspondence with Hitler (which she initiated without her husband's permission), the judges argued the gender-biased position that it constituted a betrayal of the marriage. "In such cases," they emphasized, "only by acting in agreement with her husband [could] the defendant avoid damaging her marital duties." Because the judges felt that women should not act politically without their husbands' support, they declared both spouses guilty.[87]

The overall impact of the Marriage Law of Greater Germany varied. It had its most dramatic impact in Austria. In the first months of the new law, from 1 August through 31 December 1938, 36,716 people ended their "bed and board" marriages.[88] In Germany, the impact was less dramatic: the total number of divorces varied from 54,402 in 1934 to 46,786 in 1937 to 49,497 in 1938. The "dissolution of the marital household" clause became the new law's most popular. After the war began, the overall divorce rate fell from nearly 20 percent throughout the 1930s to closer to 10 percent.[89] The likelihood of a couple's actually being permitted to divorce differed from one judge to the next. In Dortmund in 1933–1934, one set of judges denied 20.7 percent of couples divorce, while another denied divorce to only 8.7 percent of couples. The overall success rate of couples seeking divorce remained high as the war began, with 88.2 percent of divorces granted in 1939 and 99.2 percent in 1940.[90]

Throughout the Nazi era, economics and gender expectations remained important factors in limiting the accessibility of divorce. Lawmakers, judges, and most Germans viewed husbands as breadwinners, and men who failed to provide for their families often found themselves in court. In 1933–1934, 25.9 percent of German women who filed for divorce did so because their husbands failed to provide by refusing to support their families, deserting them, being thrown in jail, or falling into excessive debt.[91] German judges worried that allowing all these marriages to dissolve would create too great a

87 SaM, Landgericht Dortmund, 10.R.4/39.
88 By the end of 1940, the number had risen to 48,970. In 1939, the total number of divorces within the former German boundaries was 60,789, or 38.3 per 10,000 (compared to 55.5 per 10,000 in Austria). Blasius, *Ehescheidung in Deutschland*, 211.
89 SaM, Landgericht Dortmund, Ehescheidung 5.6.7.R.33, 3.R.33, 3.R.40, 3.R.41.
90 Calculated based on the cases in box 3.R.33 versus box 4,5,6.R.33, all found in SaM, Landgericht Dortmund, Ehescheidung.
91 SaM, Landgericht Dortmund, Ehescheidung, boxes 5.6.7.R.33, 9.R.34, 3.R.40, and 3.R.41.

burden of unsupported wives for the state to bear.[92] Although they expected husbands to provide for their wives, judges took extenuating circumstances into account.[93] In 1933, Marian D., the wife of an unemployed lathe operator, moved in with her parents after her husband sold their furniture to get money. During her divorce trial, her husband testified that it was his unemployment, not a lack of will, that had prevented him from supporting his wife. Although the court sympathized with Marian's anger, they also understood her husband's precarious position and refused to grant her a divorce, stating: "The fact that as a result of the reduction in his income, her husband is not in a position to pay for his own furniture does not give her the right to live separately. She must also stay by her husband's side during the most difficult times and share joy and misery with him."[94] Many judges, who themselves experienced hard times during the Depression, may well have sympathized with their fellow breadwinners and refused to allow the hard economic times that gripped Germany in 1933 to undermine marriage.

Although judges tried to secure a livelihood for all parties involved in a divorce, they considered neither joint residence nor financial partnership as absolutes in determining marital viability. In 1934, Frau B. filed for divorce, complaining that her husband had failed to support her and their two children. She claimed that although he received welfare, he spent most of it on himself, forcing her to move in with her parents. Herr B. in turn accused his wife of destroying the marriage, first by deserting him and then by refusing to follow when he moved. The judges recognized that "the denial of support constitutes a serious breach of the marital duties" but argued that it only constituted grounds for divorce if the defendant was capable of paying and yet failed to do so, thus causing "distress" to the plaintiff. In this case, Frau B.'s parents had stepped in to support her and her children, so that her husband's lack of support had caused minimal hardship. Since Frau B.'s parents would have terminated their support had she moved back in with her husband, they saw reason in her refusal to do so.[95] Under better economic circumstances, the court decided, the marriage would still be sustainable. Similarly, during the Second World War, many judges viewed "support for soldiers' dependents" (*Familienunterstützung*) as an alternative to divorce,

---

92 In other national contexts, historians have also found economics to be a major driving force behind divorce. See Soland, "Gender and the Social Order"; May, *Great Expectations*, 80.

93 The Danish welfare system supported women whose husbands failed to provide for them after divorce. Soland, "Gender and the Social Order," 207.

94 SaM, Landgericht Dortmund, Ehescheidung 9.5.R.20/33.

95 Ibid., Ehescheidung 9.5.R.36/33. Already during the Depression, Weimar courts held other family members responsible for helping before the state stepped in. See StaD, L 80 IC, Gruppe XXII, Fach 70, 1.

since the benefits could sustain a family when the husband was unable to provide.[96] In an attempt to ensure an economically stable population, judges and lawmakers tried to shore up marriages on terms advantageous to men during periods of extended stress.

German judges' concentration on economics in the context of divorce often clashed with couples' interests. German women's reasons for filing for divorce suggest that their attitudes toward marriage shifted during the Nazi era. In 1933, 25.9 percent of women listed failure to provide as their main reason for filing, compared to 19 percent who listed adultery, 27.9 percent who listed abuse (14.7 percent physical abuse and 13.2 percent mental abuse), and 20.6 percent who listed heavy drinking. By 1940–1941, the number of women filing for lack of support had fallen to 22.1 percent, while other reasons increased: 22.9 percent cited adulterous behavior, 35.4 percent cited abuse (26 percent physical abuse and 9.4 percent mental abuse), and 6.3 percent cited heavy drinking. Clearly, these women's expectations for marriage went beyond mere financial support to encompass a code of behavior as well. Even when their financial well-being was not in jeopardy, some women found their marriages sufficiently damaged by their husbands' behavior as to make divorce desirable.[97]

Women's willingness to file for divorce for reasons other than economics may seem surprising given that women remained the more vulnerable partner in divorce after 1933, just as they had been before. Nazi lawmakers worried that making divorce more accessible might further disadvantage the weaker spouse, usually the woman. To protect women, judges enforced with greater rigor the "countercomplaint," by which defendants who chose to remain with a guilty spouse in a marriage that judges deemed viable could override their spouses' divorce petition. Judges honored countercomplaints with extra vigilance if children were involved or if they believed the woman had sacrificed more than usual for the marriage – for example, if she had struggled especially hard to maintain the family during her husband's lengthy unemployment or if she had ruined her own health in repeated childbirths.[98] Lawmakers' desire to protect women had very definite limits, however, since

96 When one woman tried to divorce her husband for failure to support, the judge rejected her argument because the soldiers' benefits adequately provided for her. SaM, Landgericht Dortmund, Ehescheidung 3.R.641/40.

97 In contrast, at least until the war broke out, 28 percent of men filed because their wives failed to run proper households, and 44.9 percent filed because their wives had committed adultery. By 1940–1941, adultery had fallen to 33.3 percent of cases, and household issues fell to 10.5 percent. SaM, Landgericht Dortmund, Ehescheidung 5.6.I.R.33, 9.R.34, 3.R.40, and 3.R.41.

98 "Die Regelung des Unterhalts der geschiedenen Frau," Anlage zum Rundschreiben F 18/41 vom 26 February 1941, BaK, NS 44, 36.

even here the interest of the *Volk* took precedence over that of individual spouses. The law emphasized that "the countercomplaint is not to be
heeded if the preservation of marriage is not morally justified."[99] Because
Nazi lawmakers' highest priority lay not in protecting innocent spouses from
desertion but in freeing "healthy" people from "unhealthy" marriages, the
countercomplaint option could not be used to entrap healthy Germans in
childless marriages. Judges retained the right to override countercomplaints
they found inappropriate.

Substantially more men went to court to get injunctions to force their
wives to reestablish their marriages than did women. In 1933, judges ordered
women to return to their husbands in 10.2 percent of the cases men filed,
compared to the only 1.2 percent in which judges ordered husbands to
return to their wives.[100] Despite the seeming legal advantage held by men,
however, men frequently later returned to court to divorce wives who failed
to return home after their own divorce attempts were dismissed.

Like their left-wing predecessors in Weimar, Nazi policymakers had initially hoped to create a system of alimony payment focused on divorcees'
needs and not on guilt. They ultimately failed to achieve this goal. The
only alimony-related innovation they managed to effect in the 1938 law
declared the spouse who was assigned the majority of the guilt (in cases
where spouses shared guilt) responsible for paying alimony.[101] In a change
from Weimar, then, women who shared guilt did not necessarily lose all their
financial support. Technically, the law was gender neutral, and guilty wives
bore responsibility for supporting their ex-husbands, but this only applied if
the man could not support himself. The law also assigned the spouse who
had filed for divorce responsibility for alimony in cases in which guilt was
not assigned. Judges did take into account the formation of new families,
however, to ensure that men who divorced unworthy women were not
prevented from founding new families.

Alimony was set at "the standard of living appropriate to both spouses"
and took into account each spouse's earning potential. The law emphasized
that "to work is an honor and can never be labeled dishonorable [since] in
principle every healthy, able comrade [*Volksgenosse*], male or female, is obligated to work for the community [*Gemeinschaft*] according to their age."[102]

99 Ibid.
100 SaM, Landgericht Dortmund, Ehescheidung 5.6.7.33.
101 GEG §66. This was previously governed by BGB §1578.
102 They emphasized that for mothers with small children and elderly women for whom paid labor
    would be too burdensome, the evaluation of whether they could work had to be made carefully.
    Das Großdeutsche Ehegesetz, 240–41.

If a woman was employed, her alimony was reduced accordingly if her ex-husband could show that his ex-wife's work should offset the alimony payment. Only if a woman had young children or elderly parents to care for did the law waive her responsibility to seek employment.[103] The Nazis even expected women with older children who had never worked outside the home to find work. By expecting women to work and by reducing alimony when they worked, the law protected men's money, undercut women's ability to lead unhampered domestic lives, and won workers for the state.

Other regulations governing alimony focused similarly on protecting men's money rather than preserving women's well-being. Men whose ex-wives had private savings upon which to live were freed by the law from paying alimony. Although designed to ensure that women with private means did not prevent their ex-spouses from beginning a new family, the law was worded so loosely that any woman with any savings could be denied alimony. By 1940, this matter had come to the attention of the Sicherheitsdienst (literally "security service"), which recommended that a distinction be made between wealthy women and women with small savings accounts that would be rapidly depleted, leaving them penniless.[104] The law imposed further constraints on women by denying them the freedom to choose a postmarital lifestyle: judges often gave women who refused to work unfavorable court settlements. The law also made alimony contingent upon a woman's behavior. Men had the legal right to contest their obligation to pay alimony if their ex-wives did not lead "moral" (*sittliche*) lives. An ex-husband could challenge a woman's right to continue to use his family's name if he disapproved of her lifestyle, in particular if he felt her behavior damaged the family name. Thus, the Nazis provided men multiple options for protecting their money and their honor. They even sacrificed women's privacy by giving men an incentive to monitor their ex-wives' behavior.

Once the war began, the state extended its effort to protect ex-husbands' money to protecting state resources as well. The guidelines for replacing alimony payments with welfare for soldiers' dependents put the livelihood of ex-wives in further jeopardy. Because the state limited the distribution of welfare for soldiers' dependents to those people who received the majority of their income from a soldier, it excluded ex-wives who (in accordance with the law) supplemented their alimony payments with earned income.

---

103 It also waived this responsibility in cases in which a woman took care of the households of unmarried brothers or sick relatives. Oberbürgermeister to Fürsorgeamt A, 1 November 1940, Stadtarchiv Bielefeld (StaB), Sozialamt 50, 8.
104 Boberach, *Meldungen aus dem Reich*, 4 July 1940, 1345–6.

The welfare department in Bielefeld announced in 1940 that since Frau K.'s ex-husband "had not been primarily responsible for supporting his ex-wife before he was drafted, she [was] not eligible for support." Their seven children, whom he supported, however, continued to be eligible for child support payments.[105] Thus, although the Nazis broadened alimony awards to include cases in which both spouses were declared guilty, by strictly limiting the cases in which women were eligible for support, they ultimately severely compromised the protection they offered ex-wives.

In regulating remarriage, Nazi policymakers found themselves caught in a by-now-familiar contradiction: they wanted to uphold traditional moral values and at the same time encourage the establishment of prolific marriages. The Marriage Law of 1938 preserved the idea that "a marriage cannot be entered into between a spouse divorced on the basis of adultery and the person with whom he committed the adultery, if this adultery was identified as a cause for the divorce."[106] But because of the state's pronatalist stance – its awareness that many adulterous relationships promised to produce healthy children – Nazi lawmakers tried to limit the instances in which judges issued "marriage hindrances." Under the new policy, marriage hindrances were created only when adultery was the primary complaint cited in the divorce hearing, not if it came to light through a countercomplaint. This meant that an adulterous spouse received a marriage hindrance only if the innocent spouse filed for divorce primarily on the basis of adultery.[107] Ironically, by encouraging adulterous spouses to be the first to file for divorce, the law may have punished wronged spouses who wished to overlook adultery and save their marriages.

Individual Germans defended their decisions to remarry using arguments that closely resembled those made during the 1920s. Some couples applied because their mutual children needed a "real" family; others applied because society pressured them to legalize their relationships. As one woman explained in a letter to the Führer: "It cannot go on like this any longer. The apartment is supposed to be taken from us because we live together. They say 'yes, they just live together like that.'" The judge had denied the woman's fiancé permission to remarry because it would have been his third marriage

---

105 Children also continued to be awarded to the innocent parent. The NSV announced at the end of one trial that even though the mother had cared for her child during the trial, since she "was assigned the entire guilt, the child must be separated from her." NSDAP Volkswohlfahrt to Ortsamtsleiter der NSV, 15 June 1936, Stadtarchiv Paderborn (StaP), G 2, 5665.

106 GEG §9.

107 If adultery was committed with more than one partner, the marriage hindrance applied only to the person named in the divorce settlement, and the question of alimony was made much less stringent.

and he doubted the man's ability to make it succeed.[108] As this example suggests, judges under the Third Reich continued to base their decisions about divorce on a couple's financial viability, their marriage's chances of success, and its potential benefit to the state. In 1935, for example, the Arnsberg Landgericht judge opined that a marriage should be permitted although the man had been arrested for participating in the Communist Party, because "the legitimization of the child and the legalization of the immoral relationship through the intended marriage . . . [spoke] in favor of issuing an exemption."[109] The state valued marriage if a child stood to benefit, but unsustainable marriages were believed to devalue the institution as a whole and were to be forbidden.

Germans seeking permission to remarry shaped their justifications of remarriage in ways that show they understood that the state was interested in healthy marriages and healthy children. When Maria M. wrote in 1936 to request permission to remarry, she emphasized that her marriage would not only provide her eleven-year-old child with a caring father but "would immediately lift a burden from the state," since she relied on welfare. In another case, Gertrud M. wrote the court, "Now that I am old and sickly, I would like to found a household in order to avoid becoming a burden on the public welfare." The welfare department cut her off because its employees believed her fiancé, Heinz L., could support her. The Landgericht judge rejected the application for exemption, stating, "On the basis of both the applicant's and her fiancé's personalities, their moral attitudes, and their inferior characters, I do not believe that the intended marriage will last long term." He felt that the marriage "[did] not lie in the state's interest." Undeterred, Gertrud reapplied, arguing that she was now pregnant and needed to marry for the child's sake. Ultimately, she failed to produce proof of pregnancy, raising the suspicion that it had been invented to sway the court. Her fiancé's later threat "to present the entire state of affairs to the Führer" if the local court did not permit the marriage failed to move the court.[110] Though the couple had based their argument on economics and a child's well-being and finally had threatened to turn to Hitler, due to the judges' negative assessment of the couple's genetic health and the long-term viability of the marriage, they refused to be swayed without proof that a child's well-being was really at stake.

---

108 Frau S. to Führer, 14 February 1936, in application for remarriage, SaM, Oberlandgericht Hamm, 360.
109 StaD, Landgericht Arnsberg, 712.
110 Herr L. to Landgerichtspräsidenten, 22 May 1936, SaM, Oberlandgericht Hamm, 360.

Whereas during the Weimar era courts had focused on balancing the support of prior families with the benefit of founding new families, after 1933 they emphasized the need to found new "racially pure" families. In its guidelines for dependents, the Deutscher Gemeindetag in Westphalia/Lippe noted that "If the spouse ordered to pay [child support and/or alimony] is responsible for supporting a young child or a new spouse, the extent to which they are required to support their prior family diminishes to the level deemed fair in light of the needs" of the new family.[111] An SD report from October 1942 recommended canceling all marriage hindrances, since generally it was only ex-wives who had a stake in them. Although judges granted most people's request to remarry, many judges, like those who heard Gertrud and Heinz's case, continued to place value on the creation of racially pure, prolific, moral, and economically responsible families.[112]

CONCLUSION

During both the Weimar and National Socialist eras, lawmakers struggled to create divorce law that reflected national needs. For Weimar lawmakers, the disagreement over whether divorce would bring about greater human happiness or usher in the end of German civilization proved insoluble and prevented legal change. The verdicts issued by Weimar judges – who believed that Germany's future depended upon their saving marriages and not facilitating frivolous efforts to escape it – clearly supported traditional values. Still, Weimar judges did selectively apply modern, gender-based standards as they increasingly declared women guilty in divorce and demanded that they seek employment to support themselves afterward.

After 1933, Nazi lawmakers approached divorce reform with racial and population goals central in their minds. After the Marriage Law for Greater Germany was introduced, "racially healthy" Germans generally faced little opposition in their petitions to divorce Jews or individuals who had been sterilized, who suffered from a genetic disease, or who could not or would not reproduce. The Nazi law subordinated individual happiness to the public good, and divorce was acceptable only after evaluation of the public benefit of the marriage. Divorces were rarely granted to "unhealthy" Germans (unless the marriage blocked a "healthy" German from reproducing) or to Germans whose remarriages did not promise to produce racially and

---

111 Richtlinien über die Heranziehung unterhaltspflichtiger Personen Herausgegeben vom Deutschen Gemeindetag, Provinzialdienststelle Westfalen/Lippe, received by Oberpräsident der Provinz Westfalen, 4 July 1939, LSVA, C60, 354.
112 Boberach, *Meldungen aus dem Reich*, 22 October 1942, 4362–3.

genetically healthy children. Moreover, unlike Weimar law, which declared gender equality, Nazi divorce law explicitly favored men over women. Not only were men given greater freedom to leave their wives, but the law restricted women's access to alimony payments, especially if a newly founded family depended on the man's income.

The fact that conservative conceptions of marriage and family continued to hold a prominent place in Nazi divorce legislation has led some historians to conclude that aside from the added racial elements, the new divorce law largely preserved the traditional family.[113] This understates the degree to which divorce law changed. Not only did the Nazis distort what constituted a healthy marriage, but they also broadened the grounds for divorce to encourage prolific marriages. Their readiness to subvert the traditional family in the name of state interests extended far beyond anything that preceded it.

As Nazi policymakers revised divorce law, judges tried to combine the traditional values they attached to marriage with new Nazi racial ideology. In the end, most of their decisions reflected the priority placed on founding racially pure families. But judges continued to hear testimony and to investigate marital circumstances in such cases rather than make divorce pro forma. They still considered men breadwinners and women homemakers, they hesitated to divorce couples with young children, and they tried to ensure the economic viability of both spouses after divorce.

Individual Germans, for their part, continued to expect the law to provide both traditional protections and modern freedoms. Although there is little evidence that they challenged the Nazis' racially based divorce policy, many Germans used Nazi ideology to their own advantage by, for example, citing their pressing desire to reproduce to justify divorcing "unhealthy" spouses.

---

113 Ramm, *Die Nationalsozialistische Familie*. In contrast, Dirk Blasius has argued that Nazi divorce law "lay entirely in line with National Socialist racial and population policy." See *Ehescheidung in Deutschland*, 210.

3

From Mother's Day to Forced Sterilization

Promoting Motherhood as the Solution to the Population Crisis

Maternity ... no longer oppresses and burdens the individual woman but becomes the concern of the public at large.

– Adele Schreiber, SPD delegate, 1924

The future of the *Volk* is only secure when it is prepared to give the highest sacrifice for mother and child.

– Government propaganda campaign, 1935

During both the Weimar and Nazi eras, politicians across the political spectrum, clergy, feminists, and doctors were united in the belief that the promotion of motherhood was necessary to boost the birthrate and improve national health. Perceiving women's resistance to motherhood as central to the nation's problems, many Germans advocated rallying women to resume their duties as mothers, while others argued that Germany's health depended on controlling who became a mother. Profound differences in how politicians on the Right and Left envisioned motherhood – and hence how to rehabilitate it – opened debates on Malthusianism and neo-Malthusianism, racial hygiene, pronatalism, and even sterilization.[1]

Celebrating and honoring mothers presented itself to Weimar politicians as a way to unite the divided nation and strengthen the population. With the strong support of the churches, state officials increasingly recognized mothers' crucial contribution to society. Yet as they weighed welfare and pronatalism against the implications of sexual equality as enshrined in the Constitution, they found that no consensus existed about how to celebrate mothers. They disagreed about whether mothers should be publicly or privately honored and whether all or just some mothers deserved recognition.

---

1 The epigraphs are drawn from Usborne, *Politics of the Body*, 39, and a Nazi propaganda campaign, 1935, BaK, NS 1033, 37.

Budgetary limitations overlapped and conflicted with eugenic concerns as officials debated which mothers should be honored and how. Throughout the 1920s, Weimar politicians sought to find a balance between these seemingly irreconcilable factors. Ultimately, they made only token gestures to promote motherhood and left its regulation untouched.

The Nazis, on the other hand, went beyond honoring mothers to alter dramatically the relationship between motherhood and the state. As Gisela Bock has demonstrated, Nazi pronatalism had as its flip side a vicious antinatalism that prevented those people the Nazis deemed unfit from reproducing. The Nazis defined the "good" mother not solely by the number of children she bore – though in an era of declining birthrates prolific mothers were admired – but also by other social, political, and ultimately racial qualities. And for healthy mothers they dramatically increased the number and publicity of state honors. The Nazis believed, however, that improving the *Volk*'s health necessitated both increasing the number of healthy children born and decreasing the number of unhealthy children born. Both women and men who did not meet the racial standards of National Socialism were deemed unworthy of bearing children. The Nazis used their belief that the interests of the *Volk* took precedence over those of the individual to justify state intrusion into motherhood and fatherhood, and they wielded state power to encourage "desirable" births and prevent "undesirable" ones.

This chapter begins with an examination of Weimar policymakers' efforts to influence women and honor mothers. It then turns to state-sponsored pronatalist programs the Nazis created. Yet equally central to the Nazi project was the prevention of unhealthy births through forced sterilization. After a survey of Nazi pronatalist policy, the remainder of this chapter investigates antinatalist policy against women and men.

THE WEIMAR REPUBLIC: HONORING MOTHERS

After the First World War had ended, the birthrate in Germany, which had been 28.6 per 1,000 people in 1911, fell to a low of 14.3 in 1918. Together with the high number of war casualties, this seemed to portend an especially grim demographic future. Although other countries also experienced a decline in their birthrates, the trend was most pronounced in Germany, where by 1933 the birthrate was the lowest in Europe. Berlin had the lowest birthrate of any city in Europe.[2] Though a brief postwar baby boom brought

2 Grossmann, *Reforming Sex*, 4.

the birthrate up to a high of 25.8 in 1920, this did little to calm fears, since it declined thereafter to 23.2 in 1922, 20.9 in 1925, and 17.5 in 1930.[3]

Although the declining birthrate represented the continuation of a trend that had begun at the turn of the century, lawmakers across the political spectrum regarded it as a new problem. At the center of their debates about what to do stood the question of the appropriate role for women. Politicians on both the Right and Left attributed the low birthrate to women's greater participation in the labor market, lamenting the fact that between 1925 and 1935, 29 percent of married women had non-houschold employment.[4] Politicians objected most vehemently to women's industrial work. The connection between women's work and the low birthrate was "proven," as Cornelia Usborne has pointed out, by means of many narrow and unbalanced studies that ignored critical factors that affect the birthrate, including levels of poverty and environment. Much of the perceived increase in the number of female workers can in fact be attributed to more accurate counting – for the first time, both family helpers and domestic workers were taken into account – but contemporaries believed that the numbers reflected a drastic and potentially detrimental shift in women's attitudes and behavior.[5]

The consensus among politicians on the Right and Left, churchwomen, and feminists that women should mother and that mothers should be honored by the state seemed to offer common ground upon which to build policy. Yet profound differences existed in the ways these various groups envisioned motherhood. Politicians on the Right "upgraded motherhood from a responsibility to a calling" and blamed women's selfish motives for their increasing hesitance to bear children.[6] Basing their recommendations on medical reports that held women's gainful employment responsible for the low birthrate, they proposed banning women's factory labor and more rigorously enforcing laws against abortion. The Social Democrats agreed "unequivocally that maternity was women's social task" but saw an expanded social welfare system as the solution to falling birthrates.[7] Adele Schreiber and Louise Schroeder, both SPD legislators, cited women's triple burden of wage labor, childcare, and housework as the obvious reason they were choosing to have smaller families.[8] Delegates from both the Independent Socialist Party of Germany (Unabhängige Sozialdemokratische Partei, USPD) and the SPD asserted that if it did not provide jobs, housing, and food to

3 *Statistisches Jahrbuch für Preußen* 30 (1934).   4 Hausen, "Mothers, Sons," 394.
5 Usborne, *Politics of the Body*, 53–5.
6 Bridenthal and Koonz, "Beyond Kinder, Küche, Kirche," 43.
7 Usborne, *Politics of the Body*, 58.
8 Grossmann, *Reforming Sex*, 35–6.

struggling families, the state had no right to demand that women have more babies. The Communists likewise argued that "'a society not able to provide women with the material means for motherhood' also had 'no right to demand that women take on cares and burdens derived from motherhood.'"[9] They, too, advocated comprehensive social welfare programs.

Beyond the political arena, women from all walks of life affirmed the values of motherhood. Clara Bohm-Schuch, the editor of *Die Gleichheit* (Equality), the Social Democratic Party's women's newspaper, claimed that "women had a duty as 'protectors and rearers of the species' and that education should instill the 'will to maternity' in the younger generation."[10] The members of the bourgeois Federation of German Women's Organizations also touted motherhood for women, claiming that women should apply their maternal qualities to both the private and public realms, including the fields of education, health care, and especially social work. Churchwomen joined the chorus praising motherhood. They believed that men and women were fundamentally different and that "the gift of maternity and motherliness would... not only restore social health" but also "gain... [women] a special status in the new republic."[11] Protestant women made an explicit connection between women's motherliness and Germany's national interests. Both the Catholic and Protestant churches set up extensive programs to educate mothers-to-be, take in unwed mothers, and provide needy mothers with advice, health care, and material supplies. Even the more radical feminists in the Organization for the Protection of Motherhood (Bund für Mutterschutz) saw motherhood as women's "highest achievement." Unlike most men, however, they believed strictly in voluntary motherhood and "the principle of reproductive self-determination."[12]

The near unanimous support for motherhood found expression in the adoption of Mother's Day, a holiday developed in America and Norway and then exported to Germany in 1923.[13] Dr. Rudolf Knauer, the head of the Association of German Florists (Verband Deutscher Blumengeschäftsinhaber) and the first vocal advocate of Mother's Day in Germany, cited "the inner conflict of our *Volk* and the loosening of the family" as his inspiration for introducing Mother's Day in "our fatherland."[14] He hoped that Mother's Day would unite the politically divided

---

9 Usborne, *Politics of the Body*, 39.   10 Ibid., 57.

11 This position put Catholic women in conflict with Pope Leo XIII's assertion that motherhood was the only acceptable occupation for married women. Ibid., 64–6.

12 Ibid., 66.

13 Karin Hausen claims that Mother's Day began in Sweden, not Norway. "Mother's Day," 132–5.

14 Rudolf Knauer, BaK, R36, 1028.

An affirmation of the family unit as portrayed in Weimar film. Still from unknown film ca. 1930. Courtesy of Getty Images.

and economically troubled Germany. As one observer noted, "Mother's Day should bring about a spiritual unification of the *Volk* on neutral ground."[15] When in 1925 Knauer's Reich Committee for Mother's Day joined the independent Task Force for the Recovery of the *Volk* (Arbeitsgemeinschaft für Volksgesundung) led by Hans Harmsen, the movement became separated from commercial interests and firmly connected to population concerns.[16] The task force strongly believed that the moral crisis besetting the German *Volk* could only be cured by drawing women back to their responsibility as mothers. Nationalism also became intertwined with Mother's Day, since motherhood was celebrated as a means of rejuvenating the nation. What all the supporters of Mother's Day shared was a hope that the holiday would inspire more young women to assume the responsibility of bearing children.

15 Archiv für Wohlfahrtspflege, 1924, BaK, R36, 1028.
16 Rudolf Knauer, BaK, R36, 1028. The task force was created in 1924 and expanded in 1926 to incorporate the German Society for Population Policy (Deutsche Gesellschaft für Bevölkerungspolitik). Hausen, "Mother's Day," 132–5.

Not everyone saw Mother's Day as inherently good, however. Because so many conservative forces, including Catholic and Protestant churches, backed Mother's Day, people of a more progressive persuasion saw it as a reaction against women's equality and especially against the New Woman, whose independent lifestyle allegedly threatened families. The Social Democrats, Communists, and progressives objected that the Mother's Day rhetoric omitted any recognition of the economic hardships that made many women's lives more difficult. Rather than providing mothers with concrete financial or material aid, as they advocated, Mother's Day obscured mothers' needs with an honorary celebration.[17] The anti-emancipatory ideals connected to Mother's Day may account for the unwillingness of *Die Frau*, the newspaper of the Federation of German Women's Organizations, even to recognize the holiday.[18] As Karen Hausen has stressed, the promoters of Mother's Day did not view mothers as individuals but rather focused on the "idea of the mother and hence the mother as an embodiment of idealized qualities and ways of behaving."[19] Paul Weindling has pointed to the even more negative function of Mother's Day as "the antidote to the problems of abortion, contraception and decadence."[20] Although this may be an overstatement, it is certainly true that many Germans hoped that Mother's Day would unite the nation across class, regional, generational, and gender lines – and do so without draining the budget or raising contentious social policy issues.

The Mother's Day celebration, rightly interpreted by historians as conservative and ideologically based, was not always as empty of substance as has been suggested. Many local city authorities viewed it not only as a day to honor all mothers symbolically but also as an opportunity to support mothers with large families materially. In Westphalia, the Reich League of Child-Rich Families (Reichsbund der kinderreichen Familien) led the crusade to win national recognition for Mother's Day and to shift it from a day of symbolic honor to one that offered mothers financial and material benefit. Beginning in 1925, officials in many Westphalian towns engaged in an animated dialogue about whether to distribute gifts on Mother's Day to mothers who had several children. In Hagen, city officials invited "child-rich" mothers to attend a coffee social. In Bochum, they held a concert to honor mothers, after which they awarded mothers of seven or more children with five Reich marks per child if the family had only one breadwinner. Roxel

17 Hausen, "Mothers, Sons," 386.   18 Hausen, "Mother's Day," 146–7.
19 Hausen, "Mothers, Sons," 384.
20 Weindling, *Health, Race and German Politics*, 423.

city officials also gave prolific mothers gifts, and they connected eligibility to both the number of children a woman had and her material need.[21] Bochum's policy implied a nonworking mother, and Roxel's emphasis on need made a single breadwinner seem more likely, but neither city explicitly mandated that women not work. In 1926, Münster awarded child-rich mothers a cup and saucer with the inscription "To the German Mother – the City of Münster, German Mother's Day, 1926." Other cities also gave gifts, though sometimes bureaucratic complications, financial constraints, or both hampered the process. Osterfeld city officials had planned to give mothers with ten children a gift on Mother's Day, but when this became too complicated, they opted instead to give any mother who had ten children one hundred Reich marks at the birth of the tenth child. In Gladbeck, officials granted mothers with ten living children, 140 in all, savings accounts of one hundred marks. When Recklinghausen city officials decided that their city could not afford to distribute money, the welfare department began to use social workers to distribute packets of linens worth ten to fifteen marks.[22] With such a proliferation of celebrations, the meaning and purpose of Mother's Day took on different nuances. What was initially designed as a private holiday for the honoring of mothers also became the occasion for public ceremonies in which women with large families received extra recognition. As cities began to connect financial awards to neediness, Mother's Day awards became less honorable in the eyes of some, even as the financial aid undoubtedly provided some relief for needy "child-rich" mothers.

In 1927, Prussian state officials expanded their awards for prolific mothers with a child welfare program that provided large families – those with more than twelve children – a bonus for education and an honorary gift for the mothers: either an honorary cup or hundred marks.[23] These honors, awarded in conjunction with child subsidies, had to be applied for through the mayor's office and distributed by the district welfare office. The awards were based solely on the number of children borne by one woman

---

21 Regierungspräsident Münster to Oberbürgermeister Roxel, 28 March 1928, Stadtarchiv Münster (StaM), Amt Roxel A Fach 33, 5.

22 Letters from Oberbürgermeisters of Recklinghausen, Gladbeck, Bochum, and Hagen, StaM, Armenkommission, 864.

23 Of the thirty-eight applications from 1931–1932 in the district of Lippe, roughly half received both child subsidies and an honorary mother gift. The remaining women were disqualified largely because some of their children were from their husbands' previous marriages. On 19 August 1929, the Reich minister of the interior limited the grants to families whose youngest child was born on or after 1 October 1927. In 1931, mothers with twelve children also received a framed certificate (*Ehrenurkunde*). Applications for child subsidies, StaD, M1 IM, 888.

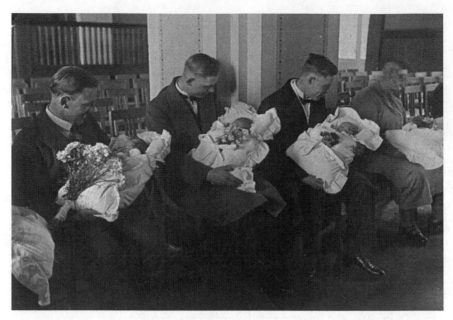

Though no official Father's Day was introduced during the Weimar era, fathers were featured as part of the family, as shown here awaiting the baptism of their children. Courtesy of Getty Images.

within her present marriage. Nonbiological children, including adoptive or foster children, were not included in the total count. The application detailed family size, economic status (including everything from the number of chickens owned to the size of a family's debt), and past welfare history. The family's reputation was also evaluated. The guidelines explicitly stated that "only families in which both parents and grown children have impeccable reputations and financial need is proven will be awarded this subsidy."[24]

The burden of assessing families for child subsidies and honorary gifts fell to social workers, who as state employees in youth and welfare departments found themselves at the crossroads of social welfare and state intervention. Social workers' ability to investigate and evaluate family reputations was marred by the limitations of their profession. Although they enjoyed the respect that came with the recent professionalization of their field, during the 1920s they increasingly felt that their male colleagues in administration treated them like "errand girls" (*Laufmädchen*) whose duty was to

24 Ibid., 889.

deliver the bureaucrats' messages.[25] Moreover, hard economic times meant there were fewer jobs available for social workers, and those who remained employed did more work for less pay. These conditions hampered social workers' ability to act as "mothers of the *Volk*."[26] As a result, most social workers assessed reputation only in general terms, and the distribution of honors remained somewhat flexible. None of the mothers or families in the files I examined were denied honors or aid on the basis of reputation, suggesting that applications may only have been completed for families that social workers considered to have good reputations. Sometimes, officials disagreed among themselves about who deserved honor. In 1931, Frau Brand, the wife of a worker in Büren, applied even though her youngest child had been born in 1926, one year before the program was instituted. Local authorities approved her application, noting that in addition to her thirteen children, she had had three miscarriages. They called hers "an extraordinary case which should still receive consideration, despite its belatedness." Notwithstanding this encouragement, however, the president of Minden refused to bend the rules in the absence of economic need.[27] His narrow interpretation of the guidelines for eligibility meant that only prolific mothers whose families faced economic hardship received the honor.

At the national level, Weimar politicians failed to reach consensus on whether to emphasize pronatalism or social welfare in their programs to honor mothers. Honorary programs never received full state support, and Mother's Day continued to straddle the line between being a public holiday and being a private one. Even cities that did celebrate publicly continued to debate whether to expand their celebrations to support prolific mothers financially. By requiring proof of economic need, child subsidies excluded many prolific mothers – and revealed that the programs' intent lay at least partly in social welfare and not pure pronatalism. But while some Weimar authorities were willing to assess economic need, they stopped short of applying eugenic requirements to their assessments of mothers. Though the guidelines for child subsidies required that women and families have impeccable reputations, no evidence exists to suggest that social workers used their access to families to apply eugenic criteria in their evaluations of families or that state authorities pressed them to do so.

25 Zeller, *Volksmütter*, 152.
26 Physical and mental breakdowns became so prevalent among social workers that in 1925 the Prussian Volksminister distributed a detailed questionnaire to social workers. The responses he received attributed their distress to their need for better pay, smaller districts, more help, better transportation in rural areas, and better insurance. Ibid., 157.
27 Applications for child subsidies, StaD, M1 IM, 889.

NATIONAL SOCIALISM: HONORING MOTHERS, 1933–1945

When the National Socialists took power, they tried to erase any ambiguity in women's roles by increasing the number of public ceremonies and lauding mothers for the sacrifices they made for the nation. Almost from their first day in office, the Nazis inundated Germans with propaganda exalting motherhood. Government-sponsored advertisements and posters, carefully designed for shop windows and for blitz campaigns, loudly and publicly proclaimed, "The care of mothers and children is the holiest duty of the entire German *Volk*," "The future of a *Volk* is only secure when it is prepared to give the highest sacrifice for mother and child," and "Only a healthy and strong mother can give her *Volk* healthy sons and daughters."[28] When asked whether she was aware of the state's pronatalist attitudes, one woman I interviewed (b. 1916) claimed that there was an atmosphere in which motherhood "was so self-evident, it hung in the air."[29] Another woman agreed, telling me: "Yes, then, well, somehow we were all so 'in' [the spirit of motherhood] that we all wanted to marry and also gladly have children. I don't even know whether we were aware of it [the propaganda]. It was just the general propaganda which influenced us."[30] In celebrating motherhood, the Nazis echoed similar public celebrations in Europe, including England and France. But the Nazis differed in their simultaneous development of an intense and invasive antinatalist campaign aimed at prohibiting the "unworthy" from reproducing that existed side-by-side with pronatalism.[31] All mothers who were candidates for honor had to be evaluated by doctors and social workers to assess their genetic and racial value to the *Volk* in terms of their physical, social, and mental well-being. The Nazis also collected information from teachers, mayors, employers, and party leaders to create a more complete picture of families. The consolidation of information drawn from different perspectives was meant to enhance authorities' overall ability to assess a woman, but conflicts often arose among the various assessors over control and turf as well as over questions of definition, all of which directly affected Nazi authorities' ability to honor mothers.

One of the Nazis' first steps after seizing power was to declare Mother's Day a national holiday. Dr. Rudolf Knauer acknowledged that it was with joy that the Reich Committee for Mother's Day celebrated the day the National Socialists came to power, since they realized that "the pure idea

---

28 This particular campaign took place in 1935. BaK, NS37, 1033.
29 Frau Schnabel, interview.
30 Frau Frandsen, interview.
31 Bock, "Racism and Sexism," 271. See also her book, *Zwangssterilisation im Nationalsozialismus*.

Gesunde Jugend — Glückliches Volk!

"Healthy Youth – Happy Volk!" This mother met the Nazi goal of bearing four healthy children. The father's absence reflects the Nazi de-emphasis on the paternal role. (*Du und Dein Volk*, Volksverlag, Publication of Hauptamt für Erzieher der NSDAP Reichsleitung, ca. 1940/41).

of German Mother's Day could be laid in the hands of men, who were [committed] . . . to the high goal of popular rejuvenation . . . [and who made] the mother the leitmotif of their struggle." Henceforth, Mother's Day would not only celebrate mothers but also "awaken motherly responsibility toward the *Volk* in the souls of German women." Children would learn to use

Mother's Day to express their deep respect, thankfulness, and love for their mothers. The state stepped in to honor mothers who had lost sons in war and to free child-rich and poor mothers from "front line work in factories."[32] Even members of the SS and SA were given the day off to celebrate motherhood.[33] Mothers were invited to come together to listen to radio broadcasts that informed them of their duty to populate the nation and ensure Germany's future. In 1934, Minister of the Interior Wilhelm Frick, announced, "We stand now at a turning point! The salvation of Germany depends not only on love for the fatherland, but equally on women's and girls' devotion to the idea of motherhood." He even claimed that "the state would step in where fathers had stepped out" for any reason by supporting all wage-earning wives and mothers if they preferred not to work.[34]

Although the elevation of motherhood at the rhetorical level was quickly accomplished, unifying local celebrations under Nazi leadership proved more difficult. Both the Catholic and Protestant churches resented the Nazi effort to bring Mother's Day under the control of the National Socialist People's Welfare Organization (NSV) and the National Socialist Women's Organization (NSF). In many cases, conflict broke out at the local level. The Bielefeld branch of the Protestant Women's Aid (EFH), for example, balked at the Nazi intrusion into its celebrations. On 30 April 1934, the district head of the NSV, Herr Hausmann, called a meeting of all women's organizations in Bielefeld to discuss his plans for one central Mother's Day celebration. He wanted to honor not only child-rich mothers, war widows, and war mothers but also all the isolated, lonely mothers in Bielefeld. A lack of space foiled his plan to hold one large celebration, and instead Hausmann agreed to decentralize the celebration. Each organization would coordinate one celebration, and the NSF would advertise all the celebrations and distribute invitations. After this preliminary meeting, however, Hausmann never contacted any of the individual organizations or planned another group meeting. Then, after individual programs had been completely arranged, a leader of the NSF appeared and abruptly announced that she had been appointed to run the celebration. When she refused to carry out any of the planned programs, the women of the Protestant Women's Aid protested but ultimately backed down to avoid a fight. Thus, on Mother's Day Sunday, the NSF ran the program, while the EFH women "occupied a subordinate position and only participated where help was necessary." In the aftermath of the celebration, it became evident that both the Patriotic Women's Association

---

32 Rudolf Knauer, "Die Entwicklung des deutschen Muttertages," n.d., BaK, R36, 1028.
33 Klinksiek, *Die Frau im NS-Staat*, 84.
34 Dr. Frick, *Wir bauen das Dritte Reich* (Oldenburg, 1934), quoted in Koonz, "Ethical Dilemmas," 25.

For its Mother's Day issue, the *NS Frauenwarte* chose this idealized image of a mother and her children. 1939. *NS Frauenwarte* Heft 23, 7 (1939).

(Vaterländischer Frauenverein, VFV) and the Catholic Women's Organization had had similar experiences, causing widespread resentment.[35]

35 Stadtverband der Evangelische Frauenhilfe, Bielefeld, to Evangelische Frauenhilfe, Soest, 15 May 1934, Archiv Evangelische Frauenhilfe (EVHA), 118–0. When the Katholischer Mütterverein distributed gifts to newborns in October 1939, the Gestapo forbade the "secular activity."

Only by controlling the celebrations themselves could the Nazi leadership ensure that its ideological goals were met. Reiterating and building upon the views of conservatives from the Weimar era, NSV authorities called motherhood a "duty" for healthy women, greatly strengthening the connection between women's patriotism and childbearing. Harking back to Dr. Knauer's 1923 suggestion that Mother's Day "should become a . . . celebration of the fatherland," Nazi policymakers used Mother's Day to praise mothers publicly for their patriotic spirit and for their "readiness to sacrifice" both for their children and for the nation. For women, childbearing was presented as the equivalent of military training for men – both were ways of serving the country.

Although Nazi rhetoric continued to designate Mother's Day a private family holiday, its patriotic elements took on elevated importance, particularly after the war began, when the celebration of Mother's Day assumed a strongly militaristic tone.[36] Nazi authorities conscientiously tried to include all Aryan mothers in the celebration, claiming that "no mothers, especially not soldiers' mothers, should feel alone on this day!"[37] They brought together mothers who lived alone for small group celebrations in the company of the youth groups. Even after the war had begun and the Central Department for Publication and Propaganda had outlawed large-scale public celebrations, Mother's Day remained an important holiday heavily imbued with National Socialist ideology.

From their first Mother's Day celebration, the Nazis also connected motherhood to racial politics. Eugenic ideals of racial purity dictated which mothers were worthy of honor. The Nazis redefined women's "worthiness" and reshaped the concept of the ideal mother by creating a standard against which all women were judged. Some of the qualities the Nazis expected of mothers did not differ dramatically from traditional notions: "A German mother's 'worth' consisted . . . in her being peaceable, frugal, orderly, and clean. The 'worthy' mother was a good housewife. She had a tidy, clean, orderly and straightened home; she wore clean, feminine clothes, had a husband to whom she was faithful, and bore only legitimate children. If she became pregnant, she bore the child under all circumstances. She did not smoke, and drank alcohol only sparingly."[38]

But the dimensions of a mother's worthiness under National Socialism extended beyond the sum total of the woman's behavior, style,

36 Weyrather, *Muttertag und Mutterkreuz*, 24.
37 Reichsfrauenführung, Rund Schreiben F 53/41, 1941, BaK, NS44, 36.
38 Weyrather, *Muttertag und Mutterkreuz*, 123–4.

The integral connection between a woman's duty to bear children and a man's duty to provide for and defend the nation was often overt. *NS Frauenwarte*, Heft 20, 6 (1937/38).

and stature to include those of her family as well. A worthy woman's husband might smoke, but he drank only small amounts of alcohol and did not have a criminal record. Together with her husband, she worked industriously and paid the rent and debts punctually. If any member of the family was identified as "asocial" or a "work dodger," it reflected badly on the whole family, but especially on the mother. Alcohol or drug abuse by any family member similarly revealed a fault in the family and the mother. While families that found themselves in economic trouble might accept welfare or aid from the NSV, too much reliance on the state for money was viewed as evidence of unworthiness. NSV officials believed that children who had trouble in school reflected their mother's shortcomings. Parents who had not demonstrated political reliability by showing their electoral support for the NSDAP early or by joining a Nazi organization could be dubbed unworthy. Finally, a worthy family was racially pure according to Nazi racial guidelines. Jewish and Gypsy mothers, as well as mothers who were themselves or whose family members had been identified as hereditarily ill, were considered to be unworthy. Women who were not "German-blooded" also were not honored. Only if a woman and the members of her family passed all these tests did Nazi authorities hold her to be worthy of public honor.

In addition to Mother's Day, the Nazis adapted other Weimar programs to the new governing ideology. The 1931 decree providing certificates and honorary cups or monetary awards to mothers of twelve or more children continued after 1933, albeit in an altered form: a decorated swastika, the symbol of the Third Reich, appeared prominently on each certificate, and a new emphasis was placed on determining the racial worth of applicants. Whereas before 1933, mayors, pastors, and the welfare office had filed applications for mothers in their communities, in the Nazi era doctors also participated in the nomination process. The character of the evaluation that was carried out also changed. Weimar authorities typically described a family's reputation with the single word "good," but after 1933 doctors and other evaluators described reputation in much greater detail.

The Nazi attempt to apply racial guidelines to the already existing Weimar programs met resistance from authorities at all levels. Many authorities had used both the gifts associated with Mother's Day and the monetary awards for prolific mothers to help needy families. They had even made exceptions for couples whose behavior did not match national guidelines – a privilege they were loath to forfeit. When the Dietrich family applied in 1939, the doctor argued that although Herr Dietrich tended to drink too much, the family was "worthy" because he noted "no other genetic illnesses or inferiorities."[39] Similarly, many mayors took personal circumstances into account in their assessments of individuals, even if it meant bending the rules. In 1939, the mayor of Lichtenau supported the application for the Stemmer family although the parents often fought, two of the children from the husband's first marriage showed signs of delinquency, and the youngest son had undesirable "hereditary" (*erbbiologisch*) characteristics (which made him ineligible to have Hitler as his godfather).[40] The mayor chose to overlook these flaws because the father worked as a butcher and the mother "was trying to get ahead."[41] The fact that the aid was granted reveals that the mayor was not alone in his belief that one assessment of hereditary inferiority did not necessarily preclude future aid.

The Nazi leadership was dismayed at local authorities' willingness to interpret racial guidelines loosely. In attempting to correct this, the Reich minister of the interior wrote the *Regierungspräsident* (district president) of Minden in 1940 to find out how he and his subordinates prevented the honoring of child-rich families deemed to be asocial. The *Regierungspräsident* assured him that the doctors in the health departments and the Criminal Police worked together with the welfare department to ensure the high quality of recipients.[42] Nevertheless, many local leaders who refused to forfeit federal aid despite the new racial guidelines used whatever flexibility they could in their selection of aid recipients.

The NSV leadership had somewhat more control over the shape of programs they introduced. Pressure from the national level was exerted to make sure that towns supported prolific mothers and families. This led to competition among towns for the reputation of being most "child friendly."[43] Some towns sponsored outings in decorated carriages for child-rich, worthy mothers, while others held coffee hours to honor them. Many mothers with large families seem to have appreciated these events. As Sopade (Social Democratic Party in Exile) reporters noted after one state-sponsored occasion where elderly child-rich mothers were honored with coffee, cake, and a postcard with a picture of the Führer, "Many of these women were truly taken in by this propaganda trick, and they feel they are being specially treated by the Führer."[44] More significantly, some towns tried to offset the financial burden children imposed on families by establishing savings

39 Kreiskommunalarzt 1, June 1939, StaD, M1 IM, 888.
40 This program was designed to honor families with seven children or five sons.
41 StaD, M1 IM, 888.
42 Even after this assurance was given, sterilization did not eliminate a family's chance of receiving aid. StaD, M1 IM, 888.
43 *Sopade Berichte* 5, no. 6 (1938): 649.
44 Boberach, *Meldungen aus dem Reich*, 29 April 1943, 5207.

accounts for babies newly born into families that already had four or more children. Other towns waived rent or lowered the cost of school for children from large families. Some companies paid fathers more than bachelors and nationally, bachelors were assessed an extra "bachelor's tax." Before awards of any kind were granted, women and their families were evaluated, since these programs were limited to racially pure, desirable mothers. Social workers made house visits to determine whether a potential award recipient's house was tidy, the family was "orderly," and the children were cared for. One former social worker (b. 1907) told me that she assessed whether the family "had the right attitude toward life [*Lebenseinstellung*], and if they did not – if the man always went to the pub and drank or the woman was dirty or the children were not cared for – then they could not expect that they would receive state subsidies."[45]

The Nazis were not alone in creating programs to help large families raise children. A monthly child allowance, introduced by the Nazis in 1936, was similar to child allowance programs in most other European countries. Nazi programs differed from other countries (except Italy and Spain), however, in privileging fathers over mothers. Child allowances and marriage loans were paid to fathers, not mothers. This, together with the effort to ensure that fathers were not disadvantaged vis-à-vis bachelors, has even prompted Gisela Bock to call National Socialism "a modern cult of fatherhood."[46] Rather than create a cult of fatherhood, however, the Nazis disregarded fatherhood and viewed men as breadwinners instead.

Beginning on Mother's Day 1939, the Mother Cross, "the German *Volk*'s visible sign of thanks to child-rich mothers," became the primary Nazi honorary award for mothers. From its inception, the Nazi Mother Cross fused the ideas and feelings associated with Mother's Day with Nazi racial and population policy. The crosses were distributed according to the number of children a woman had: bronze (level three) for four to five children, silver (level two) for six to seven children, and gold (level one) for eight or more children. Stepchildren, adoptive children, and stillborn children were not included in the reckoning. The guidelines specified that both parents had to be "genetically fit" (*erbtüchtig*) German citizens and that mothers had to be "worthy." The blue and white enameled metal cross bore a black Nazi swastika in the center; it was surrounded by the words "To the German Mother" and hung on a blue and white band. The back of the cross was

45 Frau Gethmann, interview.
46 Bock, "Antinatalism, Maternity and Paternity," 124–5.

supposed to read "The Child Honors the Mother" followed by Hitler's signature, but in reality it was inscribed with 16 December 1938, the date the program was announced.[47] Hitler himself took credit for the Mother Crosses, stating, "I award the German Mother Cross to honor German mothers for their services to the German *Volk*."[48]

The introduction of the Mother Cross met with particularly warm approval from the Reich League of Child-Rich Families, which hoped that "this high honor would spur German women to raise youth ready for action for Germany." League members were optimistic that Mother Cross recipients would set an example for all German women, thus helping to overcome the low birthrate. The Nazis intended for the cross to earn respect for mothers at home and in public, where members of the Hitler Youth (Hitler-Jugend) were ordered to greet them.[49]

Town mayors, heads of local branches of the NSDAP, and district leaders of the Reich League of Child-Rich Families recommended women for the crosses. Other people, including husbands and older children, could also nominate a woman they believed to be particularly worthy. In rare instances, women themselves applied. The list of applicants then progressed through various hands, including social work and welfare agencies, health departments, National Socialist mother and child organizations, the local NSDAP party office, and, on occasion, individual teachers and police officers. Although during this process women usually became aware that they were under consideration, in unusual cases women claimed to have been surprised when they were awarded a cross.[50] In most towns, Mother Crosses were distributed during a celebratory ceremony – initially on Mother's Day, but later at other intermediary ceremonies as well. Recipients and their families were invited to the ceremonies where they received their crosses, and those not attending were visited by Nazi officials or members of the BDM.

The process whereby officials selected mothers for the Mother Cross was multifaceted to ensure that only "racially pure," politically reliable, and socially worthy mothers received them. From beginning to end, however, distribution of the Mother Cross, as well as women's perception of the crosses, remained anything but uniform. On 16 December 1938, Hitler

---

47 At least, this is true of the Mother Crosses that I have seen.
48 *Reichsgesetzblatt*, Jahrgang 1938, Teil 1.
49 Telegram to Führer, 7 December 1938, BaP, NS 10, 13, 39.
50 Frau Frandsen, interview; Frau Ludwig, interview; Frau Wolff, interview. This contradicts Irmgard Weyrather's findings that every application had to bear a woman's signature attesting to her racial purity. The fact that some women refused the crosses makes it unlikely that all women knew ahead of time.

The trend toward smaller families in Germany meant that the Nazis' highest award for women, the Gold Mother Cross, was awarded mostly to elderly women with grown children. The cross was a true honor among women supportive of the Nazi regime. *NS Frauenwarte* Heft 4, 7 (1938).

decreed that the distribution of the crosses would begin on Mother's Day, 1939. When by 7 January 1939 no further explanation had been issued, many mayors began to worry that they would lack the lead time necessary to identify candidates before Mother's Day in May. The high mayor of Nuremberg wrote to ask for clarification of the meaning of such terms as "German-blooded," "genetically healthy," "worthy," and "unworthy" and to point out that in Nuremberg alone there were 165,000 women who deserved the cross. Because it seemed to him "completely unclear whether the remaining four months [would] be adequate to process this plethora [of applications]," he suggested restricting the first distribution to those women who deserved the gold cross (those with eight or more children).[51] The Herford high mayor noted, "Because until now there has been no office, not even the civil registry, which recorded how many living children a woman had borne, ascertaining which mothers come into question for honor ... will be impossible, especially for the older women."[52] On 6 February 1939, policymakers issued a new decree to alleviate the mayors' fears and to explain that on the first Mother's Day only those women over seventy years old would be honored. Communities that did not have eligible mothers over seventy were to honor those between sixty-five and seventy or, failing that, those between sixty and sixty-five.[53] Even this plan proved unworkable for some cities. The city of Lemgo, for example, decided to have a second distribution later in the year, since not all mothers could receive their crosses on Mother's Day. But by 30 September 1941, 4.7 million Mother Crosses had been awarded nationwide: 1.2 million crosses each of gold and silver and 2.3 million bronze crosses.

Even after the distribution date had been set and cities began to evaluate applicants, the process did not proceed smoothly. According to Nazi guidelines, mothers were either worthy or unworthy and their children were either burdens or welcome members of the *Volksgemeinschaft*. For each mother the authorities assessed, they had to determine "whether by bearing her children, a mother ... had sacrificed ... with the interest of preserving the German *Volk* or whether ... [her] children were a burden and danger for the future of the German *Volk*, and hence should not have been born."[54] Nazi policy allowed for no gray area between one mother's sacrifice for the country and another mother's burden on society. Local authorities took their role in assessing mothers very seriously, since they rightly feared that honoring unworthy mothers might cause worthy mothers to refuse to wear their Mother Crosses. A Sicherheitsdienst (SD) report underscoring the crosses' success at raising the value of child-rich mothers stressed that "the valuation of Mother Crosses will inevitably sink if asocial mothers or otherwise undesirable mothers are awarded the cross."[55] And it is clear that such mistakes were made. An NSF report lamented: "Again and again we receive complaints that the grossest mistakes occur in the distribution of Mother Crosses. On the one hand, there are 'unworthy' [mothers] who are awarded

---

51 Oberbürgermeister Nürnberg an den Deutschen Gemeindetag, 7 January 1939, BaK, R36, 1158.
52 Letter Herford Oberbürgermeister an den Deutschen Gemeindetag, 26 January 1939, BaK, R36, 1158.
53 Decree of 6 February 1939, BaK, R36, 1158.
54 Reichsminister des Innern, Bericht vom 14 February 1939, III Pol 7/14.39, BaK, NS18, 255, cited in Weyrather, *Muttertag und Mutterkreuz*, 59.
55 Boberach, *Meldungen aus dem Reich*, 29 April 1943, 5207.

this honor, and on the other hand politically and biologically valuable families and mothers are being ignored."[56] The problem, of course, was that it was by no means as easy to distinguish the "worthy" from the "unworthy" as the Nazis made it out to be.

Furthermore, the National Socialist definition of "worthiness" showed inherent class bias. One of the most important characteristics of a good housewife was her ability to conduct a proper household, and records reveal that officials denied many women Mother Crosses because their homes were found to be "disorderly," "dirty," or "neglected." Women with limited budgets faced considerable difficulty keeping their homes up to the National Socialist standards of cleanliness – as judged by middle-class social workers. Furthermore, women of the middle and upper classes who had maids did not have to demonstrate their housekeeping skills.[57] Indiscretions in private life, which could also disqualify women from consideration, were much more visible among working-class than middle- or upper-class women, since privacy among the lower classes was scarce.[58] In wealthier neighborhoods, where residents enjoyed greater distance between living quarters, co-residents in apartment buildings were less likely to report neighbors who received male visitors. Nazi authorities themselves felt less comfortable pointing out social indiscretions among the wealthy than they did among the poor.[59] And, finally, if a poor family had applied for extra financial support and thus brought itself to the attention and scrutiny of various agencies, it became more likely that a "genetic flaw" would be identified, thereby reducing the woman's chances of receiving a Mother Cross.[60]

Despite the rigorous standards for the award of Mother Crosses, officials only rejected some 5 percent of applicants, a number which suggests that "unworthy" women either did not apply or were identified and disqualified before the application process formally began.[61] Denials were issued on a multitude of grounds. Some files contain only a one- or two-word condemnation of the family: "inferior," "genetically unhealthy," "asocial," "feeble-minded." Other files offer brief explanations of the family's shortcomings,

---

56 NSF monthly report, January–March 1941, BaK, NS22, 952.
57 Weyrather, *Muttertag und Mutterkreuz*, 106.
58 Ibid., 117.
59 Gellately, *Gestapo and German Society*, 158.
60 Among Hamburg applications for the Mother Cross, most of those that were denied came from working-class women. Weyrather, *Muttertag und Mutterkreuz*, 108.
61 Although the exact number of Mother Crosses awarded cannot be ascertained because the files of the *Präsidialkanzlei* in Berlin were destroyed, Irmgard Weyrather estimates that not more than 5 percent could have been rejected in addition to the many women who for racial reasons were never nominated. Ibid., 87.

including "not politically reliable," "family history contains inferior blood," and "indicted and imprisoned." Specifically female faults were sometimes cited in judgments against a woman's morality. Women who led "immoral" lifestyles or bore illegitimate children – especially multiple illegitimate children with different fathers – were labeled bad mothers. Women whose daughters acted immorally or who failed to establish respectable households were also judged harshly.[62] Although it happened less frequently, some applications were rejected for specifically racial reasons. Those filed by women who themselves or whose husbands had either Jewish or Gypsy blood were denied. Even contact with Jews was sufficient cause for denial, as in the case of one widow who was disqualified for having rented a room to a Jewish man and his Aryan wife and children.[63]

Identifying and confirming the suitability of women for honor proved a bafflingly complex problem. The processing of applications for Mother Crosses varied tremendously from one region to another. Mothers were supposed to be nominated by government authorities or Nazi party officials who set into motion a process that ran according to plan. In reality, however, the procedure often went awry. Some women found advocates who pushed their applications through even when pertinent information was missing. Others were overlooked by authorities altogether. In December 1941, for example, the mayor of Bad Salzuflen personally orchestrated the presentation of the Mother Cross to Frau Kortfunke, whom authorities had ignored. Her eleven children had finally come forward and applied directly to him. He, in turn, wrote the government that "Since in the case of the K. family we are dealing with 'worthy,' respected citizens of good repute, I comply with this wish and support the application warmly." He emphasized that Frau Kortfunke had recently celebrated her sixtieth wedding anniversary but "live[d] a very withdrawn life" and preferred not to come forward in public, a fact he thought was understandable given her advanced age of eighty-one years. Furthermore, since in his estimation the family was German and the woman was "worthy," and since the children had all been born alive, he doubted that there was cause to consult a doctor. (Perhaps he also recognized the negative impression that forcing a medical exam on such "worthy, respected citizens" would have made on the family – and potentially others as well.) To ensure the woman's privacy, he even personally wrote the

---

62 Applications for Mother Crosses, StaD, L 80 IC, Gruppe 24, Fach 12, 41, and Fach 11, 40a. According to an exhibit titled "The Public Health Service" (*Die öffentliche Gesundheitsdienst*), "anti-social family" and "inferior offspring" were the most common reasons for denial of Mother Crosses. Cited in Weyrather, *Muttertag und Mutterkreuz*, 88.
63 Applications for Mother Crosses, StaD, L 80 IC, Gruppe 24, Fach 11, 40a.

NSDAP county leadership and requested that "any possible reservations based on political grounds" be sent to him immediately.[64]

As was the case for marriage loans, the burden of evaluation fell on doctors, health departments, and social workers, who quickly became overwhelmed by their new responsibilities. Even doctors sympathetic to the program found the task difficult to carry out. The Brake *Amtsarzt* wrote in 1939 that he was already struggling with the demands created by the applications for Mother Crosses within Brake itself when two smaller counties, Hohenhausen and Extertal, were added to his workload. These areas were managed by assistants who "knew the population only to a limited extent," and he feared that "the danger existed that they would be unable to provide an accurate verdict." Given the gravity of the task, he did not feel he could trust their assessment, and he requested more time to complete his research on families.[65] To help facilitate the process for the party officials who managed it, the leaders of the NSF and the German Women's Enterprise (Deutsches Frauenwerk, DFW), who stood in closer contact with mothers and families than did most party leaders, volunteered to review the applications. But despite their urgent need for help, party officials refused to incorporate these women into the decision-making process, and it remained primarily in the hands of male party members, who were assisted by female social workers.[66] Even the logistics of distributing the crosses remained a problem, with officials constantly worrying about missing and misplaced Mother Crosses.

Social workers constituted the only group of women to play a significant role in evaluating mothers for the Mother Cross. They did not uniformly support the Nazi interest in eugenic health. Not only were their personal convictions diverse, but the profession as a whole found itself in something of a quandary. At the end of the Weimar era, in the depths of the Depression, social workers' employment prospects had worsened to the point that in June 1930 the Prussian minister of welfare limited the number of new social work students to thirty-five per year for the entire state.[67] As unemployment and extreme need increased, many social workers had grown disillusioned with the Weimar Republic's ability to "cure" social ills and began to favor greater state intervention into families as a solution. They were also inclined to agree with Nazi authorities on a variety of issues pertaining to social hygiene, education, and public health. The combination of their dedication to the

---

64 StaD, L 80 IC, Gruppe 24, Fach 12, 41.
65 Amtsarzt to Landrat Brake, 20 June 1939, StaD, D 102 Lemgo, 187.
66 NSF monthly reports, January–May 1941, BaK, NS22, 925.
67 Soziale Arbeit 7/130, Heft 3, Ausgabe A, quoted in Zeller, *Volksmütter*, 118.

profession and their hope that the new National Socialist leadership would solve the pressing problems left by the Weimar welfare state encouraged them to cooperate with the new regime. As the board of one social work guild wrote shortly after the Nazis came to power, "We are certain that . . . out of a feeling of responsibility toward our work each individual will place his or her full strength and practical experiences in the service of the new order."[68]

By vastly expanding the need for social workers, moreover, the Nazis won the support of many.[69] They created an array of new family-oriented programs and demanded household assessments for all manner of reasons. In addition, they drove Jewish social workers, including Alice Salomon (a leading bourgeois feminist and social work educator), from the profession, opening up more space for new recruits. The Nazis simplified social workers' training by reducing it from four years to two years and added courses that emphasized the National Socialist worldview. Social work students took exams on topics that included "The educational goals of the Führer," "What type of state does the National Socialist Worldview suggest?" and "The National Socialist Household."[70] The Nazis wanted social workers to care for the "healthy" *Volk* and not waste their energies by indiscriminately helping all who were needy.[71] In contrast to the Nazi-trained "brown sisters" (the name referred to their brown uniforms), both social workers trained in the spirit of Alice Salomon and confessional social workers influenced by the teachings of the church approached their work from the perspective of their own more inclusive training, and they did not uniformly implement Nazi policy toward families.

Officials interpreted the criteria for the Mother Crosses differently. Many mayors, like the mayor of Bad Salzuflen mentioned above, believed Mother Crosses should honor upstanding citizens regardless of their medical histories. Social workers, similarly, often supported applications from people they believed tried hard under adverse circumstances. In most such cases, the advocates argued in favor of bypassing doctors' invasive exams and potentially harsh verdicts. Their willingness to overlook medical exams clearly demonstrates that racial policy was not the overarching concern of all authorities. In practice, this meant that racial guidelines were implemented inconsistently, and applications received a variable amount of attention as authorities

68 Open letter of the Gilde Soziale Arbeit (GSA, Social Work Guild) board to members announcing its voluntary disbandment, 2 May 1933, quoted in Schnurr, "Why Did Social Workers," 126–7.
69 Schnurr, "Why Did Social Workers," 130.
70 Individual social workers' records for state certification, SaM, Regierung Arnsberg, 18 no. 18, Bd. 1. See also *Sopade Berichte* 4, no. 9 (September 1937): 1310.
71 Zeller, *Volksmütter*, 96.

sometimes waived regulations. When Frau B.'s husband applied for a Mother Cross for his wife, the *Amtsarzt* who examined the family reported that several of the children were "mentally inferior and partially feebleminded" and attended a special education school (*Hilfsschule*). The doctor's report outweighed the Lemgo mayor's glowing recommendation, and authorities rejected her application. Two years later, in 1941, however, authorities reconsidered the case when they realized that the denial of a Mother Cross was negatively affecting the family's chances of receiving child subsidies. They wrote to the head of the county administration, who resumed the investigation. Instead of challenging the doctor, he collected other evidence to corroborate the mayor's positive evaluation. The children's teacher denied that the children were feebleminded, claiming instead that "the children's bad [school] work can be mostly attributed to the fact that they do not have adequate supervision and care." Under normal circumstances, this might have confirmed the doctor's negative evaluation of Frau B., but the district leader argued that it was understandable that a mother with eleven children who worked on a farm during the day "[could not] raise and supervise her children in the way that is possible with fewer children." He further emphasized that the children, like their parents, were hardworking and orderly. With this more sympathetic evaluation of the family, the doctor's conclusions were discounted, and Frau B. was awarded a Mother Cross.[72]

Though not unique, Frau B.'s case was also not typical. More often, authorities exhibited significantly less diligence and proved unwilling to reconsider their decisions or to ignore disqualifying evidence. When Frau Kurtin's application for a Mother Cross was rejected in 1940, her husband wrote to find out the reason why. In his inquiry, he told the government that since he had never been convicted of a crime, neither he nor his wife had any debts, and their children were healthy, he could not understand its decision. Furthermore, he had been a member of the Reich Military Service (Reichskriegsdienst, RKD) for six years, which he felt illustrated his patriotism. His file reveals that although the mayor approved the Mother Cross, it was once again a doctor's discovery that had undermined the case: "With the mother as well as the sons," the doctor reported, "there is suspicion of feeblemindedness." As in the previous case, authorities also rejected the family's application for child subsidies, probably on account of the doctor's report. Rather than probe the meaning of the word "suspicion" or investigate further, the county administrator informed Herr Kurtin that his wife

---

72 Applications for Mother Crosses, StaD, L 80 IC, Gruppe 24, Fach 11, 40a.

had been rejected because of "proven genetic weakness."[73] The doctor's "suspicion," formed on the basis of a single interview, proved sufficient to rule the family out for any future support. Thus, the consequences of a rejection could outweigh the potential benefits of the Mother Cross, as the application process itself brought women to the attention of authorities – in particular the health departments – that might otherwise not have paid them heed.

Being awarded a Mother Cross did not guarantee permanent recognition of worthiness or ensure continued state support. A Mother Cross could be revoked if a woman's behavior changed, most commonly if she neglected her children or did not remain true to her husband. Because revocation could be taken as a sign that worthiness was not permanent and that the regime was fallible, it was not taken lightly. In fact, authorities granted some women the opportunity to improve their behavior. In one case, nurse hygienists discovered that while Frau Tielker's husband was at the front, she had neither kept up the household properly nor helped her children with their homework. Worst of all, she had become involved in a relationship that threatened her loyalty to her soldier husband. On the basis of these discoveries, the nurse assigned to the case concluded that Frau Tielker had ceased to be a good mother and applied to have Frau Tielker's cross revoked. The local party leader confirmed that the negative behavior had only started subsequent to Frau Tielker's husband's draft and her receipt of the Mother Cross, and he agreed that revocation of the cross was appropriate. Nevertheless, ten months later, he reversed his decision, explaining: "After we threatened to take her child subsidy away and reduce her family support, Frau Tielker's [behavior] improved significantly. She gave up her immoral lifestyle and takes care of her household and children satisfactorily."[74] It is clear in this case and others that the authorities did not hesitate to use the Mother Cross to shape women's behavior. From Frau Tielker's perspective, however, it may well have been the financial threat and not the revocation of the cross that forced her to conform.

The advent of the war placed new pressures on the award and distribution of the Mother Crosses that resulted in a relaxation of the eligibility standards. In 1942, the Minden government suggested to the Reich minister of the interior that it would have a positive influence on the population if mothers whose sons and husbands were at the front or had died in battle were compensated with the honorary Mother Cross even if they would not otherwise have qualified. The minister of the interior responded that

73 Ibid.   74 Ibid.

while in some instances this might be a good idea, he did not consider it good policy in general. He especially encouraged awarding Mother Crosses if something could be done to improve a mother's (or family's) failings, but he warned that "in borderline cases the population's response to the conferral of a Mother Cross . . . must be taken into consideration." Above all, the value of the crosses was not to be undermined by awarding them too liberally.[75] Despite this warning, as the war escalated and more soldiers died in battle, the government attached greater importance to recognizing and honoring mothers with Mother Crosses.[76] Nazi authorities would have found it untenable to have no Mother Crosses to distribute on Mother's Day, "since this might [have been] construed as a sign that the birth rate was receding, that mothers had no interest in the Mother Cross, or that no one was 'worthy.'"[77] They deemphasized the health and racial requirements that had governed prior Mother Cross selection and used the crosses to help restore and maintain women's loyalty to the regime. Policymakers' decision to broaden the criteria for the Mother Cross to include war widows even when they did not meet standard guidelines reflected a state effort to bolster women's support for the war. It also exposed the program's failure to create a sufficiently large number of prolific mothers to honor. Mothers whose applications for the cross had previously been rejected because of "asocial" conditions reapplied and received crosses after they lost loved ones in the war.[78] Many local authorities expressed frustration that they could not reject women they deemed unworthy. Far from worrying about the changing meaning of the crosses, however, many women agreed with Frau Kemper (b. 1919), who reported that the Mother Crosses were one of so many honors bestowed on the German population by the end of the war that they lost any significance they had originally had.[79]

Despite publicity and ceremony, control over the meaning of the crosses eluded the Nazis. "At the time, we more or less just laughed about the golden Mother Cross," remembered Frau Schnabel (b. 1912), who held a leadership position in the upper echelons of the BDM.[80] In strongly Catholic areas, the population rejected the idea that mothers needed any recognition for

75 Reichsminister des Innern to Herrn Regierungspräsident Minden, 16 April 1942, StaD, D 102 Lemgo, 187.
76 At the beginning of 1945, Mother Crosses were awarded to a woman posthumously if a child or her husband applied immediately after her death. Weyrather, *Muttertag und Mutterkreuz*, 42–4.
77 Ibid., 80.
78 Boberach, *Meldungen aus dem Reich*, 29 April 1943, 5209.
79 Frau Kemper, interview.
80 Frau Schnabel, interview.

childbearing beyond the recognition that came from God.[81] Some women scorned or refused to accept the cross. Frau Wolfe (b. 1903) opted not to receive her Mother Cross, claiming that she had borne her fifth child not for Hitler but rather because she and her husband wanted another child.[82] Refusing to accept a cross was a risky step, since it could be interpreted as a statement against the regime and as such bring on reprisals. Although the Nazis never specified consequences for refusal, women recognized that they "would certainly be looked at askance" if they declined the honor.[83] In some cases, it was not the refusal of a Mother Cross alone that caused trouble for a family but rather that the refusal was used as evidence of a family's political unreliability if its members found themselves in other conflicts with the government. In many such cases, Nazi authorities were probably correct in interpreting the behavior as low-level resistance. In the case of Frau Wolfe, the authorities permitted her to decline the cross, but when a short time later her son wrote a letter to his mother of questionable political content, she was called in for interrogation.

Other women expressed their criticisms more forthrightly. Frau Brielmann received her cross on Mother's Day in 1941. She complained to her neighbor that "they should have given me fifty marks instead." To another neighbor, she expressed her wish that she could exchange the cross for 100 marks. During the award ceremony, she allegedly intensified her criticism and told the women at her table, "They should have given me the means to avoid having more children instead [of the cross]." After the ceremony, she gave her children the cross to play with. Frau Brielmann's actions suggest that she assumed that the women at her table would share her scorn of the cross – or maybe even of the regime – but it was one of these women who reported the comments to the authorities. Perhaps she found Frau Brielmann's attitude reprehensible; perhaps she merely disliked Frau Brielmann and decided to use this opportunity to lash out at her. Frau Brielmann was investigated and found guilty of having sought an abortion. Her public show of disdain together with her illegal attempt to limit her family size could not be overlooked, and her cross was revoked. The county administrator declared: "Frau Brielmann is behaving in ways contradictory to a 'German' mother. She is unworthy of the honor of the honorary cross."[84] Clearly, even after being honored with the cross, Frau Brielmann did not accept the value placed on it by Nazi policy. Rather than inspiring her to have more children,

81 Boberach, *Meldungen aus dem Reich*, 29 April 1943, 5209.
82 Frau Wolff, interview.
83 Frau Neske, interview.
84 Applications for Mother Crosses, StaD, L 80 IC, Gruppe 24, Fach 11, 40a.

the cross underscored her desire to have fewer. Although no further information is available about Frau Brielmann, she would have faced grave, if not insurmountable, difficulty winning any future state support.

Yet Frau Brielmann's contempt for the cross suggests that the Nazis' efforts to promote a culture of motherhood were as much a failure as their attempts to raise the birthrate. Initially, Nazi authorities combed the population for prolific mothers who could be honored, even if their youngest child was already an adult. A large number of crosses were distributed very quickly: in 1939, Detmold officials nominated 134 women for the gold cross, 110 women for the silver cross, and 123 for the bronze cross. After 1941, the backlog of elderly prolific mothers had been honored, and most mothers who were awarded the cross became eligible through the recent birth of a child. The number of crosses distributed fell dramatically, in part because the Nazis lacked a systematic method of locating women who had borne their fourth child. Many women and their families also hesitated to apply for a cross, believing the state should find them.[85] As a result, in May 1942, Detmold officials nominated only ten women for the gold cross, eighteen for the silver cross, and seventy-two for the bronze cross. Furthermore, only four women needed to have their crosses upgraded. The inflated number of crosses distributed early in the program did not correlate with the birthrate, and the birthrate's failure to rise after the introduction of the Mother Cross suggests that few women saw the cross as an impetus to bear more children, especially in a time of war.[86] Even as the Nazis distributed Mother Crosses, the general population largely dismissed the idea of large families.

Nor did the Nazis' other pronatalist programs work. Some people claimed they would rather pay higher taxes than support extra children in a lower tax bracket. Others complained that the extra benefits the Nazis offered parents did not compensate for the lower wages they had introduced. One Sopade report included the assertion that "those who bear fewer children are still better off than the 'child-rich.'"[87] Nor did the population take kindly to the blatant state propaganda to encourage large families. In 1938, the Ministry of Film and Propaganda released a film entitled "Papa's Birthday" depicting Goebbels's many children dancing and praying for their father. The first audiences that saw it recognized that this brash propaganda "was clearly an advertisement for having lots of children." Rather than marvel at the children's dedication to their father, some people speculated subversively that the

---

85 Boberach, *Meldungen aus dem Reich*, 29 April 1943, 5208; Weyrather, *Muttertag und Mutterkreuz*, 78–82.
86 Applications for Mother Crosses, StaD, L 80 IC, Gruppe 24, Fach 12, 40 and 40a.
87 *Sopade Berichte* 5, no. 6 (1938): 650.

children danced in socks to hide the fact that they had inherited their father's club foot, while others pointed out that Goebbels "badly needed somebody to pray for him." In the face of such public scorn, the Nazis quickly withdrew the film.[88] After the war began, the state's call to reproduce was met with cynicism by citizens who found it hard enough to feed themselves.[89] The increased rate at which women were called in to do the work of men sent to the front lines, especially in rural areas, caused the miscarriage rate to rise.[90] Despite Nazi pronatalism, then, women continued to practice birth control and to limit their family size throughout the Nazi era. And regardless of stiff penalties for both doctors who performed abortions and women who underwent them, abortion remained a not infrequent occurrence. One 1937 report found that in every small town in Westphalia, at least one woman was hospitalized per week for the aftereffects of abortion.[91]

Nazi officials continued to search for new ways to encourage "healthy" marriages to be more prolific and to prevent "unhealthy" couples from reproducing, and in doing so they risked crossing the line between acceptable and unacceptable levels of state intervention. In 1938, before being sent to a bride school (a requirement for women marrying members of the SS), Frau Siebold (b. 1912) was taken aback when she was rigorously interrogated about any miscarriages she might have had. Although she understood that the technique was intended to confirm her fertility, she was outraged at the suggestion that she might have engaged in premarital intercourse.[92] Nazi officials and doctors conducted such intimate interrogations in the hope of discouraging from marrying women who suffered from "internal diseases" that could cause difficult pregnancies or deliveries.[93] They also threatened to force divorce on couples whose marriages remained childless. Frau Dewald (b. 1913) explained that in 1944, after years of childless marriage, her husband was warned by the Reich Labor Service leader that he saw "trouble" for their marriage and that unless they bore a child before the end of the war, their marriage would be dissolved.[94] Because blame for the couple's childlessness fell entirely on Frau Dewald's shoulders, she underwent medical exams to determine the nature of the problem. Implicit in all such examinations, interrogations, and threats was the unequal fertility

88 Ibid., 645.
89 Boberach, *Meldungen aus dem Reich*, 17 April 1940, 1019.
90 Ibid., 13 December 1939, 570.
91 *Sopade Berichte*, 4, no. 7 (1937): 1353–4, and 5, no. 6 (1938): 654.
92 Unfortunately, Frau Siebold could not remember whether it was a member of the NSF in charge of SS wives or a civil registry official who interrogated her. Frau Siebold, interview.
93 Czarnowski, *Das kontrollierte Paar*, 213.
94 Frau Dewald, interview.

WINTERSONNENWENDE 1943

During the Second World War, Nazi pronatalist propaganda intensified, often drawing a direct connection between the war fatalities and the need to raise the birthrate. Here the newborn seems to replace the fallen soldier. The lack of religious symbols on the Christmas tree and the title "winter solstice" reflect the Nazi emphasis on German mythology. *NS Frauenwarte* Heft 4, 12 (1943).

standard for men and women. Whereas women were examined for their suitability as German mothers, a role that implied the ability to bear and raise a healthy child, men were neither examined nor questioned. Although the state did not actually take action against Frau Dewald and her husband, the fact that both they and Frau Siebold were interrogated at all reveals a climate in which such actions were a possibility. Clearly, some Nazi authorities were willing – and, moreover, eager – to see the state go beyond the traditional boundaries of privacy in the name of state interests, and they designed antinatalist programs that clearly did so.

No discussion of National Socialist policy toward mothers can adequately cover the topic by focusing only on pronatalist programs. The reverse of the honor Nazi policymakers bestowed on "worthy" women was the dishonor in the form of violence and invasion they aimed at "unworthy" women. At their least hostile, Nazi policymakers withheld aid and support from "unworthy" mothers. At their most malignant, Nazi authorities used sterilization to prevent the "unworthy" from reproducing. The 1933 Law to Prevent Hereditarily Sick Offspring (*Gesetz zur Verhütung erbkranken Nachwuchses*), which legalized compulsory sterilization of the "unworthy," far exceeded any prior attempt to shape motherhood. Moreover, in contrast to pronatalist programs, which honored mothers in their biological role, Nazi antinatalist policy was not limited to mothers. Instead, it targeted all men, women, and children believed to be carrying genes unworthy of the German *Volk*. Integral to state ideology was the belief that the state had a responsibility to prevent these people from passing their "defective" genes on to the next generation.

The Law to Prevent Hereditarily Sick Offspring has been labeled the "first attack on highly personal individual rights."[95] But even before the sterilization law went into effect, the Nazis had enacted an array of other legislation that attacked the rights of Jews, Communists, and others to work, worship, and live. What made the sterilization law different was the medical method of assault and the group it targeted. When candidates for sterilization were selected, the collective interests of society and the race took precedence over individual rights. The law identified nine "diseases" whose carriers were labeled unsuitable parents: hereditary feeblemindedness, schizophrenia, manic depression, hereditary epilepsy, Huntington's chorea, hereditary blindness, hereditary deafness, hereditary malformations, and severe alcoholism. To prevent individuals with these conditions from passing on their "inferior" genes, Nazi officials made every effort to eliminate their reproductive potential.[96] Between 1934, when the law went into effect, and 1945,

---

95 Ramm, *Das Nationalsozialistische Familien*, 17.
96 Although there was considerable discussion about creating a sterilization law at the end of the Weimar era and in 1931 the German Racial Hygiene Society adopted a program to sterilize the "degenerate" voluntarily in an effort to distribute "differential welfare benefits," sterilization was initiated only on a very limited basis. Weindling, *Health, Race and German Politics*, 451–2.

a total of 360,000 people, approximately 1 percent of the German population between the ages of sixteen and fifty, were sterilized in accordance with the law. Women comprised roughly 50 percent of those sterilized.[97] Every German man, woman, and child stood at risk. In fact, as Irmgard Weyrather has pointed out, even women who wore the Mother Cross and who supported National Socialism lived with the knowledge that another birth might reveal a genetic defect that would lead to their sterilization.[98]

The process of identifying and nominating individuals for sterilization was a painstaking one. Responsibility for monitoring hereditary health fell to state health officials, who in effect became the gatekeepers of Nazi racial policy. Doctors had the greatest access to personal and family histories and therefore became the primary source for nominations for sterilization. Many doctors who had already supported sterilization measures during the Weimar era enthusiastically backed the new law, which they believed was the antidote to the steady decline of national health. To make the system work, however, doctors needed support from all other health employees, including social workers, midwives, and welfare employees. One study of nominations in Kreis Herford found that state authorities, among them the NSV workers, state health officers, and the mayoral staff, nominated 46.3 percent of candidates. The remaining half of nominations came from local health departments, individual doctors, and insurance agencies.[99] Health departments then collated the reports and, beginning in April 1935, stored them in the newly established clinics for hereditary and racial care (*Beratungsstellen für Erb- und Rassenpflege*), where officials worked to create a hereditary index.[100] Nominations were passed on to the new hereditary courts (*Erbgesundheitsgerichte*), where three judges and two doctors decided the fate of those nominated for sterilization. Many physicians, especially psychiatrists, benefited from the sterilization law: administering and adjudicating on the law enhanced their status as professionals and increased their income.

Though theoretically the sterilization law applied to all Germans equally, in practice sterilization policy targeted indicted criminals, residents of psychiatric institutions, and those who attended – or had attended – schools for the disadvantaged. The criteria upon which people were judged to have many of the diseases deemed cause for sterilization, particularly "hereditary feeblemindedness," reflected social prejudices or a class-based lack of

97 Vossen, "Gesundheitsämter im Kreis Herford," 94; Bock, *Zwangssterilisation*, 372.
98 Weyrather, *Muttertag und Mutterkreuz*, 216–17.
99 Vossen, "Gesundheitsämter in Kreis Herford," 95.
100 For more discussion, see Weindling, *Health, Race and German Politics*, 522–8.

understanding. Social workers often attributed a mother's failure to keep a clean household to genetic deficiencies, for example, rather than to economics. Virtually anyone who defied normal behavior could be characterized as suffering from hereditary feeblemindedness. Families who relied on welfare exposed themselves to a greater degree of state scrutiny and hence were more likely to find their members nominated for sterilization. As a result, certain groups of the population were more likely to be sterilized. One historian has even argued that "in general the entire sterilization policy focused on simple people [*einfache Leute*] or members of fringe groups [*Randgruppen*]" – that is, the underprivileged.[101] Through their contact with needy families, NSV welfare office employees may well have played a larger role in nominating people than the records reveal.

At the local level, doctors found evaluating candidates for sterilization to be as labor intensive as assessing applicants for marriage loans or the Mother Cross. Although technically the law required extra personnel to collect information, examine people, and answer letters of protest, in reality the burden fell most heavily on doctors. In March 1934, the director of Bethel Psychiatric Institute wrote that his work in conjunction with sterilization had "become extensive and time-consuming beyond all expectations."[102] Because locating detailed family histories proved labor intensive and difficult, doctors often sent incomplete reports to the courts, thus hampering the courts' ability to prosecute the cases efficiently.[103] Like other facets of Nazi policy, the bureaucracy that evolved to cope with sterilization was complicated, redundant, and, in the eyes of many, excessive. The director of one provincial psychiatric institution (*Provinzialheilanstalt*) concluded that building a case for sterilization "[could] be tremendously accelerated if one [did] not adhere strictly to the bureaucratic regulations."[104]

Bureaucratic confusion caused long delays before sterilization actually took place. In 1934, officials at the Gütersloh Psychiatric Institute protested that of the ninety-three people they had nominated for sterilization, only fifty-one cases had been decided, and only thirty-eight of these had actually been sterilized.[105] These delays persisted even in later years. As late as 1941, the Eickelborn Psychiatric Institute authorities reported that of the 2,099 people they had nominated for sterilization, the cases of only 519 had

101 Vossen, "Gesundheitsämter in Kreis Herford," 89.
102 Letter from Bethel Chief Doctor, StaD, D23 C, 2097.
103 Oberlandesgerichtspräsident Hamm to Herrn Oberpräsident der Provinz Westfalen Landesfürsorgeverband, 20 April 1934, LSVA, C60, 258.
104 Letter Direktor der Provinzialheilanstalt, 14 August 1934, LSVA, C60, 260.
105 Heilanstalt Gütersloh zu dem Landesfürsorgeverband, 13 August 1934, LSVA, C60, 260.

been decided.[106] Some people got lost in the system; others were nominated repeatedly. The *Landschaftsverband* (Regional Association) authorities complained, "Recently, it has . . . occurred that applications for sterilization have been filed for people who have already been sterilized."[107] The courts found themselves so overwhelmed that they were unable to act quickly on nominations.

Implementation of the Law to Prevent Hereditarily Sick Offspring depended on the participation not only of medical professionals and judges but also of social workers, teachers, and individual Germans. Therefore, despite the widespread support for the law among physicians, Nazi policymakers met resistance at each turn, particularly from church officials. They postponed the passage of the law until after the Concordat had been signed with the Catholic Church, emphasizing only their pronatalist opinions during negotiations. The ramifications of the new law were not lost on Church authorities, who objected to the Nazi state's intrusion into the realm of reproduction. Many religious personnel who worked in hospitals and health establishments, in particular nuns, refused to identify candidates for sterilization. As Claudia Koonz has demonstrated, they often did so without the explicit support of the Church, since Church leaders worried that objecting too vociferously to Nazi eugenics would jeopardize the civil rights the Concordat had won them.[108] Although Nazi leaders sought to replace anyone who refused to support the new legislation, this proved impossible. In 1934, the Reich minister of the interior ruled against any removal of religious employees, emphasizing that "Pressure may not be placed on confessional nursing personnel."[109] Throughout the Nazi era, religious hospitals and institutions continued to harbor potential victims of the law.[110]

Individual Germans' failure to accept Nazi antinatalism – as it applied to themselves, if not in principle – also confounded state aims. Many "asocial" couples denied that the law was intended for them and acted on the state's pronatalism, continuing to bear children.[111] Others who aggressively protested sterilization verdicts posed an even more significant hindrance to

---

106 Of these, only 455 were ordered to undergo sterilization, 437 were sterilized, and 306 of them were then released. Report of Eickelborn Anstalt, 30 December 1941, LSVA, C60, 260.

107 Oberarzt, Erbiologische Zentralstelle der Provinzial Verwaltung Westfalen to Herrn Landesrat Schulte, 28 April 1936, LSVA, C60, 262.

108 Koonz, "Ethical Dilemmas," 27–33.

109 His solution was to hire only "secular personnel" (*weltlicher Hilfspersonal*) in the future, thus gradually diminishing the number of opponents of the law. Reichs Ministerium des Innern, 14 August 1934, LSVA, C60, 258.

110 For example, the nuns at Stift Tilbeck outside Münster moved all the psychiatric patients to the attic to protect them from Nazi inspections. Schwester A., interview.

111 *Sopade Berichte*, 5, no. 6 (1938): 650.

the smooth implementation of the sterilization law. The Reich minister of the interior received daily complaints from doctors and other informers whose identities had been revealed to the victims of state sterilization. To avoid this problem, nominators' identities were frequently not specified in official records. Still, the fear of being found out may well have reduced some people's willingness to nominate others, thus diminishing the efficacy of the program.[112] In another act of protest, some women, determined to defy their label as "unworthy," became pregnant before their sterilization verdicts could be carried out. These "pregnancies of defiance" (*trotz Schwangerschaften*) sometimes occurred with the explicit support of the Catholic Church.[113] They forced many courts to delay sterilization until a pregnancy had ended. Gradually, however, more and more courts agreed with the assessment by the director of one institute that "it cannot be in the spirit of the law, that such pregnancies be carried to full term."[114] In 1935, the abortion law was revised, and the pregnancies of women who were ordered to be sterilized were regularly aborted.[115]

Individuals directly protested sterilization verdicts in more than one-third of all cases. While the sterilization law itself permitted protest, it limited both the time in which that protest could be registered and who could file it. Only the victims of sterilization, their fathers (but not their mothers), or their guardians were allowed to protest. When Frau M. nominated her daughter for sterilization because she was epileptic, for example, the court discounted her opinion, since her husband was alive and he alone had the right to file a petition.[116] The reasons people gave for protesting sterilization varied widely. Some objected out of fear for their families. One father protested his son's proposed sterilization "because this would be very disadvantageous for [his] other children." He feared that even if the case were handled discretely, information would leak out and make the lives of his other children more difficult.[117] Others feared the operation itself.[118] While the deaths caused by sterilization were few, the psychological effect of these deaths was far-reaching.[119] In July 1934, the

---

112 StaD, D 23 C, letter M, 752; Carola Sachße, *Siemens*, 45.
113 Bock, *Zwangssterilisation*, 386–7.
114 Quoted in ibid., 386.
115 It is not known how many such pregnancies were aborted, but Gisela Bock estimates that there were 30,000 "racially motivated abortions" (*rassenhygienische Abtreibungen*). Ibid., 398.
116 In some cases, parents nominated their own children for sterilization, most often in cases of indisputable mental illness. StaD, D 23 C, letter M, 1178.
117 Case from 1936, StaD, Erbgesundheitsgericht, 805.
118 See, for example, a case from 1936, StaD, Erbgesundheitsgericht, 45.
119 Gisela Bock estimates the rate of deaths at 0.5 percent for women and 0.1 percent for men. *Zwangsterilisation im Nationalsozialismus*, 376.

Prussian minister of the interior noted with concern, "It is without a doubt true that the appearance of more such 'incidents' [deaths] will make implementing the law more difficult." To counteract this problem, he made doctors responsible for the health of patients after sterilization, stating, "The doctors who are entrusted with executing this 'intervention' are hereby notified that the hereditary courts or the higher hereditary courts' decision to sterilize does not release you from the responsibility for the 'intervention.'"[120]

Much more commonly, it was the grounds for the sterilization themselves that people challenged. Even in the case of medically specific diseases, doctors did not always agree in their diagnoses. When Heinrich A.'s doctor nominated him for sterilization in 1934 because he was deaf, he protested the diagnosis that his deafness was genetic. Heinrich's teacher testified that upon entrance to school his hearing had been fine and that he had lost his hearing only gradually, suggesting that it stemmed from an ear infection.[121] With this, the *Amtsarzt* overruled his colleague's nomination, and Heinrich was spared. Although Heinrich's case never went to court, other similar cases did, and individuals appealed their cases and forcefully fought doctors' opinions they deemed flawed.[122]

Because of the pressures on their time, doctors often rushed their decisions, with the result that many people found fault with them. In 1935, the Weidenbrück county doctor nominated Mathilde M. for sterilization on the grounds of feeblemindedness, citing as evidence her father and siblings, who also suffered similarly. Mathilde M., the mother of seven children, protested the decision. First, she claimed that the decision was based on shoddy evidence, since she had only been cursorily examined. Second, she argued that the questions she was asked were inappropriate. "Of course I cannot answer a question about calculating interest, which ninety of one hundred women could not have answered," she complained, continuing, "Another question about the winnings in the large lottery was clearly unreasonable, since the doctor did not know the answer." She stressed that she had worked for the railway before she married and no one had thought her feebleminded. And she underscored the inappropriateness of the doctor's evaluation to her own situation: "If in the oral meeting, my voice shook, one should be able to understand that a rural woman like me ... does not gain an exceptional social intelligence working with children and on a farm. During the day,

---

120 Letter from Preußische Minister des Innern, 21 August 1934, LSVA, C60, 259.
121 StaD, D 23 C, letter A, 1777.
122 Ibid.; StaD, Erbgesundheitsgericht, 796.

I have no hours to read or the like, since with the children and 30 acres of land, as well as the animals, I work from early morning until late night without rest. . . . The experience I had with the intelligence test, someone else would have had with questions about agricultural farming or preparing fodder, so this cannot possibly be based in feeblemindedness." Just as middle-class standards for housework failed to take into account working-class reality, so too the Nazi definitions of average intelligence were based on urban, not rural, lifestyles.

At the end of her meeting with the doctor, he told her she should not have any more children, and she responded smartly: "Thank God, we have enough children already!" But despite Mathilde's willingness – in fact, her desire – to stop bearing children, she did not want the state to sterilize her.[123] Mathilde's protest shared characteristics with many other protests. She believed she had a right and power to contest medical and, ultimately, state authorities. Like many others, she believed herself capable of controlling her own reproduction without state interference. Some childless couples accepted the state's judgment of their unsuitability for parenthood and agreed not to have children but asked not to be sterilized. One couple wrote, "We would have liked to have children, but if it is in the state's interest, we will refrain."[124]

In other cases, however, the erroneous charges leveled against individuals gave them the courage to challenge not just their verdict but the state's right to sterilize people. When the Verl Kreisamt (district office) nominated Herr Otto for sterilization on account of his feeblemindedness in 1935, Herr Otto was so outraged that he protested the way his exam had been conducted, the doctor's conclusions, and the way the law itself was being carried out. Three years later, at the request of the social worker, both he and his son were examined by a neurologist. After examining him, the neurologist told Herr Otto that he had contracted tuberculosis on the front lines during World War I and had subsequently passed it on to his son. Herr Otto dismissed this as "nonsense," explaining that his son "was born in 1913 before the war" and hence could not have inherited tuberculosis from him. Because the doctor was clearly rushed and his conclusion was so obviously false, Herr Otto had not contradicted him at the time. Only when he learned that the

---

123 In the end, her protest was successful and she was not sterilized. Case from 1935, StaD, D 23 C, letter M, 796. Parents of children with disabilities frequently argued that sterilization was unnecessary, since their children never came in contact with members of the opposite gender. This rarely swayed the courts. See SaM, Erbgesundheitsgericht, 16178 and 55. Others argued that the illness was not genetic and hence did not fit the requirements of the law. See ibid., 796.
124 Case from 1938, SaM, Erbgesundheitsgericht, 16183.

doctor had nominated him for sterilization on the basis of this cursory exam did he challenge the verdict.

Though Herr Otto criticized his own nomination for sterilization, he did not challenge the law itself. He did, however, cast doubt on the character of its implementation. He questioned whether the law was really intended to target for sterilization a sixty-one-year-old war veteran and widower with a healthy family. He also accused social worker S. of having trumped up the case, and he marveled at the fact that "despite her previous condemnation of the current regime, today she can do exactly what she wants." Her behavior seemed to him reprehensible, and the regime's willingness to listen to her at his expense represented an especially egregious miscarriage of justice. Herr Otto emphasized, moreover, that the improper execution of the law was having a detrimental effect on the population. He warned the authorities that this incited the *Volk* "to rage," threatening "the Führer's and the government's work of justice." He cautioned: "The population here is upset enough with it that sometimes one could imagine that the next day another revolution will take place." In his protest, Herr Otto made a clear distinction between the government and the Führer, both of whom he saw as just powers, and the local authorities, who he felt wielded their power irresponsibly, undermining the very justice he believed Hitler and the government strove to establish. In the end, Herr Otto's protest proved successful and his sterilization was canceled.[125]

In contrast to Mathilde M. and Herr Otto, not everyone believed they possessed the power to overturn the court's decision on their own. Frequently, parents sought help from friends or authorities. In 1934, when Elisabeth N.'s doctor nominated her for sterilization, her mother, a widow, enlisted the aid of a social worker and the mayor because she did not trust the strength of her own petition. In Elisabeth's case, it was in part her mother's ability to run a household that saved her from sterilization. The district social worker visited their house and found "a household [that] makes a very good impression." She reported that Frau N. and her daughter lived together on the pension left by the late Herr N. and seemed to have a good relationship with one another. The social worker concluded her report by stressing that "Even the fact that the family is not known at the welfare office suggests that the girl and her family are on the right track." The mayor also assured the court that Elisabeth's feeblemindedness was acquired, not genetic, and

125 StaD, D 23 C, letter M, 752. For other examples, see SaM, Erbgesundheitsgericht, 52 and 56; StaD, D 23 C, letter A, 94 and 1777.

hence did not need to be controlled by sterilization. In the end, since there was no firm evidence of a genetic basis for Elisabeth's feeblemindedness and the women led respectable and orderly lives, Elisabeth's nomination for sterilization was revoked.[126]

Because an inability to function in the *Volksgemeinschaft* constituted one of the criteria for sterilization, other people tried to overwhelm the court with evidence of their loved ones' abilities. When the *Amtsarzt* in Gelsenkirchen nominated Ernestine G. for sterilization, her father protested, claiming that her childhood had been completely normal and that her later failure to achieve in school stemmed from several abusive teachers. Outside that school environment, she had resumed normal life. She had been an active member of the League of German Girls for the previous three years and, since her mother died, had competently run his household. To prove Ernestine's competence, her father enlisted a neighbor's help. The neighbor gave Ernestine a complicated list of errands, which she completed flawlessly — hence demonstrating her ability to function normally, according to her father. Finally, he entreated her employer to write a letter on Ernestine's behalf, which she did. The employer argued: "I myself am a believer in the law and hold it as a good deed for the future of the German people. In this case I voluntarily offered to submit a reference for the girl because I believe the entire case is an injustice against [Ernestine] G." In the face of such concerted protest and the proof of her ability to function in society, the court became convinced that Ernestine would make a competent mother and dropped the sterilization case.[127]

When Emma G. was nominated for sterilization on account of feeblemindedness, her father disputed the diagnosis. As evidence for this, he claimed, "My daughter Emma is now enrolled in the sewing school and her work is well accepted by her supervisors." The courts decided to postpone the decision for three years, since Emma's ability to sew, cook, and run the household for her family made more observation necessary before a definite verdict could be reached. As they pointed out, "The fact that all the siblings went to a school for the disadvantaged and that the parents drink suggests the existence of feeblemindedness. On the other hand, the practical talent and the good moral behavior as well as the possibility that the lacking school work is the result of the household conditions [speak against this diagnosis]."[128] In another case, the court spared Frieda S.

126 Case from 1934, SaM, Erbgesundheitsgericht, 52.
127 Ibid., 9284.
128 Case from 1935, SaM, Erbgesundheitsgericht, 9289.

sterilization because "she [had] a well-run household . . . [and] there are no debts." The judges concluded, "From this one can deduce that she is frugal and spends her husband's income wisely." These abilities compensated for her low score on the intelligence test.[129] The courts assessed different skills in men. In 1936, when Anton W. was diagnosed with genetic feeblemind-edness, his father protested, claiming that Anton did perfectly competent field work. Moreover, he argued, Anton's low score on the intelligence test was the result of the myriad responsibilities he had on the farm, which had caused him to neglect his schoolwork. When the examiner retested Anton, he discovered that "he [knew] the price of livestock, grain, and other such things." Made aware of Anton's farming knowledge, the court concluded, "He will be able to succeed in life."[130] Thus, in some cases, both women and men could overcome verdicts of hereditary feeblemindedness if they proved themselves competent in the gender roles expected of them.

Gender roles also affected men's and women's chances of having their sterilization nominations thrown out. My examination of sterilization verdicts suggests that women succeeded less frequently than men in getting their verdicts reversed in cases of hereditary feeblemindedness. The primary reason for women's sterilization, hereditary feeblemindedness was often diagnosed as a result of women's allegedly "loose morals." Girls were nominated because they "gave themselves up to men without discretion," "flirted," were "wild," or had borne multiple illegitimate children – or in some cases just one illegitimate child. In such cases, the girl or woman's behavior implied an inability to fulfill the role of wife and mother properly and thus was considered an endangerment to the German nation as a whole. The residents of many delinquent girls' homes were examined and, when found morally lacking, sterilized.[131] Outside institutions, sterilized girls suffered a much higher incidence of rape because many men viewed them as "safe." The state's solution to this acknowledged problem was to institutionalize many, though not all, sterilized girls. In contrast, it was the inability to work or to hold a job that most often marked delinquent boys as incompetent. But whereas a letter from an employer could testify that a boy had become a good worker, no such letter could vindicate a girl. In fact, no one could testify that girls' innocence and morals were intact after a wild adolescence. Thus, while both boys and girls could protest a verdict of feeblemindedness,

---

129 SaM, Erbgesundheitsgericht, 8030.   130 Case from 1938, StaD, D 23 C, letter W, 2245.
131 See Bock, *Zwangssterilisation*, 392–3. This was a vicious circle, since institutionalized girls were less likely to have someone willing to protest for them. It is not clear how many sterilized girls were institutionalized for their protection.

girls found it more difficult to collect the evidence necessary to overturn a sterilization verdict.

Not everyone agreed with the state's right to intervene in families even in the name of improving the health of the *Volksgemeinschaft*. When in 1936 the *Amtsarzt* recommended fifteen-year-old Luise A. for sterilization because of her low IQ, her father objected, challenging both the law's "immoral" basis and the state's right to intervene in his family. Grounding his protest in his Catholicism, he argued that if they forbade Luise to marry he would comply, but sterilization was not an acceptable option. Moreover, he questioned the court's entire line of reasoning. He agreed with the Paderborn hereditary court's assessment that his daughter was not the same as all other children, but he asked: "Is everyone equally talented? How many inferior people are there?" He emphasized Luise's "ability to survive in life [and to] . . . do all house and farm work." Furthermore, he promised to keep her home with him and to ensure that she never married. The court could not abide Herr A.'s protest, however, maintaining that "this [sterilization] deal[t] with the nation's highest moral goals." Luise's father then escalated his objection. He wrote an irate letter in which he stated: "Today I voted for the Führer; the Führer promised me freedom and peace. Therefore I *demand* the *right* to decide about my child. Otherwise I will turn to the Führer." As Luise's father, he believed that he, not the state, had the right and responsibility to decide what was in his daughter's best interest, especially when his decision did not jeopardize the state's purposes. He also saw a distinction between the Führer's promise to support paternal authority and the authorities' implementation of the law. In the end, the court officials overruled him, and one month later Luise was sterilized.[132]

CONCLUSION

During both the Weimar and Nazi eras, motherhood was celebrated as women's most valuable contribution to society, and state officials created and sustained programs to honor, encourage, and assist mothers. Weimar officials saw in motherhood an institution that could simultaneously unite the divided nation and guarantee its survival. Alarmed by women's apparent refusal to bear children, Weimar politicians, doctors, and church leaders united in stressing the benefits of educating Germans of all classes about public health and the importance of family. Lawmakers agreed that creating state-supported programs to honor women would encourage more

132 Case from 1936, StaD D 23 C, letter A, 2269.

women to become mothers; however, they failed to reach consensus on the shape programs should take. As Cornelia Usborne has made eminently clear, the concept of motherhood took different forms in the minds of socialists, nationalists, feminists, and clerics. The disparate programs they proposed and supported reflected their diverse agendas. Throughout the era, moreover, Weimar efforts to raise the status of motherhood clashed with women's increasingly clear delineation of what constituted their best interests. As Atina Grossmann has argued, an ever-growing number of Weimar women regularly practiced some form of contraception. Moreover, Karen Hagemann has demonstrated that even among working-class women, efforts at "modernizing" and "rationalizing" everyday life – including family life – demanded family limitation.[133] In light of these modern influences on private behavior, no Mother's Day celebration or honorary cup could alter the sea change in attitudes. Although young women may have honored their own mothers on Mother's Day, they continued to marry comparatively late and to practice birth control, and they did not feel pressured – or inspired – to rush into motherhood themselves. For their part, Weimar officials never created a uniform policy toward mothers. Though they added to the ways in which mothers, in particular "child-rich" mothers, were honored, they did not sacrifice the sanctity (and privacy) of the family in the name of pursuing national interests. They also retained important constitutional and legislative language that opened more modern paths for women and that constituted alternatives to motherhood.

After 1933, the Nazis redefined motherhood according to racial, health, and social guidelines. They honored "racially pure," prolific mothers on Mother's Day and with the Honorary Cross for German Mothers. Simultaneously, however, Nazi authorities joined together to implement a vicious antinatalism, labeling certain women – and men – "undesirable" and sterilizing them to prevent the spread of their genes. Thus, by redefining what constituted a good mother according to racial ideology and preventing those they defined as unworthy from reproducing, Nazi authorities transformed motherhood from a private role into a public duty.

The implementation of the Nazis' newly delineated standards for the good mother proved difficult. Although social workers, mayors, welfare workers, and party leaders helped to collect the information on individual families, doctors bore the brunt of evaluating women and their families, and their evaluations usually carried the most weight. In many cases – perhaps

133 Hagemann, *Frauenalltag und Männerpolitik*, 642–3.

because of the more subjective nature of the information upon which they based their assessments – doctors' reports were more negative than others'. But doctors, overwhelmed by the responsibilities related to Nazi racial policy, did not always render accurate decisions or decisions that were in line with Nazi guidelines. Individuals who fell victim to incompetent medical opinions frequently succeeded in obtaining a second opinion to overrule the first. Social workers, whose access to private homes made them especially aware of mothers' and families' shortcomings, did not always use their access to families against individual mothers. Mayors and teachers, who tended to know families on a less intimate and more social level than doctors, tended to offer sympathetic readings of people's virtues. Even dedicated Nazi leaders manipulated policy at the expense of racial guidelines to fit current and changing national needs.

The Nazi program to honor mothers and raise the birthrate depended to a great extent on German women and their families. Irmgard Weyrather has asserted that "insofar as [they] did not in general reject [the mother cult] – German women (irrespective of whether they were aware of it) were drawn to it."[134] The evidence in this chapter suggests, however, that German women and their families proved an even greater obstruction to the smooth application of a uniform, racially guided policy designed to encourage prolific motherhood than state officials did. Although many women appreciated Hitler's promise to save women from employment and involvement in "dirty politics" and to honor them in their homes,[135] efforts by the Nazis both to encourage motherhood and to prevent it met with stiff opposition. In spite of financial and honorary incentives, the birthrate did not rise as much as the Nazis had hoped. The plan to test women's fertility before marriage fell on deaf ears as women astonished by the proposal continued to abide by their own traditional moral code. Throughout the era, SD and Sopade reports revealed that Germans scorned Nazi pronatalist policies and publicly expressed their opinion that "despite all the bonuses and supports every additional child means a lowering of the family's standard of living."[136] After the war, the situation worsened as the German birthrate fell precipitously. Most women avoided the "mother cult" by limiting their family size and managing their homes just as they had in earlier eras. Even if by receiving Mother Crosses and celebrating Mother's Day women lent credibility to the

---

134 Weyrather, *Muttertag und Mutterkreuz*, 219.
135 Bridenthal and Koonz, "Beyond Kinder, Küche, Kirche," 56.
136 *Sopade Berichte* 5, no. 6 (1938): 655.

Nazi regime, the data overwhelmingly reveal women's rejection of the cult of motherhood. Societal attitudes toward childbearing may have shifted, especially after the Nazis began to celebrate motherhood more publicly, but individual women's decisions regarding motherhood continued to be influenced by economic, social, and familial circumstances. To the extent that they could, many women who did not match the Nazi ideals stayed out of the public eye by refusing to apply for honors or assistance that would have brought them to the attention of authorities. And neither women nor their families hesitated to challenge state definitions of a "good mother" if they felt they had been judged unfairly.

4

Alleviating the Burdens of Motherhood

In 1940, when Frau Ludwig bore her fourth child, Uli, she was awarded the Honorary Cross for German Mothers. Shortly after her daughter's birth, a recent high school graduate was sent to her by the National Social-ist Women's Organization (NSF) to help Frau Ludwig with housework and childcare and fulfill her own *Pflichtjahr* (Service Year) obligations. Frau Ludwig, who had heeded her mother's advice – "Hilde, don't put your children in a kindergarten! You have them only so long for yourself" – was grateful for another pair of hands to help with her older children (ages five, three, and two). The teenager remained with the family during the war and helped when the fifth and sixth Ludwig children were born.[1]

Though she partook of some of the benefits the Nazi state extended to child-rich mothers, Frau Ludwig opted out of others: she attended no courses on mothering, never visited a recuperation home, and did not recall bringing any of her children to advice centers. And she did not otherwise recognize any state influence on her experience as a mother. Moreover, she categorically denied having had her children because the Nazis wanted large families, attributing her decision instead to a belief that "better situated people" needed to have big families for Germany's sake. Frau Ludwig told me that she fundamentally believed that mothering was a woman's private responsibility, but she did not turn away the help proffered to aid child-rich families.

Beyond the general agreement in both the Weimar and National Social-ist eras that childbearing and child rearing were a woman's responsibility, policymakers in both eras surmised that if motherhood were less burden-some, young women would be more likely to bear children and family size would increase. But no consensus existed about the cause of mothers'

1 Frau Ludwig, interview.

troubles or whether their goal was to shape motherhood or merely to support mothers. Were economic and social problems the root cause of mothers' troubles or did young mothers lack basic knowledge and maternal competence? Did women limit family size because they were selfish and unaware of the nation's needs, or because of the financial burden posed by children? Would an emphasis on "scientific motherhood" and rationalized household management solve the problem or did women need more traditional social and economic support?[2] Policymakers also realized that many women, like Frau Ludwig, viewed motherhood as a private affair in which state involvement was undesirable. And yet if such mothers stayed away, might not the programs look more like welfare than support intended for all mothers? Some people, especially in the National Socialist era, asked whether mothers should be forced to participate in a broad range of state programs.

This chapter explores the programs that Weimar and National Socialist policymakers designed to alleviate the burdens of motherhood and women's reception of the programs. The state helped women get medical assistance when their children were born, advised them on childcare and health, watched over children when mothers worked, and sent women to the countryside to rest and recuperate. Most state programs existed already during the Weimar era, but took on a new form when the Nazis added ideological guidelines.

PROGRAMS FOR MOTHERS DURING THE WEIMAR ERA

When the First World War ended, German policymakers recognized that innumerable crises plagued German families and began to debate what policy might help them. Two urgent problems seemed integrally connected: infant mortality and maternal morbidity and mortality. The infant mortality rate was so alarmingly high[3] that immediately after the war an atmosphere prevailed in which any "resistance to the creation of a public child welfare system might have seemed vaguely unpatriotic."[4] Although there was no clear consensus on the state's right to intervene in families, across the political

---

2 Some people viewed family as the central location of hygienic lifestyles and the housewife as the agent. Carola Sachße, *Siemens*, 30. See also Nolan, *Visions of Modernity*. Others even argued that motherhood had become internationally "rule-bound, embodying a body of scientific knowledge that had to be mastered." Turner, *Myths of Motherhood*, 233.

3 For each 1000 children born alive, 13.8 legitimate children and 25.1 illegitimate children died in 1918. *Statistisches Jahrbuch* 21 (1925).

4 Dickinson, "State, Family and Society," 615.

spectrum, religious and secular leaders agreed that maternal responsibility, education, and ability were central to reducing infant mortality and raising the birthrate. As one call to help mothers declared, "No mother was in a position to help her child, if she lacked the essentials herself."[5]

But how were mothers to be helped? Before effective policy could be drafted, the source of what ailed mothers had to be identified. Even on this question, disagreement was rife. Politicians on the Right blamed women's reliance on abortion for the increase in maternal mortality and morbidity, while those on the Left blamed poverty, poor housing, and ill health.[6] In light of this insoluble difference of opinion, politicians agreed to target the financial woes that forced many pregnant women and nursing mothers to work until late in their pregnancies and to resume work too soon after they gave birth. The Law for Maternity Benefits and Maternity Welfare (*Gesetz über Wochenhilfe und Wochenfürsorge*) of 16 September 1919 and 30 April 1920 extended the wartime maternity welfare benefits to women with incomes of less than 2,500 marks per year.[7] Eligible women received food and medical care before, during, and after delivery, money for delivery (100 marks), and additional money (256 marks) to compensate a midwife or doctor if necessary. To ensure that women had a respite from employment, the law also offered new mothers daily subsidies (*Wochengeld*) of at least 3 marks for up to ten weeks after delivery. Because breast-feeding improved an infant's chances of survival, women who breast-fed their babies received an extra daily bonus of 1.5 marks for twelve weeks.[8] As impressive as these maternity benefits were on paper, however, the success of the maternity welfare law was limited. The law excluded many needy women, since only women covered by insurance (or who had been covered by their husbands' insurance for six months prior to delivery) were eligible for state maternity benefits. The unstable economic situation in Germany meant that despite adjustments for inflation, by 1923 the payments fell far short of meeting women's needs, and many pregnant women were forced to continue to

---

5 Prussian Minister of Welfare, "Aufruf zur Gründung einer grossen, alles umfassenden Organisation zur Rettung der deutschen Jugend," received 12 February 1920, BaP, R 43 I, 835.

6 The maternal mortality rate increased from 21.9 per thousand in 1913 to 47.0 per thousand in 1923. Weindling, *Health, Race and German Politics*, 370.

7 Usborne, *Politics of the Body*, 47.

8 Reichstag Gesetz 26 September 1919/30 April 1920 (*Reichsgesetzblatt* 1920, 1069), BaP, Tape 36218, 9407. If the mother died during delivery or during the period of time covered by insurance, the money was paid to the person who assumed the child's care. Actual amounts varied depending on the cost of living in a particular area. Grundsätze über Voraussetzungen, Art und Maß der öffentlichen Fürsorge in Herford, Westfalen, 1 May 1931, StaD, M1 IS, 7.

work until just before they delivered their babies and to resume working very soon afterward.

Lawmakers across the political spectrum recognized the inadequacies of the Law for Maternity Benefits and Maternity Welfare. As a solution, the Social Democratic Party advocated German ratification of the Washington Convention of 1919, which called for paid maternity leave before and after delivery, but economic constraints in 1920 forced the postponement of ratification until 1925, when a report from the German Textile Workers' Union (Deutscher Textilarbeiter Verband) that detailed miscarriages, low birth weight babies, and complications in 70 percent of union members' pregnancies prompted the government to ratify the convention. As of July 1927, all female factory workers were supposed to receive maternity leave of eight to twelve weeks and two half-hour periods per day for breast-feeding. The 1927 law was the most far-reaching maternity benefit passed during the Weimar Republic, but it still left agricultural and household workers outside its scope.[9]

In Westphalia, an array of private organizations provided help at the time of delivery to mothers who were ineligible for state benefits. Some organizations, like the Catholic Mathildenstift, provided beds, medical support, and grants to women who could not afford to stay at home and who did not receive state benefits.[10] The Home Care Association of the Catholic Association (Hauspflegeverein im Katholischen Verein) also helped needy, expectant women in Westphalia regardless of religious denomination by providing in-home care, linens, clothing, and nurses to advise needy women.[11]

It soon became evident that maternity benefits alone would not reverse the demographic decline in Germany. Because Weimar lawmakers believed that "the business of procreation was politically far too important to be left to the individual,"[12] on 20 August 1920 the minister of welfare, Heinrich Hirtsiefer, proposed the creation of mother advice centers. Hirtsiefer worried that too many needy mothers did not receive aid because they did not understand their rights and that gaps between private organizations

9 For further discussion of the maternity benefits and maternity welfare, see Usborne, *Politics of the Body*, ch. 1.

10 The Catholic Mathildenstift took in 325 women between 1 January 1932 and 31 January 1932, of whom ten were given a free bed and many received financial aid. Katholischer Verein zur Pflegebedürftiger verheiraten Wöchnerinnen jeder Konfession, Jahresbericht, 1932, StaM, Armenkommission, 1339.

11 Report of Hauspflegeverein im Katholischen Verein zur Pflege bedürftiger Wöchnerinen jeder Konfession zu Münster, 23 June 1924, StaM, Stadtverordeten Regierung, 388.

12 Usborne, *Politics of the Body*, 35.

and the state led to poor distribution of resources. He further emphasized that although "the shortage of apartments, clothing and food affected the entire population, [it was] the mothers, limited by employment before and after delivery, and their infants [who] were the first victims of the sad economic conditions." The new mother advice centers would aim to "grasp the entire realm of welfare questions and find solutions" and to coordinate the efforts of doctors, midwives, social workers, the labor office, and private organizations. Advice center staff would inform pregnant women about the guidelines of the maternity welfare laws, provide advice to single and married mothers, and distribute financial and material support to needy families. The minister also made it the duty of the advice center staff to notify officials when requests for help overwhelmed the existing welfare agencies "so that the paths could be sufficiently expanded."[13]

Mother advice centers were not the invention of the minister of welfare. During the First World War, the Federation of German Women's Organizations had created mother advice centers to help needy families, and after 1918 the centers proliferated as both the Protestant and Catholic churches reached out to support needy mothers and their children.[14] But with state support, the number of clinics increased from 1,000 to 2,600 between 1920 and 1921, and by 1928 the number had nearly doubled again. Advice centers were far less expensive than treatment facilities, making them especially attractive for the state. In Westphalia, local governments and churches designed and established programs and clinics to help infants, children, and mothers.[15] The programs and personnel who staffed them varied tremendously. In the city of Hamm, the mother advice center was staffed by three active nurses; in Horde, by five social workers. In Münster, the Catholic Welfare Association (Katholische Fürsorgeverein) and the Protestant parish (Evangelische Kirchengemeinde) together ran an advice center for infants and children. Using the city's list of all newborns to locate clients, staff visited all new mothers, examined children, advised mothers, provided bed linens and infant clothes, and, to large families, distributed groceries. They also conducted house visits to identify and monitor troubled homes and,

---

13 Der Minister für Volkswohlfahrt Berlin, Runderlass über Mütter und Säuglingsfürsorge, 20 August 1920, StaP, Amt Neuhaus G 2, 844.

14 Christoph Sachße, *Mütterlichkeit als Beruf*, 164–70. Although the *Arbeiterwohlfahrt* and the Inner Mission ran mother advice clinics in some areas of Germany, I never found records of their activity or mention of them in the Westphalian archives.

15 Report from the Quakers' Aid Association (Vereinigung der Quakers Speisung), 1922, StaM, Stadverordneten Registeur, 388; Letters to the Regierungspräsident Arnsberg from Kreis Hamm, 27 November 1922; Horde, 27 November 1922; and Witten, 25 November 1922, SaM, Regierung Arnsberg 18, bd. 1.

in the most desperate cases, helped to place children in alternate homes.[16] While the Ministry of Welfare encouraged the creation of advice centers throughout Germany in 1920 and established some regulations for how they should function, the state neither sought uniformity among the clinics nor committed to finance them.[17] Rather, advice centers were meant to supplement the already existing welfare and youth departments without draining state coffers. How exactly this was to be done was "left to the discretion of the individual towns."[18]

For the duration of the Weimar era, then, local authorities debated how to create, finance, and administer advice centers. The *Regierungspräsident* of Arnsberg strictly opposed making the youth departments responsible for all health care, since he assumed a lay administration (*Laienverwaltung*) would be unprepared to grasp or address "the most important aspect of human life encompassed by welfare." He believed that only those with the combined knowledge of nursing lounges, infant homes, day cares, and school health care could run the mother advice centers.[19] On 1 April 1931, the Bielefeld youth department turned over control of both the infant welfare and mother advice centers to the Central Welfare Department (Zentrales Gesundheitsamt des Wohlfahrtsamts).[20] In some rural towns where transportation posed a serious problem, authorities chose not to establish advice centers.[21] In other towns, authorities hesitated to do so because local doctors ran private advice centers or infant advice centers that doubled as clinics for mothers.[22] In most places, however, doctors visited advice centers on a regular basis, but social workers and nurses provided most of the advice and identified women in need. In many Westphalian towns, religious organizations, including the Catholic Association for Girls, Women, and Children,[23] the Protestant Women's Aid Society, and the Association of Patriotic

---

16 StaM, Armenkommission, 1614.

17 Der Minister für Volkswohlfahrt, Runderlass über Mütter und Säuglingsfürsorge, 20 August 1920, StaP, Amt Neuhaus G 2, 844.

18 Administratively, advice centers were classified variously as affiliated with youth departments, legal advice centers, vocational guardianships, and county welfare departments (*Kreisfürsorge*). Runderlass über Mütter- und Säuglingsfürsorge, Der Minister für Volkswohlfahrt, Berlin, 20 August 1920; Letter Regierungspräsident Arnsberg to Oberpräsidium, 11 August 1922, both in SaM, Oberpräsidium Münster, 6034.

19 Regierungspräsident Arnsberg to Oberpräsidium, 11 August 1922, SaM, Oberpräsidium Münster, 6034.

20 Jahresbericht des städtischen Jugendamtes Bielefeld, 1 April 1930–31 March 1931, StaD, M1 IM, 842.

21 This problem continued to plague authorities during the Nazi era. Amt Neuhaus Report, 30 November 1920, StaP, Amt Neuhaus G 2, 844.

22 Report from Regierungspräsident Minden to Herrn Preussischen Minister des Innern in Berlin, June 1934, StaD, Dezernat 24 D 1, 211.

23 Application for financial aid, 20 January 1924, StaM, Stadtverordneten, 388.

Women, ran their own advice centers. Though there were striking differences in the kind of help offered by advice centers and in the ideology on which they were based, by 1928 most cities in Westphalia had some form of center run either by the county welfare department, a private organization, or a church. Herford established a city mother advice center only in 1929.

Because Weimar state authorities backed the creation of advice centers but never dictated how they should function, advice center staff faced the question of how to attract mothers and who exactly should benefit from the services they offered. The minister of welfare implied that the advice centers' first goal should be to help needy mothers, but he also emphasized that advice centers should be "official" (*behördlich*) in nature to avoid getting caught up in the "damaging pettiness" that might discourage the attendance of middle-class women, "whose inclusion was urgently desired" and who might be deterred from attending a "welfare office for the poor" (*Armenamt*).[24] As individual women decided for themselves when to seek aid, some sought out the centers and made enthusiastic use of their offerings. But many more mothers turned to the centers for help only when they were truly desperate. The Patriotic Women's Association had very well-attended advice centers when it distributed supplementary coupons for groceries and nursing certificates that qualified women for breast-feeding subsidies. Later, when the same benefits became available from individual midwives, attendance at the advice centers fell so precipitously that the organization had to shorten the centers' hours.[25] Though the advice center staff realized many needy mothers received no help, they had no mandate to force women to attend.

Mother advice centers, which stood at the crossroads of the expanding state welfare program and an older private system of social aid, put the question of the state's willingness to intervene in families – and whether it had a right to do so – in stark relief. Advice centers provided women with material aid and advice to raise their children. State maternity benefits afforded more women medical assistance at birth and brought more women to the attention of health professionals. But neither program ensured that all needy children came to the attention of state authorities. It was children who most poignantly forced politicians to address the issue of state intervention in families. Not until 1922, and then only after heated debate did the Reichstag ratify the Reich Youth Welfare Law (*Reichsjugendwohlfahrtsgesetz*, RJWG)

---

24 Der Minister für Volkswohlfahrt, Berlin, Runderlass über Mütter- und Säuglingsfürsorge, 20 August 1920, StaP, Amt Neuhaus G 844.
25 Tätigkeitsbericht der Vaterländische Frauenverein, 1921, LSVA, CI, 764.

which gave the state the right and responsibility to support German youth. Newly founded youth departments employed a growing number of professional social workers to monitor children's well-being. Doctors employed in local health departments and mother advice clinics raised the caliber of care by bringing medical supervision to all children. The law encouraged midwives to visit unmarried pregnant women before and after delivery and required them to report all miscarriages. They visited mothers of legitimate children only if the child was at risk physically. Teamwork between physicians, case workers, nursing staff (*Pflegepersonen*), and midwives brought support within the reach of many needy families for the first time. All parts of this system increased the state's opportunities to observe families. Gradually, the pieces of a comprehensive state system were put into place.

Greater contact with mothers and children allowed social workers and doctors to develop a standard by which to assess whether mothers were raising their children "properly." One early problem was the perception that mothers spent maternity welfare benefits irresponsibly. Rather than base support for pregnant women and nursing mothers on a minimum income, in 1924 it was linked to neediness as determined by social workers.[26] In 1926, the Detmold magistrate of the welfare department declared that since mothers might use their maternity benefits money improperly, he was inclined to pay them in kind with food and clothes. In more serious cases of suspected impecuniousness, he proposed giving the money to a social worker, who could monitor the way it was spent.[27] As social workers' scrutiny of mothers increased, many mothers began to question whether social workers represented their best interests and hesitated to participate in programs designed to help them. In 1926, one caseworker made a proposal for greater maternal surveillance that suggests how intrusive social workers' surveillance could be: "After discussing it with the department doctor I propose that in order to...increase the effectiveness still further, [and to ensure] that all children are brought to the mother advice centers, payment of maternity welfare be made dependent on [mothers'] bringing children to the mother advice centers regularly. This would offer the opportunity to influence the mothers repeatedly so that they feed, care for, and raise their children in the *right way*."[28] Some social workers, frustrated by their inability to improve their clients' behavior, criticized not just their clients' lifestyles and need but also "the bureaucratization and juridification of the welfare

---

26 Letter Kreiswohlfahrtsamt, 19 May 1924, StaP, Amt Neuhaus G 619.
27 Magistrat der Fürsorge Amt Detmold, 16 August 1926, StaD, D 106 Detmold, 277. See also Magistrat der Fürsorge Amt Brake, 3 September 1926, StaD, D 106 Detmold, 277.
28 Schwester R. to M. M., 10 March 1926, StaD, D 106 Detmold, A 277. Emphasis mine.

system, the neutrality of public welfare, and the penetration of parliamentary politics into the welfare and youth welfare offices."[29]

Although there were social workers who continued to emphasize the importance of relationships with clients and the advisory nature of their work, others became more receptive to racial and eugenic thought. An unusual set of service instructions (*Dienstanweisungen*) for the social workers in the district of Brake from 1925 suggested that children and mothers should receive different treatment based on their "worth." The instructions declared that the purpose of the mother advice center was "to provide information and advice about infant care and nutrition for mothers whose small children are not hereditarily ill." In contrast, small children with hereditary illnesses were to be sent directly to the doctor's office.[30] Although the distinction may well have been intended to ensure that children with serious health problems received extra care, the chosen terminology hinted at a more sinister reason for the differential treatment. Eugenics was not yet widespread (or state-mandated, as it would become after 1933), but it is evident here and elsewhere that eugenic concepts had begun to creep subtly into public discussion.[31] Social workers were held to professional standards of silence, privacy, and impeccable (*einwandfrei*) behavior and required to avoid bringing attention to "unworthy" families, but the labeling of children and mothers hinted at what Paul Weindling has called an inadequate "protection of the individual when confronted by the guardians of state welfare."[32]

As it became clear that advice centers and maternity welfare alone were insufficient to reverse demographic stagnation or restore traditional gender roles, many bourgeois politicians came to believe they faced an attitude problem: young women demonstrated less interest in becoming wives and mothers than they once had.

They argued that this dangerous trend might be halted and women's widespread rejection of the "career" of motherhood rectified if women received proper training in household management and motherhood. Social Democrats, bourgeois feminists, religious groups, and organized housewives agreed that educating girls to be efficient housewives and "modern" mothers would strengthen the nation.[33] They believed that girls' lack of household skills hurt children and damaged the "entire national economy," which

---

29 Hong, *Welfare, Modernity*, 179.

30 Dienstanweisung für Fürsorgerinnen in Verwaltungsamtbezirk Brake, Lippische Verwaltungsamt, Bezirksfürsorgestelle, 28 April 1925, StaD, D 102 Lemgo, 30.

31 For more on the history of eugenics during the Weimar era, see Peukert, "Genesis of the Final Solution."

32 Weindling, *Health, Race and German Politics*, 348.

33 Nolan, *Visions of Modernity*, 206ff.; Harvey, *Youth and the Welfare State*, 82–5.

Dance, music, and cabaret were among the controversial activities that for some represented thrilling, modern opportunities for women and for others seemed to distract young women from motherhood, putting the nation at risk. Courtesy of Getty Images.

depended on "the punctual and methodical work of mothers."[34] Training young women – especially from working-class backgrounds, where girls' lack of knowledge of home economics was believed to be particularly severe – promised to rectify the perceived deterioration of morals, make motherhood and housework seem more attractive, and ensure the future of the race.[35] Many people argued that the "future of the race required the successful transformation of the working-girl into a thrifty housewife, conscientious mother, and custodian of the health and morals of future generations."[36] Whether the "spirit" women needed to learn was "shorthand for the traditional womanly virtues of moral rectitude, diligence, self-sacrifice, and nurturance" or the "domestic virtues plus nationalism" remained open to debate.[37] It was clear, however, that the ideal 1920s housewife was to be different from her predecessors.

34 Advertisement for Mütterschulung und Mütterdienst, ca. 1932, EVHA, 118–2.
35 Harvey, *Youth and the Welfare State*, 33.
36 Ibid.
37 Nolan, *Visions of Modernity*, 213.

The belief that women needed to be trained as mothers led to a proliferation of religious and secular vocational schools for women. In some cities, including Hamburg, city officials made attendance at vocational schools mandatory for unskilled girls, who were trained in a curriculum of basic home economics.[38] In Westphalia, the curriculum varied, but all the courses emphasized infant care, health care for the sick, and national birth and population policy. In addition to these standard topics, the Protestant Women's Aid Society courses also emphasized Luther's role as the founder of the Protestant family.[39] In 1920, the high mayor of Münster, responding to calls that society needed "to care not only for the scientific training of women and girls, but also for the domestic areas and to prepare them for their work in family and career," asked a Catholic order, the Sisters of Providence, to found a home economics school for women. In 1921, what began as a one-year women's school was expanded into a two-year school and then in 1926 into a three-year school – the first upper-level women's school (*Frauenoberschule*) in Prussia with financial backing from the state.[40] Some large companies also sponsored mother courses for their employees' wives, trusting that better wives and mothers would in turn make better workers.[41] In many cities, youth department employees and social workers also received extra training in the legal protection of expectant and nursing mothers.[42]

Household and motherhood training could not alter the fact that many German girls and women worked outside the home or that the nature of women's work was changing. After the First World War, the number of women employed in agriculture and domestic service dropped significantly and the number in white collar jobs rose. The rationalization and mechanization of business led to the creation of new jobs in such fields as typing and bookkeeping, while the consumer boom created myriad positions for women as sales clerks. Even within industry, women's work shifted as mechanization opened up some previously male fields in the electrical, iron, and metal industries to women.[43] Though women earned less than half as much as their male counterparts, many families depended on their contributions for survival. For working women, household responsibilities

38 Harvey, *Youth and the Welfare State*, 83–4.
39 Advertisement, "Ferien für unsere Mütter!" Klara Schlossmann-Lönnies, ca. 1931, EVHA, 118–2.
40 Welzenberg, *Die Westfälische Provinz*, 68–9. By 1932, fifty-four mother schools had been founded. Denkschrift des Mütterdienstes der Evangelischen Reichsfrauenhilfe, 1933/34, BaP, R15.01, 26330.
41 Nolan, *Visions of Modernity*, 218.
42 Kursus des Landesjugendamtes Westfalen und des Städtischen Jugendamtes Bielefeld zur Fortbildung von Beamten und Fürsorgerinnen des Regierungsbezirks Minden in der Jugendwohlfahrtspflege, 25–6 May 1925, SaM, Oberpräsidium Medizinalwesen, 6034.
43 Winkler, *Frauenarbeit im Dritten Reich*, 17–25.

constituted a double burden. Bourgeois feminists, Social Democrats, and especially doctors stressed that even in the aggregate, maternity bene-fits, medical care, and education could not eradicate the exhausting real-ity of motherhood for many women. As a result, Weimar authorities, religious and secular, designed three different programs for mothers of small children: kindergartens for working mothers, recuperation homes for fatigued and ill mothers, and household help for pregnant and "child-rich" mothers.

Kindergartens were not a Weimar invention. According to Ann Taylor Allen, the kindergarten movement, aimed at caring for three- to six-year-old preschool children for half or full days, had grown during the second half of the nineteenth century in response "to the class conflict caused by the decline and impoverishment of the small-town artisan class, the growth of an urban proletariat, and the economic crises of the 1840s."[44] In 1919, a national school conference convened to discuss the future of kindergartens. The Socialists present argued that kindergartens should be public and universally available on a voluntary basis. They were outnumbered by the religious and political conservatives, who opposed expanding public kindergartens because "the right and duty of raising children of preschool age belongs basically to the family."[45] As a result, instead of being incorporated into the state educational system, kindergartens remained under the umbrella of the welfare department.

During the 1920s, many Westphalians recognized the important function kindergartens served for working mothers and supported them. Yet the capacity of kindergartens did not increase during the Weimar era, and many working mothers were forced to find "a relative, friend or neighbor, who would watch and care for children in return for a nominal compensation" and who, if well-chosen, would offer a "thankful and beneficial sphere of influence."[46] The predominantly female teachers of the kindergartens believed that getting children off the street and into "healthy," supervised environments would improve children's health and physical safety and help "to raise a new generation of Germans as citizens, not as subjects."[47] City authorities in Unna applied to the *Oberpräsidium* for money to create a kindergarten in a largely working-class neighborhood populated with child-rich families who "because of health, social or educational reasons . . . are not

---

44 Ann Taylor Allen, *Feminism and Motherhood*, 60.
45 Die Reichsschulkonferenz, 1921, 692, quoted in Ann Taylor Allen, "Children," 31.
46 Niederschrift über die Verhandlung des Fürsorgeausschusses des Landkreises Münster, 19 November 1922, StaM, Kreisarchiv B, 298; Hagemann, *Frauenalltag und Männerpolitik*, 428.
47 Ann Taylor Allen, *Feminism and Motherhood*, 63–5.

in a position to care for their preschool age children sufficiently." Making a strong plea to nationalism, they emphasized that the kindergarten would "be important for the recovery and reconstruction of our *Volksleben*."[48] Some large companies ran their own kindergartens.[49] Private financing also supported other kindergartens, like one in Bielefeld for poor children run by a deaconess and financed by donations from a wealthy citizen.[50] Cities, churches, and private organizations all ran kindergartens, and though their ideological basis varied, the state supported many financially.[51]

If kindergartens provided a safe haven for the children of working mothers, in the eyes of religious and secular Weimar authorities they also constituted an essential part of a multilayered welfare system designed to further the national goals of lowering infant mortality and raising the birthrate. State authorities set safety and health guidelines and sometimes helped to bring kindergartens up to standards.[52] In 1931, state assessors denied a permit to a kindergarten in Freudenberg because the building conditions did not meet standards. The mayor protested that the kindergarten which had cared for children since 1864 was essential "especially for mothers who are unable to dedicate themselves sufficiently to the education and supervision of their smaller children." Because the town of Freudenberg could not afford to improve the kindergarten, the national government contributed to bring the kindergarten to national standards.[53] The state did not always step in with financial aid, however. State regulations called for doctors to visit kindergartens regularly to examine children. When the pastor at the Protestant kindergarten in Siegen protested that they were unable to provide medical supervision for the children, the mayor insisted that "the Protestant parish find doctors . . . who [could] assume responsibility for examining the

---

48 Verein von Velsen-Stiftung to Oberpräsidium, 1 February 1930, SaM, Oberpräsidium Medizinal-wesen, 6275.
49 Gutehoffnungshütte in Oberhausen is one example. Siemens in Berlin also offered health care for the children of men who worked at Siemens. Nolan, *Visions of Modernity*, 218; Carola Sachße, *Siemens*, 219–20.
50 When the purchasing power of the money was greatly reduced in the inflation, another resident who had immigrated to the United States donated more money to restart the kindergarten. Report, Städtisches Jugendamt Bielefeld, 1 April 1930–March 1931, StaD, M1 IM, 842.
51 Verein von Velsen-Stiftung to Oberpräsidium, 1 February 1930, SaM, Oberpräsidium Medizinal-wesen, 6275; Jahresbericht Städtisches Jugendamt Bielefeld, 1 April 1930–31 March 1931, StaD, M1 IM, 842.
52 In 1930, the minister of welfare demanded "that every kindergarten be examined by the state for safety at least every three years, more often if necessary." Preußische Minister für Volkswohlfahrt, Berlin, 2 December 1930, SaM, Oberpräsidium Medizinalwesen, 5873; Bürgermeister Freudenberg, application for support, 20 November 1931, SaM, Kreis Siegen Kreis Wohlfahrt, 11.
53 Bürgermeister Freudenberg, application for support, 20 November 1931, SaM, Kreis Siegen Kreis Wohlfahrt, 11.

children." He could not "imagine that a Protestant doctor [would] refuse this small request from his church."[54]

The state's aim throughout was to improve children's health and well-being. Increasingly, kindergarten teachers made house visits to check on children's home environments, held parent and mother evenings, and met individually with parents. In some cases, they even exchanged information about families with youth leaders to better meet the needs of children and families. These meetings were thought to have the added benefit that "the processing and reporting about the toddler's inner and outer world done by the responsible teacher" would "better enabl[e] mothers to perform the difficult task of raising their children with a happy spirit."[55] Many mothers saw in their child's kindergarten teacher someone who could support and advise them about their children. At the same time, meetings with kindergarten teachers gave parents a greater opportunity to influence their children's care. Although this network of observations and contacts with families did allow teachers to be more helpful to mothers, not all kindergarten teachers looked favorably on parental participation.[56] Some also felt a new level of authority in their ability to intervene "when the mother neglects childrearing."[57]

Government officials respected the fact that kindergartens benefited the children of working mothers. They also appreciated the opportunity to monitor children's health that kindergartens presented them. But they became greatly alarmed when they discovered that kindergartens designed to help working mothers generally closed during school vacations, since this was precisely when the demand for childcare was at its greatest. In 1921, the Reich labor minister requested that childcare and day care centers stay open during vacations.[58]

Officials worried not only about whether mothers' needs were being met but also about whether they were using the programs exactly as they had been intended. Some felt that mothers were taking advantage of the kindergartens to run errands, rest, or complete other tasks more easily done alone, and they were determined to prevent kindergartens from replacing mothers or diminishing mothers' responsibility for their children. One government report in 1922 stated, "It has repeatedly been observed that

54 Oberbürgermeister to Pfarrer Dr. Schmidt, 16 November 1932, SaM, Kreis Siegen Kreis Wohlfahrt, 11.
55 Minister für Volkswohlfahrt Regierungspräsident Münster, 12 April 1924, StaM, Kreisausschuss Amt 43 E, 292.
56 Hagemann, *Frauenalltag und Männerpolitik*, 427.
57 Niederschrift über die Verhandlung des Fürsorgeausschusses des Landkreises Münster, 19 November 1922, StaM, Kreisarchiv B, 298.
58 Der Reichsarbeitsminister, Berlin, 25 May 1921, SaM, Kreis Siegen Kreis Wohlfahrt, 13.

mothers are being released from their responsibilities unnecessarily and as a result are growing accustomed to giving up to others the duty of watching their children in school free time."[59]

Although kindergartens relieved many mothers during the workday, they did not eliminate the burden of housework and child care. Many people continued to worry that "mothers and housewives, many of whom are overworked, suffer[ed] the most."[60] As a result, a variety of organizations, including both the Catholic and Protestant churches and city welfare offices, sponsored "mother recuperation" (*Müttererholung*) programs. The Protestant Women's Aid Society began its mother recuperation program in Westphalia immediately after the First World War, sending women to rented resort homes. The number of mothers it sent increased steadily from 25 in 1921 to 300 in 1925, 1,800 in 1930, and finally 2,400 in 1932.[61] The cost of the health spas varied, but women unable to afford to pay their way could receive subsidies.[62] In 1931, the Catholic Church established its own program for providing recuperation for needy "child-rich" mothers under the auspices of Caritas, the Landesfürsorgeverband (regional welfare association), and the German Catholic Women's Organization.[63] In groups of thirty, mothers would "vacation" in a home that provided physical and emotional recuperation under the leadership of dependable and knowledgeable staff. Although each organization selected mothers by means of its own criteria, all targeted exhausted women with four or more pre-school children for relief.[64] Women typically stayed at the recuperation homes between ten and forty days, during which time the sending organization made arrangements for their children at home, enlisting the help of relatives when possible. If no appropriate relatives could be found to run the household and care for the children, neighbors or other women associated with the sending organization stepped in. Children who also needed recuperation were sent at the same time as their mothers, though every effort was made to send mothers and children to separate homes to ensure that the mothers could rest.[65]

---

59 Der Regierungspräsident Arnsberg to Oberpräsidium, 11 August 1922, SaM, Oberpräsidium Medizinalwesen, 6043.

60 Regierungspräsident Minden, 27 May 1932, StaD, M1 IM, 842.

61 Report of Mutterdienst des Westfälischen Frauenhilfe, EVHA, 118–2C.

62 Kreisausschuß des Landkreises Münster Abt. Wohlfahrt to Amt Roxel, 30 April 1929, StaM, Amt Roxel A Fach 33, 4.

63 Katholischer Deutschen Frauenbund, Zweigverein Münster to Wohlfahrtsamt der Stadt Münster, 7 July 1931, StaM, Armenkommission, 856.

64 In Münster, the number of women who benefited from these programs increased from 640 women in 1928 to 969 in 1930. The population of Münster was 116,040 in 1928. *Provinzialhauptstadt Münster, Statistischer Bericht über die Zeit v. 1938–1948*, hrsg. von Statistischen Amt der Stadt Münster, 18.

65 "Ferien für unsere Mütter!" Klara Schlossmann-Lönnies, ca. 1931, EVHA, 118–2.

Even as late as 1931, when Germany's economy was at its worst, mother recuperation programs continued.[66] Rather than discontinue programs, authorities screened applicants more carefully and reduced the length of stay. The Münster State insurance reduced the length of retreats from six weeks to three but reassured the authorities in Amt Dützen, "Our experience reveals that a shorter retreat is adequate to rebuild mothers weakened by everyday burdens and the present economic misery." They also restricted retreats to women whose husbands were insured and who had four children under sixteen years of age.[67] When insurance companies and welfare funds ran out of money, churches stepped in to alleviate the burden. The Protestant Women's Aid Society advertised its program as providing essential help in difficult times: "When the work never stops, when the money never stretches to the end of the week. When the children never cease to ask questions, when the unemployed husband's complaints never subside, when the mending basket needs attention, when during the washing, the back hurts so badly – then hundreds of thousands of German mothers of all classes think: 'Oh how wonderful – a day just to lie peacefully in the sun with nothing to do but think about beautiful, sunny rest!'"[68]

Although sending mothers to recuperation homes did not permanently change women's lives, many women savored the retreats and the state's generosity. Together with the many other maternal support programs created by the Weimar state, recuperation homes reflected the widely held belief that mothers were key to restoring and strengthening the German state. As the depression swept Germany, many social services had to be curtailed and the belief that what resources existed should be saved for the worthy grew more prevalent. Though this call was not uniformly heeded under Weimar, after 1933 it changed the shape of all state programming for mothers.

RESHAPING PROGRAMS FOR MOTHERS, 1933–1945

From their first day in power, the Nazi leadership touted motherhood as the most important role for "healthy" women and considered "protecting the pregnant mother and the unborn child one of [the state's] . . . most essential responsibilities."[69] The National Socialists expanded, supplemented, and

---

66 Der Landeshauptmann der Provinz Westfalen Landesfürsorgeverband to Amt Dützen, 6 May 1931, Kommunal Archiv Minden (KaM), Amt Dützen, 1808.

67 In 1936, when economic conditions improved, this was reduced to three children at home. Münster Landesversicherungsanstalt Westfalen to Amt Dützen, 21 February 1936, KaM, Amt Dützen, 1808.

68 "Ferien für unsere Müttern!" EVHA, 118–2. In 1934, the one hundred mothers they sent to one spa averaged five children each, and thirty-four had unemployed husbands. Ibid., 118–2a.

69 Reichsminister des Innern to alle Regierungen, 2 November 1933, BaP, R15.01, 26479.

focused Weimar era programs, modifying the Maternity Benefit Law of 1927, for example, to give mothers more time off from work and restrict the work of pregnant women.[70] In contrast to their Weimar predecessors, however, the Nazis devised their programs with an eye specifically to National Socialist ideology. They made clear that they only intended to support mothers who met their racial, social, or biological guidelines. Women past child-bearing age, Jewish women, and other women deemed "unhealthy" were excluded from programs directed toward mothers during the Nazi era.[71]

The Nazis created the NSV Mother and Child Relief Agency (Hilfswerk Mutter und Kind, HMK), an organization dedicated specifically to mothers and children.[72] Upon its creation, the Reich minister for press and propaganda announced the agency's goal: "To stand by a German mother in physical, spiritual, or emotional need [and] to help a hereditarily healthy [*erbgesund*] German child to healthy development."[73] The agency tried to create a ubiquitous presence throughout Germany by establishing aid centers (*Hilfsstellen*) that provided family social services. By 1935, the Nazis had founded 18,195 aid centers, and by 1939 almost 30,000 centers provided educational, health, and economic aid to families.[74] The Nazi leadership repeatedly stressed to all local party leaders that mothers needed to be treated with special care to ensure their continued dedication to the National Socialist movement.[75] Women's sacrificial role as the bearers of children for the German nation framed Nazi ideological attitudes toward them. One contemporary publication stated: "To be a mother means giving life to healthy children, bringing to fruition all the physical, mental, and spiritual faculties in these children and creating a home for them that represents a nurturing center for *völkisch*-racial culture. It means realizing in the community of the family a part of the ideal *Volksgemeinschaft* and giving to the nation, in grown children, a full development of the *Volk* in body and soul who are able to

---

70 Women were entitled to maternity benefits from the sick insurance fund six weeks before and after delivery, and they could receive more if the birth had entailed complications. Pregnant women had the right to refuse to work more than forty-eight hours a week, and work was forbidden immediately after delivery. Kirkpatrick, *Nazi Germany*, 226.

71 *Sopade Berichte*, 4 (1937), 1314–15.

72 The NSV Mother and Child Relief Agency was one branch of the NSV. The NSV was founded in September 1931 as a registered *Verein* with a local presence and a conflicted status in the party. In March 1933, Erich Hilgenfeldt was appointed leader of the NSV and given Goebbels's support to publicize the organization. In May, the NSV was officially declared a party organization and introduced nationwide. Sachße and Tennestedt, *Der Wohlfahrtsstaat im Nationalsozialismus*, 111.

73 Ibid., 128.

74 Arbeitsrichtlinien für die Hilfstellen Mutter und Kind, BaK, NS37, 1031; Sachße and Tennestedt, *Der Wohlfahrtsstaat im Nationalsozialismus*, 129.

75 Rundschreiben des Gauorganisationsames Nr. 16/35, 27 February 1935, StaD, L113, 255 bd. 1.

cope with life and face it boldly, who are aware of their responsibility to the *Volk* and race, and who will lead their nation onward and upward."[76]

Integral to the Nazi system was the centralization of all programs so that genetic, social, and ideological guidelines could be applied uniformly. During the first meeting of the NSV and the Protestant Women's Aid Society, the NSV authorities announced, "The counseling of mothers and infants, which up until now has been [the] responsibility of the confessional organizations, must now be placed in the hands of the NSV."[77] They created a hierarchical system of informants, each of whom contributed to identifying needy mothers and children. Aid center directors and neighborhood leaders (*Blockwalter* and *Zellenwalter*) widened the scope of information available to the state to evaluate mothers. HMK employees were expected to cooperate with social workers, kindergarten teachers, and doctors and to use house visits as an opportunity "to cast a first glance into the economic and personal relationships of the family."[78] From the outset, then, National Socialist programs were intended to be interventionist.

Along with the new degree of intervention, Nazi authorities applied racial guidelines to all programs for mothers. They explicitly stated their intention to help only "worthy" mothers and children at Nazi aid centers. Doctors, social workers, and other state agents determined worthiness based on their observations and interactions with mothers and their children. The Nazis planned to replace the vast number of private and state programs with one ideologically driven, state-run organization. Churches were left with the responsibility of caring for the "unworthy."

Nazi policymakers hoped to provide long-term medical, nutritional, and economic aid to all mothers, children, and families identified as worthy. HMK advice centers offered mothers direct material support, aided unemployed fathers in job searches, located apartments for homeless families, and organized food and clothing for infants and children.[79] In conjunction with the health department, they organized programs to send children to the countryside for health spas, ran kindergartens, and selected which mothers to send to recuperation homes. Finally, the HMK provided infant welfare centers to care for children whose mothers were ill or pregnant or whose home environment "threaten[ed] the child's survival."[80]

76 Marie Tscherning, "Die Erziehung unserer weiblichen Jugend," quoted in Klinksiek, *Die Frau im NS-Staat*, 84.
77 Vorsitzend Fischer, Siegen Stadtverband der Frauenhilfe to Pastor Johannes Werth, 7 June 1934, EHVA, 118–0.
78 Arbeitsrichtlinien für die Hilfswerk Mütter und Kind, BaK, NS37, 1031.
79 Frau Paula Siber to Bericht, November 1933, BaP, R15.01, 26331.
80 Dezernent für Gesundheitsfürsorge, 17 June 1933, BaP, R15.01, 26478.

Paramount among the HMK's responsibilities was to help pregnant and "child-rich" mothers in bearing and raising their children. To make this possible, NSV officials established advice centers throughout Westphalia, beginning with 383 in 1934 and running 635 by 1939. In 1935, the Gau leadership proudly proclaimed that 114,000 mothers had visited mother advice centers in Westphalia.[81] Nazi leaders emphasized the importance of the services offered even before delivery, which aimed to "awake[n] joy toward childbearing so that pregnancy would not be experienced as a burden" and to teach mothers how to raise their children independent of state support. The HMK staff prepared women for their "careers" as mothers – careers "that should not weaken them."[82]

Beyond the material, financial, and medical advice offered at advice centers, the Nazis also viewed the centers as agents for inculcating Nazi ideology and infused racial hygienic thought into all areas of clinic life.[83] Racially inspired pronatalism constituted one "essential psychological issue" (*seelische Kernfrage*) that guided work at the mother advice centers. Leaders informed mothers of every "child's right to siblings . . . because it needs them," arguing, "By the age of six the only child is, as a rule, already so badly developed that it has substantial difficulties finding its rightful place in the school class." Furthermore, the Nazis contended that children did not thrive in "small families." Only families with four or more children could offer the optimal environment for children, they claimed, "since where a boy is faced with several sisters, if he is a real boy it is easy for him to become isolated from his own play companions." "Single daughters," they added, "face a similar fate."[84] Hitler himself also emphasized the importance of large families: "The essential thing for the future is to have lots of children. Everybody should be persuaded that a family's life is assured only when it reaches upwards of four children – I should even say, four sons."[85]

The degree to which the Nazis succeeded in centralizing aid to mothers was inconsistent. Though the *Regierungspräsident* in Minden reported in June 1934 that all local advice centers had been united with the NSV, local reports paint a different picture. NSV guidelines mandated that the new advice centers be run by a doctor or trained welfare worker, but especially in smaller towns, where doctors were already burdened by the responsibilities affiliated

81 Münsterischer Anzeiger, Abendausgabe vom 6 June 1936, quoted in Kappelhoff, "Organisation und Tätigkeit," 74.
82 Reichsminister des Innern to alle Regierungen, 2 November 1933, BaP, R15.01, 26479.
83 Hansen, *Wohlfahrtspolitik im NS-Staat*, 300–301.
84 NSVolksdienst Organ des Hauptamtes für Volkswohlfahrt in der Reichsleitung der NSDAP, July 1937, BaP, 62 DAF 3, 19521.
85 Hitler, 19 October 1941, Trevor-Roper, *Hitler's Table Talk*, 74.

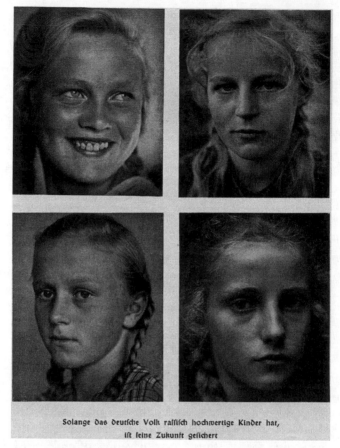

Solange das deutsche Volk raffisch hochwertige Kinder hat,
ist keine Zukunft gesichert

"As long as the German Volk has racially worthy children, its future is guaranteed." These four girls with their long, braided hair depicted the ideal girlhood. *Volk und Rasse,* June 1942.

with their role in policing "racial health," this level of staffing proved difficult to reach.[86] Even in Lübbecke, where the strong Nazi presence in the city hierarchy lent support to the expansion of the new mother aid system, authorities were unable to provide sufficient supervisory staff.[87] The new goal of monitoring all families put significant additional pressure on clinic

86 Arbeitsrichtlinien für die Hilfswerk Mutter und Kind, BaK, NS37, 1031.
87 Regierung Minden, report about Kreis Lübbecke to Herrn Preussischen Minister des Innern, June 1934. Similarly, despite noting a deterioration in the quality of the food children brought to school and in the children's clothes, the center in the city of Wiedenbruck was forced to curtail its hours in 1933. Amtsarzt Weidenbruck to Regierung Minden, 10 February 1933, both in StaD, Dezernat 24 D1, 211.

staff, who had been shorthanded even before the new guidelines were issued. In Lübbecke, where a trained community nurse had visited all newborns to advise mothers about proper nutrition and infant care, the National Socialist guidelines forced the addition of volunteer staff, who were inconsistent in the care they provided. The Nazis warned that volunteers "must be forbidden from any health counseling" and limited what volunteers could do.[88] As a result, some families were compelled to repeat their stories for both volunteers and social workers, an imposition that caused considerable distress. As the Nazis limited the churches' influence in advice centers, some communities were forced to shorten advice center hours and women lost support they had previously had.[89]

Even after the economy improved, Nazi authorities found that some town mayors and other local authorities continued to thwart the full-scale adoption and support of NSV mother advice centers.[90] In January 1937, leaders of the Reich Mother Service (Reichsmütterdienst) appealed to the *Regierungspräsident* of Minden for help forcing county and city governments to provide greater economic support for the RMD. In his response, the *Regierungspräsident* lauded the RMD's goals wholeheartedly, but refused to interfere with local budgetary decisions.[91] In Herford, authorities refused to expand their mother advice center at the Nazis' request because they believed "without a trained staff it would be wrong."[92] Local authorities' reasons for resisting Nazi guidelines varied. Some towns lacked funds to support an NSV advice center, while others saw no reason to interfere with already well-run clinics. For authorities who resented the Nazis' effort to impose their will or who disagreed with the policy itself, it was far safer to obstruct Nazi goals on account of local conditions than to protest outright. Some local authorities also wanted to avoid antagonizing the church leaders who ran the existing clinics. Both the Catholic and Protestant churches protested the Nazi effort to assume leadership. In 1942, one community nurse in Lippe reported that she had just then replaced the Protestant nurses with National Socialist nurses in the mother advice centers, but even then some German mothers maintained their allegiance and visited the women

---

88 Regierung Minden to Herrn Preussischen Minister des Innern, June 1934, StaD, Dezernat 24 D1, 211. This concern was serious enough that the HMK guidelines stated, "An accumulation of house visits by many people to one family is absolutely to be avoided." Arbeitsrichtlinien für die Hilfswerk Mutter und Kind, BaK, NS 37, 1031.

89 Büren to Regierung Minden, 18 February 1933, StaD, Dezernat 24 D 1, 211.

90 Regierungspräsident Minden to Reichsmütterdienst, 8 March 1937, StaP, Amt Neuhaus Neuhaus Bestand G 2, 4901.

91 Ibid.

92 Kreisausschuß Herford to Regierung Minden, 4 June 1934, StaD, Dezernat 24 D 1, 211.

in the churches for advice.[93] Although nurses at the NSV centers blamed the denominational nurses for undermining their work, National Socialist nurses, who were "appointed with great pomp and speeches,"[94] were notorious for their lack of sympathy and their strict political outlook, which emphasized larger racial goals and prevented them from focusing on individuals and families. Not surprisingly, many mothers preferred the more personalized attention they received from Catholic, Protestant, or Red Cross nurses.[95]

Despite large-scale propaganda campaigns celebrating mother advice centers, by 1942 a full 50 percent of mothers still had not brought their children in to be seen. Many of those who came did so not for advice and guidance but to benefit from free medical care, immunizations, and, during the war, cebion sugar (a synthetic vitamin C supplement)[96] or for specific material help, such as infant clothing and supplies and support after delivery.[97] One National Socialist nurse reported that she did not win over many wary parents until she took charge of the immunization of children. She stressed that it was only through caring for pregnant mothers, allocating household helpers, and organizing neighborhood help during and after delivery that she had gained the confidence of some hesitant mothers.[98] Another frustrated nurse concluded her report with the statement, "The Lemgo population is partially very reserved and can only be won over slowly."[99]

Though the new mother advice centers were not uniformly successful, the Nazis found other ways to promote the health of mothers. Soon after taking power, Nazi authorities, who emphasized the "infinite damage...to the German *Volk* caused by mothers' and women's ignorance," began to centralize mother training and to eliminate all competitors for mothers' attention.[100] The two party-affiliated women's organizations, the National Socialist Women's Organization (NSF) and the German Women's

---

93 Stimmungsbericht 1943, StaD, L113, 943.   94 *Sopade Berichte* 2, no. 7 (July 1935): 842–3.
95 Brehmer, "Frauen um 1945."
96 Frau Kemper, interview; Merkblatt über die Zusätzliche Vitamin C Versorgung der Säuglinge im Winter 1940/1, BaK, NS37, 1037, 1031.
97 Kundrus, *Kriegerfrauen*, 356.
98 Bericht über Gemeindearbeit in Lemgo to NSDAP Kreisleitung Lippe, Amt Volkswohlfahrt, 19 January 1943, StaD, L113, 932.
99 Bericht Schwester N., 27 January 1943, StaD, L113, 932.
100 Because the Nazis could not simply eradicate other organizations that were popular, the Association to Protect Catholic Girls (Verband der Katholischen Mädchenschutzverein), Caritas, and the Inner Mission continued to receive government subsidies for their programs even after 1933. To reduce the significance of this competition and to gain experience and access to other groups' members, the NSV sometimes offered courses in conjunction with other women's organizations. Petition for financial support, Verband der Katholischen Mädchenschutzverein in der Erzdiözese in Minden an BM, 29 July 1933, SaM, Oberpräsidium Münster, 6275.

Enterprise (DFW), bore responsibility for teaching women to be good mothers. Their teachers delivered the National Socialist message to women by "awaken[ing] a quasi religious consent and excitement through talking about emotions."[101] The practical side of National Socialist mother courses echoed Weimar efforts to improve health and hygiene. Women were introduced to the "expedient national feeding of the *Volk*," learning that meat was not essential at every meal and that vegetables lost flavor and nutritional value when overcooked. After the war effort began to require food rationing, cooking courses were further revised to use available foods creatively. Another popular course, hygiene, taught women the essentials of health as well as how to fight heat stroke and how to use vitamins.[102] Many women found the courses informative and helpful. Course leaders, who reported encountering "a great deal of superstition and ignorance,"[103] found them especially helpful for women employed in factories, who often lacked any training in household management.[104]

Yet the Nazi courses were designed to move far beyond practical goals to indoctrination. Although it is true, as others have suggested, that the courses were not intended to open political debate, it is also clear that Nazi attempts to introduce women subtly to the Nazi worldview often encountered trouble.[105] While many women appreciated the cooking and hygiene instruction offered in courses, they often balked at their political content. Some leaders limited discussion of politics because they encountered resistance arising from the women's religious sensibilities. One reported with astonishment that her students insisted that "even the Jewish question is to be answered from the perspective of Christian brotherly love," and she exclaimed, "many still shop in Jewish stores!" This instructor realized that in order to maintain her position in the group, she had to avoid criticizing anything considered "holy" (*heilig*). In Büren, one of the instructors found that "the clergy seems to hold women back from participating on account of a higher church order."[106] Another leader complained that the local women "do their work, go to church on Sundays, listen to what the pastor tells them, bring a child into the world every year and don't need any joy or any innovations."[107] Because they quickly learned that "especially in rural areas the Catholic clergy [had] a decisive influence, in particular on

101 Dammer, "Kinder, Küche, Kriegsarbeit," 226. 102 See, among others, StaD, M1 IS, 34.
103 Frau Conradi, interview; Aus den Wochenbericht der Lehrkräfte des Reichsmütterdienstes, Gau Westfalen, ca. 11 December 1936, StaD, M1 IS, 34.
104 Reichsmütterdienst Bielefeld to Regierung Minden, 16 March 1935, StaD, M1 IS, 33.
105 Schnurr, "Why Did Social Workers," 129.
106 Büren Reichsmütterdienst, report, 15 March 1935, StaD, M1 IS, 33.
107 NS Schwester H. G. to Frau E., NS Frauenschaft 31, August 1935, SaM, NS Frauenschaft, 536.

the women," many course leaders realized that their success depended on clergy support.[108] Interestingly, some topics did gradually open for discussion despite the Church's opposition. One leader claimed, "If we . . . speak about genetics and sterilization, the women are initially reserved, but slowly they prick up their ears, one after another and breathe deeply – an inner burden that the Church irresponsibly laid upon them becomes lighter."[109] But some course leaders were less enthusiastic than this one about mixing politics into their courses. The amount of propaganda taught in mother courses thus depended on the leaders' interests, the group members, and the churches' influence in a given area.

If some women were less enthusiastic about the mother courses because of their political content, other women were hesitant to participate in part because the NSF and DFW often recruited ideologically trained instructors from outside the community instead of using local instructors, as was traditional.[110] Many women viewed the new Nazi teachers as offensive intruders and, in rejecting them, also rejected National Socialism. As National Socialist leaders tried to replace tradition with modern science in mothering, they encountered women who were singularly uninterested in racial and political ideology. One leader reported with frustration that despite their lack of knowledge, women refused to participate: "Our farmers' wives . . . are a grim chapter because they inherited the traditions from their grandmothers and continue them generation after generation."[111]

Because attendance in the courses was mandatory for only a minority of women – the wives of SS, SA, some soldiers, and some marriage loan recipients – National Socialist leaders felt compelled to make their courses more attractive to other women.[112] In addition to advertising, some leaders tried to lure women in by convincing their husbands of the importance of the courses. They attended SA and SS meetings to talk to the men "so that they

---

108 Outside the city of Büren, the Reichsmütterdienst reported on 15 March 1935 that the Catholic clergy were waiting for an order from the higher church authorities before participating in the courses. Allegiance to the church was so strong among women that RMD leaders were frustrated because they did not think the courses would be accepted until the church accepted them. RMD Büren to Regierung Minden, StaD, M1 IS, 33; Aus den Wochenberichten der Lehrkräfte des Reichsmütterdienstes Gau Westfalen Nord, ca. 11 December 1936, StaD, M1 IS, 34.

109 Aus den Wochenberichten der Lehrkräfte des Reichsmütterdienstes, Gau Westfalen Nord, ca. 11 December 1936, StaD, M1 IS, 34.

110 Reichsmütterdienst reports, among others, from Oelde 4 April 1936, SaM, NS Frauenschaft, 536. NSF and DFW teachers had to be ideologically trained, and trained teachers were always in short supply. StaD, Dezernat 24 D 1, 211.

111 NS Schwester H. G. to Frau E., NS Frauenschaft, 31 August 1935, SaM, NS Frauenschaft, 536.

112 *Sopade Berichte* 4, no. 9 (1937): 1315.

Die Zahl der Bräute, die so schnell wie möglich die Kurse des Mütterdienstes besuchen wollten, nahm in unserem Gau ständig zu. Ein Teil von ihnen wollte der ihnen von der Führung der SS. auferlegten Pflicht genügen, sich hausmütterlich zu schulen; aber ein mindestens ebenso großer Teil hatte von sich aus den Wunsch, sich in richtiger Weise auf die Ehe vorzubereiten. Schon viermal hatten wir für Bräute einen Sonderkurs, in dem alle Kurse des Mütterdienstes zusammengefaßt waren, abgehalten, und die von auswärts kommenden Mädchen in einer Jugendherberge untergebracht. Nun bot sich uns die Möglichkeit in der Universitätsstadt Tübingen ein Studentenhaus mietweise zu erhalten, um dort eine Bräuteschule einzurichten. Allerdings: Ein Studentenhaus und eine Bräuteschule dienen recht verschiedenen Zwecken. Eine Bräuteschule braucht z. B. keinen Kneipsaal, keinen Unterrichts- und Festräume, keinen Hauboden, aber eine Lehrküche.

Wir wollten ein Haus schaffen, das selbst ein Heim sein sollte den jungen Bräuten, das ihnen aber auch durch jedes einzelne Stück seiner Einrichtung und durch die Gesamtwirkung zeigen sollte, wie ein solches Heim gestaltet wird. Wohl muß die Bräuteschule Unterrichtsräume enthalten, aber nirgends darf sie den Charakter eines Schulgebäudes tragen, es sei denn in dem Sinne, daß sie lehre durch sich selbst.

Eine
Bräuteschule
entsteht

"A Bride School is established." Special bride schools prepared the wives and future wives of members of the SS and SA. At the schools, women were trained in housework and childcare and prepared for their roles as National Socialist wives and mothers. *NS Frauenwarte*, Heft 8, 22 (1940).

[would] demand the necessary interest from their wives."[113] Leaders who visited women at home to invite them personally did so at some peril. Frau E., who made house visits to discuss the National Socialist courses with women, admitted that many of the women she visited would have liked to have thrown her out of their houses: "If my uniform had not protected me," she said, "they would have set the dog on me."[114]

Women's general lack of interest in home economics courses sparked a debate that was carried on virtually until the end of the war.[115] One desperate leader concluded that women needed "to be forced to attend." Women who depended on welfare benefits were especially likely to feel pressure (if not actual compulsion) to attend courses.[116] At one Gau Women's Leadership Meeting (*Gaufrauenschaftsleitung*), leaders decided to threaten women who refused to attend "with sanctions like revocation of their parental rights or removal of their children to another home."[117] A Nazi leader, Nurse M., complained that the same women who refused to attend mother courses lived in families where unemployment was pervasive and, as a result, "there are not shirts to be found in many [of these] households." Conflating economic and moral problems, she said: "The greatest immorality rules here. Small girls and big boys live in the absolute worst environment." She won the mayor's support for making marriage loans contingent upon attendance of the mother courses.[118] While this policy never became law, it is clear that Nazi policy articulated from Berlin charged women's ideological training with erasing economic and moral problems, and that in this instance the local NSF leader and the mayor envisioned immorality and unemployment as one problem that mother courses might solve.

The popularity of mother courses fluctuated, especially as the economy changed. In 1936, one leader in Gladbeck noted that the miserable economic conditions there dramatically increased the popularity of all courses, but especially the cooking classes, where some of the course members commented enthusiastically, "Here for once, we can actually fill our bellies." The leader happily added that some of the women had gained as much as

---

113 NS Schwester H. G. to Frl. E, NS Frauenschaft, 31 August 1935, SaM, NS Frauenschaft, 536.
114 Report on Mütterschulung von Schwester to Frau E., 31 August 1935, SaM, NS Frauenschaft, 536.
115 Technically, only women engaged to members of the SS and adoptive and foster mothers were obligated to attend. Brides of SS members were sent to "bride schools," where they learned to cook, sew, grow potatoes, work with children, and exercise. Frau Siebold, interview.
116 Dammer, "Kinder, Küche, Kriegsarbeit," 235; Kappelhoff, "Organisation und Tätigkeit," 76.
117 SaM, NSDAP Volkswohlfahrt, 28.
118 Bericht der Mütterschulleiterin Schwester J. S. in Brassert, 13 July 1935, SaM, NS Frauenschaft, 536. The Nazis also believed that the courses would dissolve class lines, though they fell short of this goal. Dammer, "Kinder, Küche, Kriegsarbeit," 239.

three pounds during her six-week courses.[119] This example underscores the fact that women attended and used the courses for their own purposes – purposes that sometimes coincided with political goals and at other times did not. Some leaders acknowledged the potential benefit of allowing the courses to serve purposes other than those designated by policymakers. One reflected: "The need is very great here. Therefore mothers should get lost in joy and the feeling of relief" in the courses.[120]

If mother courses met with mixed reactions, the issue of kindergartens proved equally thorny, though for different reasons. Nazi rhetoric that touted motherhood as a woman's primary role in society rendered the position of kindergartens somewhat tenuous after 1933. Especially distressing to the Nazi leaders was the fact that most Westphalian kindergartens were run by the Protestant and Catholic churches. Instead of directly challenging the well-established kindergartens upon which so many mothers depended, the Nazis regarded them as another realm in which the state could, through indirect means, further its own aims while helping to alleviate mothers' burdens. As one *Kreisamtsleiter* put it, "It is the intention of the NSV to take over fully all Kindergarten work."[121] The Nazis standardized kindergarten guidelines to help parents "raise children in the spirit of the National Socialist state."[122] All kindergartens were to be uniform in appearance and organization, Hitler's photo was to be hung in a prominent place, and the raising and lowering of the swastika flag became standard practice. Kindergarten teachers were forced to introduce the Nazi greeting, and patriotic songs became a regular part of the kindergarten day.[123] Above all, every child attending kindergarten had to be "healthy" according to Nazi racial guidelines. After 1935, all children had to present a medical certificate of health provided by a "responsible National Socialist doctor or department doctor." Doctors were also expected to hold office hours at kindergartens weekly.[124] Though the Nazi kindergartens were limited to "racially pure"

---

119 Stimmungsbericht Gladbeck, October 1935, SaM, NS Frauenschaft, 536.
120 NS Schwester H. G. to Frl. E. NS Frauenschaft, 31 August 1935, SaM, NS Frauenschaft, 536.
121 Kreisamtsleiter NSV to Kreisleiter Detmold, 26 October 1937, StaD, L113, 442.
122 Richtlinien über die Errichtung, Beaufsichtigung, Leitung und Einrichtung von Kindergärten, 1934, StaD, D102 Lemgo, 238. On 17 July 1934, the NSV Westfalen North wrote all the Kreisamtsleiter to emphasize the importance of educating children in National Socialist ideology in kindergarten. SaM, NSDAP Volkswohlfahrt, 86.
123 Not all the kindergartens complied, but kindergarten teachers' monthly reports reveal that they understood that uniformity was expected. SaM, NSDAP Volkswohlfahrt, 86. Even the Catholic kindergartens had to comply or they risked state intervention. Schwester O., interview.
124 Kindergarten Ordnung for Detmold, Brake, and Westfalen Provinzial Kindergartens, 1934, and revision, 18 September 1935, both in StaD, D 102 Lemgo, 393. Frau Schmitt told me that a medical student examined the children in the kindergarten she ran. Frau Schmitt, interview.

children, Jewish children could continue to attend Jewish kindergartens until the Nazis closed them down in the fall of 1942.[125] Nazi kindergarten teachers, like their predecessors, tried to increase the flow of information between parents and teachers, but they also had the responsibility "to work their way [*hineinwirken*] into the German family."[126]

The degree to which the Nazis succeeded in imposing uniform standards on kindergartens varied according to local conditions, party leaders, kindergarten teachers, and the local population's acceptance of the changes. In Westphalia, Nazi authorities ran into immediate conflict with both the Catholic and Protestant churches. Because it was politically costly to take over church kindergartens outright, the Nazis instead reduced the state resources available to them, introduced new kindergarten guidelines, and made themselves responsible for evaluating kindergartens and granting permits.[127] They also competed with the churches by opening NSV kindergartens staffed by trained National Socialist kindergarten teachers in areas served only by church kindergartens.

The Nazis' attempt to compete with the churches not only failed to alleviate the perennial shortage of Kindergarten spaces for children but ultimately exacerbated the shortage. During the Nazi era, many mothers continued to find it difficult to place their children in a kindergarten. In some areas, shortages of space became so dire that apartments vacated by fleeing Jews were used for kindergartens.[128] After the war began, the shortage of kindergartens also gave many mothers an excuse not to fulfill the Nazi call to work.[129] Some companies' managers, recognizing that the shortage of kindergartens jeopardized mothers' ability to work, founded company kindergartens in response.[130]

Despite the Nazi efforts at centralization, religious kindergartens persisted.[131] At the beginning of 1937, the Nazis had established forty-five

125 Kreisleiter Wedderville to Kreisamt, 4 May 1937, StaD, L113, 442; Kaplan, *Between Dignity and Despair*, 176.

126 NSV kindergartens cared for children daily except Wednesday and Saturday afternoons and all day Sunday for a cost that was income-based. Bericht über die Tagung der Gauabteilungsärzte in München, ca. 1939, SaM, NSDAP Volkswohlfahrt, 28.

127 Applications for waivers to run kindergartens, 1935, StaD, D 102 Lemgo, 238. Historically, many private kindergartens, including those of Caritas, Inner Mission, the Patriotic Women's Association, and the Red Cross, depended on government subsidies. In 1935, all the money was given to the NSV to be distributed to other groups. Landesoberinspektor to Oberpräsidium der Provinz Westfalen Landesjugendamt, Münster, 8 April 1935, SaM, Oberpräsidium Medizinalwesen, 6275. For elaborate discussion about the negotiations between Nazi Party leaders and church organizations, see Hansen, *Wohlfahrtspolitik im NS-Staat*.

128 Boberach, *Meldungen aus dem Reich*, 1938, 210.

129 Ibid., 27 May 1940, 1186; 22 July 1940, 1411.

130 *Sopade Berichte*, 6, no. 6 (1939): 752.

131 Although many more Protestant kindergartens than Catholic kindergartens accepted Hilgenfeldt's 1941 order that confessional kindergartens be voluntarily turned over to the NSV, ultimately

NSV kindergartens in northern Westphalia, and eighty-two more were in the planning stages.[132] The allegiance many mothers showed church kindergartens, however, confounded NS kindergarten teachers. Local city authorities sometimes even resisted the establishment of NSV kindergartens. For years, Detmold city officials successfully thwarted NSV attempts to locate an appropriate space. In 1937, the Nazis noted: "After five years of National Socialist building, it can be described as irresponsible that in a city like Detmold with 20,000 inhabitants, the kindergartens which exist are not only inadequate, but also contradict the National Socialist worldview."[133] Despite Nazi agitation, Hans Keller, the mayor, a long-time NSDAP member and staunch Catholic, persistently avoided meeting the Nazi demands, blaming his lack of action on budget constraints.[134] In Hiltrup, a small town outside Münster, the Nazis found their plans obstructed by the refusal of the Catholic Church to sell a piece of land for the kindergarten. Unable to force the sale, the NSF retaliated by blocking the opening of a new Catholic kindergarten, for which 285 people in Hiltrup had petitioned, leaving the city without a kindergarten until 1938.[135] In Rheda, another small town, the mayor evaded all political discussions and continued to finance the Protestant toddler care institution, offering the explanation that many local families depended on two incomes and the institution was necessary.[136] Ironically, during the war, when labor demands made women's work increasingly vital, the Nazis themselves had to rely on church kindergartens to meet some of the demand for childcare.[137]

The Nazis deliberately selected the locations of their kindergartens for political reasons as well as to compete with churches. In Recklinghausen, the NSV created a kindergarten to help coal mining families and because

---

the number of Catholic and Protestant kindergartens that were nazified was approximately equal. Regional differences continued to exist, however, and resistance was especially high in Westphalia. Hansen, *Wohlfahrtspolitik im NS-Staat*, 229.

132 Kappelhoff, "Organisation und Tätigkeit," 101.

133 Kreisamtsleiter to Herr Landrat des Kreises Detmold Schweiger, 26 October 1937, StaD, L113, 442.

134 In fact, Keller, who was unanimously appointed mayor after his predecessor was driven out of office by the Nazis, continuously caused trouble for the party. Kreisleiter Wedderwille complained to the *Gauleiter*, "The cooperation between Mayor Keller and the party has always left much to be desired. All the local party leaders have had conflicts with Keller." Bender, "Die 'NS-Machtergreifung' in Detmold," 245.

135 Pfarrer St. Clemens, Hiltrup, to Ortsbürgermeister, 9 July 1935, Bistums's Archiv Münster, PfA Hiltrup St. Clemens, A 156.

136 Rheda Bürgermeister to Regierungspräsident Minden, Abt. Medizinalwesen, 21 July 1933, StaD, M1 IM, 859.

137 Despite the Nazi order to the contrary, in Münster, church kindergartens continued to refuse to admit children of other religions. Letter an Kreisleiter der NSDAP, 30 April 1943, SaM, NS Kreis und Ortsgruppenleistungen, 126.

adults there "remained distant from National Socialism."[138] Many of the most successful Nazi kindergartens were those created in rural areas where the need was great and no kindergarten had previously existed. One woman I interviewed, Frau Schmitt (b. 1910), remembered that many local women appreciated the kindergarten she opened under the auspices of the NSV because it was the first one in the area.[139]

Though the Nazis claimed to create kindergartens to offer mothers a respite, they did not necessarily take mothers' self-defined needs into account. In 1936, they proposed the creation of temporary "harvest kindergartens" to help rural mothers at harvest time. The officials of some rural towns, including Lüdinghausen and Burgsteinfurt, rejected the idea of harvest kindergartens because the population was spread so far apart that parents would have to commute long distances to and from the kindergartens. Others felt no need for another kindergarten. In Minden, town residents rejected the idea of a harvest kindergarten because it was customary for families to take their children to the fields or to leave them with relatives.[140] Despite these uniformly negative responses, on 21 April 1936, the Gau Westfalen North leadership announced that harvest kindergartens were essential.[141] Furthermore, in order to keep the state's costs low, they required the rural population to provide the necessary milk, potatoes, and vegetables for the kindergartens so that mothers and children could receive the food free of cost.[142] As Clifford Kirkpatrick noted, already in 1938, the harvest kindergartens revealed "an awareness of an unfair balance between work and reproduction but hardly a fundamental or permanent solution to the problem."[143] They merely allowed mothers to devote their energies to another state-desired task. Historian Gisela Bock has criticized the fact that the Nazis offered mothers kindergartens "not...as a right, but as poor relief."[144]

Nazi leaders, like the Weimar authorities before them, worried that some mothers used the kindergartens to shun their maternal responsibilities. One National Socialist doctor pointed with concern to the growing propensity "of many mothers...to get rid of their children as soon as possible"

138 Kappelhoff, "Organization und Tätigkeit," 101.
139 Frau Schmitt, interview.
140 Responses regarding Harvest Kindergarten, Burgsteinfurt, 25 March 1936; Ahlen, 25 April 1936; Bocholt, 28 May 1936; Wiedenbruck, 6 May 1936; Ludinghausen, 2 April 1936; Minden, 18 May 1936 to NSDAP Volkswohlfahrt Münster, SaM, NSV 86.
141 Notiz Besprechung mit dem Reichsnährstand betr. Erntekindergarten am, 21 April 1936, SaM, NSDAP Volkswohlfahrt.
142 Hauptamtsleiter NSV to Gauamtsleiter der NSDAP Leiter der Ämter für Volkswohlfahrt, 19 May 1937, SaM, NSDAP Volkswohlfahrt, 81.
143 Kirkpatrick, *Nazi Germany*, 275.
144 Bock, "Antinatalism, Maternity and Paternity," 125.

Beim fröhlichen Spiel im Erntekindergarten

"Playing happily at a harvest kindergarten." To portray itself as both supportive of farm women and child friendly, the Nazis published photos of happy, healthy children in the harvest kindergartens. *NS Frauenwarte*, Heft 23, 7 (1939).

by putting them in kindergartens, and he proposed a three-year age minimum as a solution.[145] In contrast, the priests in the Catholic parish in Haarbrück stressed that kindergartens were important for rural women who

145 Der Amtsarzt, Staatliches Gesundheitsamt des Kreises Lemgo, 12 September 1938, StaD, D 102 Lemgo, 393.

were burdened by work in the fields and lengthy shopping trips for house-hold necessities. Because all children over fourteen years of age also helped with farm work or were employed, rural families in the parish could not hire someone to watch their young children. The priests explained, "It is self-evident that the kindergarten provides the most relief for mothers who use it to gain some protection and relaxation, [especially] rural moth-ers, since they do not have the opportunity, as in the cities they would, to visit the swimming pool, or to enjoy themselves in one of the many recuperation homes [*Erholungsstätten*]." They continued to praise kinder-gartens as an essential aid for rural mothers who were known for their "unbending love of children."[146] What the Nazis viewed as irresponsible, the priests saw as an essential break for mothers from their otherwise constant responsibility.

Mothers clashed with Nazi ideals presented at the kindergartens in part because the Nazi ideology was internally inconsistent. Despite their outspo-ken desire to have mothers stay home with their children, the Nazis also saw kindergartens as a perfect opportunity to intervene in families and indoctri-nate children. As one *Kreisleiter* (district head) put it, "By educating children in the spirit of National Socialism from the youngest age up, we are ful-filling a duty to the Führer."[147] To ensure the uniformity of kindergartens, all teachers, whether they planned to work at a confessional or an NSV-sponsored kindergarten, were obligated to pass a state exam designed to test their knowledge and commitment to Nazi ideology – especially its gender and racial laws. Kindergarten teachers were expected to build children's self-confidence and train them to act appropriately to their gender. Boys were encouraged to be soldiers and leaders, while girls learned the importance of mothering. During celebrations, these gender stereotypes became more tangible, as boys donned helmets while girls were decorated with a cross and carried a bouquet of flowers. Frau Roessner remembers her kindergarten class singing at the houses of SS members whose wives had just borne chil-dren.[148] Moreover, although the Nazis permitted no religious instruction in the NSV kindergartens, the children were still "urged to thank God daily for sending the great Führer in time to save the German *Volk*."[149]

Because Nazi authorities envisioned kindergartens as an opportunity for indoctrination, many women like Frau Ludwig (b. 1915) refused to

146 Das Katholische Pfarramt in Haarbrück an Regierung Minden Sozialamt, 16 May 1935, StaD, M1 IS, 37.
147 *Sopade Berichte* 4, no. 9 (1937): 1319.
148 Frau Roessner, interview.
149 *Sopade Berichte* 4, no. 9 (1937): 1319.

send their children to NSV kindergartens.[150] Many kindergarten teachers similarly refused to introduce politics into the kindergarten curriculum; others were inconsistent. Though the kindergarten teacher exams were deeply imbued with Nazi ideology, one Catholic nun told me, "It was really not so difficult to pass the exam: one just had to know which ideas National Socialism promoted. And if you mentioned them in your answer or in explaining education, then you were scored highly."[151]

Because kindergartens did not fundamentally reduce mothers' housework – or inspire larger families – the Nazis sought other ways to make motherhood more attractive and less burdensome. Domestic helpers (*Haushaltshilfe*) had become increasingly rare after World War I because young women were drawn to jobs with set hours and regulated pay. The Weimar regime's failure to regulate domestic working conditions or to extend maternity benefits to domestic workers further discouraged young women.[152] In response, the Nazis devoted considerable energy to attracting young women to do domestic work, both to prepare girls for their future roles as mothers and to alleviate some of the daily burdens of motherhood in the hope that mothers might be inspired to bear more children.

In 1933, the NSV in Westphalia paired needy mothers with members of the female work service organization. The Reich Labor Service (Reichsarbeitsdienst) sent girls into largely rural areas, where they worked on farms on an hourly basis so that mothers could rest.[153] Receiving families generally welcomed the help.[154] In rural areas like Paderborn, where the population largely rejected National Socialism, the NSV felt confident that "the best propaganda" was provided by the "household help and kindergartens." Nonetheless, the program failed due to its limited appeal with girls: in 1936 in Warendorf County, 213 "suitable" households sought domestic helpers, but only four girls applied to do household work.[155] The Sicherheitsdienst (SD) noted, "The vast majority of young girls have absolutely no interest in working in domestic service, to say nothing of such work in child-rich families." Notes from the SD attribute girls' lack of interest to their desire

---

150 Frau Ludwig, interview.
151 Schwester O., interview.
152 Wittmann, "Echte Weiblichkeit."
153 Richtlinien für die Wohlfahrtsarbeit der NSV, SaM, NSDAP Volkswohlfahrt, 251. In addition to making the Reich Labor Service mandatory for all girls after 1936, the Nazis made university study contingent upon completion of a Reich Labor Service program.
154 Frau Ludwig, interview; Frau Otto, interview.
155 Of the suitable households, 191 were in small towns, and 141 were farm families. In the end, the NSF found household help for 134 of the 213 requesting families. NSF Jahresbericht über Hauswirtschaftliches Jahr für Mädchen im Familienhaushalt 1936, Kreis Warendorf, SaM, NS Frauenschaft, 233.

for set work hours, free Sundays, higher pay, and better cultural opportunities.[156]

The demand for household helpers intensified after Germany went to war. In November 1940, the Reich minister of labor announced that the labor departments, NSV, DFW, and the Reich Farmers (Reichnährstand) would henceforth work together to expand the household help program into a motherhood aid program (*Mütterschaftshilfe*). Under the new provisions, all expectant eligible mothers, especially those in rural areas, would receive a trained helper for two weeks before and four weeks after delivery.[157] Though all Hitler Youth and BDM members were required to perform two to four weeks of "vacation work" during the summer, the demand for domestic helpers continued to outstrip supply. In February 1942, only eleven of nineteen rural districts polled received the desired number of household helpers.[158] In Kreis Herford, the NSF asserted that it was more important to have household helpers than bureaucrats in each district, since "through the latter no garden work is completed, no child led, no food for the families of workers cooked."[159] To increase the number of girls willing to participate, the Nazis sent girls only to healthy and morally impeccable families (they worried that bad placements would damage the program's reputation) and sent them to towns in groups with a leader. They regulated domestic helpers' working hours and required that families permit the girls to attend all NSDAP events, including BDM meetings. They also made it the "self evident duty of every family member to treat the household helper with the appropriate respect and willingness."[160] Although Nazi authorities tried to ensure that girls' experiences as mothers' aides were positive, and though they assiduously avoided sending girls to homes

---

156 Boberach, *Meldungen aus dem Reich*, 18 September 1941, 2785–6.
157 Rundschreiben from the Reichsarbeitsminister in Berlin to the Hauptamt für Volkswohlfahrt, Berlin, forwarded to the Gauamtsleiter der NSDAP and Leiter der Ämter für Volkswohlfahrt, 12 December 1940, BaK, NS37, 1004.
158 Survey of household helpers in Gau Westfalen Nord, 10 February 1942, SaM, NSDAP Volkswohlfahrt, 565. One survey in North Westphalia found that fewer than 30 percent were Reich Labor Service or female work service (*Frauenhilfsdienstmädel*) helpers. Fragebogen NSDAP NSV, Gau Westfalen Nord, SaM, NSDAP Volkswohlfahrt, 565.
159 Report from NSF DFW Kreis Herford, February 1942, StaD, M15, 48.
160 Household helpers were also to be given at least ten hours of uninterrupted rest at night, one afternoon free each week, and their own room. Many girls complained about the bossy nature of the mothers to whom they were assigned. Mothers in turn complained that girls were inexperienced and unwilling to learn. Moreover, many families believed that in order to provide their helper with a moral base and prepare them to become good members of the *Volksgemeinschaft*, they had to monitor the helpers' private behavior. Reichsleitung der NSDAP Reichsfrauenführung, Hauptabteilung Hilfsdienst, ca. 1941, SaM, NSDAP Volkswohlfahrt, 565; Guideline for Durchführung des Pflichtjahres, 1943/44, StaD, M15, 65; Reichsminister des Innern Rundschreiben no. 12, 30 April 1934, BaP, R15.01; Wittmann, "Echte Weiblichkeit," 40–41.

where they might come in contact with "foreign workers" or prisoners of war, most girls remained hesitant to participate.[161] As competition for the few household helpers available intensified, girls who were willing to take the positions could often pick from multiple options. One advertisement placed in a newspaper that read, "Simple, 21-year-old girl from a rural area seeks a position as a household helper or aide with knowledge of cooking," yielded seventy letters, twenty telephone calls, fifteen personal visits, and two telegrams.[162]

The shortage of girls prompted more official scrutiny of applicant families and greater public irritation with the program's shortcomings.[163] Many Germans protested when wealthy childless couples were assigned domestic helpers.[164] After his wife's request for a helper was rejected twice, Herr P., a lawyer, reapplied, framing his wife's need in terms likely to elicit Nazi sympathy. He wrote: "The comparatively large age difference between . . . [our] two children can be attributed to two miscarriages which my wife suffered on account of the double demands of pregnancy and housework, which she has to do without help." He assured the authorities that if his wife had a helper, they would bear another child.[165] Despite the many desperate pleas for help the Nazi authorities received, the extremely limited number of helpers prevented them from expanding the program. The problem was so great that the SD warned authorities that promising domestic help to "child-rich" families when they could not deliver was unwise.[166]

Realizing that some mothers needed more than a temporary escape from their maternal responsibilities, the National Socialist government continued to send mothers to recuperation homes. The Nazis designed three kinds of mother recuperation to liberate mothers from the daily demands of housework and children. First, they sent some mothers to stay with other families. This inexpensive, uncomplicated system usually relied on the women's relatives' willingness to take them in. Second, the Nazis created health centers and spas, administered primarily by the public welfare department, for women who were physically ill. The third and most popular type of

---

161 NSVolkwohlfahrt, Betr. Einsatz von Schülerinnen in den Einrichtungen der NSV durch den Kriegseinsatz der HJ, SaM, NSDAP Volkswohlfahrt, 90. Hitler Youth and BDM members could opt to work in farming, commercial enterprises (*Gewerbetrieben*), NSV kindergartens, or an NSV kitchen instead of with child-rich families. Notiz, 20 August 1940, StaD, L113, 502.

162 Boberach, *Meldungen aus dem Reich*, 4 June 1942, 3822–3.

163 Applications for household helpers, 1944, StaD, L113, 946.

164 Boberach, *Meldungen aus dem Reich*, 22 April 1943, 5172.

165 Heinz P., Gerichtsassessor, Herford-Elverdissen to Kreisfrauenschaftsleiterin Adelheid C., 10 February 1944, StaD, M15, 68.

166 Boberach, *Meldungen aus dem Reich*, 22 April 1943, 5172.

During the war, BDM girls helped the war effort both by helping women at home with childcare and housework and by creating parcels for soldiers on the front lines. *Das Deutsche Mädel*, November/December 1943.

mother recuperation, which affected the greatest number of women, sent mothers on vacation. After 1933, women who previously would have been sent for recuperation by churches, private organizations, and the welfare department were increasingly selected by the NSV in conjunction with the NSF and social workers.[167] In April 1934, the Nazis separated recuperative programs into two components: one for women with health problems, the other for healthy but exhausted women. The former remained under the auspices of the public welfare department (*öffentlichen Wohlfahrt*), while the latter became the domain of the NSV's Mother and Child Relief Agency.[168]

Recuperative vacations, designed to reward racially, genetically, and socially healthy mothers, were most often granted to overburdened, new, or child-rich mothers. Mothers with at least three children under sixteen and those who had supported the Nazi Party prior to 1933 received special consideration.[169] Nazi pronatalist interests meant that women who had completed their families were sometimes overlooked, as were those who received help from Catholic rather than Nazi nurses.[170] Most women were sent during the summer months, but special winter trips were available for rural women who could not leave their crops during the summer.[171] Their children were housed with relatives, friends, or neighbors. If no relative could be found, the NSF and NSV found suitable homes or placed children in kindergartens temporarily. When money was tight, Nazi authorities sometimes limited participation to women whose relatives could watch their children or whose children were old enough to stay alone.[172] Because government officials feared that mothers placed with families might feel obligated to help with housework, they favored sending mothers to resorts.[173]

Mother recuperation programs, which quickly became one of the most popular Nazi initiatives for mothers, presented an opportunity to

---

167 Bielefeld Oberburgermeister, report, 4 June 1934, StaD, Dezernat 24 D 1, 211.
168 The actual selection of mothers continued to be influenced by the NSF, German Women's Enterprise (DFW), Inner Mission, Caritas, and the German Red Cross, with additional help from the Organization for Child-Rich Families and the German Labor Front's (DAF) Department for Women's Issues. Richtlinien für die Müttererholungsfürsorge, BaP, R15.01, 26480. Even within the Nazi ranks, the Gauamtsleitung and the HMK competed, as the Gauamtsleitung decided mother recuperation should be interconfessional and not, as the HMK wished, based on confession. Kappelhoff, "Organisation und Tätigkeit," 81.
169 The mandatory number of children was raised during the war, when resources were scarce. Richtlinien für die Müttererholungsfürsorge, 8 May 1934, BaP, R15.01, 26480; NSDAP Westfalen Nord Abteilung Volkswohlfahrt to Amt für Volkswohlfahrt Kreis Emscher/Lippe, 13 May 1939.
170 *Sopade Berichte* 3 (December 1936): 1299; 2 (December 1935): 1446; 4, no. 9 (1937): 1311.
171 Anordnung Nr. V.7/34, betr. Hilfswerk Mutter und Kind, BaK, NS, 1034.
172 *Sopade Berichte* 4, no. 9 (September 1937): 1318.
173 Richtlinien für die Müttererholungsfürsorge, 8 May 1934, BaP, R15.01, 26480.

incorporate National Socialist ideology into women's daily lives. In 1935, the Nazis proclaimed, "In light of the National Socialist educational goals, mother recuperation will only be permitted to take place if it can be guaranteed that National Socialist influence and educational ideas will be embraced" by the women.[174] Because many recuperation homes continued to be staffed by churchwomen, the Nazis assigned a "comradeship leader" (*Kameradschaftswalterin*) to each home, whose job it was to ensure that "the entire home life is organized according to the principles of National Socialist philosophy of life" and to report on vacationing women or home staff who clearly opposed the Nazi government.[175] Ensuring that all recuperation homes ran according to the National Socialist plan proved difficult. Church influence posed an intractable problem. In a desperate drive to negate church influence and take control, the Nazis overextended themselves. In 1934, NSV leaders took over all the programs to send "healthy" women to special spas and refused to send women to many of the church-run homes, a decision that reduced the number of homes nationwide by one-third.[176] Also, because the Nazis believed that building their own homes would demonstrate the National Socialist dedication to the welfare of mothers, they turned their energy to construction rather than filling and running the homes already in existence. In 1937, as it became clear that the Nazis lacked both the financial and organizational capacity to run the homes themselves, they returned some control to the churches.

Nazi authorities even had trouble ensuring that the ideological atmosphere in the homes under their control met national standards. Often, inspectors who evaluated the homes expressed dismay at the scarcity of National Socialist influence. In 1934, Frau R., an NSF leader, discovered to her horror that the home in Nettelstedt lacked the most basic symbols of National Socialism. Neither Hitler's picture nor the swastika flag were hung prominently; the women did not assemble to listen to the Führer's speeches on the radio; even Nazi publications and newspapers were absent. In her report, Frau R. stressed that she had immediately detected "that the mothers feel like strangers here," a particularly grave problem since the homes were supposed to tie women into the *Volksgemeinschaft*. She attributed the problems to the youth and lack of life experience among the house leaders, who

---

174 NSDAP Reichsleitung to alle Gauleiter der NSDAP und Gauamtsleiter des Amtes für Volkswohlfahrt, RS Nr. V 38/35, 25 February 1935, BaK, NS, 1033.
175 Kappelhoff, "Organisation und Tätigkeit," 82; Rahmenplan für die Arbeitstagungen der Heimleiterinnen von Müttererholungsheimen und örtlichen Erholungsheimen, January 1938, BaK, NS, 1030.
176 Kappelhoff, "Organisation und Tätigkeit," 83.

were unable to command the necessary respect to run the home properly.[177] But the absence of ideological training may also have resulted from the home leaders' disinclination to introduce politics. Another report found that in one home thirty of the thirty-eight mothers felt oppressed when the leader read long prayers before dinner and encouraged them to convert to the Confessing Church.[178] As late as 1944, the leaders in some homes refused to greet the women with "*Heil Hitler.*" When some of the guests in one house challenged the staff, they were told that "the home community constitutes a large family and it is also not usual in families to greet other family members with *Heil Hitler.*" When the women continued to greet the staff with "*Heil Hitler,*" the staff conceded to return the greeting, though they went on greeting the other mothers with "Good day." When this episode came to the attention of the district chief leader (*Kreishauptleiter*), he was outraged, since "sending women to the mother homes [was] not solely for the purpose of rejuvenating them, but also simultaneously to train them to be National Socialists."[179] Nonetheless, the overall scarcity of staff made eliminating all uncooperative staff impossible.

Many women, exhausted from the demands of motherhood, enjoyed their time away. Word of the recuperation homes spread rapidly, and the Nazis quickly became overwhelmed by the number of women who wanted and needed to be sent.[180] Some women even argued with the authorities who denied them permission to go to a recuperation home.[181] In other cases, husbands and family members applied for their wives, mothers, and sisters. When Frau Neske's husband returned from the Russian front in 1943 to find his wife completely exhausted from caring for their two young daughters, he complained to the Detmold NSDAP office. As a result, Frau Neske was immediately sent to the North Sea coast for a month while her parents cared for her children. Today, Frau Neske (b. 1917), a woman who never supported National Socialism and who suffered substantial hardships during the war, remembers this respite as a lifesaving and entirely apolitical

---

177 Furthermore, too much work was demanded of the women. Mütterschulleiter to NSF, Bericht über die Frauenkur in Nettelstedt, SaM, NS Frauenschaft, 534.
178 Mütterschulleiterin about Erholungsheim in Soling b. Dassel Dries, Einbeck to NSF Westfalen Nord, 7 im Christmond 1934, SaM, NS Frauenschaft, 534.
179 Kreisamtsleiter, Recklinghausen, to NSDAP Gauamt für Volkswohlfahrt, 19 July 1944, SaM, NSDAP Volkswohlfahrt, 830.
180 See, for example, Münster Volkswohlfahrt to Deutsche Arbeitsfront, 7 September 1936, SaM, NSDAP Volkswohlfahrt, 830.
181 For example, when Frau T. from Bad Salzuflen was told that she did not qualify, she turned to the county leader, who wrote a letter on her behalf. When she reapplied, she was again told that she was not "child-rich" and hence could not be sent. She turned to the district social worker for a special permit. StaD, L113, 200 bd. 1.

Durch Ruhe, aber auch durch Bewegung, Gymnastik und Spiel wird für die Erholung und Entspannung der Mütter in den Mütterheimen der NSV. gesorgt

"Through rest as well as movement, exercise and games, mothers' relaxation and recuperation is provided for in the NSV mother homes." The Nazis also intended to use the mother homes to win mothers' support for the regime. Mothers responded positively to the program, but mostly for the relaxation and freedom from responsibility they enjoyed while at the homes. *NS Frauenwarte,* Heft 8, 22 (1940).

vacation.[182] The appreciation many mothers felt can be seen in their letters to the NSV to express their thanks. Some women even wrote Hitler himself.[183] One letter that was used to advertise the mother rest homes (and may be the work of a Nazi bureaucrat) claimed: "We live as though in a fairy tale; when we wander through the forest, I always look to see whether one of the seven dwarfs with Snow White or an enchanted princess or some other fairy tale figure will appear. We have landed in a truly heavenly place."[184]

The absence of politics in Frau Neske's memory may reflect the genuine lack of politics in the mother home to which she was sent, her personal decision not to participate in the political activities that did take place, or her effort to cleanse politics from her memory of the homes. Because the goal was to give women a much-needed rest, staff often did not pressure women to participate, a fact confirmed by the *Sopade* reports that "if a mother prefers to sit in a garden chair [rather than] attending [edification] hour, she can do just that."[185] Many mothers tailored their stays to meet their own needs, for example, making presents for their friends and families at home, even though doing so contradicted the Nazi definition of rest.[186] In one home, some mothers spent so much money on frivolous items that it alarmed the staff and undermined the collective spirit of the home.[187] Frau Neske remembered that the majority of the war widows in her home spent their time going to the movies.[188]

Not all women appreciated the Nazi effort to provide recuperative vacations. Already before the war, some women refused to be sent because they "had no desire to have a strange woman run her household and snoop [in her things]."[189] After the war began, many women from rural areas refused to leave their land,[190] while others categorically refused to leave their children, even after a trip had been arranged.[191]

182 Frau Neske, interview.
183 Telegram to Adolf Hitler, 10 December 1935, BaP, NS 10, 13.
184 Aus Mütterbriefen: Wie die Mütter ihre Erholungszeit erleben, 1934, BaK, NS37, 1035.
185 *Sopade Berichte*, 3, no. 5 (1936): 630.
186 Report from Müttererholungsheime to NSV, 11 June 1938, SaM, NSDAP Volkswohlfahrt, 28.
187 NSV Notiz für NS Schwestern Tagung des Gauamts Bezirks in Hallern, 1937, SaM, NSDAP Volkswohlfahrt, 28. In addition, to relieve the financial burden on the NSV and counteract the problem of mothers having extra money to spend at the homes, mothers were increasingly asked to contribute to the cost of the vacation if they were capable. Mothers who refused to pay although they were able were excluded from the trips. NSV Mitteilung 3/41, 4 July 1941, BaK, NS37, 1009.
188 Frau Neske, interview.
189 *Sopade Berichte*, 4, no. 9 (September 1937): 1320.
190 Letter from NSDAP Herford to the Gaufrauenschaftsleitung, Abteilung Landfrauenarbeit, Herford, 15 September 1944, StaD, M15, 65.
191 Kundrus, *Kriegerfrauen*, 355–6.

After 1939, the war forced some changes to the program. War widows and pregnant women were given priority, and only mothers with large families were sent.[192] When the army confiscated the recuperation homes, the NSV sent mothers to guesthouses and hotels for up to six weeks. As the war progressed and more mothers refused to be separated from their children, children sometimes accompanied their mothers.[193] Nazi authorities continued the recuperation program until late 1944, when most of the homes had been taken over by the army or turned into wartime maternity hospitals.[194]

CONCLUSION

Throughout the period 1918–1945, maternity benefits, mother advice centers, kindergartens, and mother recuperation homes together created a new safety net for struggling mothers and their children. During the Weimar era, the absence of any consensus on what kind of help mothers needed and, more importantly, what right the state had to intervene in families resulted in programs for mothers that varied widely in both intent and impact. Weimar state authorities supported and depended on private initiatives, both religious and secular, to expand and bolster state programs. Even maternity benefits, by far the most far-reaching and important state program for mothers, were coordinated with private organizations to assist in implementation and to aid those women not eligible for state benefits. Many women proved receptive to the Weimar programs: they brought themselves and their children for health exams, enrolled in household classes, and enjoyed recuperative trips. They accepted and supported state efforts to improve their health. But the support Westphalian women accepted tended to be practically grounded and bore little resemblance to the loftier agenda of modernizing and rationalizing households.[195] From lawmakers' perspective, the inability to ensure that every weak and exhausted mother received the training to run a modern household and to raise a healthy child was frustrating, but not frustrating enough to override their strong belief in the sanctity of the family.

192 NSDAP Richtlinien to die Gauamtsleiter der NSDAP und Leiter der Ämter für Volkswohlfahrt, 14 May 1940, BaK, NS37, 1004; NSV Münster Fürsorge für die werdende Mütter, ca 1942, SaM, NSDAP Volkswohlfahrt, 47.
193 NSV Gau Westfalen Nord, Münster to alle Regierungen, 3 September 1942, SaM, NSDAP Volkswohlfahrt, 815.
194 NSV Gau Westfalen Nord to Berlin NS Volkswohlfahrt, 28 October 1944, SaM, NSDAP Volkswohlfahrt, 28.
195 Nolan, *Visions of Modernity*, 217, 219–26.

The structure of programs for mothers changed dramatically after the Nazis put a state mandate and uniform ideology behind them. The National Socialists, who disparaged Weimar authorities' inability to make Germany a more populous nation, envisioned a wide array of programs that would provide much-needed knowledge of home economics and proper child care to racially desirable women, who would use their knowledge to create large National Socialist families. The Nazis trained instructors, social workers, and advice center and recuperation home staff in National Socialist ideology so they could provide women with both material and ideological support. They also terminated all support to women deemed racially impure.

The practical form that Nazi programs took fell short of Nazi ideological aims, however. At the structural level, the process of centralizing the programs under the NSV and adding racial guidelines often pitted the National Socialists against local officials. Doctors, mayors, and church authorities all obstructed the smooth implementation of Nazi programs. Moreover, the speed with which the Nazis tried to centralize programs under their own control sometimes undermined their overall goals.[196]

In addition, the programs' impact on women varied. Many women happily and gratefully partook of the Nazi offerings, and others vociferously protested their exclusion. Whether or not they endorsed National Socialism, such women's enthusiastic participation lent a degree of credibility to the Nazis' claim to help mothers. But for many women, religious belief continued to dominate their thoughts on reproduction, creating a buffer against Nazi ideology. Much to the Nazis' chagrin, the churches continued to provide aid, support, and guidance throughout the Nazi era.

The Nazis' belief that programs directed at mothers would make the regime look supportive of mothers and encourage childbearing without necessitating significant financial or material resources also compromised the programs' success.[197] Even before the war broke out, but especially afterward, the Nazi leadership made the military, not social programs, their priority. The consistent shortage of consumer goods dramatically increased the burden placed on mothers.[198] Although the Nazis tried to spare the hereditarily healthy members of the *Volk* "every avoidable difficulty," they

---

196 This closely resembles what Dieter Pohl has called "the central characteristic of National Socialist rule ... namely, the disjunction between utopian projects and scarce resources and contested jurisdictions." See "Murder of Jews," 85.

197 In fact, already in 1938, Clifford Kirkpatrick noted that "motherhood is rewarded with propaganda and philanthropy rather than with solid economic security." See *Nazi Germany*, 278. See also Bock, "Antinatalism, Maternity and Paternity," 124–7.

198 Overy, *War and the Economy*, 192–3.

failed.[199] During the war, in addition to "rationing, bad quality, long lines and rising prices," the scarcity of everything from beds in delivery homes to bottle nipples to children's clothing and food discouraged women from bearing children.[200] By greatly increasing the daily burdens of motherhood, especially after the war began, the Nazis effectively undermined the positive impact of their programs for mothers.

199 Kundrus, *Kriegerfrauen*, 309.   200 Ibid., 314.

5

Maternal Morality versus Infant Mortality

Negotiating Policy toward Single Mothers
and Their Children

Lina E. was employed as a maid when she became pregnant in 1922 at the age of twenty-three. One month before she gave birth to her daughter, Martha, she quit her job and moved in with her parents. When her lover, August K., denied paternity and refused to pay child support, Lina and Martha's case became embroiled in a complex system of legal and social policies governing illegitimacy and single motherhood. During the fifteen years of Lina's involvement with the courts and child welfare agencies, children born outside of marriage and their mothers were at the center of debate at the national level, and policy implementation underwent substantial change at the local level.

For Weimar politicians, single mothers represented a breach of traditional morality, while their children promised to ameliorate the falling birthrate. Repeatedly, Weimar policymakers asked: How could the state admonish single mothers without hurting their children – or, inversely, how could it help illegitimate children without condoning the behavior of their unmarried mothers? What would deter childbirth outside of marriage if the state removed the stigma of single motherhood? The high infant mortality rates after the First World War prompted all politicians to agree with the general goal of improving the health and well-being of illegitimate children. Given the financial cost of raising a child, however, few wanted the state to shoulder the burden. Most believed fathers should support their illegitimate children. But what if paternity could not be proven? And equally troubling, how could a man be punished for his irresponsible behavior without so encumbering him that founding another family became impossible?

Although the infant mortality rate had fallen by 1933, National Socialist leaders saw a need to revise policy toward single mothers and their children. For them, however, the compelling interest was raising the birthrate. Nazi policymakers worried that the great disparity between the number of men and women would prevent many "racially pure" women from contributing children to the *Volksgemeinschaft*. For them, the question was how to design a policy that would raise the birthrate regardless of mothers' marital status and at the same time improve social morals. Since they did not want "unworthy" women to bear children at all, this necessitated a two-tiered policy for single mothers. Equally troubling was the question of how the German population could be convinced to accept single mothers and their children when many Germans still believed that children were best off in two-parent families. The fact that opinions regarding illegitimacy were anything but unanimous even among Nazi leaders only compounded this problem.

This chapter examines the concerns that shaped policy toward single mothers and their children, the implementation of policy by courts and public agencies, and the ways individual men and women negotiated the laws governing paternity. It explores how modern understandings of sexuality and parenthood, the realities of modern technology, strongly held public opinions, and a devastating war all came into play, shifting the grounds for debate. As a result, individuals like Lina and Martha negotiated a path through an often-changing maze of bureaucratic agencies, laws, ideologically based policies, and state agents designated to help them.

BALANCING CHILDREN'S NEEDS AND MOTHERS' RIGHTS UNDER THE WEIMAR REPUBLIC

When the First World War ended, Germans held single mothers partly responsible for the decadence whose inexorable spread they saw as a threat to both the family and the nation. Although the illegitimacy rate in Prussia rose from 7.7 percent in 1910 to reach a high of 12 percent in 1918, by 1921 it had returned to 9.7 percent, suggesting that public concern was out of proportion to the actual problem.[1] Still, as Richard Bessel reasonably argues, the debate about moral standards was particularly intense not because morality was lax but rather because "it involved anxieties arising from the strains of war, defeat, political revolution, economic upheaval, and inflation."[2]

The illegitimate children who attracted public attention became a concern for Weimar politicians due to the high mortality rate of infants born to unmarried women: in Prussia in 1918, the illegitimate infant mortality rate was 25.1 per 100, as compared to a legitimate infant mortality rate of 13.8. In 1922, the rate for legitimate children had dropped to 11.6, while

---

1 *Statistisches Jahrbuch* 18 (1922).   2 Bessel, *Germany after the First World War*, 251–2.

the illegitimate infant mortality rate actually rose slightly to 25.5.[3] In consequence, illegitimate children became the focus of attention in parliamentary debates as politicians of all persuasions agreed that the high illegitimate infant mortality rate had to be addressed. Social Democrats, Communists, and liberals on the Left blamed the extremely high illegitimate infant mortality rate on class bias and the unfair treatment of single mothers, and they recommended the passage of new laws and social programs to address these problems. A small group of Social Democratic women went further and, echoing August Bebel, called for a new sexual ethic and the redefinition of marriage based not on state acknowledgment of the couple but rather on an individual's relationship to a child. Conservative politicians and members of the Catholic Center Party, however, worried that any attempt to lessen the legal distinction between illegitimate and legitimate children would wreak havoc on inheritance laws and thus endanger the rights of legitimate children.[4] Many also heeded DNVP representative Paula Müller Olfried's warning that "if the status of unmarried mothers [were] . . . improved [through legal reform] many more women [would] imitate them."[5]

Like the political parties, women's organizations also disagreed about the social status of single mothers and their children. After the First World War, the Association for the Protection of Mothers became more vocal in its criticism of "the inequity of a system under which single mothers were burdened with all the duties of parenthood, while their seducers escaped with the payment of a minimal financial contribution."[6] In contrast, most members of the increasingly conservative Federation of German Women's Organizations joined conservative politicians in voicing their fear that raising the status of single mothers and their children would destroy the family.[7] Despite these divergent interpretations of the problem of illegitimacy and the differing proposed solutions to it, most Germans agreed that the problem was important – that the German family, the very core of the nation, was at stake.

Weimar politicians' strong belief that the state had a fundamental responsibility toward its citizens inspired the passage of the Reich Youth Welfare Law of 1922. This law, specifically designed to bring endangered children under closer state control, targeted illegitimate children and foster children

---

3 *Statistisches Jahrbuch* 17 (1921); 20 (1924): 14.
4 For a more detailed discussion of the views of political parties after the First World War, see Scott, "Governmental Laws."
5 Wagner, "Die Reformbestrebungen zur Neugestaltung des Nichtehelichenrechts," 148; quotation in RT Proceedings, 6 April 1922, 6921–4, quoted in Usborne, *Politics of the Body*, 82.
6 Dickinson, "State, Family and Society," 516.
7 Hagemann, *Frauenalltag und Männerpolitik*, 179.

(many of whom were illegitimate) for greater state supervision.[8] By far the most dramatic effect the law had on illegitimate children was to declare them wards of the youth departments. Throughout Germany, local officials founded these youth departments to implement the law and transferred guardianship of illegitimate children and foster children from public guardians to youth department personnel. The newly assigned guardians supervised illegitimate children's upbringing regardless of whether they lived with their mothers, in foster care, or in public or private institutions.[9] The law called for guardians to be assigned to illegitimate children immediately after their birth, since the earlier in a child's life the guardian was assigned, the more timely and consistent the child's support payments were likely to be.[10] Seeing that public expenditures would decrease if fathers were compelled to pay child support, local officials rushed to assign youth department guardians.

A central aim of the Reich Youth Welfare Law was to make a trained guardian responsible for representing every illegitimate child in Germany. Before 1922, German law granted single mothers the right and duty to care for their children, but it did not grant them parental authority (*elterliche Gewalt*) or the right to represent their children in court. Instead, legal representation of illegitimate children fell to a court-appointed guardian, who also bore responsibility for ensuring that the father paid child support.[11] Judges unfamiliar with individual towns relied on priests or mayors to recommend guardians, thus ensuring that guardians were known locally. As the population grew and became more mobile, however, courts found it increasingly difficult to identify suitable guardians. One solution was to appoint a county social worker to oversee all paternity cases; by 1918, one-quarter of all counties in Prussia had at least one such social worker.[12] An alternative system required the county welfare office to assign a trustee to each town to "keep a watchful eye on all cases of interest to the youth department" and to inform the department of specific problems.[13] Yet this system was not working sufficiently well to ensure the well-being of illegitimate

---

8 Foster children were defined as those under twenty-four years old who spent a long time in care outside their families.

9 It was hoped that *Berufsvormundschaft*, the use of public legal guardians, would draw more attention to children and hence compel more fathers to pay. On 1 October 1921, *Berufsvormundschaft* was declared automatic for illegitimate children, poor children, and children supervised by the state's social welfare agencies. Dickinson, "State, Family and Society," 299–305.

10 Previously, guardians had been assigned when children were six to twelve weeks old.

11 Guardians were named by the court in conjunction with the youth department. BGB §1707.

12 Dickinson, "State, Family and Society," 548.

13 Jugend Amt Brilon to the Jugend Amt Medebach, 13 December 1926, SaM, Landgericht Arnsberg, 342, bd. 2.

children. Weimar lawmakers hoped that the creation of youth department guardians would pressure fathers to more readily acknowledge paternity and more consistently provide child support. Proponents of the new law believed that this alone would lower the mortality rate of illegitimate children. In addition, they hoped that if youth department workers learned more about single working mothers' circumstances, they could help ease mothers' burdens in myriad other ways: in the hope of keeping illegitimate children with their mothers and out of foster care, they could advocate and support the establishment of kindergartens, homes for infants, and advice centers for mothers; they could bring local resources to the attention of needy mothers and find suitable housing; and, as a last resort, they could help locate adoptive parents for children whose mothers were unable or unwilling to care for them.[14]

Although the law explicitly called for increased "scrutiny and supervision" of youth, it did not specify who exactly was to supervise children.[15] It also did not establish a rigorous, standard treatment for all children, stressing instead the need to adapt to individual children's needs. In the end, the system, "a mixture of advice and sanction," relied on responsible participation at all levels. But youth department personnel rapidly became overburdened and could not make the system work effectively. Not all courts could depend on members of the youth department to serve as guardians. When youth department workers refused, courts struggled to find guardians. Because the reimbursement level was low and many people viewed the responsibilities as abetting state intervention in the family, finding guardians often proved difficult. Most courts narrowed the potential pool of guardians, moreover, by appointing only men, a reflection of their desire not to challenge traditional gender roles. One judge explained: "The vast majority of rural women live domestic and reserved lives, and have only vague notions about public affairs and private legal transactions. I would like to hold this as an advantage and view home and family as women's natural sphere of activity."[16] Of the twenty-four guardians selected by the court of Medebach, Westphalia, in

---

14 In 1928, 73 percent of the children who came under the youth departments' guardianship were newly born illegitimate children. *Statistisches Jahrbuch* 26 (1930): 252.

15 In addition to its paid staff, the Hamburg Youth Department, one of the most advanced departments, relied on volunteers, primarily members of private welfare organizations. Harvey, *Youth and the Welfare State*, 181.

16 This judge appointed women only if three male recommendations failed. Amtsgericht Hilchenbach to Landgericht Arnsberg, 17 September 1919, SaM, Landgericht Arnsberg, 342, bd. 2. Before World War I, some feminists in the BDF had argued that public guardianship was an opportunity for women to hold a public office, but only after the war had begun and many male guardians were drafted did Community Orphans' Boards consider women. Dickinson, "State, Family and Society," 439–41.

1929, only one was a woman (a schoolteacher), and she was assigned as a guardian to female youth. All the others were men: teachers (five), curates (three), priests (seven), community leaders (three), as well as a businessman, a deacon, a school principal, a pastor, and a farmer.[17] Once appointed by the court, guardians received a "Guidebook for Guardians, Foster Parents, Legal Advisors and Representatives, and Aides" and were entrusted to make sure their wards grew into "decent people" (ordentliche Menschen).[18]

Despite its shortcomings and its locally variable implementation, the Reich Youth Welfare Law helped to lower the infant mortality rate for illegitimate children, which dropped significantly from 25.5 per 100 in 1923 to 15.5 in 1929.[19] Following the enactment of the law, the percentage of fathers who actually paid child support rose, and by 1929 more than three-quarters of unmarried Westphalian fathers were providing some level of support.[20] After 1920, illegitimate children were also eligible for public social welfare (öffentliche Fürsorge), so that even in cases in which fathers could not be identified or did not pay support, the children's mothers received some financial assistance. By 1926, 34.6 percent of illegitimate children in Germany received public social welfare.[21] State assistance in getting support from fathers improved the economic situation of many single mothers. But because state officials assumed fathers paid once they were ordered to do so, they were often slow to recognize a mother's or child's neediness. The new law also brought an increased level of state intervention in the family. In fact, as Karen Hagemann has pointed out, "It was only through an intensive

17 In contrast, when the Catholic Welfare Organization for Girls, Women, and Children composed its list of recommendations for guardians, it included the mayor's wife, a teacher, a nun, social workers, and the wives of men important in the community. The striking gender difference between the lists reflects the different opinions members of the state and nonstate philanthropists had about the kind of help illegitimate children needed. The state tended to emphasize their need for financial and career guidance, while church organizations emphasized their need for moral and maternal guidance. List of trustees, Amtsgericht Medebach, n.d., SaM, Amtsgericht Medebach, 4.

18 The term ordentlicher Mensch has connotations of health, industriousness, responsibility, success, and dedication to family. The system of trustees was approved on 1 December 1927 by the county youth department and the court representatives under the condition that the list of trustees be solicited from mayors and other community men. Judges emphasized that trustees had to inform the courts when they deemed court intervention necessary. The youth department continued to be solely responsible for financial matters.

19 Despite this, illegitimate children under the guardianship of the youth department still had a much higher death rate than legitimate children, at 10.5 percent as opposed to 0.1 percent. Statistisches Jahrbuch 26 (1930): 252, and 21 (1925): 11.

20 In 1929 in Westphalia, 52.3 percent of fathers of illegitimate children paid child support, and of these 26.1 percent paid in full. In contrast, 22.5 percent of those ordered to pay paid nothing at all. Ibid.

21 After 1920, illegitimate children were also eligible for public social welfare (öffentliche Fürsorge), so that even in cases in which fathers could not be identified or did not pay child support, children received some support. Winter, Sozialer Wandel, 41.

control of the mother that the state believed it could care for the well-being of illegitimate children."[22]

The mixed impact of new legislation can be illustrated by looking again at the case of Lina E., with whom this chapter began. After the birth of her daughter, Martha, in December 1922, Lina informed the youth department that the bricklayer August K. was the father of her child. When the youth department contacted August K., he denied paternity and thus economic responsibility. Because no guardian had been appointed, the case languished, and Lina received no money from the state or from her child's father. It was not until the Langenholzhausen Youth Department reported that Lina was "truly penniless and in an extreme state of need... [and had] lived only from the compassion of citizens of this city" that her case was reopened.[23] Because of the scarcity of their own resources, the Langenholzhausen youth department requested that Brake take over the case and proposed Lina's uncle as a potential guardian for Martha. Three months later, it was the youth department that finally brought the case to court. On 25 May 1923, the youth department, representing Martha, called a hearing in which Lina appeared as a witness to testify about the nature of her relationship with August K. Generally, such court hearings consisted of the woman and the alleged father each telling their version of the truth. Judges usually believed a woman's story unless a man could prove he had not had intercourse with her around the time of conception or could find a witness who would swear that he had also slept with the woman during the same time period. Lina swore on oath that she had had intercourse only with August K. around the time of conception, and he did not appear in court to challenge Lina's story (perhaps he hoped that by his not coming the case would be dismissed). On 20 September 1923, he was declared Martha's father in absentia and ordered to pay monthly child support payments of fifteen Reichsmarks for sixteen years.

Courts in Westphalia set the amount of the child support payments based on the mother's status at the time of conception. As a maid, Lina was at the bottom of the income scale, and the support she was awarded was meager. Setting child support according to the mother's economic status had the effect of making the consequences of relationships with some women more expensive than with others. Because women earned less than men in the aggregate and because single mothers tended to have small incomes,

---

22 Hagemann, *Frauenalltag und Männerpolitik*, 190–93; Crew, "German Socialism."
23 Langenholzhausen Youth Department to the Brake city administration, 27 February 1923, StaD, D 23 Hohenhausen, 523. Whereas in Westphalia child support levels were based on the mother's status, outside Westphalia some cities set child support according to the city's standard of living.

economic support for illegitimate children was generally fairly paltry. This problem, which the Reich Youth Welfare Law did not address, contributed to illegitimate children's higher mortality rates. Courts occasionally changed a child's support if a mistake had been made about the mother's employment. The Dortmund Youth Department reopened one case because the woman had been the head of household staff, not an unskilled worker, when she became pregnant: "In this position she more or less presided over the household. In other words, she responsibly led it. This means she had an elevated social status." In her case, child support payments more than doubled from twenty marks a month to fifty.[24]

The Reich Youth Welfare Law made youth departments responsible for supporting illegitimate children when no father could be identified or when he could not be forced to pay.[25] Money was so scarce at the local level in many areas that debates ensued between youth departments as to who was responsible for transient mothers.[26] As a result, not only mothers but also the youth departments had a vested interest in finding the fathers of illegitimate children and forcing them to pay. Judges were aware of the youth departments' limited resources, and – given the difficulty of determining fatherhood with any certainty – their bias toward saving state funds seems to be reflected in the high proportion of paternity cases in which fathers were ordered to pay. Of the paternity cases decided in Westphalia in 1929, only 14 percent were decided in men's favor. The statistics of men's success in denying paternity for the cities of Minden (9.6 percent) and Arnsberg (10.1 percent) are consistent with the overall Westphalian numbers.[27] While the courts aimed to keep the well-being of illegitimate children a matter of public concern, they did not want the state to become financially liable for replacing fathers in families. Yet men were generally not passive participants in paternity cases. Some fathers fled the country after being ordered to pay; others married different women than those with whom they were accused of fathering a child.[28] One judge stated, "It is easy for a young man to thwart a child's interests through changing his employment, moving from

24 StaM, Amtsgericht 20. This case, which was allegedly brought to court by a six-week-old infant, underlines the absurdity of not allowing women to bring cases to court themselves. Ibid., 22.
25 When fathers did not adequately support their children, youth departments tried to collect from other relatives and, if she put her child in foster care, the mother herself. Crew, *Germans on Welfare*, 123–5.
26 StaB, Sozialamt 13.
27 The percentage of cases lost by fathers was 63.2 in Minden and 66.7 in Arnsberg. The remaining cases (27.2 percent and 23.2 percent, respectively) were still pending at the end of the year. Interestingly, perhaps because of the large Catholic population, Münster differed dramatically, with 46.4 percent of women winning and 45.1 percent losing in 1929. *Statistisches Jahrbuch* 26 (1930).
28 SaM, Amtsgericht Altena, 87.

city to city, and even through pure idleness."[29] The courts had to balance their desire to force fathers to support their illegitimate children against their fear that overburdening fathers would lead them to flee their responsibility (and force the local youth department to take up the slack). This calculus generally worked to the disadvantage of single mothers and their children, as the courts tried to set child support payments low so that they would not overburden fathers.

Initially, August K. made his payments, and for nearly two years, Lina received fifteen marks a month.[30] Then, in January 1925, August's lawyer appeared in court to have the decision reversed. He argued that the mere fact that August had not appeared in court should invalidate the court's decision. (The law did not directly address what to do in the absence of one of the concerned parties. Many fathers attempted to undermine their cases by refusing to appear, but their absence was often interpreted as a sign of guilt.) The lawyer told the court that August had followed the court's order for two years – although he had always believed the decision to be erroneous – because he had not realized its far-reaching implications. Now that he understood that his obligation would last fourteen more years, he felt it was necessary to protest the injustice. August also asserted that through his own investigation he had discovered the promiscuous nature of Lina's life at the time she became pregnant. This new information prompted August to take the matter in his own hands, and the child support payments came to an abrupt stop.

August thus used the most common method by which an alleged father challenged a woman's allegation: he accused Lina of "promiscuity."[31] A man proved a woman's promiscuity by finding a witness – in most cases another man – who had been the woman's lover at approximately the time of conception. German Civil Code section 1717 identified a man who slept with a woman around the time of conception (*Empfängniszeit*), which was defined as 181–302 days before delivery, as the father unless he proved that

---

29 Amtsgericht Hilchenbach to Landgericht Arnsberg, 17 September 1919, SaM, Landgericht Arnsberg, 342, bd. 2.

30 Lina told the court that August provided her only income. The average amount an adult on the welfare rolls received in Münster in 1926 was forty Reich marks per month, while children received twelve marks. This seems very little, though it was later raised to an amount that seems more reasonable. *Statistisches Jahrbuch* 22 (1927).

31 "Promiscuity" (*Mehrverkehr*) in this context means that a woman had more than one sexual partner. Two other less common methods of undermining a woman's accusation were advancing medical proof to dispute the date of conception and to reveal the woman to be an unreliable witness. How exactly a woman's integrity was determined is not stated in the records, but it seems to have been established with reference to her appearance, style, and the consistency of her story. SaM, Amtsgericht Dortmund, 27.

she had slept with another man during the same time. An accused man did not have to prove that the woman in question had actually had intercourse with two men within this time period to win a case – simply that it might have happened. When businessman Felix D. in Dortmund challenged his paternity status, he called as witnesses both the man he suspected of being the child's father and several other people who testified that the woman had had multiple relationships. Because the suspected father could not swear that he had not slept with the child's mother around the time of conception, Felix won, and the mother lost child support.[32] Locating and bringing witnesses to court took time and often prolonged cases so that many mothers did not receive support promptly; some men doubtless used this as a strategy to avoid being forced to support their children.

Of course, the court had to determine whose story was most believable. Though men often called many witnesses, most ended up denying having slept with the woman in question around the time of conception or claimed never to have slept with her at all. It was not uncommon for as many as five witnesses to take the stand and then deny having had intercourse with the mother of the illegitimate child, which suggests two possibilities: either accused men tried desperately to find witnesses and often chose the wrong ones or they found the right men but those men decided on the stand that the risk of confessing was too great.[33] The difficulty men encountered in finding suitable witnesses worked in favor of single mothers and their children. However, the mere prospect of court hearings about promiscuity undoubtedly deterred some mothers from identifying their children's fathers. The existence of a system that often humiliated women and denied support to those who were revealed to have had more than one sexual partner strongly reinforced traditional moral judgment against sexual promiscuity.[34]

Because August K. failed to locate a witness who could confirm Lina's alleged promiscuity, the court disregarded his complaint and ordered him to resume payments. Challenges of initial court judgments like August's were common. Both parties petitioned the court, sometimes repeatedly, to alter payment levels to adapt to economic changes, particularly in the unstable economic conditions of the Weimar years. During inflationary years when prices rose daily, child support payments often lagged hopelessly behind the

---

32 Ibid.
33 In contrast, many American men brought friends to court to testify that they had had intercourse with the mother of the child they were accused of fathering so that the case would be dismissed. Solinger, *Wake Up Little Susie*, 37.
34 This stands in stark contrast to Sweden, where all men who slept with an unmarried woman who became pregnant were forced to pay child support.

cost of living. Courts repeatedly renegotiated support levels for illegitimate children: between 9 October 1922 and 9 August 1923, one train conductor in Warburg had the amount of his child support payment changed from 25 marks a month to 500 and then to 3,000, 5,000, 20,000, and finally to 72,000. This whole process, magnified by thousands of cases, overwhelmed the courts, and while parents wrangled and courts delayed, many children suffered.[35]

In March 1923, the minister of justice recommended that the courts create an alternate system of adjusting payments to lessen the detrimental effects of inflation on illegitimate children. Most local courts in Westphalia created their own ways of contending with economic instability.[36] Some, like those in Bielefeld and Minden, followed the suggestion of the minister of justice and published government statistics in the local newspapers to set child support payments. Other communities devised their own systems. In Vlotho, the calculations for child support payments were based on the cost of a liter of milk; in Werl, on the price of rye and potatoes, the most important subsistence foods; and in Kamen, on the average income of a coalminer from a single shift. In Dortmund, an industrial city where the legal guardians maintained constant contact with the fathers of illegitimate children, payments could be adjusted without court involvement.[37]

While child support payments were often adjusted relatively uniformly to match national economic trends, adjustments based on life changes required more personal attention. Mothers often returned to court when they could no longer live on the set award. The court then faced the task of balancing a child's needs against that child's father's economic capabilities. On 3 February 1928, Lina returned to court to claim that the fifteen marks per month she received from August was, as her only income, insufficient.[38] The Brake court contacted August, who asserted that since his limited income also had to provide for his mother and running his family's land, he could not afford to afford to pay more. The court disagreed and doubled his support to thirty marks per month. When Lina tried again in 1930, however, the court ruled against her even though thirty marks per month was below the city limit.

---

35 Declarations of *Vaterschaftsanerkennung*, Amtsgericht Warburg, StaD, D 23 Warburg, 93 (1921–28); Justizminister to Oberlandesgericht Hamm, 7 March 1923, StaD, Oberlandesgericht Hamm, 379.
36 Landgericht Hagen to Oberlandesgericht Hamm, 5 June 1923, SaM, Oberlandesgericht Hamm, 379.
37 Landgericht Bielefeld to Oberlandesgericht Hamm, 5 June 1923, SaM, Oberlandesgericht Hamm, 379; Landgericht Dortmund to Oberlandesgericht Hamm, 25 June 1923, SaM, Oberlandesgericht Hamm, 379.
38 The fact that BGB §1709 dissolved a man's responsibility to pay child support if the mother or her relatives were able to provide may well have discouraged some women from seeking employment.

Fathers could also petition to be allowed to pay less support, although they were rarely successful. In 1932, August K. wrote the court to say that he had fallen on hard times and therefore could no longer afford to pay thirty marks per month. The court rejected his offer to pay fifteen marks but, without consulting Lina, lowered his payment to twenty-two marks per month. This was unusual, as most men found the courts unwilling to negotiate and had to cease to pay entirely before the court would listen. The fact that the court was willing to adjust August's payments in this case probably reflects the small size of the town in which he lived, as well as the consistency with which he had made his payments for eight years.

When men formed new families, they commonly requested that the amount of their payments be lowered. The potential conflict between enforcing child support payments for illegitimate children and encouraging the founding of new, "legitimate" families fueled protracted debate. Especially in light of fears about declining population and most Germans' belief in the sanctity of the family, no politician or judge wanted to stand in the way of the founding of new families. Judges worried, in fact, that men burdened by child support payments stemming from their youthful sexual encounters might be viewed as undesirable future partners. This was especially problematic, since it was also feared that mothers who received child support for their illegitimate children might be considered more desirable marriage partners than more "moral" single women. In a society that judged a woman's breach of respectability more harshly than a man's, the idea that a woman might in the end benefit while the man suffered was deeply troubling to many. The tendency to judge single mothers as morally reprehensible years later while agonizing over hindering a man's ability to start a new family reveals a double standard in court policy. On the other hand, judges worried that canceling fathers' responsibility toward their illegitimate children might lead to other undesirable – and irresponsible – behavior. As one judge pointed out, "The married man – like all others – can withdraw from his obligations without difficulty; as soon as he has children of his own, he can rest easy that his wages will not be garnished."[39] This complicated set of priorities forced the courts to evaluate each case individually.

Paternity cases also forced an examination of maternal roles inside and outside of traditional families. Judges usually felt that mothers were best off married and in families, but many women did not consider marriage to their children's fathers a desirable option, even if the alternative was single motherhood. Sometimes, judges were inclined to agree. One worker told

---

39 Amtsgericht Hilchenbach to Landgericht Arnsberg, 17 September 1919, SaM, Landgericht Arnsberg, 342, bd. 2.

the court in 1925 that he was unable to pay child support for Marie's child because he already paid eight of his twelve marks in weekly income to support two other illegitimate children. He offered, "If Marie F. is willing to marry me today, I am willing at any time." Given his questionable ability to support a wife and child, however, Marie's refusal to marry him seems understandable – even courageous. The Warburg court supported her decision and demanded that the father pay twenty marks a month in support, despite his previous obligations and the fact that he could not possibly have done so with his current income.[40] In Westphalian court records, there are numerous other cases in which women declined marriage proposals from men who had no means to support a family. Many judges accepted this as a legitimate reason to refuse marriage. During a hearing in Hohenlimburg, one father agreed to support both the mother and child, but only on the condition that the mother marry him. When the woman declined to do so, claiming only to want support, not marriage, he refused to pay. The judge in this case declined to force the man to pay but was also unwilling and unable to force the woman to marry. His response to the woman's logic was critical and confused: "I believe this is a logic upon which the best of intentions make no impression," he said.[41] Though judges considered child support essential when family formation failed, they refused to aid alternative families when the parents simply did not desire marriage.

It was not unusual for judges to question the motives of women who came to court in pursuit of support. Many unmarried parents worked actively to keep their cases out of court, avoid public humiliation, and limit state involvement in their personal economic matters. In a context in which many "honest" parents privately arranged for the support of illegitimate children, reliance on the courts implied a certain level of irresponsibility or immorality. One judge contended that "the people who are conscientious and do not doubt their paternity usually prefer to pay a lump sum."[42] Judges recognized that victory in court seemed to separate a virtuous single mother from other, more "promiscuous" women; many believed that through a court victory a mother "earn[ed] not only a capital for the child, but also rehabilitate[d] her own honor."[43] Some judges incorrectly assumed that any father who recognized paternity would responsibly pay without court intervention.[44]

---

40 In cases of nonpayment, the court could compel a man to work and garnish his wages, but if child support already consumed his income, little could be done. StaD, D 23 Warburg, 1925, 93.
41 Amtsgericht Hilchenbach to Landgericht Arnsberg, 17 September 1919, SaM, Landgericht Arnsberg, 342, bd. 2.
42 Ibid.
43 Ibid.
44 Fathers frequently evaded payments, denied paternity, and even backed out of prearranged agreements.

Because no official historical record exists for the cases that did not go to court, we can only speculate about how they complete the picture of care for illegitimate children. In 1929, there were 4,804 illegitimate children born in Westphalia, and 1,673 of these children's fathers voluntarily acknowledged their paternity. This number suggests that less than 35 percent of fathers acknowledged their illegitimate children without being forced to do so.[45] In Hamburg, the likelihood that a man would recognize his illegitimate child varied according to his income. While 67.9 percent of working-class fathers recognized paternity, only 10.5 percent of white-collar workers and only 2.2 percent of civil servants did so.[46] Men with status and financial resources were less likely to recognize paternity voluntarily but were probably also more likely to negotiate privately to avoid scandal. These differences increased the variability of experiences among illegitimate children.[47]

In addition to the courts, the relationship between the mother and her child's guardian could have an enormous influence on the child's life. The German Civil Code guaranteed all illegitimate children a guardian, who had the "right and responsibility... to care for their wards."[48] Frequently the guardians were relatives of the child. The mother's father – the child's maternal grandfather – was the first choice as guardian for most courts. The degree to which these guardians directly intervened in families varied widely. When mothers were close to their families, such court assignments had little negative effect on the child's upbringing. But when no relative was available, the court appointed the youth department itself or a nonrelated person acted as guardian, increasing the potential for unwanted intrusion. In Martha's case, the guardian at least sporadically took an interest in his ward. Initially Lina filed petitions for increased child support payments without the aid of Martha's guardian. Later, in 1936, Martha's guardian investigated August's resources in an attempt to procure more money for her. His conclusion that August could not afford to pay more reveals that apparently he was not unduly biased in favor of his ward.

Although most guardians, like Martha's, limited intervention and permitted mothers to raise their children as they saw fit, the legal description of the guardian's role left considerable room for greater intrusion. Guardians, charged with observing children's upbringing and informing the

---

45 *Statistisches Jahrbuch* 27 (1931): 91.
46 Hagemann, *Frauenalltag und Männerpolitik*, 185.
47 Of the total of 5,500 children who left the guardianship of Westphalian youth departments in 1928, 25 percent left after being legitimated through the marriage of their parents, 4.7 percent were adopted, and 10.5 percent died. *Statistisches Jahrbuch* 26 (1930): 30.
48 BGB §§1708, 1800.

courts when something was amiss, sometimes recommended that children be removed from their mothers' homes. Katrin K.'s guardian determined that Katrin's mother's home was unsafe and recommended that she be put in foster care. Only his revised decision to ask a social worker's opinion saved Katrin's mother from losing her daughter.[49] Technically, fathers paid child support directly to the youth department, which then distributed it to mothers (or foster families), setting aside part of each payment in an account for the child's education. When mothers were deemed irresponsible, however, youth department authorities sometimes gave the money to the guardian instead. When Frau P. wanted to buy shoes for her son, the court told her the guardian would have to be present when she shopped, clearly revealing the power vested in the guardian's role.[50] Animosity often arose between mothers and guardians they deemed excessively inquisitive, yet single mothers needed guardians to help them negotiate state laws. Even when a single mother subsequently married, she and her husband did not have free rein to raise the child. If they wanted to give the child the new husband's name, the guardian had to submit the application for them.[51] Because a guardian's legal responsibility for a child necessitated observation of the mother as well, guardianship provided the state with one more way to control mothers' behavior.

Interestingly, despite the extensive intrusion into single mothers' households, women did retain custody of their children, even though they were not allowed to represent them in court. These custody rights remained intact whether a mother decided to raise her child herself, put the child in foster care, or place the child in an institution. Only if the court explicitly revoked a mother's custody rights (which happened rarely) or if she placed her child for adoption did she lose these rights. Furthermore, even when mothers chose not to raise their children themselves, custody did not automatically fall to fathers, whose importance in a child's life was treated as insignificant. Nor were youth departments legally permitted to bypass a mother's custody rights on behalf of either foster parents or biological fathers. A father could spend months, if not years, in negotiation to get custody rights for his child even when the mother was not herself caring for the child. Finally, children in foster care could not be adopted without their mothers' permission.[52] Thus, despite the courts' control over child support payments and state-appointed guardians' surveillance of their lives, single mothers

49 StaD, D 23 Hohenhausen, 1924–1941, 85.   50 StaD, L 80 IC, Gruppe XXIV, Fach 11, 40.
51 Amtsgericht Arnsberg to Landgerichtpräsident, 16 October 1924, SaM, Landgericht Arnsberg, 686.
52 See, for example, SaM, Amtsgericht Hohenlimburg, 78.

retained significant control over their children's well-being. Although the stigma attached to single motherhood and illegitimacy persisted during the Weimar era, the greater likelihood that illegitimate children would receive child support and/or state welfare improved the lives of both illegitimate children and their mothers. This improvement was reflected not least in the decline in infant mortality rates among illegitimate children.

SHIFTING MORALS: ILLEGITIMACY UNDER NATIONAL SOCIALISM

When the Nazis rose to power in 1933, their party program promised to rejuvenate German society – a promise that, in the minds of Nazi policymakers and much of the populace, necessitated rebuilding patriarchal families. From the beginning, however, a vociferous debate ensued about whether racial and population concerns should take precedence over morality. The Nazis ultimately gave priority to preserving and expanding the Aryan race, and with that goal in mind they tried to redefine morality in terms of race. Rather than condemn all single mothers out of hand, they were willing to make accommodation for "genetically healthy" German women and their "racially pure" children.

Leading Nazis argued that policies for single mothers and illegitimate children should be tailored to meet National Socialist racial and population goals. Walther Darré asserted that the distinction between married and unmarried mothers – a distinction created solely by the church – should be of secondary importance. Alfred Rosenberg agreed, asserting that unless the state recognized its own interests and sanctioned out-of-marriage birth, the "oversupply" of German women would relegate many women to childlessness.[53] Henry Picker, an official of the Youth Leadership, claimed that any legislation that supported "racially pure" single mothers would benefit the entire nation, not only by increasing the population but also by helping "to give the German woman back her self-confidence and thus leave her with a healthy emotional life." This new self-confidence would in turn enable German women to work "for the good of the family and *Volkstum*."[54]

Support for a progressive revision of the laws could be found within the legal profession as well. Echoing the SPD's Weimar-era position, some

---

53 War mortalities meant that there were approximately 2 million more German women of marriageable age than there were men. Rosenberg, *Der Mythos des 20. Jahrhunderts*, 593.

54 Many people believed that encouraging women to bear children would simultaneously strengthen the German family (thus rebuilding society's traditional base) and allow men to act in their "natural" roles as patriarchs (thus, one might add, restoring men's self-confidence). Dr. Henry Picker, Mitarbeiter des Jugendführers des Deutschen Reichs, in "Das uneheliche Kind im deutschen Recht."

argued that illegitimate children deserved essentially the same treatment as legitimate children, not the second-class status they received. They contended that children should have a right to take their father's name regardless of their mother's marital status and that an illegitimate child's relationship with both the father and paternal relatives should be formally recognized, since doing so would be mutually beneficial. In an article in *Deutsches Recht* (German Law), several authors argued that when paternity could be established, fathers should be forced to take parental control and become involved with their illegitimate children.[55] Others opposed nonparental guardians on the grounds that "the guardian should in principle be the mother."[56]

Within Nazi organizations, efforts were made to raise the status of single mothers and their children. The National Socialist Women's Organization stressed that under all circumstances "a single mother, who has a racially pure child, will be seen as a positive member of the *Volk* [*Volkskörper*] in National Socialist thinking."[57] Although Hitler did not publicly take a position on single motherhood or illegitimacy, his private conversation suggests that he agreed that since the war had eliminated the possibility of marriage for two and a half million women, Germany had to "be forbidden to despise the child born out of wedlock." He stated, "I've much more respect for the woman who has an illegitimate child than for an old maid."[58] This line of argument was used to justify supporting single mothers and in some cases to claim that single Aryan mothers who lacked families to protect them needed extra protection from the state.

The Nazi assertion that some single mothers should be supported rather than scorned flew in the face of traditional morality, however, and Nazi attempts to change laws governing single motherhood and illegitimacy met widespread opposition. Even within the party, many people worried that improving the status of single mothers and illegitimate children would encourage irresponsible and immoral behavior and would undermine the traditional family. Within the National Socialist People's Welfare Organization and the NSF, many people suggested that instead of revising the law the courts should put pressure on fathers to marry the mothers of their children, thus making honorable women of them. The National Socialist Frauenwarte pointed out that since single women generally only bore

---

55 This did not mean that they wanted fathers to become caregivers, however, a role that they relegated to the mother. Klinksiek, *Die Frau im NS-Staat*, 96.
56 SaM, Oberprasidium Munster, 5767.
57 Themenbeispiele for Nationalsozialistische Volkswohlfahrt, ca. 1933–34, SaM, NSDAP Volkswohlfahrt, 227.
58 Trevor-Roper, *Hitler's Table Talks*, 352.

one child whereas married women bore many, supporting single mothers contradicted population policy aims.[59] The Committee for Family Law (Familienrechtsausschuß) agreed, citing the frequency with which fathers married other women in order to avoid paying child support. They argued that if men married the mothers of their illegitimate children, it would guarantee that all children grew up with the support of both father and mother, stop men from being irresponsible, and rid society of the problem posed by fatherless families.[60] One legal author went so far as to advocate forcing all men who could plausibly be the father of any given illegitimate child to pay child support, positing that this would teach men to be more responsible.[61] The Catholic and Protestant churches vocally opposed any legal change on moral grounds, as they had during the Weimar era. In 1935, both Caritas and Inner Mission published articles rejecting any radical change in state policy regarding single motherhood and illegitimacy.[62] Grounding its opposition in the Bible, the Protestant Women's Aid Society declared that "unmarried intercourse is an act which threatens the order of the nation."[63] Although churchwomen ran homes to help "fallen" women and to care for illegitimate children, this by no means lessened their condemnation of the "sinful act" of premarital intercourse. Many Germans supported the churches on this issue.

Ultimately, faced with such opposition, the Nazis sought a way to make their ideas more palatable to the German populace. They devised a new racially based system that divided single mothers into two categories: "Racially pure" German women and their children born outside of marriage were viewed as desirable members of the *Volk*, and hence both these mothers and their children deserved support. In contrast, women deemed hereditarily sick or asocial and their children were perceived as a burden on the German nation. By dividing single mothers into two groups, the Nazis claimed to be upholding high moral standards and traditional values while pursuing pronatalist aims.

To encourage "racially pure" unmarried women to bear children outside of marriage without tainting their status as respectable women, the

---

59 Kundrus, *Kriegerfrauen*, 357.
60 Leo Pelle, "Rechtsprechung und Gerechtigkeit in der Unterhaltsbeitreibung für uneheliche Kinder," ca. 1935, BaP, 62 DAF 3.
61 Proposal by Rudolf Bechert and Friederich Cornelius, quoted in Klinksiek, *Die Frau im NS-Staat*, 96.
62 Caritas published "Neugestaltung des Unehelichenrechtes" in July 1935, while the central office of the Inner Mission published a *Denkschrift* containing its positions in November 1935. SaM, Oberpräsidium Münster, 5767.
63 Richtlinien zur Unehelichenfrage, 1937 or 1938, EVHA 118–6b.

Nazis introduced the motto, "Bear a child for the Führer." The Mother and Child Relief Agency provided medical, physical, and psychological help to "racially pure" mothers regardless of their marital status. In addition to providing state support to single mothers, the Nazis made a concerted effort to change social attitudes about single motherhood. New guidelines required teachers to treat legitimate and illegitimate children equally in the classroom. Nazi tax law allowed "worthy" single mothers to pay taxes at the same lower rate as divorced and widowed mothers. The Nazis outlawed the dismissal of unmarried civil servants purely on the basis of pregnancy. At all levels of society, Nazi authorities tried to help unmarried mothers rekindle broken relationships with their families. Finally, they ordered National Socialist organizations, among them the League of German Girls and the Reich Labor Service, to treat unmarried pregnant women without scorn.

Despite National Socialist attempts to lessen the discrimination against single mothers, changing popular attitudes proved difficult. While young girls were among the most receptive to Hitler's call to reproduce because their active participation in the BDM and the Reich Labor Service brought them in close contact with Nazi ideology, their parents often stood in staunch opposition to "modern" notions about single motherhood. In a letter to her parents, one girl wrote that she would return from the Reich Labor Service as a "German mother." She admonished them not to complain, since she had "only acted according to the Führer's wishes." A thirteen-year-old mother informed the nurses who tended her after delivery, "I am a mother and want to be treated as such; the Führer wishes it so." In the face of such ideologically motivated defiance, many parents felt furious, frustrated, and confused. Those who continued to shun their unmarried pregnant daughters found that expressing their outrage publicly was dangerous.[64]

The German populace's reluctance to accept unmarried motherhood among "racially pure" women led the SS to found the first of the *Lebensborn* ("fountain of life") homes in 1935. Ultimately, there would be six *Lebensborn* homes in Germany, nine in Norway, one in Belgium, and one in France. These homes provided a safe place where select single, "racially pure" women could deliver their children away from the scrutiny of their neighbors. The *Lebensborn* homes promised women secrecy, fictional addresses, permission to register with the police as widows or divorcees after they left the homes, employment help, and adoption assistance. Since Heinrich Himmler (head of the SS) realized that assigning a social worker or guardian from the established youth department would undermine these women's

64 *Sopade Berichte* 3, no. 10 (1936): 1316–18; 2, no. 6 (1935): 692–4.

privacy, the *Lebensborn* program assumed the functions of a youth department, with its own independent staff and the authority to appoint guardians and control adoptions. By providing single mothers a private place to bear their children and helping them to recreate their lives after delivery without shame, Himmler hoped the *Lebensborn* homes would make single motherhood more acceptable.[65] Himmler also planned for the *Lebensborn* homes to serve women and children well beyond the delivery itself. He intended to encourage single mothers to give up their children – ideally products of unions between "racially pure" women and members of the SS – for adoption by members of the SS so that they could be raised in National Socialist families.

All such state efforts to encourage unmarried women to "bear a child for the Führer" took place against the backdrop of publicly declared support for a more conservative definition of marriage and the family. Even within the party, very few people advocated equalizing motherhood inside and outside marriage. In 1937, the Reich minister of the interior announced: "The primordial cell of society is the family. The family is based on marriage. Marriage is the long-term relationship between two people of the opposite sex recognized and promoted by the state. Even if the state does not explicitly forbid other relationships, it also does not offer them its special protection. Such relationships are often short-term and thus true family life does not develop in them. They do not offer the necessary security for childrearing."[66] Thus, the Nazis did not redefine motherhood per se; rather, they tried to separate the rearing of children from the bearing of children. They encouraged "racially pure" women to bear children outside of marriage but discouraged them from raising the children they bore. They also tried to conceal the most obvious pronatalist and racist aspects of their policy to avoid the moral outrage of the German population.

The reverse side of Nazi pronatalism was the vicious condemnation of those single mothers deemed "unworthy." The line that divided worthy from unworthy, which was determined by a combination of contemporary science and National Socialist racism, meant that single motherhood in combination with other characteristics could mark a woman as "unworthy." Fritz Lenz, a leading eugenicist, denounced illegitimate children

---

65 Himmler also intended to eliminate the youth departments' scrutiny – and their surveillance of children's well-being. Lilienthal, *Der Lebensborn e. V.*, 88–9.

66 Richtlinien für die Erhebung des Widerspruchs gegen die Gewährung von Kinder Beihilfe Berlin, StaD, D 102 Lemgo, 183.

because he claimed they were "predominantly feebleminded, psychopathic and according to their physical condition less favorable than children born legitimately."[67] He judged mothers who bore illegitimate children equally harshly. NSV authorities also judged single mothers who applied for welfare more severely than other women.[68] Middle-class social workers often labeled single mothers who failed to keep their apartments up to middle-class standards "genetically asocial" or "feebleminded" rather than economically underprivileged. Because the Nazis believed "unworthy" single women placed an unnecessary burden on state resources, moreover, they sometimes went beyond denying aid to pursue compulsory sterilization. The accusation that single mothers were "morally compromised" put them at much greater risk of being sterilized.[69] Single women with multiple illegitimate children were especially likely to be considered immoral and nominated for forced sterilization, especially if those children had different fathers.[70] Moreover, because the belief that daughters of single mothers were genetically inclined toward "feeblemindedness" was widespread, they were frequently labeled "morally endangered," and their behavior was more strictly controlled than the behavior of most women.[71]

By condemning some single mothers and creating the illusion that they were maintaining – even strengthening – traditional morals, the Nazis attempted to make their pronatalist program for "worthy" single mothers more palatable to healthy, Aryan members of the *Volksgemeinschaft*. In fact, policy toward single mothers went far beyond what preceded it in terms of state intervention in family life and in the addition of race as a determinant of worthiness in single motherhood. "Unworthy" single mothers joined other "unworthy" women in their exclusion from Nazi benefits and often from motherhood itself. In contrast, the Nazis tried to equate single "worthy" mothers with married "worthy" mothers, giving them access to almost all state benefits for mothers. Although the *Lebensborn* program, the most radical pronatalist policy, was under the direct control of the SS, it was

---

67 Fritz Lenz, "Brauchen Wir mehr uneheliche Kinder?" *Neues Volk*, April 1937, 21, quoted in Pine, *Nazi Family Policy*, 42.

68 The guidelines also stated that illegitimate children were not eligible for child support (*Kinderbeihilfe*), whereas those of women in long-term relationships (*eheähnliche Gemeinschaft*) were eligible if nothing else precluded them.

69 StaD, D 102 Halle, 21; Bock, *Zwangssterilisation im Nationalsozialismus*, 405–7.

70 Bock, *Zwangssterilisation im Nationalsozialismus*, 406–7; Richtlinien für die Erhebung des Widerspruchs gegen die Gewährung von Kinderbeihilfe Berlin, StaD, D 102 Lemgo, 183.

71 The term "feebleminded" was applied to single mothers in the United States also. See Kunzel, *Fallen Women, Problem Girls*, 53.

but one part of the larger program to raise the birthrate. It is hence incorrect to view the Nazi state's efforts independently of either the *Lebensborn* program or the fundamental division of single mothers according to their racial worth.[72]

Not surprisingly, neither local authorities nor the general populace fully accepted Nazi policy for illegitimate children and their mothers, with the result that the actual legal, bureaucratic, and popular response to single mothers changed far less dramatically than Nazi policymakers had hoped. As in the Weimar era, a great deal of interest was focused on single mothers and their children in the courtroom. Using racial ideology as a foundation, Nazi policymakers claimed, "During the Third Reich, it is more important to identify the father of a child [for racial purposes] than that a potential father relieve the state of the burden of paying child support."[73] Despite their attempt to alter radically the grounds for paternity claims, the Nazis encountered institutional inertia. Many judges were holdovers from the Weimar era, and they did not share Nazi priorities in this matter.[74] Although the Nazis attempted to staff youth departments and the judiciary with party members, they lacked a sufficient number of suitable candidates. As a result, throughout the 1930s, single mothers and children, assisted by youth departments, still sought fathers not simply to confirm their identities "for racial purposes" but rather to force them to pay child support – that is, they continued to be motivated primarily by financial, not ideological, concerns in court hearings.

The Nazis' most significant impact on paternity cases came in the late 1930s with the wide-scale introduction of blood tests to identify fathers. The use of blood tests during the Nazi era comes as no surprise given the Nazis' emphasis on blood to define people and relationships. Although some courts had introduced blood tests at the end of the Weimar era, most rejected them as inaccurate.[75] Not until the latter half of the 1930s did the tide turn, and especially during the Second World War the use of blood tests became common legal practice. In most cases, the putative father, the mother, and the child underwent two sets of blood antigen tests. These tests could disqualify a man definitively, but they could not positively identify

---

72 Dorothee Klinksiek has separated the *Lebensborn* program from other Nazi programs for unmarried mothers because the *Lebensborn* program was controlled by the SS, and this separation has allowed her to argue that Nazi policy toward single mothers was beneficial. *Die Frau im NS-Staat*, 94–8.
73 Kreisausschuß Herford Kreisjugendamt to Herrn Regierungspräsident Minden, 11 January 1939, StaD, M1 IS, 31.
74 Berghahn, *Modern Germany*, 171–2.
75 SaM Amtsgericht Dortmund, 25, 28.

him. In practice, however, the courts labeled an accused man as the father if he was not definitively disqualified by blood tests, even when another male witness was potentially culpable.[76]

Blood tests dramatically changed the role morality played in paternity cases. Before the advent of blood tests, proof of a woman's promiscuity usually released a man accused of fathering her child from paternal responsibility (BGB §1717). But blood tests allowed the court to identify a father regardless of a woman's promiscuity. In one 1943 case in Wanne-Eickel, for example, the public guardian filed for child support for Jürgen, the son of Agnes G., a maid. The alleged father, Kurt B., a hunter, admitted to having had intercourse with Agnes but claimed he could not be the father because he had consistently used birth control. He also asserted that throughout her pregnancy Agnes G. had assured him that he was not the father. After Jürgen's birth, however, Agnes's parents convinced her that since the child looked like Kurt B., he must be the father. As a part of his defense, Kurt B. identified a local farmer, Heinrich S., who had also slept with Agnes around the time of conception, and Agnes admitted that she had done so. Both men, Agnes, and the child were given blood tests, which disqualified Kurt B. but not Heinrich S. The youth department promptly dropped the case against Kurt B. and sued Heinrich S. He, too, called a witness to attempt to deflect the verdict, but without success. Whether Agnes had in fact slept with a third man remains unclear, but the court ordered no further blood tests.[77] The youth department's willingness to use the blood tests to pursue a second man and the court's willingness to hear the case reveal a new disinclination to discuss morality combined with an ongoing concern to find a plausible father. In some cases, like that of Agnes G., where promiscuity alone might have put a mother in the "unworthy" category, the new blood tests dramatically increased a mother's chances of winning child support. Both the financial constraints on youth departments and the Nazi emphasis on determining racial genealogy pushed judges to rely increasingly on blood tests to determine paternity.

Though blood tests aided in deciding paternity cases, judges continued to rely on testimony. When the guardian of Peter, the son of factory worker Elizabeth O., sued another factory worker in a paternity case in 1944, the judge summed up the case, saying, "Even though the witness, as mother of

---

76 Two exceptions were when a woman refused to testify (see SaM, Amtsgericht Altena, 95) or when she was considered a bad witness (see SaM, Amtsgericht Dortmund, 64).
77 SaM, Amtsgericht Altena, 93.

the plaintiff, has a not insignificant interest in the outcome of the lawsuit, her testimony, strengthened by her oath, is believable."[78] Judges often based decisions on a combination of a "believable" story and a positive blood test.

The Nazi effort to aid "worthy" single mothers and their children increased the degree to which these families were placed under the observation of authorities. Through the NSF, the NSV, and the HMK, the Nazis provided "worthy" single mothers with child support, prenatal care, milk before and after birth, and items essential to infants. Expanding the system developed by the Reich Youth Welfare Law for oversight of illegitimate children, the Nazis assigned social workers and midwives to make house visits to young mothers in order to check on children's physical well-being and evaluate the state of their households.[79] Social workers examined households for cleanliness and order – including the timeliness with which dishes were washed and beds were made – and to make sure that children had their own beds. These visits allowed social workers to judge the mother's ability to raise a "good" child. In addition to requiring social workers and midwives to file reports, the state required mothers to bring their illegitimate children to see the county doctor every two months for the first year, every four months until age four, and twice a year thereafter.[80] Mothers who failed to comply risked losing their children. Block leaders, who were assigned to apartment buildings, also observed households and individuals and reported irregular behavior. In many cases, these leaders and neighborhood spies proved more effective as monitors of individual behavior than even the Gestapo.[81] Taken together, social workers, midwives, doctors, and block leaders enabled the state to monitor illegitimate children and both "worthy" and "unworthy" mothers.

Even as the Nazis tried to tighten control over single mothers, however, some mothers figured out how to manipulate the system. At least until the war started, Nazi rhetoric upheld full-time motherhood as the ideal. Although not all mothers accepted this ideal, some women used it to their own benefit. Ingrid M. was unmarried when her daughter, Susanna, was born in 1932. She elected to put Susanna into foster care with her sister, Frau E., so that she could work and earn money to help support the child. Susanna was granted child support from her father, a married auto mechanic who was also supporting two legitimate children. During lapses in support,

78 Ibid., 106.
79 StaD, D 100 Detmold, 900. For the role of midwives, see StaD, Dezernat 24 D1, 209.
80 Kreisjugendamt letter of instruction to single mothers, 1935, StaD, D 100 Detmold, 900.
81 Mallmann and Paul, "Omniscient, Omnipotent, Omnipresent?" 179–80.

the state stepped in to help Susanna. Ingrid did not earn enough to support Susanna alone, but she retained a large role in ensuring her daughter's financial well-being. She assumed that as Susanna's mother she had the right to control her daughter's finances and make the important decisions about her life. When in 1939 Ingrid discovered that after an interruption in payment Susanna's father had begun to send his support directly to Frau E., she was outraged. She told the youth department that there was no reason to bypass her, maintaining, "I provide the majority of the support for my child and I work hard for it." She felt the youth department had violated her rights by negotiating with Susanna's foster parents behind her back, and she complained: "I do not understand why Frau E. is informed about my earnings. If I refuse to tell her, I have my reasons." The youth department authorities found themselves caught in an awkward legal position, since Ingrid still had parental rights and partially supported the child. Though they would have liked to exclude Ingrid, the law forbade doing so when questions about her daughter's well-being arose.

Ingrid also understood National Socialist ideology on motherhood well enough to keep the system working for her. When she learned that Frau E. had begun to work for the Red Cross, Ingrid took Susanna and began to search for a new foster home. She refused to give Susanna to the child's biological father because she suspected that his only motive for wishing to take her was to lessen his financial responsibility. She scoured the newspapers herself to see if she could find new foster parents. Knowing that the youth department had a responsibility toward Susanna, she demanded a social worker pay more attention to her case and even turned to the NSF and NSV to see if they could help. Having decided not to raise Susanna herself, Ingrid refused to settle for less than a full-time mother for Susanna, and she readily used the state's new willingness to intervene on behalf of children.

When Frau E. learned that she had lost Susanna on account of her Red Cross work, she in turn challenged the youth department, citing another aspect of the Nazi family ideology. She pointed out that as a German citizen she had a duty to contribute to the war effort, but she said that she could not bear to lose her role as a mother. She pleaded with the county NSDAP leader for help getting Susanna back. On 21 April 1941, the Nazi county official wrote the youth department on Frau E.'s behalf, asserting that she and her husband had taken excellent care of Susanna; Herr E. had even done schoolwork with her. The letter emphasized that Frau E. only worked as a substitute for the Red Cross and concluded, "Given this, it would not be necessary to remove the child from this foster family." Ingrid continued to search for alternatives, and when the file ended in 1943, she was considering sending Susanna to a boarding school.[82]

What makes this case especially striking – aside from the fact that the mother and foster mother were sisters – is that both women understood the contradictory nature of Nazi policy and used it to their own advantage. Far from fearing state authorities' judgment of her as a single mother, Ingrid actively sought out and challenged state officials in her quest to find a full-time foster mother for her child. When her chosen foster mother started working, Ingrid searched for a better situation for Susanna. Though state authorities sometimes used single mothers' attempts to move their children from one foster family to another as proof that they were unfit mothers (a judgment that could result in the revocation of child custody), Ingrid suffered no such ill consequences. Frau E., on the other hand, pointed out to Nazi authorities that they could not simultaneously demand that she support the war effort and also impose full-time maternal responsibilities.

The state's treatment of Ingrid stands in stark contrast to the treatment received by women labeled "unworthy." Frau B. and her three illegitimate children lived on public welfare when the state decided she was not raising them properly. In 1938, the Warburg Amtsgericht transferred the two eldest children to an institution and sent the youngest to live with her grandmother. The county welfare office then bluntly informed Frau B. that she had to work and that any further children she bore would be put into foster care at birth. She responded by moving to Marburg to await the birth of her next child. Even in her absence, however, the *Landrat* and county welfare office organized the removal of her child from her. When the child was born, it was immediately taken from Frau B. and placed in a children's home in Arolsen. Youth department authorities informed her that they would never again permit her to run her own household or raise her children.[83] Other "unworthy" women found that scrutiny by welfare agencies was the first step toward forced sterilization.

For some women, single motherhood alone made them "unworthy" and put them on the path toward sterilization. In 1936, Maria A., a maid, was nominated for sterilization by her doctor because she had borne two illegitimate children by different men. The father of one child was married to another woman and paid no child support; the other child had died. When the court interviewed her, they found her answers punctuated with

---

82 Case of Ingrid M., StaD, D 100 Detmold, 471.
83 Correspondence between Landrat, Bezirksfürsorgeverband, and Regierungspräsident, 29 July 1938, StaD, M1 IS, 511.

pauses and her appearance suggestive of feeblemindedness and confirmed the doctor's opinion that "sterilization is urgently needed to prevent further children." Although both Maria and her father protested the proposed sterilization, her pregnancy with twins was terminated and she was sterilized.[84]

Sometimes Nazi nurses nominated women whose behavior they deemed "unworthy." Heidi H., a factory worker, was nominated for sterilization in 1939 by a Nazi nurse because she had three illegitimate children, none of whom was in her care. She discounted Heidi's claim that she had planned to marry her children's father until he left her for another woman. The nurse identified the roots of Heidi's genetic deficiency in her family: her mother was feebleminded, if industrious; her father, a drunk, had been sterilized for mild feeblemindedness. Her sister described Heidi as "dumb and [unable to] succeed in life" even while conceding that she was hardworking. The nurse also pointed to Heidi's poor performance at the special education school (*Hilfsschule*) she attended in 1923. The staff at the girls' home where she lived reported that she lacked any moral perspective. Heidi's teacher disagreed with the nurse's negative assessment, recalling Heidi as a friendly, punctual, and well-dressed student. Since Heidi was the only sibling to attend the special education school, the teacher doubted her problem was genetic. But after a doctor confirmed Heidi's feeblemindedness, she was sterilized.[85] Once identified by authorities, neither Heidi nor Maria were able to prove their "worthiness," especially in the face of the possible future offspring they might bear.

Occasionally women were able to overturn a label of "unworthiness" even if they had borne illegitimate children. In 1940, the Hagen *Amtsarzt* diagnosed Erna N. as feebleminded and nominated her for sterilization. Among the flaws he cited were her below-average intelligence and the three illegitimate children (ages twelve, seven, and ten months) she had by three different men. The doctor claimed "a weakness of judgment and a lack of restraint" had resulted in the children and necessitated sterilization. The nurse confirmed the doctor's impression that Erna displayed a "high degree of moral feeblemindedness," adding that she "was sexually very compulsive and indiscriminate in her choice of acquaintances and sexual partners." Erna challenged this negative assessment of her character, claiming that her status as a single mother was not intentional. She had planned to marry the first child's father, but had been stopped by his criminal record. The parents of the second child's father had prevented her intended marriage to their

84 StaD, Erbgesundheitsgericht, D 23 C, Detmold, 1420.
85 SaM, Erbgesundheitsgericht, 311.

son on religious grounds. Finally, she still planned to marry the third man, even though a schizophrenic episode had caused him to be sterilized. Erna's employer spoke highly of her, claiming that "nothing negative can be said about her." With this conflicted record before them, the judges on the herditary court granted Erna a lengthy interview, at the end of which they discarded the accusation of feeblemindedness and voted against sterilization, even granting her permission to marry.[86] Although the odds were against single mothers, some women succeeded in convincing the court that they were good mothers in unfortunate circumstances and that sterilization was wrong.

The Second World War brought new challenges to the Nazi programs directed at illegitimate children and their mothers. After 1939, the Nazi pronatalist agenda fell into crisis as the increasing number of deaths again outnumbered births. Pressures to increase the birthrate were intensified, and in 1943 abortion was declared a capital crime. Himmler's argument that "every victory with weapons is meaningless unless it is accompanied by the victory of a child" gained new significance as SS men died by the hundreds on the battlefields.[87] In his position as head of the SS, he began to exert pressure on soldiers to father children, calling it their duty as "last sons" to make sure they left offspring behind. Early in the war, he had issued a decree recommending that each SS man should impregnate a woman before leaving for the front lines, since "The greatest gift for the widow of a man killed in battle is always the child of the man she has loved." Later, he promised SS soldiers immunity from child support suits, emphasizing that the SS would care for all legitimate and illegitimate children.[88] Himmler even arranged for vacation time, hotel rooms, and train fares for wives and girlfriends so that soldiers fighting on the front could meet their loved ones for a few days away from the battlefield. Care was taken to schedule these visits during the optimal time for conception.[89] Beginning in 1942, Himmler established centers to advise childless SS wives and brides about childbearing. The *Lebensborn* homes became an open secret as they and their residents became more numerous during the war. By the end of the war, the Nazis' inability to place children born in the homes and the growing propensity of women to leave their newborns behind in the homes until they were able to provide

---

86 Ibid., 49.

87 Himmler speech from 1934, quoted in Lilienthal, *Der Lebensborn e. V.*, 132.

88 Himmler to all men of the SS and Police, Führer Headquarters, 28 October 1939, in Noakes, *German Home Front*, 368.

89 "Ausführungsbestimmungen zum Befehl des Reichsführers – SS vom 28. October 1939," 19 June 1940, Anordnung über planmäßigen Urlaub, in Lilienthal, *Der Lebensborn e. V.*, 135–8.

for them led to dangerous overpopulation of the homes and a rapidly rising infant mortality rate in the *Lebensborn* program.

Even in the context of war, not all party leaders agreed with Himmler's radical departure from convention. In 1939, Rudolf Hess, deputy führer, received a letter from a pregnant woman whose fiancé had been killed in battle. She complained that despite the fact that both she and her husband were Aryan, she found herself condemned to the social scorn traditionally directed at single mothers. In his widely published response, Hess expressed sorrow and outrage at her situation: "What would it help if a people were victorious but became extinct through the sacrifice for the victory?" he asked. Unlike Himmler, however, Hess's proposals to remedy the situation stopped short of suggesting that the status of all mothers be equalized. He, like most Germans, believed that the ideal place for children was in families, since only the family could teach a child how to be a member of the *Volksgemeinschaft*.[90]

Although the war posed obvious challenges to the Nazis' hopes of expanding the Aryan population, it did little to change most Germans' thinking about illegitimacy. The simple fact that most women of child-bearing age were separated from men after 1939 lowered the likelihood of reproduction. Even when men were not on the front lines, war-related work on the home front demanded so much time and energy from both men and women that there was little left for building families. For many women, uncertainty about their husbands' and fiancés' return after the war and the desire not to enter the postwar era as single mothers discouraged motherhood.[91] Difficult wartime conditions – which rendered everything scarce, from baby bottles to strollers to food itself – also convinced many women not to have children or to limit the size of their families.[92] Even in this context, however, the German populace resisted changing its opinions about illegitimacy. Most Germans' widespread opposition to what they saw as the immoral forced breeding of women caused both the *Lebensborn* program and the idea that women should "bear a child for the Führer" to be discussed largely in muffled tones. Many BDM and Reich Labor Service leaders refused to accept or teach the "new morals," and some parents removed their daughters from the BDM when they heard hints that what they perceived to

90 Heinemann, *What Difference*, 31–3; Kundrus, *Kriegerfrauen*, 357–8.
91 Frau Schnabel, interview; Boberach, *Meldungen aus dem Reich*, 28 May 1942, 3766–7; Heinemann, *What Difference*, 50–51.
92 Amtsarzt to Oberburgermeister der Stadt Bielefeld, 8 October 1941, StaD, Dezernat 24 D1, 212; Runderlass no. 240/44 Der Oberpräsident der Provinz Westfalen Landeswirtschaftsamt Münster to Landräte, Obergurgermeister, Wirtschaftsämter, 19 August 1944, StaD, M15, 65. See also Boberach, *Meldungen aus dem Reich*, 28 May 1942, 3766–7.

be immoral topics were being discussed.[93] In some BDM units, girls who became pregnant were expelled.[94] As a result, Himmler's ideas remained more rumor than reality – a thing of "adolescent fantasy." Many people I interviewed claimed to have known *of* someone who had borne a child for the Führer, but no one was personally acquainted with a woman who had done so.[95] Parents facing their daughter's illegitimate pregnancy often continued to push for abortion or marriage.[96] The outrage caused by Himmler's 1939 promise to free members of the SS from the burden of child support prompted him to issue a new order on 30 January 1940 reassuring SS men and the populace that he was not advocating illegitimate birth.[97] The very fact that *Lebensborn* homes placed such emphasis on helping women conceal their out-of-wedlock pregnancies reveals the ongoing lack of acceptance of illegitimacy in German society. Even within the *Lebensborn* homes themselves, married women and SS wives, who went to the homes for support during delivery and thereafter when husbands were away at war, asked for private rooms and expected better treatment than unmarried women. Delivery homes not run by the SS also continued to separate married and unmarried mothers until the end of the war.[98]

Even in the context of war, moreover, neither Himmler nor other Nazi leaders were prepared to openly disregard the traditional family or revise the sexual double standard that judged men's adultery less harshly than women's. *Lebensborn* homes opened their doors to married men's pregnant mistresses, but married women who became pregnant extramaritally could not turn to the *Lebensborn* homes for help, since the homes feared they might be accused of helping to deceive husbands. Thus, though they encouraged women to bear children and to raise the birthrate, Nazi leaders refused to offer women sexual freedom.

The *Lebensborn* program never gained the importance Himmler had hoped it would. Though he touted the selectivity with which women were chosen, claiming to admit only 40 to 50 percent of applicants, evidence

---

93 *Sopade Berichte* 2, no. 6 (1935): 695, and 3, no. 10 (1936): 1317–18.
94 Ibid., 2, no. 6 (1935): 693.
95 Herr Meyer, interview; Frau Schnabel, interview.
96 Jugendamt to Amtsgericht, report about the Riepings, StaD, D 106 A Detmold, 115. The desire to abort could have wider consequences, for example expulsion from the BDM. BDM Obergauführerin S. to NSDAP Kreisleitung Lippe, 1940, StaD, L113, 1038 bd. 2.
97 Himmler, Order for the whole SS and Police, 30 January 1940, in Noakes, *German Home Front*, 372.
98 Even the NSV homes kept careful records of each mother's marital status. Tätigkeitsberichte, NSV "Mutter und Kind" Heime, 1944, StaD, L113, 932; Lilienthal, *Der Lebensborn e. V.*, 64.

suggests that closer to 75 percent were admitted.[99] Moreover, the *Lebensborn* homes served a mostly middle-class population, likely reflecting middle-class Germans' unwillingness to accept illegitimate birth and the relative ease with which they proved their "worthiness." Single women seem to have gone to the homes more to avoid shame than because they wished to bear children for Hitler. The fact that only 5,000 of the 12,000 women who bore children in the *Lebensborn* homes between 1939 and 1945 were single mothers is indicative of the moral qualms raised by Himmler's attempt to adjust morality to ideology.[100]

Despite the small number of women involved, the *Lebensborn* homes are symbolically important because they illustrate the extent to which the Nazi state was willing to redefine morality in the name of pronatalist racial goals and highlight the gulf the Nazis tried to create between motherhood and reproduction, as even "racially pure" single women were expected to give their children up for adoption in SS families. In practice, this aspect of the politics of illegitimacy broke down at all levels: single mothers refused to place their children for adoption, married women did not consider single mothers their equals, SS families did not want to adopt, women deemed "unworthy" did not forswear reproduction, and, finally, the rising infant mortality rates in the *Lebensborn* homes severely compromised the effort to raise the birthrate.

The policy toward illegitimate children encountered further complications after 1939 as many alleged fathers left for the front lines. In the context of war, pursuing soldier fathers in paternity cases raised fundamental questions of national priorities as well as practical questions of which court had jurisdiction and how to identify witnesses.[101] The difficulties inherent in conducting court proceedings from a distance encouraged some soldiers charged in paternity cases to list as many potential fathers as possible – a sometimes successful tactic. In 1944, one soldier listed seven, a list that the mother claimed was completely fabricated. Another soldier listed as a possible alternative father a seventy-six-year-old man. When Gustav S., a truck driver turned soldier, named Markus K. as a witness, he did not know that Markus K. was in an English prison. While the court sometimes commented

99 This was the number cited by head leader of the *Lebensborn*, Willy Ziesmer, at the Nuremberg trials, but Georg Lilienthal estimates the total to have been between 7,000 and 8,000 in *Der Lebensborn e. V.*, 92.

100 Ibid., 229–30.

101 It was decided that career soldiers would use the courts where they were stationed, whereas drafted soldiers would continue to deal with the courts at home. SaM, Amtsgericht Altena, 86.

with disbelief on the choice of witnesses, it usually did not refuse to hear the testimony.[102] Markus's inability to testify prevented the court from determining fatherhood, and the case languished until after the war ended.[103] Waiting for witnesses to testify was detrimental to mothers and children, and many mothers complained about the delays, since during the wait they usually received only limited state support.

Finding adequate representation for soldiers and collecting the relevant information for the court became almost impossible in time of war. Blood tests proved all but impossible to administer on the front lines. Even when military doctors agreed to conduct them, their lengthy transport back to a laboratory at home frequently rendered the samples unusable. Soldiers' lawyers argued that the war made it all but impossible to communicate with their clients and locate witnesses. Battles over paternity regularly drew the most intimate details of relationships into the courtroom – details to which no remote representative was likely to have access. In 1941, one soldier who denied paternity claimed through his representative that he had always used contraceptives and accused the mother of promiscuity. In court, the mother defended herself by providing further details of their sexual relationship. The soldier's representative, who had only limited information about the relationship, "groped around in the dark" for a response. In the end, he wrote the soldier to inquire about the woman's testimony and to ask whether there were witnesses who could testify to the woman's promiscuity. The representative's letter was returned stamped "Addressee no longer with the unit. Await new address." Meanwhile, the mother continued to push the case forward, since her child's well-being depended on her receiving child support. Ultimately unable to contact his client, the representative conceded defeat on the assumption that the decision could always be challenged at a later date.[104]

Some legal experts argued that, in principle, soldiers should be protected from paternity allegations during the war. In an opinion in *Deutsches Recht*, a judge by the name of Hellbach stressed that a soldier's dedication to fighting for the nation ought to protect him from the burden of having to pay child support.[105] But disagreement on the topic was widespread. While some judges postponed cases, another argued that "identifying a father and

---

102 Ibid.   103 Ibid., 98.

104 Boberach, *Meldungen aus dem Reich*, 15, January 1941, 3169–71.

105 Judge Hellbach, "Unterhaltsklagen außerehelichen Kinder gegen Soldaten im Kriege," cited in Heinrich Webler, "Dienst in der Wehrmacht: Ein Freibrief für ledige Väter?" Sonderdruck aus *Deutsche Jugendhilfe* (Berlin: Carl Heymanns Verlag, [October/November 1940]), StaD L113, 930. This piece is undated, but the date of a response to the piece by Heinrich Webler suggests that it was most likely published in 1940.

making him pay child support belong[ed] among the matters critical to war."[106] In November 1940, Heinrich Webler, a front-line army officer, wrote in reply to Judge Hellbach that "every soldier in the war has the duty to clear up his personal matters as quickly as possible." He argued that it was contrary to family law and state interests to allow soldiers to escape their paternal responsibilities. He went on to warn, "We [in the army] would like to take a stand against the not insignificant danger that a certain sentimentalization that is completely unknown on the front lines is being mobilized for selfish reasons and a superficial view of sexual intercourse and its consequences is being supported where duty and responsibility need to be strengthened."[107] The government was of a different opinion, however: on 13 October 1942, soldiers were promised protection from personal matters, including paternity suits, that might interfere with their war-related responsibilities.

Protecting men from paternity suits did nothing to help men whose paternity had already been established. To these men, the state offered another escape from paying child support. In May 1940, illegitimate children were declared eligible for family allowances if their paternity had been determined by a court and their fathers had – or would have – supported them. Rather than face a mountainous debt of child support payment after the war, many soldier fathers were willing to see their illegitimate children receive state benefits. For illegitimate children and their mothers, the impact of the state's decision was less straightforward. Once children were awarded state support, they lost their right to receive child support from their fathers. While this had the advantage of ensuring that children received support consistently and promptly, in many cases the amount of state support illegitimate children received was considerably lower than that ordered by the court. After the Russian campaign brought the German death toll into the millions, the rules for receiving family allowances were further eased so that in the case of a soldier's death, if an intent to marry could be proven, both illegitimate children and their mother became eligible. This right was cancelled only if the solider was married to someone other than the mother, if more than one woman filed for a single soldier's benefits, or if a woman was proven to have Jewish blood.[108]

The effect of this change on women's and children's chances of winning illegitimacy cases remains unclear. Although fewer paternity cases were

106 SaM, Amtsgericht Altena, 88.
107 Webler, "Dienst in der Wehrmacht," StaD, L113, 930.
108 Boberach, *Meldungen aus dem Reich*, 17 July 1941, 2539–40; Kundrus, *Kriegerfrauen*, 359.

brought to trial after 1939 (3,313 in Westphalia compared to 4,428 in 1929), this may reflect the declining birthrate rather than a lower proportion of illegitimate births or the existence of a smaller proportion of single mothers willing to request support for their children. In Westphalia, the number of cases won by fathers increased from 15 percent in 1929 to 25 percent in 1939. (In the city of Minden, the numbers were 9.6 percent and 16.7 percent, respectively.)[109] This might be evidence of the courts' changing perception of soldiers' responsibility toward illegitimate children. The court records I examined suggest, however, that in the overwhelming majority of cases throughout the war, the determining factor in paternity cases continued to be blood. This would imply that the courts did not dramatically change their attitudes toward fathers.

Further suggestions for helping illegitimate children arose from various sources during the war. Many party members and civil registry authorities proposed creating a less thorough registration – one that would hide a child's illegitimate birth, especially for school purposes.[110] Others argued that illegitimate children whose fathers died in the war deserved special consideration. In 1940, the minister of the interior offered soldiers' fiancées the option of taking the soldiers' name even if he died before they could marry. Because this did little to help illegitimate children, however, they also insisted that the word "illegitimate" be omitted from the birth certificates of the children of deceased soldiers.

Reports filed by the SD make it clear that the German population was well attuned to the problems posed by paternity in wartime. Many Germans believed that paternity suits should be postponed until after the war. Rather than leaving illegitimate children to languish, however, they asserted that the state should support illegitimate children until a case could be heard.[111] Of greater concern for many was the growing number of children whose alleged fathers died before they acknowledged paternity, extinguishing any hope of paternity being established. According to the law, a man had to acknowledge paternity either in court or to his battalion commander for it to be legally established. In some cases, however, a man's intention to marry was patently obvious even though he had failed to follow the correct legal steps. One officer in the Luftwaffe, for example, failed to marry his fiancée before their baby was born because the military doctor had hindered the wedding. When the baby arrived during his leave, he nonetheless

109 *Statistisches Jahrbuch* 26 (1930); 58 (1940).
110 Boberach, *Meldungen aus dem Reich*, 29 January 1940, 703–4.
111 Ibid., 15 January 1941, 3169–72.

celebrated and very publicly acknowledged his paternity. After his return to Russia, he reinforced his claim to fatherhood, referring to "our little daughter" in numerous letters. Despite the officer's unequivocal acknowledgment of his paternity, when his plane was shot down, state authorities denied his fiancée state support. Of this and similar cases, the SD was aware, the population "[did] not hold back its criticism": the German people demanded that the law be changed to protect such clear miscarriages of justice.[112] Some argued that soldiers needed to acknowledge paternity even before their children were born to avoid the all-too-common occurrence of soldiers being transferred – or dying – before their paternity could be established.[113]

In the many discussions about how to alleviate the problems caused by sexually active soldiers, few people criticized moral latitude granted sexually active soldiers. In contrast, for women sexual activity outside marriage was one of the easiest ways to earn the label immoral.[114] Westphalian illegitimacy cases from the Second World War confirm that a woman seen together with a soldier was enough to stir suspicions in the welfare department and the courts. And yet, at a time when so many men were in uniform, it would have been difficult to find a man who was not. Far worse were relationships with the many foreign workers stationed in Germany. Nearly one quarter of all political crimes in 1940 – 1941 were for "forbidden contact" and most resulted in guilty verdicts.[115]

Accusations of immorality were often based on the observations of neighborhood spies, who monitored people's social contacts. Especially for single mothers, neighborhood spying constituted a loathsome intrusion into their private affairs. In 1942, Frau S., a war widow, began a paternity suit against a worker to get child support for her child. At the request of the accused man, a number of people from her apartment testified about her behavior and lifestyle. The landlord testified that he had heard a man's voice in her apartment at 12:20 one night when he was hauling water. Furthermore, he told the court that the woman who lived below Frau S. had heard men's footsteps in the apartment in the early morning hours. Another neighbor remembered hearing someone leaving Frau S.'s apartment at 5:40 A.M. Although Frau R. had not actually seen anyone that morning: "I assumed

---

112 Ibid., 17 July 1941, 2539–40; 6 March 1941, 2082–3.
113 Ibid., 20 February 1941, 2029.
114 Susan Gubar sees a direct connection between the emasculation men felt at their own helplessness on the battlefront and their fear that women were betraying them at home, which fueled stories of female spies, syphilitic whores, and other similarly threatening women. See "This Is My Rifle," 240.
115 This included both married and unmarried women. Heinemann, *What Difference*, 59.

that it was the soldier I had seen in the apartment the previous night." This witness went on to note: "I observed that she left her child alone at home and went out with this person." Thus Frau S. stood accused of two immoral acts – sleeping with a soldier and neglecting her child – and had no chance of winning support for her child.[116] Because Frau S. stood accused of two serious offenses, few judges would have shown leniency toward her despite her status as a widow.

Another problem, common already during the Weimar era, that became more complicated after the war began was how youth departments should deal with men who shunned their obligation to pay child support. Like their predecessors, the National Socialists garnished men's wages or, if they refused to work, sent them to workhouses. Though the Nazis often attributed the problems of delinquent fathers to their "asocial" natures, they did not propose forced sterilization for men, as was common for "asocial" women. After the war began, state authorities worried that supporting illegitimate children would diminish men's ability to work for the war effort. This concern had some validity, as men were known to switch jobs regularly to avoid having their wages garnished. But after 1939 the problem took on national significance, because tracking down delinquent fathers demanded scarce time from youth department authorities, thus threatening the war effort. When one father in Bielefeld refused to pay the child support ordered in his court settlement in 1935, he was put in a workhouse, where authorities collected his child support payments until he disappeared. In October 1938, the mayor wrote five companies searching for him before finally locating him. The company began to garnish his wages, but by August 1940 he had disappeared again, and it was not until December of that year that he was relocated – only to disappear again in April.[117] During the war, many people felt that the time, expense, and work that went into locating fathers was counterproductive, and they questioned the value of collecting child support under these conditions. As the courts and youth departments debated whether failing to pursue fathers encouraged irresponsible behavior, many single mothers and their children fell victim to lapses in child support.

CONCLUSION

Both Weimar and National Socialist authorities considered single mothers and their children a troublesome issue and revised their policy. During the Weimar era, widespread fear that raising the status of single mothers

---

116 SaM, Amtsgericht Altena, 97.   117 StaB, Jugendamt-Amtsvormundschaft, 67.

and illegitimate children would destroy the traditional family and increase social immorality prevented the sweeping legislative changes advocated by the Social Democrats. Despite this, real reform went considerably further than the rhetorical changes noted by Cornelia Usborne.[118] The Reich Youth Welfare Act compelled the creation of youth departments that after 1922 increasingly took over guardianship of illegitimate children. These guardians – in conjunction with judges' awareness of the state's limited budget – forced a growing number of fathers to support their illegitimate children, thus improving single mothers' situations as well. Moreover, the focus on identifying a man to provide support pushed single mothers' immorality into the background unless their "promiscuity" was blatant. Karen Hagemann is correct to stress that the traditional "proletarian" sense of morality that pressured working-class men to marry their pregnant girlfriends went a long way toward restoring the honor of many single mothers while simultaneously legitimizing their children. This should not, however, detract from our awareness of the growing number of illegitimate children whose lives were improved because the courts ordered their fathers to pay child support and they did pay. Nor should we lose sight of the fact that Weimar efforts to help illegitimate children resulted in a decline in illegitimate infant mortality.[119]

Unmarried mothers' relationship to both single motherhood and the state also changed during the 1920s. All but the poorest young women and men practiced some form of birth control, and many who nevertheless became pregnant resorted to abortion. As Atina Grossmann has pointed out, popular culture encouraged New Women to enjoy sex but avoid pregnancy.[120] Thus, women who became pregnant were increasingly viewed as stupid rather than immoral.[121] Rather than cower in poverty, many single mothers began going to court and fighting for child support. While some found the state's escalated interest in the well-being of their illegitimate children meant intrusion into their homes and surveillance of their housekeeping and mothering skills, the degree to which this was true varied from case to case. Some guardians intervened often and intrusively, confirming Karen Hagemann's claim that "the state welfare measures were directed not at providing autonomy and equality for single mothers, but rather [they] increased their dependence on the 'Father State' and promoted the discrimination

---

118 Usborne, *Politics of the Body*, 61–2.
119 Infant mortality rates among illegitimate children dropped from 25.5 per 1,000 in 1923 to 15.5 in 1929. *Statististisches Jahrbuch* 23 (1925): 11; 26 (1930): 252.
120 Grossmann, *Reforming Sex*, 100.
121 Ibid., 99–101; Usborne, *Politics of the Body*, 212; Hagemann, *Frauenalltag und Männerpolitik*, 175–6.

and stigma [they suffered] as a societal fringe group."[122] But many others encountered significantly less state presence. Nonetheless, the potential for state control, together with the economic hardship and social stigma – to say nothing of the responsibility of single parenting – likely restricted the number of women who proudly and defiantly became single mothers.[123]

Like their predecessors, Nazi policymakers worried about social immorality and infant mortality, but for them, single mothers and illegitimate children represented one more avenue for furthering a racist and pronatalist agenda. In a strong challenge to tradition, the Nazi policy on illegitimacy made "worthy" single mothers and their children eligible for state support but barred "unworthy" mothers and their children from any support. Social workers, doctors, nurse hygienists, party officials, and neighbors were all enlisted to evaluate single mothers' worthiness. Women deemed unworthy risked losing their children or being forcibly sterilized.

Many factors obstructed the smooth application of Nazi policy toward illegitimate children. Chief among the obstacles was the German populace's unwillingness to change its traditional, often religiously based notions of morality. Throughout the Nazi era, single mothers found the easiest way to prove their "worthiness" was to marry, and about half did.[124] Even some prominent Nazi leaders rejected the idea of equalizing the status of all mothers without regard to their marital status. Within the wider German population, there was widespread refusal to accept the Nazi idea that there was such a thing as a "worthy" or desirable single mother. Parents responded with outrage and horror when their daughters were taught that single motherhood could be a noble contribution to society. The very fact that the *Lebensborn* homes remained cloaked in secrecy demonstrates the Nazis' failure to effect significant change in attitudes toward single motherhood.

But the Nazi policy on illegitimacy also faltered on the painstakingly difficult and inaccurate process of distinguishing "worthy" from "unworthy." Although the law was not changed, blood tests prevented many fathers from using a woman's sexual history to avoid paying child support. By enabling women to win support for their children even when they had had multiple partners, moreover, blood tests also rendered the distinction between "worthy" and "unworthy" largely irrelevant to youth departments and courts interested primarily in finding a father to pay child support. Despite the validity in Dorothee Klinksiek's claim that Nazi authorities preferred to

---

122 Hagemann, *Frauenalltag und Männerpolitik*, 196.
123 Cornelia Usborne argues that some middle-class women "who could not or would not marry" decided to bear children anyway. See *Politics of the Body*, 212.
124 Heinemann, *What Difference*, 36.

overlook one "desirable" child rather than to risk allowing one "non-Aryan" into the *Volksgemeinschaft*, blood tests went a long way toward separating questions of morality and worthiness from determinations of who was awarded child support.[125] At the same time, some "worthy" single mothers who believed the Nazi promise to support mothers regardless of their marital status demanded support only to discover that authorities were unprepared to give it to them and unsure of how to deal with them.

The high mortality rate in the Second World War, especially after 1942, posed further challenges to the Nazi policies towards illegitimate children. The high death rate in the war dramatically increased the state's need to raise the birthrate even as it simultaneously reduced married couples' time together and hence their ability and desire to bear children. The war also dramatically complicated the situation for single mothers and their children. With soldiers away at the front, establishing paternity often became impossible. Nazi authorities genuinely worried about illegitimate children whose only possibility of being legitimized – or of ever proving their "Aryan heritage" – died on the battlefield. SD reports reveal the German population's active interest in resolving such war-related problems. Many Germans also worried about the war's impact on young, pregnant women whose boyfriends and fiancés were stationed on the front lines. Widespread support for postponing paternity suits until after the war went hand in hand with support for making soldiers' benefits more easily accessible to illegitimate children even when their soldier fathers had died. Both Germans' wartime concerns about single mothers and their children and the Nazi effort to find solutions to these concerns largely disregarded race and questions of worthiness, thus undermining the core of the Nazi policy toward illegitimate children.

---

125 Klinksiek, *Die Frau im NS-Staat*, 95.

6

Forming Families beyond Blood Ties

Foster Care and Adoption

Furthermore, the foster parents commit themselves to keeping the child out of factories, mines, and other such business operations altogether and allow work around the house only insofar as it is in keeping with the child's strengths and does not put the child's physical, psychological or moral development at risk.

— Der Landeshauptmann der Provinz Westfalen, 20 July 1926

The National Socialist worldview and its effect on population policy, development of the *Volk* [*Volksaufartung*], and spiritual renewal necessarily leads to the effort to incorporate the foster child as an important member of the entire German youth, into the nurturing *Volksgemeinschaft* as a comrade.

— *Mutter und Volk*, lead columnist Klara Lönnies, 8 May 1934

During the Weimar and National Socialist eras, the belief that children were best off in families enjoyed almost unanimous support. Despite this, national demographics made it readily apparent that not all German children could be raised in traditional families. The vast number of orphans and fatherless and indigent children, together with the low birthrate and high infant mortality rate, propelled German officials to reconceptualize their role in helping families and children. It was in dealing with children whose families had broken down that the Weimar and National Socialist regimes faced their most urgent family-oriented responsibility: defining the institution of the family in such a way as to enable the creation of non–biologically based groups that functioned as families. Many of the questions they faced were similar: what defined a proper parent, how to decide what constituted a good home, how to monitor families after they had been created. But while Weimar authorities made child welfare their primary concern, the National Socialists added racial considerations, dramatically shifting the contours of both foster care and adoption.[1]

---

1 Epigraphs are drawn from StaM, Amt Wolbeck B 15, 11, and StaD, D 106 A, 588, respectively.

Weimar reformers faced the immediate and dire problem of how to handle the almost 1.2 million orphans who had been robbed of a normal family life by the war. With so many fathers dead and so many mothers unable to remarry, a near unanimous conviction existed that unless the German state could create families in which patriarchal authority and maternal nurturing were present, these children would be at risk of delinquency and promiscuity. In December 1918, Chancellor Friedrich Ebert proclaimed that the "'principal duty' of the new government" was to provide welfare for war victims.[2] Beyond a general agreement that children needed support, however, politicians disagreed about the form this support should take, making drafting and enacting legislation enormously contentious. Chief among the debated issues was how the state could encourage the creation of foster and adoptive families while simultaneously monitoring the families it created.

When the Nazis assumed power, they resolved theoretical qualms about state intervention in the family and extended the state's license to infringe on parental rights. They fashioned a new, biologically grounded definition of a good parent and applied biological, social, and racial criteria in their selection of both foster and adoptive parents. The demand for foster parents increased so dramatically during the war, however, that the Nazis expanded their definition of foster parents, even though it meant overturning the traditional definition of family.

Like their Weimar predecessors, local authorities under the Third Reich found that playing their legal supervisory role often jeopardized the sustenance of the nontraditional families they sought to create. Moreover, when prospective foster and adoptive parents balked at the convoluted application process, many of the youth department authorities charged with the task of carrying out the new Nazi guidelines for assigning children to foster and adoptive families questioned the wisdom of a state-mandated evaluation process that reduced the pool of eligible parents.

FOSTER CARE BETWEEN 1918 AND 1932

The First World War seemed to many Germans to have utterly disrupted German children's well-being – and with it, Germany's chances of recovering its prewar strength. War orphans, who constituted the largest single group of recipients of war-related state benefits during the early 1920s, forced lawmakers to recognize the dire state in which the war had left many children. To exacerbate the problem, most widows were young women with

---

2 Bessel, *Germany after the First World War*, 274.

very small children who also depended on the state for their livelihoods, but widows' pensions, calculated according to a soldier's rank and not his income before enlistment, were so meager that they left many women in desperate economic straits. Although attempts were made to shelter widows from demobilization dismissals, many "faced catastrophe" even with the help of church charity.[3] As a result, deprivation became a fact of life for children who had lost their fathers in the war.[4]

In 1919, the Weimar Constitution made national and local authorities responsible for child welfare and child protection, and Article 120 of the constitution proclaimed that "the education of children and young people to physical, mental and social fitness is the prime duty and the natural right of parents; the carrying out of these duties is watched over by the state."[5] Despite this constitutional decree and general agreement among politicians across the political spectrum that the state needed to support children, practical political disagreements mounted. While conservative politicians worried that too much state support would undermine patriarchal authority and absolve parents of responsibility, Social Democratic politicians argued that ad hoc solutions would not repair a system that was in need of a complete overhaul. The culmination of heated Reichstag debates was the 1922 Reich Youth Welfare Law, which laid the legal groundwork for defining "family" and created a norm for parenting. As the previous chapter discussed, it established a national youth department that set guidelines for youth policy. Local youth departments, funded by the city and county, were to implement national youth policy locally, supervise foster children, care for orphans, and provide legal guardians for illegitimate children. To ensure that individual children's needs were identified and met, social workers employed by the youth departments were to visit all babies born to single women and check on other children who came to the department's attention through doctors, teachers, the police, or welfare workers. For children whose families broke down or whose mothers could not or would not care for them, youth departments stepped in to facilitate foster care and adoption placements. Youth department responsibilities also included ensuring that all children received food, shelter, education, and job training. Weimar youth department authorities sought to improve children's lives by raising the quality

---

3 In 1913, a skilled worker earned an average of 120 to 150 marks a month. A widow's pension was much lower: 33.3 marks for a private's widow, 41.66 marks for a corporal's widow, and 50 marks for a sergeant's widow. They received an additional nine marks a month for each child. Whalen, *Bitter Wounds*, 76.
4 Bessel, *Germany after the First World War*, 275.
5 Weimar Constitution, quoted in Harvey, *Youth and the Welfare State*, 165.

"Children in Need." In 1920, children demonstrated in the streets of Berlin against the hunger so common after the First World War. Courtesy of Getty Images.

of foster and adoptive homes through close initial analysis and long-term supervision.

Weimar officials preferred to place children in foster families over orphanages or other institutions because doing so was less expensive than institutional care and because they believed that foster children received more personal attention when they lived with families. To raise the quality of foster care, the Reich Youth Welfare Law established new national guidelines for foster homes and mandated that foster parents obtain permits from the local youth department before taking in foster children.[6] The permit system was designed to ensure that only healthy, moral, and financially stable families raised foster children. Doctors, social workers, and building code experts all assessed a potential foster family and its home before a permit was granted. Because youth department authorities and social workers firmly believed that only responsible, upstanding foster parents could raise the healthy, strong children Germany needed, in examining potential foster parents, they felt bound to assess more than their financial stability and status. As they began to implement the law's guidelines, they tried to locate homes that matched each child's character and religious denomination.[7] Not surprisingly, these attempts added significantly to the youth departments' workload, since they required a high level of contact with both children and parents. The 1926 application of Frau B., a forty-one-year-old housewife, was not unusual. Her family included herself; her husband, a forty-five-year-old worker; and their fifteen-year-old daughter. In the letter of application, Frau B. wrote: "We are Catholic by religion. No family member has been convicted [of a crime]. We live in orderly pecuniary circumstances and own a house with five large rooms so that the supervision and care of the child can be ensured." She agreed to the conditions of care established by the Münster Youth Department and requested a monthly compensation.[8] Many potential foster parents went further and submitted letters of reference from pastors and priests confirming their suitability as foster parents.

Some people felt the youth departments went too far in their quest to find suitable parents, bypassing many perfectly good candidates. In 1926, a judge in Münster protested the rejection rate for potential foster parents. He was

---

6 RJWG §22. The RJWG defined a foster child as "a legitimate or illegitimate child under twenty-four years of age who spends a long time in the care of others." This definition stood regardless of whether the caregiver was financially reimbursed for the care or not. The children could be in the care of others continuously day and night or repeatedly for part of the day or on particular days.

7 Der Preussische Minister für Volkswohlfahrt to Regierungspräsidenten Münster, 5 May 1931, StaM, Amt Wolbeck B 15, 11.

8 Report on Frau B., 9 August 1926, StaM, Amt Wolbeck B 15, 12.

particularly incensed because in the last year, "countless cases [had] arisen in which applications from Münster city civil servants . . . were rejected." In his mind, these men's status, their financial stability, and their faithful service to their country during the war made them acceptable parents by definition.[9] Other authorities pushed social workers to visit foster homes regularly to ensure that they were suitable, and some even argued that all potential foster parents should have a medical exam before receiving a permit.[10] Every such suggestion had to be weighed against the burden it would create for parents, children, and administrators. In 1930, the Detmold county doctor, Dr. Frenzel, rejected mandatory medical exams for children because they were wholly inappropriate in a small community like Detmold, where he knew almost all foster children from either his office hours or the infant welfare centers. Other youth department and medical authorities worried that requiring extra medical certification would discourage potential foster parents. In the end, officials rejected the stricter medical guidelines, leaving it to the youth departments' discretion to check with the doctor about the placement of children on a case-by-case basis.[11]

As the qualifications for foster parents became more rigorous, locating qualified foster parents became a mounting problem, especially in rural areas.[12] Financial constraints often pitted youth departments against one another in the scramble for sufficient foster homes. Lippe, for example, had trouble appointing foster parents because it could only afford to pay twenty to thirty marks a month in compensation, whereas other neighboring youth departments like Bielefeld paid as much as forty-five marks a month. In 1921, the *Regierungspräsident* of Münster announced, "Despite all efforts, we cannot locate enough suitable foster homes."[13] As a result, he called on other organizations that had contact with parents, such as the Organization for Infant and Toddler Welfare (Verein für Säuglings- und Kleinkinderfürsorge), to work together with county social workers to identify available families. During difficult economic times, moreover, when many families fell short of the requirements for financial stability, youth department authorities struggled to determine eligibility. One youth department's authorities urged, "Foster families with tenuous economic circumstances should not be judged too critically." Even a sudden decline in economic prosperity did not

9 Amtsgerichtsrat to Oberbürgermeister Münster, 15 July 1926, StaM, Amt 10, 49.
10 Crew, "Ambiguities of Modernity," 322.
11 Sitzung des Jugendamtes, 19 September 1930, StaD, D 106 A, 588.
12 Stadt Münster Bericht des Säuglingsheims und Säuglingskrankenhauses zu Münster über das Kalenderjahr 1920 gemäss Verfügung der Herrn Regierungs-Präsidenten, 28 September 1920, StaM, Amt Wolbeck B 15, 11.
13 Letter Detmold, Lippische Regierung Fürsorge Abteilung, 18 March 1926, StaD, D 106 A, 588.

necessarily represent grounds for removing foster children from otherwise good homes.[14]

Youth department authorities also frequently found that national ideals conflicted with local ideas about foster parenting. Although state officials appealed to respectable childless couples to become foster parents, in Münster most applicants were couples who already had children and who saw their wards primarily as a source of extra income. When youth department workers realized that a family's major incentive was monetary, they did not always know how to react. In 1931, one county social worker reported to the mayor of Wolbeck that although all three of the households she had inspected were orderly, all had "stated that the main reason they wanted a foster child... was because they could earn a comfortable extra income."[15] For rural families, foster children were crucial unpaid workers.[16] These circumstances forced youth department authorities to struggle to clarify the definition of a good foster home and to recognize that, much as they wished for things to be otherwise, many foster parents had motives other than ensuring a child's well-being.

Similarly, guidelines had to be applied differently in rural than in urban areas. While Münster city officials remained adamant that every child should have his or her own bed, this requirement caused substantial confusion outside city limits.[17] Blomberg youth authorities discovered that for many rural families, allowing children of the same sex and similar age to share beds was common and necessary. To give a foster child a bed of his or her own in such a context might even have stigmatized the child. Because a literal interpretation of the regulations would have eliminated nearly all rural families from consideration as foster parents, the youth department authorities decided to bend the rules, explaining, "It seems to us unjustified that foster children should be privileged above [the foster parent's] own children."[18] In these and other cases, national guidelines had to be modified to meet local conditions.

With the passage of the Reich Youth Welfare Law, Weimar authorities hoped to supervise and monitor foster children in their new homes. By

---

14 Niederschrift über die Konferenz der mit der Pflegkinderaufsicht in Anstalten betrauten Ärzte im Regierungsbezirk N, StaM, Amt Wolbeck B 15, 11.

15 Kreisfürsorgerin report to Bürgermeister of Wolbeck, 10 January 1931, StaM, Amt Wolbeck B 15, 12.

16 Crew, *Germans on Welfare*, 126.

17 Niederschrift über die Konferenz der mit der Pflegekinderaufsicht in Anstalten betrauten Ärzte im Regierungsbezirk N, StaM, Amt Wolbeck B 15, 11.

18 Letter Jugendamt Blomberg/Land, 25 April 1931, StaD, L 80 IC, Gruppe 28, Fach 22, 1; Fürsorgerin report to Bürgermeister Wolbeck, 28 August 1930, StaM, Amt Wolbeck B 15, 12.

granting youth departments the right and responsibility to observe foster homes, this part of the law undermined foster families' privacy. Specifically, the law required foster parents "to permit the youth department representatives access to their homes and their foster child."[19] Though it recognized the potential for conflict between foster parents' rights and the state's responsibility to monitor foster children – "The regulations governing the supervision of foster children must, on the one hand, contain the necessary protective clauses [for children], while on the other hand avoiding excessive intrusion into the personal relationships of foster parents" – it put the onus of negotiating the delicate balance between protecting children and preserving families on the youth departments.[20]

From the outset, many people viewed the new regulations with skepticism. After the *Regierungspräsident* issued the Order with Regard to the Protection of Foster Children on 17 July 1924, Westphalian magistrates (*Amtsmänner*) who feared that no family would willingly put itself under the state's watchful eye "unanimously predicted that within a very short time . . . no family would be prepared to take in foster children."[21] The Reich Youth Welfare Law's novelty lay in its attempt to make supervision of foster children universal and to change from a police-directed (*polizeilich*) supervision to a welfare-directed (*fürsorgerisch*) supervision. Female social workers, who offered advice (and judgment) on household maintenance and childcare rather than merely on physical safety, were to replace male police officers as the overseers of children in foster care. Ultimately, although the state's goal was to ensure that all "foster children be treated as much as possible like children in their own famil[ies]," its surveillance of foster children clearly distinguished foster children from biological children.[22]

Many foster parents resented any state intervention in their families.[23] Some felt that the "policing of the family carried out by Weimar youth offices was even more intrusive than normal policy practices because it was

---

19 Schutz der Pflegekinder §§22, 24, 25 und 26 des Reichsgesetzes für Jugendwohlfahrt, SaM, Oberpräsidium Münster, 6034.

20 RJWG.

21 Letter from Landrat und Protokollführer Graf von Westfalen, Anordnung betr. the Schutz der Pflegekinder, StaM, Amt Wolbeck B 15, 11.

22 This point was made by Stadtarzt Dr. H. as part of a historical survey of the development of foster care. Niederschrift über die Konferenz der mit der Pflegkinderaufsicht in Anstalten betrauten Ärzte im Regierungsbezirk N, StaM, Amt Wolbeck B 15, 11.

23 Furthermore, the state's observation of foster children did not have an unblemished history. Already in 1915, the mayor of Siegen had complained about the effect of the police supervision (*polizeiliche Beaufsichtigung*), which in "many cases le[d] to hardships in which ultimately the children themselves suffer." Bürgermeister Siegen to Regierungspräsidenten in Minden and Münster, 8 May 1915, SaM, Oberpräsidium Münster, 5925.

triggered by amorphous, arbitrarily defined threats of 'neglect' [*Verwahrlosung*]."[24] Whereas some prospective foster parents decided against taking in foster children altogether, others who did take in children tried to evade the social workers. Still others refused to apply for a permit, maintaining foster parenting as a private arrangement.[25] To bring foster families under their purview, youth departments placed advertisements in newspapers, established school contacts, and sent reminders of medical exams to foster parents. Despite this, parents who felt competent to care for their foster children without state supervision failed to bring their children to the doctor regularly, denied the youth department random access to their homes, and hid their children from inquisitive youth department representatives.[26]

This placed youth department authorities in a quandary regarding whether and how to punish parents who refused to accept state intervention. Unsure of how to deal with several families that failed to bring their children to medical exams, Detmold Youth Department authorities at one point turned to the provincial government for advice. Despite its employees' frustration, the youth department emphasized: "It cannot be concluded from this fact alone that we have complaints about these homes. Some of these cases are in fact good foster homes." The department did not favor imposing either fines or "compulsory measures" (*Zwangsmaßnahmen*), both of which could have had negative ramifications for the children.[27] The Lippe government officials who were consulted failed to resolve the conflict. They recommended that the Detmold authorities inform delinquent foster mothers of their obligations. In particular, they advocated warning the mothers, "If you fail to comply with this request [to bring your child to the doctor], we will take all further steps against you."[28] They did not specify what steps should be taken if the foster mothers persisted in noncompliance. Some youth department authorities wanted to punish as criminals foster parents who did not follow the guidelines. Ultimately, it was the Prussian minister of welfare who set a limit on the measures youth departments could take against uncooperative foster parents. In 1928, he announced that allowing youth departments to punish families that denied the youth department freedom to observe a foster child would contradict the intentions of the law. He

24 Crew, "Ambiguities of Modernity," 332.
25 Detmold Kreis Jugendamt, 10 August 1929, StaD, L 80 IC, Gruppe 28, Fach 23, 5 bd. 2.
26 Schutz der Pflegekinder §§22, 24, 25 und 26 des Reichsgesetzes für Jugendwohlfahrt, SaM, Oberpräsidium Münster, 6034.
27 Magistrat Städtisches Fürsorgeamt, Abteilung Jugendamt Detmold to Lippische Regierung, Fürsorgeabteilung and Landesjugendamt, 18 June 1928, StaD, L 80 IC, Gruppe 28, Fach 23, 5 Bd. 2.
28 Ibid.

stressed: "If the youth department were permitted to bring a charge in every case in which a child was not regularly presented, the youth department's supervisory authority would assume a policelike quality, which the law did not intend." Instead, the youth departments were to "build a relationship of trust with foster parents through [their] role in supervising foster children."[29]

Imposing a coordinated system for foster care required that youth departments register all foster children. In response to a 1928 survey conducted by the Lippe state government, the Schotmar Youth Department reported, "We believe that we have now registered all the foster children in the city."[30] The mayor in Lage confirmed that they too had registered all foster children without difficulty and would henceforth use social workers to monitor the children.[31] Other youth departments designated volunteer "helpers" in the community to increase their control over foster families.[32] The courts sometimes tightened cities' supervision by requiring foster parents to submit a periodic report "about the welfare, residence, and income of their child, so that no guardian who [did] not sufficiently provide for his ward [could] remain hidden."[33] Monitoring foster children remained substantially more troublesome in rural areas. In 1928, authorities of the rural county of Detmold reported that they could not accurately monitor the foster children in their county because "the names of the children residing in the district [*Bezirk*] [were] not known to the youth department." Furthermore, when they composed lists of children, they discovered that "the lists did not correspond with reality."[34] The shortage of youth department personnel made it especially difficult for many smaller youth departments to implement all parts of the Reich Youth Welfare Law.

Despite the law's attempt to clarify the status of foster children, foster care remained fraught with potential problems for both parents and children.

---

29 Prussian Minster für Volkswohlfahrt III F 1067/28, Betr. Bestimmungen zum Schutz der Pflegekinder, 24 July 1928, StaM, Amt Wolbeck B 15, 11.

30 Stadtrat Schötmar in Lippe to Lippische Landesregierung, Fürsorgeabteilung and Landesjugendamt, Detmold, 28 June 1928, StaD, L 80 IC, Gruppe 28, Fach 23, 5 Bd. 2. After discovering that many people neither had permits nor were applying for them, Detmold Youth Department authorities advocated advertising the requirement in the newspapers. StaD, L 80 IC, Gruppe 28, Fach 23, 5 Bd. 2.

31 Bürgermeister Lage to Lippische Regierung, Fürsorgeabteilung and Landesjugendamt, Detmold. Response to inquiry of 7 June 1938, StaD L 80 IC, Gruppe 28, Fach 23, 5 Bd. 2.

32 Stadtrat Schötmar to Lippische Regierung, Fürsorgeabteilung and Landesjugendamt, Detmold, 14 June 1928, StaD, L 80 IC, Gruppe 28, Fach 23, 5 Bd. 2.

33 Income could be paid by the biological father or mother, the youth department, or state welfare. Städtische Jugendamt Lemgo to Lippische Regierung, Fürsorgeabteilung, Detmold, 19 June 1928, StaD, L 80 IC, Gruppe 28, Fach 23, 5 Bd. 2.

34 Kreisjugendamt Detmold/Land to Lippische Regierung, Fürsorgeabteilung and Landesjugendamt, Detmold, 10 August 1928, StaD, L 80 IC, Gruppe 28, Fach 23, 5 Bd. 2.

Youth departments wanted foster parents to treat foster children as their own, but courts seldom granted foster parents the power to make important decisions concerning a child's welfare. The youth department's supervisory role meant that (at least theoretically) foster parents were under perpetual observation. Even more disruptive to foster parent–child relationships was the very real possibility that a biological parent or grandparent would reclaim a foster child. Many single mothers who hoped to secure jobs or who intended to marry in the near future used foster care as a form of intermediary child care and reclaimed their children after a time.[35] Biological grandparents also created problems: Frau B. had raised Walter for eight months when his grandparents stepped forward to claim him. When the Catholic Welfare Association for Girls, Women, and Children told Frau B. she had to give up the boy, they emphasized that Walter would now grow up without having to learn about his illegitimate background. Though they promised her that she could pick up another child when she turned over Walter, this provided little solace, as she had developed a strong emotional bond with the boy.[36]

Only adoption could promise foster parents an ongoing relationship with one child, free from intrusive state supervision. As a solution to the insecurities and indignities of foster care, however, adoption raised a great many problems of its own. Prior to the First World War, adoptions in Germany took place almost exclusively among relatives. During the war, the growing number of war orphans brought adoption to national attention, and many Germans, motivated by "national excitement and gratitude," volunteered to adopt the orphans left behind by those "who died on the fields of honor."[37] After the armistice, public interest in adoption fell precipitously, even as need remained high. Though the Reich Youth Welfare Law charged the newly founded youth departments with the task of stimulating interest in adoption, some Germans viewed it as an opportunity to exploit single mothers and childless couples alike. Single mothers desperate to find homes for their children were lured into paying "seduction money" (between 100 and 1,000 marks) to middlemen, who wrote a "contract" with interested adoptive parents. In reality, however, the contracts had no legal

35 Karen Hagemann found that in Hamburg 90 percent of foster children were illegitimate. See *Frauenalltag und Männerpolitik*, 193. In Austria at the beginning of the twentieth century, many of the children who were raised in foster care were the children of servants and farm hands (*Gesindedienst*) who remained unmarried their entire lives. Ortmayr, *Knechte*, 14.
36 Katholische Fürsorge Verein für Mädchen, Frauen und Kinder to Frau B., 29 March 1927, StaM, Amt Wolbeck B 15, 12.
37 "Mitteilungen der Arbeitsgemeinschaft der bayerischen Berufsvormünder: Annahme an Kindes Statt," in *Blätter für Öffentliche Fürsorge und Soziale Versicherung* 18, no. 11 (München, June 1933): 127–8.

status to protect either the child or the adoptive parents, and the money was pocketed almost entirely by the middlemen.[38] Throughout Germany, newspapers printed warnings about "the concealment and abduction of infants on the way to purchase– and adoption contracts." Calls for the state to intervene and take control of adoption were common in the press and in academic journals. One newspaper item demanded the closure of "every bogus company . . . which takes advantage of the plight of unmarried mothers or their relatives by charging them high mediation costs without being remotely in a position or trying in good conscience to make good on their portion of the contract."[39]

Despite the large number of newspaper advertisements for state-approved adoption services during the 1920s, the number of suitable adoptive parents remained insufficient. Some people blamed the advertisements themselves, claiming that they only confused matters by attracting people who were unsuitable adoptive parents. One study found that 90 percent of adoption negotiations failed, many because the potential parents or their relatives had criminal records or contagious diseases. A further group of potential parents volunteered only for economic reasons: they were primarily interested in receiving support payments, not parenthood.[40]

Suggestions for alleviating the shortfall in adoptive parents were offered from a variety of sources. Authors of the journal *Waisenhilfe* (Aid for Orphans) believed the problem stemmed from Germans' lack of knowledge about adoption and recommended public education as a remedy.[41] Others advocated allowing the youth department to censor newspaper ads before publication to ensure that their wording would attract suitable parents. Orphanages throughout Germany volunteered to do background checks on potential adoptive parents, while in Westphalia public pressure to create central adoption centers at the communal or church level intensified.[42]

For welfare-minded Weimar policymakers, standardizing adoption proceedings and eliminating bogus and exploitative adoptions represented one way to fulfill the goal of improving children's well-being. Alongside youth

---

38 Hedwig Renner, "Aus Unserer Adoptionsabteilung," *Helfende Hände: Blätter für freiwilligen Dienst in der Jugendfürsorge* 5, nos. 2–3 (June 1921): 30–31.

39 These bogus companies functioned under many names, such as Adoption Center, Adoption and Foster Home Offices, and Trust Institutes for the Placement of Foster Children. Pressenotiz, "Gefährdung von Säuglingen durch Verschleppung," n.d., StaD, M1 I JU, 29.

40 "Annahme an Kindes Statt," in *Blätter für Öffentliche Fürsorge und Soziale Versicherung* 18, no. 11 (June 1933): 127–8.

41 *Waisenhilfe*, vol. 1 (Berlin, January 1930): 50.

42 Cologne, Magdeburg, Berlin, and Halle had centralized adoption centers as early as 1911. StaD, M1 I JU, 29.

departments, a variety of religious and secular organizations had adoption centers that helped single mothers and couples who wished to adopt but did not want to work with the youth departments.[43] Legal rules for adoption had already been established by the German Civil Code of 1900 (§§1741–72). The law mandated that adoptive parents be over fifty years of age, childless, and eighteen years older than the children they adopted. Biological parents forfeited all rights and responsibilities for a child upon adoption (§1765). The biological and adoptive parents were both promised that their identities would be withheld from one another. Once adopted, children earned the same legal status as biological children, including the family name and the right to inherit (§1757). Interestingly, while the law did not distinguish between single and married adoptive parents, if a married woman adopted a child, the child took her maiden name unless the child was also adopted by her husband (§1758).

Legal guidelines established the exact contours of adoption. When in 1923 Henriette R., an unmarried domestic servant, delivered Lucy, she realized that her job precluded her caring for her daughter herself. As a result, she placed Lucy in foster care with Herr and Frau Scheppers. After a four-month trial period, the Schepperses announced their desire to adopt Lucy, and Henriette raised no objections. Although in their nine years of marriage the Schepperses had been unable to bear children, Frau Scheppers was legally obligated to provide a written note from her doctor ruling out any future conception.[44] With the doctor's certificate and the mayor's testimony that the marriage was childless entered in evidence, the age limit was waived. Before the adoption's conclusion, the police also certified the Scheppers' Prussian citizenship and their absence of any criminal record. Finally, Henriette R. herself appeared in court to swear that she agreed to the adoption.[45] With all the legal requirements met, the Schepperses were able to adopt Lucy.

---

43 In Westphalia, both the Catholic and Protestant churches and the youth departments established central adoption centers. In addition, by 1927, the Catholic Welfare Association (Katholische Fürsorge Verein) and the Westphalian Women's Aid also ran adoption agencies in Münster. In Dortmund, the Central Authority for Jewish Foster Homes and Mediation of Jewish Adoptions (Zentralstelle für jüdische Pflegestellenwesen und jüdische Adoptionsvermittlung), run by the Jewish Women's Organization (Jüdischer Frauenbund), served Jewish children in Westphalia. It is not clear when the Central Authority for Jewish Foster Homes and Mediation of Jewish Adoptions began to organize adoptions. It announced its presence to the Detmold regional youth department in October 1929, claiming to serve Jewish children all over Germany. StaD, D 106 Detmold A, 581.

44 These descriptions were often quite graphic. One woman's doctor told her that because the development of her "uterus [was] retarded, menstruation [would] not begin." SaM, Amtsgericht Hohenlimburg, 81. The requirement of childlessness helped avoid inheritance conflicts.

45 SaM, Amtsgericht Hohenlimburg, 78.

During the course of the 1920s, however, many foster parents found that adoption was no longer governed only by the German Civil Code. Instead, as state authorities struggled to ensure the safety of adoptive children, they developed new regulations that required doctors, mayors, and police departments to be more vigilant in evaluating the quality of adoptive parents and homes. Many adoptive parents were aware of the new, more stringent requirements and preemptively collected supplementary evidence to confirm their suitability. When the painter Heinrich Eckmann and his wife Martha decided to adopt their foster daughter Herta, they brought marriage and birth certificates for themselves and the child, along with certificates from a doctor and the police. They also provided a certificate of employment from the German Machine Factory to prove their financial stability. To further bolster their case, the parish priest wrote a letter of recommendation. Even the Central Orphans' Bureau submitted a letter on their behalf, claiming that the Eckmanns had "a good reputation, a moral lifestyle, and a well-ordered way of life." It confirmed Herr Eckmann's stable income, reliability as a worker, and the suitability of the Eckmanns' apartment for raising a child. It also emphasized that the Eckmanns' interest in adopting Herta lay in their desire to parent, not their need for another worker, thus laying to rest one of the youth department's prevailing fears.[46] Processing the information the Eckmanns voluntarily collected greatly increased the bureaucratic work of the youth department, but it also gave youth department employees a much more detailed picture of the couple and their household. Youth department authorities believed that the possibility of ensuring that children ended up in good families justified this level of investigation.

Not all information pertinent to an adoption could be collected by the prospective adoptive parents, and the methods of collection themselves sometimes became intrusive. In April 1932, the German Red Cross circulated a letter of concern to the Prussian minister of justice. The letter emphasized the current desperate economic conditions, which made expediting adoption particularly urgent, but noted that "complications" had reduced some childless couples' willingness to adopt. In particular, the Red Cross complained that despite state promises that trained youth department personnel would replace police investigators in adoption cases, "in practice in many adoption cases handled by the court, information [was] still collected by the police." To make matters worse, they found that sometimes both the

46 It is also interesting to note that the entire cost for the adoption during the inflation year of 1923 was 22 million marks. SaM, Amtsgericht Wetter, 40.

youth department and the police investigated the same family, disturbing it twice. When foster parents decided to adopt, civil servants, sometimes in uniform, were sent to investigate "the neighbors, the building supervisor, and the domestic servant." These individuals "were asked about the adoptive parents' 'circumstances'" and were sometimes even interrogated about "the 'illegitimate foster child.'" The civil servants' lack of tact astonished the Red Cross staff. They explained, "adoptive parents understandably place the highest value on concealing the nature of the child's illegitimate birth from the neighborhood; often the domestic servants are not aware that the child is adopted." The letter suggested that investigations be done only by "socially progressive youth department employees trained in welfare work," who could exercise the appropriate level of discretion.[47]

Although the framers of the Reich Youth Welfare Law had intended for youth departments to be staffed with "people with some understanding of pedagogy and of the processes of childhood socialization, and [who had] . . . the independence to follow the dictates of their pedagogical expertise," reality fell far short of this ideal.[48] Cities filled the administrative positions using their long-standing systems of civil service seniority without regard to training, relegating the mostly young, female social workers to fill the lower ranks as caseworkers. The overwhelmingly heavy caseloads they carried, together with their low status in youth departments, severely compromised their ability to live up to the state's ideals and the Red Cross's desires.[49] The Red Cross's concern prompted the minister of justice to poll the courts to find out the extent of the problem with youth department personnel.[50] Though virtually all courts and youth departments recognized the need to reduce intrusions into family privacy, no consensus existed on how best to accomplish this without compromising the state's responsibility to protect children placed for adoption. Many courts reassured the Arnsberg Landgericht in words like those of the Berleberg court: "To date we have received no complaints that the parties involved found these investigations embarrassing." They attributed the scarcity of trouble to the fact that in smaller communities the courts could bypass the police and talk directly to the bailiff (*Gemeindevorsteher*), who usually had adequate knowledge of

---

47 Deutsches Rotes Kreuz, Berlin, to Preußische Justizminister, 18 April 1932, StaD, D 23 Bielefeld, 961.

48 Dickinson, *Politics of German Child Welfare*, 172.

49 Dickinson claims that of 10,712 officials employed in youth departments in 1928, only 2,667 were accredited social workers, and 2,013 had other forms of training (such as seminars or workshops). Ibid.

50 The following analysis comes from the responses to this query from the Landgerichtspräsidenten in Bielefeld, Arnsberg, Siegen, and Vlotho and the Amtsgerichte in Berleberg, Menschede, and Siegen.

local families and children.[51] But other courts identified specific problems. The Arnsberg Landgericht authorities argued that the lack of trained social workers in rural areas meant that those who were there carried such heavy workloads that they could not carefully and discreetly dedicate themselves to each case.[52] The Bielefeld Landgericht authorities feared that too often the youth department had a financial interest in arranging adoptions, which compromised good judgment.[53] In a more extensive reply, Siegen court authorities agreed with the Red Cross that "police investigations can easily create the appearance of criminal inquiries, and as such become the root of 'unpleasant rumors' in small communities." Still, they doubted that using youth department investigators would eliminate these "evils" (*Übelstände*), since smaller communities lacking well-trained social work personnel had to rely on mayors, who then called on the police to collect information. In the view of the Siegen court, the suggestion that the youth departments were to be staffed with "socially progressive" people "trained in welfare work" itself remained a "dream."[54] In response to the variety of opinions, in December 1932, the Reich minister of justice issued a judgment reaffirming that the role of the police should be limited and emphasizing that "youth welfare [was] fundamentally the responsibility of the youth departments."[55] Despite this edict, the limited financial resources and the dire shortage of trained personnel prevented youth departments from keeping their focus solely on the well-being of the children under their jurisdiction.

Though many families would have preferred to be investigated by a social worker than by a police officer, the use of social workers to supervise vulnerable people raised a host of problems of its own. From the beginning, social workers were not a uniform group. As David Crew has pointed out, they had widely varied religious and political outlooks, and only some shared a "socially progressive worldview."[56] Moreover, as I have mentioned, the limited training of some social workers, their lack of supervision, and their large caseloads meant adoption standards were applied inconsistently.

---

51 Justizangestellter, Amtsgericht Menschede, to Herrn Landgerichtspräsident Arnsberg, 18 April 1932, SaM, Landgericht Arnsberg, 685. See also StaD, D 23 Vlotho, 666.

52 Amtsgericht Siegen to Landgericht Arnsberg, 19 April 1932, SaM, Landgericht Arnsberg, 685.

53 Landgerichtspräsident Bielefeld to Herrn Oberlandesgerichtspräsidenten, Hamm, 13 May 1932, SaM, Oberlandesgericht Hamm, 364.

54 Amtsgericht Siegen to Landgericht Arnsberg, 19 April 1932, SaM, Landgericht Arnsberg, 685.

55 In his mind, even evidence of nationality and criminal records could – and moreover should – be obtained from the public prosecutor's office (*Staatsanwaltschaft*) without the aid of the police. If in specific instances the use of the police was necessary, "the sensitive nature of the task needed to be stressed." "Inanspruchnahme der Polizeihehörden und Gericht bei Annahme an Kindes Statt und bei Ehelichkeitserklärung," *Justizministerialblatt* 268 (20 December 1932).

56 Crew, *Germans on Welfare*, 47–66.

When Herr and Frau Oeller tried to adopt the then two-and-a-half-year-old Theresa after her mother's death in 1926, the Bielefeld social worker assigned to Theresa's case discovered that the Oellers had recently borrowed money to pay unexpected medical bills and that Herr Oeller had changed jobs. Taking this as evidence that the Oellers were economically unstable, she tried to have Theresa removed from their household and given to her relatives. In despair, the Oellers appealed to the Minden *Regierungspräsident*, emphatically denying the accusation of economic instability and expressing doubt that Theresa's relatives – who had had virtually no prior contact with her and could not legally adopt her because they were already parents – wanted to raise her. In their investigation, officials found that Theresa's grandfather had no complaints with Theresa's arrangements as they stood, and her doctor pronounced her a picture of health. Copies of Herr Oeller's financial records left little doubt that he was fully capable of supporting her. Finally, Theresa's relatives assured the government that they had introduced the possibility of raising her only because the youth department authorities had frightened Theresa's grandfather into thinking that she was being mistreated. From this, the Minden government deduced that the Oellers had been misjudged by an overzealous social worker and demanded that the youth department initiate adoption proceedings. Even after this decision was made, the youth department postponed taking final action on the case. It allowed Theresa to stay with the Oellers but refused to permit her adoption until its employees reassessed her situation the following year.[57]

The Oeller case was neither typical nor unique. It demonstrates the potentially devastating effect the state's effort to protect children could have on families. As David Crew has demonstrated, once families had been identified as potentially problematic, they had a hard time escaping the state's "gaze."[58] In the Oeller case, the social worker may well have had Theresa's best interests at heart, but it is likely that if the Oellers had not actively challenged the social worker's decision, they would have lost Theresa. The dueling between the Minden government and the Bielefeld Youth Department in the Oeller case also demonstrates the number of state authorities who could become involved in a case and the labor-intensive nature of implementing adoption guidelines.

Most adoptive parents celebrated adoption as the end of state supervision and of contact with their child's past. The German Civil Code, which sought to mark the beginning of an adopted child's new life, explicitly protected

---

57 Oellers' case, StaD, M1 I JU, 18.   58 Crew, *Germans on Welfare*, 149.

adoptive parents from uncomfortable – and potentially destructive – intrusions by biological parents. Only in unusual cases in which youth departments or charities believed there was a pressing reason to reestablish contact did biological parents reenter children's lives. Records of the Kinderrettungsverein (Child Rescue Association, KRV) reveal that mothers who gave up their illegitimate children were the most likely to challenge the finality of adoption. Even after the adoption of her daughter, Gertraud, had been finalized in 1931, Elise continued to beg the KRV for photographs and information about Gertraud's well-being. She even made Gertraud the sole beneficiary in her will. But when the KRV asked the adoptive parents, a pastor and his wife, whether they were willing to provide further information about Gertraud for Elise, they refused, fearing that it might jeopardize their new parent–child relationship. This should have been the end of the story. Instead, after the adoption of Gertraud, her new parents adopted a second child and then bore three biological children, putting tremendous strain on the family's limited finances. As a result, six years later, they wrote the KRV asking it to contact Elise, give her information and pictures, and see if she would contribute to the child's upbringing. The KRV's willingness to contact Elise at this point – despite its stated concern that doing so might upset her – probably reflected its officials' knowledge that Elise had tried to contact her daughter's adoptive parents. The file ends with the KRV's letter to Elise, perhaps because the communication continued without the mediation of the KRV.[59]

As the experiences of Elise and the Oellers clearly illustrate, adoptions often became entangled in the complicated web of the needs and desires of biological parents, adoptive parents, state authorities, and church agents. Although Weimar policymakers unambiguously sought to improve child welfare, at the local level, where investigations of families were conducted and adoptions were arranged, the clear guidelines met murky reality. Some families experienced straightforward and uncomplicated adoptions. Others found that even when all parties sought what was best for a child, adoption was far from easy. The state's progressive desire to strengthen youth welfare far exceeded its ability to train and finance social workers and youth department authorities. These limitations, together with the virtually endless variety of circumstances present in adoption cases, significantly complicated the state's aim of establishing guidelines that could be applied uniformly to all adoptions.

---

59 Landesarchiv Berlin, Kinderrettungsverein, 1004.

APPLYING GENETIC CRITERIA TO NON-BLOOD-BASED
FAMILIES: 1933–1945

When the National Socialists came to power in 1933, they heightened the level of rhetoric about the importance of children growing up in families. After the Great Depression had gutted youth department budgets and put child welfare in jeopardy, the Nazi promise to restore traditional values appealed to many both within the youth departments and in Catholic and Protestant charities. It became immediately apparent, however, that the Nazis were using the National People's Welfare Organization to centralize and monopolize child welfare. While the state cut funding to all private welfare programs, NSV authorities created their own programs to duplicate and ultimately to usurp control of existing private programs. The Nazis claimed that all "racially pure" youth were the sole responsibility of the Nazi state and should be cared for by the state in line with the National Socialist worldview. Simultaneously, they insisted that state resources should be limited to "racially pure" youth to facilitate their incorporation into the *Volksgemeinschaft*.

According to the National Socialist worldview, foster children were "important member[s] of the total German youth [and], as such equal members of the *Volk* [*Volksgenossen*]." With this in mind, the Nazis began to revamp the foster care system almost immediately, creating an elaborate, rigorous, and centralized bureaucracy to control who parented and which children were parented. They blamed shortcomings of the previous foster care system on "unrealizable demands," "overburdened youth departments," and "foster mothers who were repeatedly stirred up [*verhetzt*] over political and religious matters." They claimed "many German foster children fail to develop" because of these negative conditions.[60] Like their Weimar predecessors, the Nazis believed children belonged in families, not institutions, not only because it was less expensive to place foster children in families, but also because the Nazis believed that well-chosen families would educate children in National Socialism. As one welfare worker noted, "The training lacking from one's own family should always be replaced first with that of another family."[61] Home environments still had to be clean and spacious and families economically stable; in addition, the Nazis broadened requirements

---

60 *Mutter und Volk*, Hauptschriftleiterin, Klara Lönnies to Detmold Jugend Amt, 8 May 1934, StaD, D 106 A, 588.
61 Münster Wohlfahrtsamt/Jugendhilfe to Pg. Herr S., 24 September 1937, SaM, NSDAP Volkswohlfahrt, 485.

for those wishing to become foster parents to include genetic health and at least tacit support for the new regime.[62]

The Nazis evaluated all potential foster children for six to eight weeks before placing "worthy" children in families. Older, learning-disabled, "aso-cial," and "genetically unworthy" (*erbminderwertig*) children were relegated to institutions, such as orphanages, or left in the custody of their "unworthy" parents.[63] When one social worker determined that Frau K. was "incapable of raising her children properly," for example, she nonetheless concluded, "Since the older children [are] . . . mentally inferior [*minderwertig*], it is my opinion that placing them in alternative homes at the expense of public welfare is inappropriate." She added, "If the younger children develop with average intellect (we must wait until the school evaluates them), they must be removed from the mother's influence under all circumstances."[64]

State discrimination against parents and children deemed unworthy paved the way for a second tier of foster care to develop outside state control. Both Catholic and Protestant churches continued their work with the foster care children rejected by the NSV. Jewish families continued to take care of Jewish children in need of foster families. Some men and women who were deemed unworthy of parenthood also sought foster children through the churches. Although individuals sterilized for genetic reasons could theoret-ically become foster parents, the Office of Racial Policy (Rassenpolitisches Amt) suspected that most health problems severe enough to warrant steril-ization would prevent them from offering a foster child an "orderly educa-tion."[65] These parents, too, sought foster children through the churches.

Because their program's success depended on evaluating all children, the Nazis tried to limit the churches' participation. The results of their attempts

---

62 As proof, the Nazis required that foster parents obtain a "political evaluation" (*politisches Führungs-zeugnis*) from the county leader before they were granted a permit to take in foster children.

63 Carola Kühlmann, *Erbkrank oder Erziehbar?* 66. In fact, the Nazis developed a system of rural homes (*Landesaufnahmeheime*) where children would live for six to eight weeks, during which time they would be assessed genetically. In Westphalia, the home Dorsten was opened in 1938 with "the responsibility of taking in all children sent from the Westphalian Provincial Association of Juvenile Correction and assessing them according to the quality of their genes, spirit and character." On the basis of this assessment, children were transferred to families, work centers, institutions, or eventually youth camps (*Jugendschutzlager*) similar to concentration camps. Because of the finances and personnel this system demanded, as well as the almost immediate added burden of war, Dorsten only functioned with its original purpose for a short time. Ibid., 158.

64 Social Worker to Gesundheitsamt Bielefeld, 14 September 1940, StaD, M1 IS, 531.

65 Sterilized couples were also permitted to raise children "for whom the existence of a genetic defi-ciency was to be expected." NSDAP Hauptamt Volkswohlfahrt Berlin to Gauamtsleiter der NSDAP: Leiter der Ämter der Volkswohlfahrt, Hauptstellen Wohlfahrt, Pflege und Jugendhilfe, and Stellen der Jugendämter, 19 September 1940, SaM, NSDAP Volkswohlfahrt-Nord, 770.

to centralize control over foster care varied widely. Although in Düsseldorf the NSV attained an agreement ensuring that "in principle . . . evaluating foster homes in terms of political, economic, and educational [needs] as well as the routine supervision of the homes would be transferred to the NSV," a second report written shortly thereafter tempered its optimism that this principle would be put into practice.[66] In Kreis Steinfurt, the NSV assumed control over the supervision of all foster care families, but the churches continued to place children. In Kreis Coesfeld, NSV authorities failed to eliminate Caritas's influence but nonetheless tried to carve out their own sphere of influence by making the issuance of permits to take in foster children contingent on examination by and a positive statement from the NSV Youth Aid.[67] In general, the Nazi effort to control foster care depended on the perseverance of a limited staff who were consistently overworked. As a result, the struggle between the NSV and the churches over foster care persisted for the duration of the Third Reich. In 1942, the NSDAP Gau Westfalen tried again to remove all "genetically healthy" children from church-run children's homes and place them in family foster care.[68] Ultimately, however, the war diverted energy and resources from the *Gleichschaltung* project, and many plans were postponed until after the war.

Probably the most significant change the Nazis made in the foster care system was to shift its emphasis from foster parents to foster mothers. From the outset, they addressed their rhetoric about foster care directly to German women. The National Socialist *Familienzeitschrift* (Family Magazine) dedicated one section specifically to foster mothers (*Pflegemutter Blatt*), and in 1934 the Mother's Day edition of the magazine *Mutter und Volk* (Mother and Volk) was dedicated to the German foster mother "in her double capacity as guardian of 'a stranger' and as a German woman and mother." The importance the Nazis attributed to foster mothers found concrete expression in their policy. They issued permits to raise foster children *only* to women, and their policy discussions only occasionally mentioned the foster family and scarcely ever the foster father. Although they sometimes argued that a child needed a man's discipline, in general they only rarely mentioned paternal authority.[69] And while they deemed a man's income far less important than a

---

66 NSDAP Volkswohlfahrt, Berlin, to NSDAP Gauleitung Westfalen Nord, Amt für Volkswohlfahrt, Münster, 20 May 1939; follow-up note sent to Pg. Herr S., n.d., both in SaM, NSDAP Volkswohlfahrt, 482.
67 Report NSDAP Volkswohlfahrt Westfalen-Nord to NSDAP Volkswohlfahrt Berlin, 1 June 1938, SaM, NSDAP Volkswohlfahrt-Nord, 482.
68 Akten Notiz, NSDAP Gau Westfalen-Nord, 13 May 1942, SaM, NSDAP Volkswohlfaahrt, 32.
69 Hessen-Nassau Amt für Volkswohlfahrt to NSDAP Kreisleitung, Hauptamt für Volkswohlfahrt, 3 March 1943, SaM, NSDAP Volkswohlfahrt-Nord, 770.

woman's ability to raise a healthy child, they required all future foster mothers to attend twenty-five to thirty hours of mother courses in infant care, child rearing, cooking, and household maintenance that were permeated with National Socialist ideology.[70] More strikingly, the Nazis permitted single women to become foster mothers – and heads of households – thus fundamentally altering the shape of the ideal family.[71] In 1938, fully 11 percent of foster children in northern Westphalia were placed with single women.[72] For foster children, then, the Nazis did not seek to recreate the traditional family but rather to ensure that the mothers who raised them embodied the correct National Socialist ideal.

Despite the inclusion of single women as foster mothers, the restrictive nature of the new ideological guidelines for foster parenting confounded youth departments' efforts to locate suitable foster parents in sufficient numbers.[73] When word of mouth proved ineffective, they ran propaganda campaigns to encourage women and couples to volunteer as foster parents. But the Nazis encountered significant obstacles as they redefined the role of foster parents. To combat the continued perception that foster care was a money-making endeavor, in 1937 the Reich minister for people's education and propaganda (*Volksaufklärung und Propaganda*) forbade newspapers and magazines from publishing advertisements for foster and adoptive children because "experience show[ed] that the participants almost always [tried] to make money out of the care and rearing of the child."[74] Despite this decree, advertisements seeking children for foster care and adoption continued to appear in German newspapers sporadically. In July 1938, state authorities (*Reichsstatthalter*) tried to track down who had placed two advertisements reading "Will adopt healthy child in good, loving care, write the Lippe State Newspaper under Nr. 1667" and "Seeking foster home for one-year-old boy. Offered under Nr. 1670." These ads, while benign in content, threatened the Nazi system because they provided an opportunity to bypass health standards. Privately organized foster care arrangements not only simplified the bureaucratic process but also potentially allowed "unfit" men and women

---

70 By the end of the war, the number of required hours had been reduced to twelve. Amt Wohlfahrtspflege und Jugendhilfe, Berlin, to Leiter der Hauptämter für Volkswohlfahrt in den Gauleitungen ua., 13 February 1942, SaM, NSDAP Volkswohlfahrt-Westfalen Nord, 32.

71 Ausführung zum Schutz der Pflegekinder, n.d., SaM, NSDAP Volkswohlfahrt, 485.

72 This number stands in comparison to the 46 percent of foster children who were placed with childless couples. Bericht NSDAP Volkswohlfahrt Westfalen Nord to Berlin, 1 June 1938, SaM, NSDAP Volkswohlfahrt, 482.

73 This is often discussed. See, for example, Letter Detmold, 29 July 1935, StaD, D 106 A, 588.

74 Reichsminister des Interior, Betr. Anzeigen von Privatpersonen über Pflegekinder, 13 January 1937, StaD, L 80 IC, Gruppe 28, Fach 22, 1.

to raise children. In 1934, the Minden Youth Department discovered to its dismay that the Nusses, who had repeatedly been denied foster care permits, had a child living in their household. Although during a house inspection the child appeared well cared for, both Herr and Frau Nusse had been expelled from National Socialist organizations (the SA and NSF respectively) and thus were considered by the Nazis to be unfit to parent. When closer examination revealed that the biological parents had put three of their five children in unofficial foster care, the youth department began proceedings to have custody revoked.[75] It was precisely this kind of loophole that Nazi policymakers hoped to close by bringing state officials into the foster care process more directly.

The Nazi attempt to downplay the financial dimension of foster care and encourage foster mothers to view foster children as their own created a serious dilemma. The twelve principles of foster motherhood included: "Do not take in a child if you do not want it to grow in your heart" and "Only a truly motherly woman who meets the child with love will be deemed as valuable."[76] As Nazi rhetoric celebrating the bond that developed between foster mothers and their children escalated, many foster parents came to see foster parenthood as synonymous with – and in fact as a first step toward – adoption. In sharp contrast, many single mothers flatly refused to allow their children to be placed in foster families because they did not want them to be incorporated into other families. They instead continued to view foster care as a temporary solution during an unsettled period in their lives.[77] And they had every right to do so: even after children had been placed in families, mothers were permitted to remove them if they could provide for them. But in 1938 the Westphalian NSV argued against this practice, stating, "Foster parents must be given a legal protection against the random removal of children, who generally come from circumstances that do not guarantee an orderly family life."[78] Others questioned the sense of respecting

75 Case Nusse, KaM, Amt Dützen, G IV, 153.

76 *Mutter und Volk*, Hauptschriftleiterin, Klara Lönnies to Jugendamt Detmold, 8 May 1934, StaD, D 106 A, 588.

77 In 1938, 24.7 percent of all foster children were illegitimate, compared to 14.3 percent who were orphans or "half-orphans." The uncertainty connected with the presence of biological parents limited the number of interested potential foster parents. Report, NSDAP Volkswohlfahrt-Jugendhilfe to Berlin NSDAP Volkswohlfahrt, 1 June 1938, SaM, NSDAP Volkswohlfaahrt-Gau Westfalen Nord, 482; NDSAP Kreisleitung, Amt für Volkswohlfahrt Abt. Wohlfahrt/Jugendhilfe, Recklinghausen, to NSDAP Gau Westfalen-Nord Amt für Volkswohlfahrt, betr. NSV-Jugendhilfe, Pflegekinderwesen, 28 February 1941, SaM, NSDAP Volkswohlfahrt, 482.

78 NSDAP Volkswohlfahrt – Jugendhilfe, Gau Westfalen-Nord to NSDAP Volkswohlfahrt Berlin, 1 June 1938, SaM, NSDAP Volkswohlfahrt, 482.

the rights of biological parents who did not act as proper parents. One welfare worker raised the query: "With all due recognition and emphasis on blood ties, which already make the decision difficult for the National Socialist *Volkspfleger* [guardian of the *Volk*], one does have to pose the question whether the reference to blood ties is appropriate if the child will not ever be blessed with any of the benefits that arise out of the duties that such ties imply for the parents or the child's mother."[79] Nazi policymakers were willing to endorse single mothers if they cooperated, but when they jeopardized larger family policy goals, many officials viewed these mothers' rights as anything but sacred. Even so, most single mothers recognized that their influence over and contact with their children diminished once the children were placed in families and refused to relinquish their rights. Out of frustration, NSV authorities proposed, "There must be a legal hold that allows [us] to act against the child's mother's will" in cases in which mothers refused to cooperate.[80] Although such a "legal hold" was never created, this comment reveals that at least some Nazis did not see blood ties as worthy of protection if they deemed a mother's life disorderly.

Another complication that threatened the foster care system was the heavy demand for girls in preference to boys. The ubiquitous Nazi rhetoric that stressed the importance of taking any needy, healthy child fell on deaf ears: the majority of potential parents wanted girls. Sometimes, requests for foster children revealed the reason for the sex choice. One couple who sought a fourteen-year-old Catholic girl "from a good, rural, trade family" stated: "The girl is intended to care for three small children. The position is ideal for a weak girl who would like to strengthen herself in a rural area." Other parents favored a child who could later be adopted, as one couple wrote: "Childless couple seeks Protestant girl, age eight months–1 1/2 years for foster care. Fifteen marks per month compensation desired. Preference given to a child who can be adopted later." Others went further and specified that they sought an orphan, presumably to avoid having parents later reclaim the child. Potential foster parents often identified their religious background,[81] status – "orderly, clean family" – or their living arrangements – "exceptional rural living environment." In Westphalia in June 1938, four girls

79 NSDAP Volkswohlfahrt Westfalen-Nord to NSDAP Volkswohlfahrt Berlin, 1 January 1938, SaM, NSDAP Volkswohlfahrt, 482.

80 NSDAP Volkswohlfahrt – Jugendhilfe, Gau Westfalen-Nord to NSDAP Volkswohlfahrt Berlin, 1938, SaM, NSDAP Volkswohlfahrt, 482.

81 Many parents during the Nazi era identified themselves as *gottgläubig*, a term that literally means "believing in God" but was used to designate those who left the church under Nazi pressures.

were requested for every one boy; one year later, in July 1939, this ratio had increased to six girls to one boy.[82] One report described the "excessive demand for girls" as the most pressing problem in foster care.[83] Nor did the ratio change after the war began. A report from March 1942 listed four children as needing homes: three boys (ages nine, two, and one) and one girl (age eleven). In contrast, it listed seventeen people who wanted boys and fifty-nine looking for girls. The ages of the children sought are also revealing. Fifteen of the couples requested boys between six and fourteen years of age, compared to only one who wanted an infant. Though the couples did not expressly say so, they most likely wanted older boys to do work in exchange for their care. The age spread for girls was larger: nine couples wanted girls thirteen to fourteen, thirty-two wanted girls eight to twelve, ten wanted girls five to seven, and eight wanted girls two to four. Only one couple requested an infant.[84]

Potential foster parents' desire for girl children flew in the face of National Socialist ideology, which valued boys over girls.[85] The underlying cause for the gender bias is not clear. Perhaps memories of World War I made many people reluctant to take a chance in forming a bond with a foster son who might one day be called to war. After 1939, the increasingly militaristic activity of the Hitler Youth and the war itself would only have served to exacerbate these fears. Some people may also have shied away from boys because they had a greater propensity to become delinquent.[86] But, ironically, many couples' preference for girls may have been caused by Nazi rhetoric itself. From the outset, the Nazis praised women as mothers and child rearers who remained at home and performed domestic work. In contrast, the Nazi Party removed men from their families to perform myriad duties for the nation, ultimately sending many of them to war. It seems plausible that some women would have felt inclined to raise girls because girls would stay at home and help rather than be called to national duty.

During the Second World War, as pressure on the foster care system intensified, Nazi officials made placing children in homes a priority above creating traditional families. In 1943, the NSV in Hesse-Nassau asserted,

---

82 Hagen, Pflegestellenanzeiger no. 5/39 NSDAP Amt für Volkswohlfahrt Gau Westfalen-Süd, SaM, NSDAP Volkswohlfahrt-Westfalen Nord, 770.
83 NSV Westfalen Nord report about foster care submitted to NSV Berlin, 30 March 1938, SaM, NSDAP Volkswohlfahrt, 482.
84 Lists of foster children in need of homes and available homes, NSV Westfalen Nord, 1 March 1942, SaM, NSDAP Volkswohlfahrt, 485.
85 Hitler could be named godfather (*Patenvater*) upon the birth of the seventh child or the fifth son.
86 In 1932, women constituted only 12.5 percent of juvenile offenders. Harvey, *Youth and the Welfare State*, 198–9.

"The meaning and aim of our work is not primarily to give couples who love children or single, motherly women who seek a child, a child, but rather to find the proper foster home for the many children who are withering away with their birth parents or who threaten to wither away physically or emotionally."[87] In part, this new focus reflected the growing difficulty of collecting medical, political, and financial documents as records were destroyed by bombings.[88] Some authorities were willing to disregard the Nazi guidelines in the interest of providing homes for children at the critical moment. In 1944, for example, the Detmold county leadership reported that obtaining a certificate of political loyalty for all foster parents before assigning them a child had become much too complicated under wartime conditions, especially since "in many cases a home [was] needed immediately within hours after the mother's death or the father's disappearance." Doctors who were too busy to do proper medical examinations on children only added to the chaos that came to characterize the foster care system.

But even as the system for selecting foster parents broke down, the war increased the demand for foster families. To spark interest in foster parenting, the Nazis declared 1943 the Year of the Foster Child and launched a propaganda campaign to celebrate it.[89] The propaganda proved effective and attracted many people who otherwise would not have volunteered. In August 1943, for example, two retired sisters wrote the NSV: "We are very fond of children. Our small house is in a beautiful area and has a wonderful garden. We are retired post office employees. My sister is fifty years old, and I am fifty-seven, but our hearts are still young. We are both party members; I joined before the National Socialists came to power. We both stand solidly behind the Führer! We would be happy if you could send us a young girl."[90] Other applicants included women whose husbands were at war, women who were childless or whose children were grown, and couples who had lost their sons in the war.

Despite all Nazi efforts to mold families, control the foster care system, and make foster parents happy, many Germans continued to view foster care as somewhat questionable and sought adoption instead. Because of the relative permanence of adoptive relationships, however, the Nazis were even

---

87 Hessen-Nassau Amt für Volkswohlfahrt to NSDAP Kreisleitung, Hauptamt für Volkswohlfahrt, 3 March 1943, SaM, NSDAP Volkswohlfahrt-Gau Westfalen Nord, 770.

88 Partei Genosse Bernhard Schönberger, "Der Helfer in seinem Amt," in Der Helfer der NSV-Jugendhilfe, 1. Folge 1943, SaM, NSDAP Volkswohlfahrt, 770; Detmold NSDAP Kreisleitung Amt für Volkswohlfahrt to Kreisleiter Pg. W., Betr. Politische Zuverlässigkeit bei Einweisung von Pflegekindern, 23 March 1944, StaD, L113, 932.

89 Der Helfer der NSV-Jugendhilfe, 1. Folge 1943, SaM, NSDAP Volkswohlfahrt, 770.

90 Applications for foster children, 1944, SaM, NSDAP Volkswohlfahrt-Westfalen Nord, 498.

more strongly compelled to ensure that the parents and children involved in the adoption process conformed to racial and political criteria. Although little changed legally before 1938, new guidelines for and popular ideas about race began to alter adoptions much earlier. The very public celebration of the Aryan race prompted potential adoptive parents to add genetic family trees to their applications. Their requests for children reflected a general acknowledgment of racial ideology. In 1937, Protestant authorities complained that after the Nazis came to power adoptive parents began to insist that all children should "be blond and blue-eyed, of northern parentage, and have proof of high quality heritage!!"[91] Children who did not look Aryan became increasingly difficult to place.

From the Nazis' first day in office, Jews and other "racial" outsiders found themselves excluded from the NSV adoption process.[92] In the years that followed, Nazi policymakers worked to restrict and clarify their adoption policy. In 1937, the Reich minister of the interior laid out additional racial guidelines for adoption that forbade Jews and people of "second-degree mixed race" (*Mischlinge Zweiten Grades*) from entering into adoption contracts with "healthy Germans" under any circumstances. Ambiguous cases, those between couples who had "totally or partly foreign blood," and adoptions arranged outside the surveillance of the Nazi centers, while not automatically excluded, were to be decided by the Reich minister of the interior on an individual basis.[93]

Apart from hindering non-Aryan adoptions, the Nazis took further steps to facilitate adoptions among "racially pure" Germans. To bring all adoptions under their control, the Nazis made a concerted effort to reach out to the institutions and organizations that worked with mothers who were likely

91 Ibid. As a result, when Liselotte, a Jewish woman, became pregnant in 1936, she knew better than to seek help from the NSV. Instead, she requested that the KRV act as a guardian for her illegitimate child until she and the Polish father could marry. When anti-Semitic laws in Poland prevented the marriage, she doubted that as a Jew she would be able to find sufficient employment to support her child and gave the child up for adoption. Because the Nazis prevented the "three-quarters Jewish" child from being adopted by an Aryan couple, the KRV arranged an adoption by a "half-Jewish" missionary doctor in Java. His racial status and the fact that he and the child would reside outside Germany made the adoption permissible. Landesarchiv Berlin, Kinderrettungsverein, 244.

92 Adoption und Unterbringung in Pflege bei Verschiedenrassigkeit, Runderlaß des Reichs Minister des Innern, 6 August 1937.

93 A 1938 directive encouraged the "service department leaders" (*Dienststellenleiterinnen*) to contact the university and women's clinics (*Landesfrauenklinik*), midwives' schools (*Hebammenlehranstalten*), and private delivery homes personally to encourage them to refer children to the Reich adoption agencies. Professional organizations for midwives, doctors, and nurses that counseled single mothers were required to maintain ties with the Reich adoption centers (for example, the Trade Committee for Nurses (Fachausschuß für das Schwesternwesen), Department of German Midwives (Fachschaft der Deutschen Hebammen), National Socialist German Doctors' League (NSD-Ärztebund), Doctors' Professional Association (Ärztekammer), as well as organizations of lawyers (Nationalsozialistischer Rechtswahrerbund, and Anwaltskammer). Rundbrief der Reichs-Adoptionsstelle in der NS-Volkswohlfahrt e.V., 4 February 1938, BaK, NS37, 1009.

to give their children up for adoption "and downplayed the racial testing that would subsequently become necessary."[94] They began to supervise university clinics, midwives' schools, women's clinics, and private maternity homes. They also co-opted the professional organizations for doctors, midwives, and nurses who counseled single mothers. In addition, the Nazis enlisted all National Socialist party organizations – but especially the National Socialist Women's Organization, the Reich Mother Service (Reichsmütterdienst), and the Office for the Health of the *Volk* (Amt für Volksgesundheit) – to direct mothers interested in giving their children up for adoption to the Reich adoption centers. Beginning in 1938, youth departments were required to refer all children to the National Socialist adoption centers rather than arrange adoptions themselves. Church organizations like the KRV were simultaneously barred from facilitating adoptions among "healthy" Germans. The Reich adoption centers then circulated lists of potential adoptive parents and children to help pair children and parents across Germany. This high level of coordination not only facilitated "healthy" adoptions but also allowed the Nazis to create a national blacklist intended to prevent "unworthy" parents from adopting.[95]

In the process of scrutinizing the racial heritage of all potential parents and all children, the Nazis created a battery of new requirements elaborate enough to turn what had once been straightforward adoptions into lengthy, drawn-out affairs. Even prearranged adoptions between family members were delayed as couples searched for proof of racial worth. When Christa L.'s mother died in 1935, her aunt and uncle followed through on their long-standing agreement to adopt Christa. Immediately after the death, however, the Reich adoption center in Münster informed them that despite their contract with Christa's mother, they would have to submit proof of their "Aryan" origin along with their health, citizenship, and police records. Even after they had submitted all the required documents, Christa's aunt and uncle were not granted permission to adopt. Six years later, they turned in desperation to their mayor, who wrote that the adoption should be permitted without delay.[96]

The high level of documentation required for adoption discouraged people on both sides of the adoptive relationship. Some biological mothers, put off by the prospect of thoroughly documenting their pasts, decided to

94 Ibid. The blacklists were discontinued in 1943. Rundschreiben 111/43, 5 July 1943, BaK, NS37, 1010.
95 Bürgermeister Lemgo to Herrn Reichsstatthalter in Lippe u. Schaumburg-Lippe, Landesregierung, Landesjugendamt Detmold, 4 November 1941, StaD, L 80 IA, Gruppe 27, Titel 2, 3, Bd. 2.
96 Elternmeldung Eheleute F. from Amt Wohlfahrt/Jugendhilfe in Burgsteinfurt, SaM, NSDAP Volkswohlfahrt-Westfalen Nord, 497.

raise their children themselves. Some potential adoptive parents hesitated to participate in the process, especially after the war made securing documentation more difficult. One social worker reported, for example: "The Fredes have still not been able to decide conclusively to adopt the child. They are scared off primarily by the procuring of papers."[97] As a result, despite the Nazi emphasis on adoption, the number of children who left state guardianship (*Amtsvormundschaft*) through adoption in Prussia dropped from 1,432 to 1,177 between 1928 and 1938. This drop-off occurred after Nazi pro-adoption policies were instituted and at a time when the number of state wards increased from 321,000 to 383,020.[98]

Not infrequently, Nazi racial guidelines combined with more traditional complications to make adoption exceptionally difficult. Especially when people deemed "unfit" challenged social workers' evaluations, cases could drag on for years. When the Eckhoffs applied for a permit to take in Marieke as a foster child after her mother died, the youth department granted them a permit without difficulty. But several months later, when they decided to adopt Marieke, the social worker assigned to the case claimed that although Frau Eckhoff ran a "by and large well-cared-for household," she was a "very flustered and . . . nervous woman." Moreover, Frau Eckhoff was hard of hearing, so that the social worker could "hardly believe that she [was] appropriate to raise a child."[99] When she tried to gather information about Frau Eckhoff from neighbors, she found that "getting information from neighbors is impossible because either the inhabitants stick together or they make one another look bad." The two neighbors who did send testimonies on behalf of Frau Eckhoff had opposite opinions.[100] In the face of the social worker's determined effort to prevent the adoption, the Eckhoffs hired a lawyer, who submitted a medical certificate verifying that Frau Eckhoff's hearing loss was not genetic. Even though the Reich adoption center accepted that an ear infection (and not a genetic illness) was responsible for her poor hearing, the youth department still denied the Eckhoffs' request to adopt Marieke. Because they believed she would inevitably suffer when she was older, they also threatened to revoke the Eckhoffs' foster care permit eventually. Nazi eugenic guidelines left Marieke in limbo – unable to be adopted by the only parents she had ever known and at risk of losing them entirely at an unspecified future date.

97 *Statistisches Jahrbuch* 26 (1930): 252–3; *Statistisches Jahrbuch des deutschen Reich* 59 (1941/2).
98 Ibid., 26 (1930): 252–3; 59 (1941/2).
99 Eckhoff Case, StaD, D 23 Hohenhausen, 46.
100 That personal motives and jealousies often motivated neighbors, making them unreliable reporters, has been noted by other historians. Gellately, *Gestapo and German Society*; Mallmann and Paul, "Omniscient, Omnipotent, Omnipresent?"

Children born outside marriage, who represented a high proportion of all adoptions, posed other complications. When children had no contact with their biological fathers or paternal identity itself remained in doubt, verifying racial histories became extremely challenging, and Nazi authorities often responded to incomplete family histories by blocking adoption until the child was old enough to have developed any probable genetic flaws. The Blesers, who tried to adopt their foster child, Gerhard, in 1935, faced many of the problems of adopting an illegitimate child. Gerhard's biological mother, Heidi, who had married and had two children since Gerhard's birth, refused to come to the Detmold Health Department to be examined. More troubling, the doctor who examined Gustav, Gerhard's biological father, declared that although he could not identify any genetic illness (*Erbkrankheit*), he nonetheless doubted Gustav's "racial purity." Gustav had a history of arrests for theft, deceit, and embezzlement, which, together with his appearance, raised "the suspicion of a possible hereditary incrimination [*Belastung*]." Because of this inconclusive medical history, the health department advised against Gerhard's adoption by a "racially pure" couple like the Blesers. Here the case might have languished had not authorities at the local youth department come to Gerhard's rescue and insisted that a blood test be conducted. Neither Heidi nor Gustav was willing to pay for the test; Gustav, in fact, refused to be tested at all. Frau Bleser, who was rapidly becoming discouraged about the possibility of adopting Gerhard, also refused to pay. Even after authorities convinced Gustav that only adoption would end his obligation to pay child support and he underwent the test at the state's expense, the results failed to prove anything conclusively. Heidi did not appear for her test. More than a year after they started the adoption proceedings, the Blesers asked the Lemgo Health Department doctor (*Amtsarzt*) to render a second opinion on Gerhard. Based on a physical exam, he concluded: "The now six-year-old child [is] ... predominantly of the Nordic race.... His physical development... has so far been undisturbed. In terms of character, the child has developed well so far and... makes a fresh, mentally lively, impression. On the basis of appearance, German origin must be assumed." In his report, he ignored his colleague's concerns about Gerhard's father, concentrating instead on facilitating the adoption.[101] This positive medical evaluation prompted the Detmold department doctor to speculate that Gerhard's father had previously been misidentified and that Gerhard was in fact probably "racially pure." With this, he lifted the last impediment to Gerhard's adoption. This case illustrates clearly how the ambiguity of racial tests and the arbitrary nature of doctors' decisions could

101 Case of Gerhard K., 1932–1937, StaD, L 80 IA, Gruppe 27, Titel 2, 3 Bd. 2.

tremendously complicate and lengthen the adoption process for illegitimate children.

Even after adoption had been completed, some children had to revisit their biological roots to acquire the "certificate of Aryan heritage" necessary to participate fully in Nazi society. But because these children's paternal genetic heritage was often difficult to determine, the authorities at the Department of Racial Research were often forced to use a large degree of lenience in issuing certificates. They realized that denying a certificate caused both the children and their Aryan parents significant distress.[102]

The authorities at the Department of Racial Research were not alone in viewing Nazi racial guidelines with some flexibility. Other local officials, who felt pressure to place children in families rapidly due to both financial constraints and concern about children's welfare, also often found Nazi racial guidelines a major obstacle. Some authorities not only complained about the convoluted adoption process but also sought to circumvent rules when possible, even if this meant directly defying National Socialist policy. In Bielefeld, for example, youth department authorities assumed all illegitimate children were Aryan and required proof only under extraordinary circumstances. When Nazi authorities challenged this practice, Bielefeld officials justified their actions by claiming that they usually knew both the mother and the biological father already and could hence evaluate the child's heritage without formal documentation. Furthermore, they noted that during their temporary stays in orphanages, illegitimate children could be evaluated by the doctors, home directors, and nurses. In their opinion, forcing potential parents to supply papers led to crowded orphanages, punished children, and caused unnecessary delays in the adoption process.[103] To streamline the system further (at the risk of subverting Nazi efforts at centralization), the Bielefeld Youth Department conducted its own adoptions without involving the Reich adoption centers. This enabled them to conclude typical adoptions within five months "even if the child's suitability ... had not been proven beyond a doubt." This challenge to Nazi policy did not go unnoticed. In 1939, the *Kreisleitung* (county leadership) reprimanded the *Kreisamtsleiter* (county leader) in Bielefeld over these "wild" adoption arrangements, which directly contradicted Nazi policy. In their letter of reprimand, the *Kreisleitung* stressed that centralizing the adoption process was for the "greater good" of

---

102 Mouton, "Rescuing Children"; Landesarchiv Berlin, Kinderrettungsverein, 107. For another example, see ibid., 106.
103 Notiz für die Reichsadoptionsstelle from Kreisamtsleitung Bielefeld-Halle, October 1939, SaM, NSDAP Volkswohlfahrt, 497.

all.[104] In their defense, Bielefeld authorities did not address the fact that their policy all but ignored the blood evidence so critical to Nazi logic. Instead, they emphasized that, in their view, finding homes for children took precedence over genetic and biological considerations. Even though their actions constituted a direct challenge to the Nazi adoption process, no evidence suggests that the authorities sought to resist the Nazi worldview more broadly. Unable to eliminate the unregulated adoptions by pressuring local authorities, the NSV turned to the minister of the interior, who in 1941 decreed that racial guidelines had to be made paramount and tried to ensure that youth departments played "only a passive role" in future adoptions.[105]

The Nazi effort to bring adoption into line with racial guidelines did not stop at the time of adoption. In fact, the Nazis' willingness to intrude into families even after an adoption had been finalized represented one of the most serious changes the Nazis imposed on Weimar adoption policy. In September 1938, the Reich minister of the interior issued an edict entitled the Legal Annulment of Adoptive Relations, which granted the state the right to terminate at any time any adoption considered contrary to the public interest.[106] The Wolpers' case provides a telling example of how some local authorities implemented this law. Shortly after the Wolpers adopted Wolfgang in 1939, the youth department tried to dissolve the adoption because of Herr Wolper's newly discovered criminal record. When Frau Wolper protested, she received no sympathy at the local level. In despair, she wrote an impassioned letter to Hitler himself, emphasizing her faithful, long-term support of the Nazi Party. She also stressed that the child had transformed her marriage and that she "would gladly work for [her] husband's future and above all for [her] child." Her letter concluded with a plea: "My loving Führer, just allow me to remain a mother." Despite her fervent letter, which never reached Hitler but was instead immediately forwarded back to the same local authorities who were about to dissolve her adoption, the Detmold court ruled that the adoption did not reflect the public interest. Although the Wolpers were not Jewish, Herr Wolper's criminal activity proved his status as a "racial outsider." Wolfgang's unblemished origins made it impossible for Nazi authorities who accepted the Nazi hierarchy of race to allow him to grow up in a family "whose leader [was]

---

104 Notiz für die Reichsadoptionstelle, citing Vierteljahresbericht der Kreis Bielefeld-Halle, 21 October 1939, SaM, NSDAP Volkswohlfahrt, 497.

105 Hansen, *Wohlfahrtspolitik im NS-Staat*, 253.

106 Dr. Ursula Schücking, Sachbearbeiterin in der Reichsadoptionsstelle Berlin, "Annahme an Kindes Statt: Die Weiterentwicklung der gesetzlichen Grundlagen seit 1933 und die Zuständigkeit der Adoptionsvermittlungsstelle," *Deutsches Recht* 49 (December 1941), Ausgabe A.

outwardly marked with the stigma of serious conviction." In the end, the adoption was annulled.[107]

Nazi authorities also targeted for dissolution adoptive contracts in which one party was Jewish and the other Aryan. Despite the widespread acceptance of Nazi racial stereotyping, this policy met some local resistance. Though they may have supported a ban on mixed-race adoptions, many Germans objected to the Nazi effort to intrude into and destroy long-standing adoptive families. The mayor in Bad Salzuflen, Hans Briemann (a National Socialist party member since 1933), recognized that Paul D., who had been adopted by the Hortmanns many years earlier, was half-Jewish. Nonetheless, in his letter to the Lippe *Land* government, he explained that Paul's mother was Aryan, and he wrote, "In my opinion, no reservations can be raised about upholding the adoptive relationship." Paul worked as a barber in his adopted parents' barber shop and was married to the shoemaker's daughter, who was also Aryan. Furthermore, they had a healthy child. The mayor concluded by assuring the government that Paul's "behavior inside the *Volksgemeinschaft* [had] always been impeccable."[108] In a similar case, the mayor of Lage refused to remove Eugen M. from his adoptive parents' home despite the child's suspected Jewish heritage. He assured the state government: "I believe that in his later life Eugen will prove himself useful. As I have ascertained, he is also a member of the Hitler Youth."[109] Not all authorities resisted annulments so forcefully, but it is clear that even local Nazi authorities like Mayor Briemann who did not necessarily reject the edict per se nonetheless refused to enforce the letter of the law when it conflicted with the local community's interests. In their eyes, behavior could trump biology and race in determining membership in the *Volksgemeinschaft*. Moreover, they recognized that singling out individuals who had participated in and contributed to the community for racial persecution would undermine morale in their towns.

CONCLUSION

During both the Weimar and National Socialist eras, state authorities believed foster care and adoption were essential to Germany's future and sought to provide better homes for children. Youth departments, created in the

---

107 Wolper case, StaD, L 80 IA, Gruppe 27, Titel 2, 3 Bd. 3.
108 Mayor Stadt Bad Salzuflen to Lippische Landesregierung Detmold, 18 September 1939, StaD, L 80 IA, Gruppe 27, Titel 4.
109 Bürgermeister Stadt Lage to Lippische Landesregierung Detmold, 24 November 1939, StaD, L 80 IA, Gruppe 27, Titel 2, 4.

Weimar era, persisted into the Nazi era to oversee children's well-being. Social workers employed by the youth departments throughout the interwar period conducted thorough background checks on potential foster care and adoptive parents. Despite their similar goals and methods, however, the discontinuities in Weimar and Nazi national policy regarding foster care and adoption far outweigh the continuities. While Weimar authorities sought financially and emotionally stable homes that would ensure child welfare, the Nazis dramatically altered the standards for what constituted a good parent by focusing primarily on racial criteria. The NSV and the Reich adoption centers were both created to enable authorities to apply a racial hierarchy to foster care and adoption, excluding Jews and other "racial outsiders." The Nazis put the goal of achieving racial purity ahead of the welfare of many children and even dissolved long-standing and mutually beneficial adoptions that contradicted national racial goals.

But the dramatic changes that occurred at the national level were not exactly mirrored at the local level. Weimar youth departments were unable to change foster care and adoption as thoroughly as national policymakers intended. Competition that hindered progress developed between state and church authorities over control of child welfare programs. The economic turmoil that characterized much of the Weimar era increased the number of needy German children and further overwhelmed youth departments. The division of labor between youth department authorities, social workers, doctors, and police departments caused some critics to try to reform the system to protect children from overzealous social workers and indiscreet police officers. Some local youth department authorities, facing strained budgets, dismissed child welfare ideals in favor of concrete realities. Childless couples often spent considerable time and effort to prove their suitability as parents and did not hesitate to protest if they felt they had been misjudged. The result was a system in which foster care and adoption placements varied from quick and straightforward to long and drawn-out depending on the individual couple, the youth department, the social worker, and the other authorities involved in the case.

After 1933, the Reich adoption centers centralized adoption and imposed racial criteria and in the process dramatically diminished Germans' ability to evade the state-imposed guidelines. Most people had to comply with Nazi demands that they prove their racial heritage. For Jews and other "racial outsiders," the doors to adoption within the state system decisively shut. But despite their wide-ranging efforts, even the Nazis never succeeded in attaining a monopoly over adoption proceedings. Church organizations, though relegated to a far more limited role, continued to arrange some foster care and adoption placements and to emphasize religion in their placements. Individuals went on placing advertisements in newspapers and creating some foster care and adoptive relationships privately. Despite concerted Nazi efforts to the contrary, some youth departments persisted in arranging adoptions outside the purview of Nazi adoption centers. Although the Nazis mandated ideological training for social workers and doctors trained after 1933, many, especially those who had trained during the 1920s, did not accept the Nazi worldview.

But the National Socialist emphasis on racially and politically reliable families had many unexpected results. The Nazis' stricter requirements, together with the growing need for families especially after the outbreak of the Second World War, encouraged the state to redefine family. Nazi officials directed their rhetoric specifically to women and encouraged even single women to take in children. Fatherhood and the traditional family came to be regarded as less important than race in the creation of non–blood-based families. And the Nazi focus on race also sometimes hurt the very children the National Socialists sought to help. When authorities decided for racial, social, or political reasons not to permit a foster family to adopt, they did not necessarily remove the child. Instead, though they were unwilling to allow the relationship to become permanent, they were also unwilling or unable to move the child to a "better" situation.

As Nazi racial laws made already cumbersome adoptions more labor intensive, the sheer magnitude of the workload and the complicated nature of racial guidelines prevented a careful, thorough application of policy – and paradoxically made foster care and adoption placements far less consistent than national guidelines would suggest.[110] Individual social workers, doctors, and mayors decided when to comply with policy demands and when to exert their agency on behalf of their clients. Doctors' opinions could vary even when faced with the same information, thus creating a small but crucial space for some parents – and authorities – to maneuver around certain Nazi mandates. Local authorities sometimes skirted Nazi racial law when faced with an increase in needy children and a decrease in the number of available homes. Once adoptions had been completed, local authorities – even those who were themselves Nazi Party members – were often loath to dissolve relationships even if they did not comply with Nazi racial policy. Because genetic heritage could not always be proved, even authorities in the Department of Racial Research found themselves compelled to apply racial

---

110 Doctors in particular were also burdened with the responsibility of examining people for many other Nazi programs, including marriage loan candidates and those nominated for sterilization.

policy with greater lenience than the Nazi leadership intended. Such actions reveal the wide variety of responses to Nazi racial policies. While some authorities supported – even fanatically imposed – racial guidelines, others weighed the guidelines against their own values and the circumstances presented in individual adoption cases.

Just as in the Weimar era, then, the implementation of Nazi policy toward nonbiological families depended on the compliance of the German population. The widespread acceptance of Nazi racial ideology made it relatively easy for the Nazis to bar Jews from participating in adoptions but, paradoxically, made it harder to place children who did not look Aryan or for whom documentation was unavailable. Many couples and children involved in adoption prior to 1933 were later forced to revisit their adoption files in order to provide proof of their own and their adopted child's Aryan heritage. Even before Allied bombs began to destroy church and state records, a not insignificant number of Germans refused to create detailed family histories and set limits on the level of state interference they would tolerate. Some couples avoided adoption altogether, while others found opportunities to maneuver around unfair decisions. Foster care and adoption reflected priorities in the Weimar and Nazi eras. During the Weimar era, emphasis was placed on child welfare, but the respect for families' privacy and shortages in both funding and personnel meant great variation in families' experiences. The Nazis put racial guidelines above child welfare, but the need to create families for needy children eventually severely compromised the Nazis ability to insist on racial guidelines.

Conclusion

During both the Weimar and National Socialist eras, many Germans perceived the family to be the critical foundation upon which Germany's future depended. In political debate, policy formation, and unofficial discourse, Germans articulated the view that the nation's survival rested on a revival of marriage and motherhood. Providing German men and women with the security needed to bear children would, they hoped, usher in economic prosperity, create social stability, and raise moral standards. Through family-directed legislation, both Weimar and National Socialist policymakers sought to raise the birthrate, decrease infant mortality, and improve public health. Since the two regimes had a number of aims in common, some historians have viewed their family policies as developing in a continuous line. Indeed, certain programs introduced by the Weimar governments were continued by the Nazis once they took power. During both eras, policymakers advocated the use of marriage certificates, financed kindergartens, and celebrated Mother's Day. And yet, as this study has demonstrated, a dramatic transformation in family policy followed the Nazi takeover. Parliamentary debates gave way to monolithic decrees as the Nazis introduced a race-based ideology and showed a much greater willingness to intervene directly into families. The result was fundamental change in both the aim and impact of family policy.

During the Weimar era, lawmakers across the political spectrum agreed that the German family was critical to social stability and that the war had dangerously weakened the family. Not only had the war destroyed people's lives and livelihoods, but the soaring rates of divorce and illegitimacy it brought with it continued to threaten the reestablishment of order and stability even after the armistice. To help strengthen families and ensure the nation's future, legislators believed that women needed to be encouraged to bear children and that children, in turn, needed to be protected. From the

272

outset, the Weimar Constitution supported marriage and promised social welfare for all Germans.

Building upon earlier work in the field, this study has shown that Weimar social policy came into being in a context of tremendous political conflict and legislative turmoil. Throughout the Weimar era, politicians disagreed about the specific shape family policy should take and how it should be administered. The debates surrounding these issues spread well beyond the walls of parliament: church leaders, feminists, doctors, eugenicists, and many other interested parties sometimes supported and at other times challenged legislative initiatives. The common belief that the future of the nation itself was at stake in family policy ensured that each policy was evaluated not just for its specific and immediate impact but also for its broader economic, demographic, social, and moral implications. Policymakers debated how illegitimate children could be supported without condoning their mothers' unconventional sexual behavior and how failed marriages could be terminated without devaluing the institution of marriage. They sought to raise health standards and evaluate homes for foster children without discouraging potential parents from taking in needy children. And they worried about how to provide help for children without undermining parental responsibility and paternal authority.

Complicating these debates over the precarious state of Weimar families were the rapid shifts associated with modernity. Postwar rationalization of industry, advances in medicine, and new forms of popular culture all affected family life, gender roles, and intergenerational relations. Increasingly, young women felt drawn to employment options rather than to motherhood in their early adulthood, seemingly putting the birthrate in peril. The New Woman flaunted tradition as she took advantage of the wealth of modern opportunities in Weimar society. The constitution itself, by proclaiming sexual equality, seemed to condone and encourage at least some of these tendencies. Modern medical advances enabled families of all classes to practice birth control, and it was during the 1920s that the majority of German couples came to see the advantages of controlling family size. Finally, scientific and hygienic knowledge expanded, raising health standards to unprecedented levels and creating new benchmarks for household management and mothering.

In light of these shifts, Weimar policymakers struggled to create state policy that would at once respect traditional values and recognize and adapt to social change. The newly established youth departments, with their burgeoning ranks of social workers, together with advances in medicine and social hygiene created the possibility of preemptive intervention for the first time. From the perspective of Socialists, Communists, and many progressives, this invaluable opportunity – if used properly – would enable the state to improve family health. Troubled families could be provided with assistance, and overworked mothers could be given relief before children suffered. These aims met stiff and unrelenting opposition, however, from those who believed that preserving the privacy and independence of families was of paramount importance. Conservative politicians and church leaders worried that if families became reliant on the state for support, paternal and religious authority would be undermined. The fault lines shifted as the eugenics movement grew in force and Germans of the *völkisch* Right began to insist that the state take a more active role in preventing "undesirable" births while pushing German women back toward the domestic sphere. They asserted that science had been squandered on the weaker portion of the population rather than applied selectively to ensure national strength.

Beyond the contentiousness that surrounded Weimar family policy at the national legislative level, local authorities, including judges, physicians, and local administrators responsible for implementing policy, had their own perspectives on the plight of German families. As largely reluctant participants in the republic, judges were conservative skeptics of any attempt on the part of the state to modernize families. They tended to view patriarchy as the ideal family form and through their verdicts launched a backlash against modern gender roles. Even so, conservative notions of family were challenged daily in the courts. Physicians disagreed among themselves about what kind of policy would best alleviate Germany's societal woes. Some doctors allied with the Left believed that by staffing marriage clinics, distributing advice about birth control, and making abortion legal, Germans' overall welfare could be greatly improved. Others held the firm conviction that mandatory testing before marriage and compulsory sterilization of those carrying unhealthy genes would lead to a healthier society. Social workers, though empowered to make ever more home visits that enabled the state to intervene more routinely in family life, had a varied impact. For some families, social workers were simply intruders into the private sphere to be resisted; for others, they were welcome advocates.

In negotiating between national guidelines and local realities, local bureaucrats also adapted policy. In order to balance local budgets, youth department authorities sought payment from the fathers of illegitimate children but avoided making demands that would be so onerous as to undermine the formation of new families. Health department authorities sought to prevent "unhealthy" marriages without destroying young people's happiness by forbidding marriage altogether. Social workers monitored children's well-being in foster homes but tried to avoid unnecessary intervention that would discourage couples from volunteering to take in foster children. When women failed to visit state-run marriage clinics, authorities restructured the clinics to address women's desire for birth control. Acting on a case-by-case basis, Weimar local authorities balanced national guidelines, local needs, and personal circumstances.

During the Weimar years, female clients of state programs also played an important role in shaping family policy. Women's support of a wide array of Weimar political parties shows that they, too, held varying opinions as to the most appropriate governmental policy for German society. On an individual level, women used government policy to further their own interests. They generally evaded policies they felt represented undesirable and unnecessary state intervention – such as the requirement of obtaining marriage certificates – but they regularly visited mother advice centers, enrolled in mothering courses, and took their children to kindergartens. Many single mothers took advantage of the state's willingness to force fathers to pay child support. Other women tailored their divorce petitions to reflect traditional or modern notions of marriage to increase the chance of receiving a favorable hearing from a judge. Some women did not hesitate to accept assistance from nongovernmental agencies, and the state responded by financially supporting church programs. Other women sought out birth control from private organizations when it was unavailable in state clinics.

Ultimately, Weimar politicians' inability to solve social problems or to manage the economy fed the growing antirepublican critique of all that the Weimar state stood for: democracy, socialism, modernization, and feminism. As the economy worsened, social workers and others grew frustrated with their inability to help families overcome their troubles. Some became persuaded that a more aggressive state policy – one mandating compliance or even eugenics – would more readily solve German families' problems. Still, despite the crises that engulfed Weimar family programs at the end of the republic, welfare resources available to families did dramatically increase during the 1920s. Many more German women received maternity benefits and infant care than had in the past. Fathers supported their illegitimate children to a greater degree, and this, together with the support available from advice centers, lowered the national infant mortality rate. Even as Weimar legislators failed to revise divorce law, German women and men were more successful at ending unhappy marriages than they had been historically. Moreover, as this study has demonstrated, a variety of sources of aid available to families during the Weimar era – sources that included state agencies as well as church and private organizations – coexisted to provide help for families. It is characteristic of the Weimar state's plurality that so many organizations proliferated, giving families in need a much wider array of options.

When the myriad Weimar agencies and programs failed to ward off depression-induced misery and the state offered no viable alternative solutions, many Germans found solace in the National Socialists' promise to use more forceful means to restore traditional families and strengthen the *Volk*. Following early successes in reducing crime and regaining control over the economy, the Nazis turned their attention to a new, monolithic family policy whose aim it was to provide far-reaching support to members of the *Volksgemeinschaft*. Granting marriage loans, celebrating Mother's Day, and awarding Mother Crosses were all part of a program to promote marriage and childbearing exclusively among "worthy" German women. From the outset, Nazi family policy also placed a new and sinister emphasis on race, limiting marriage and forbidding childbearing by the "unworthy." In basing this policy on the "racial worth" of individual Germans, the Nazis transformed the welfare state.

This study has demonstrated, however, that while the Nazis created a policy aimed at reshaping German society and families according to a monolithic, ideology-driven plan, in this realm as in others, policy often shifted to accommodate the state's changing needs. Moreover, local authorities made further adaptations to make policy fit local circumstances. Though the Nazis initially sought to exclude women from the labor force, once the worst effects of the Depression had dissipated and the Nazi demand for prewar labor increased, marriage loans ceased to be contingent upon women leaving the labor market. After the war began, Nazi policymakers again shifted their rhetoric and actively tried to draw women into the labor pool. They justified the change with the claim that since the Nazi Reich would last one thousand years, women's temporary contribution to the war effort did not undermine long-term goals.[1] Furthermore, when doctors were called up in large numbers, women, who had been banned from the study of medicine, were suddenly encouraged to pursue medical studies.[2] The Nazis' attempts to impose a stricter sexual morality were similarly tailored to meet the nation's changing needs. Throughout the war, the Nazis supported brothels for soldiers and maintained *Lebensborn* homes for single mothers even as they continued to praise traditional morality and scorn

---

1 Ironically, in the face of new demands for their labor, many women chose to bear children rather than work. Bock, "Antinatalism, Maternity and Paternity," 128.
2 For a more detailed account of how Nazi policy toward female education shifted, see Huerkamp, *Bildungsbürgerinnen*.

promiscuous behavior pro forma.[3] Racial policy itself underwent surprising shifts to meet the changing needs of the state. Although for years the Nazis had bombarded the population with propaganda warning against "unworthy" marriages and births, once the war began, policy changed, reflecting the need to ensure a steady birthrate and to maintain morale. As collecting documents to prove racial health became virtually impossible under wartime conditions, the state waived many components of its evaluative program, with the result that many health- and socially based conditions that earlier would have prevented marriage went unchallenged during the war. Thus, although the Nazis paid lip service to a monolithic gender, racial, and sexual policy, Nazi policymakers regularly shifted some of their directives on the basis of political expediency. It must be noted here, however, that Jewish Germans and their families experienced no such relaxation of repressive policy. Instead, policy toward Jews turned from discrimination to genocide.

Nazi family policy, like Weimar policy before it, underwent further modification in the process of implementation. As this book reveals, judges, doctors, social workers, civil servants, and others interpreted Nazi policy locally in conjunction with particular local circumstances and their own beliefs and strategies. Judges' collective failure to render verdicts consistently in line with Nazi policy aims resulted in uneven implementation of family policy. Some judges attempting to "work toward the Führer" applied racial law to their verdicts even before it became law. These judges, like other German officials whom Ian Kershaw has described, helped to "drive on an unstoppable radicalization which saw the gradual emergence in concrete shape of policy objectives embodied in the 'mission' of the Führer."[4] But while some judges radicalized the law, others clearly diluted the effects of Nazi ideology. Even after divorce law had been reformed, some judges refused to allow race to trump all other legal considerations. As a result, even couples whose marriages defied racial law – and who consequently posed an alleged threat through their potential reproduction – were not always granted permission to divorce. Other judges used blood tests to determine paternity in child support decisions, even though by doing so they downplayed issues of morality and rendered "worthiness" irrelevant: despite Nazi policy aims, a "worthy" man could still be burdened with judicially mandated support payments to an "unworthy" child. Many judges also refused to allow the war to spare fathers from fulfilling their responsibilities toward their illegitimate

3 Herzog, "Hubris and Hypocrisy," 13.
4 Kershaw, *Hitler*, 530.

children. And although Nazi leaders recognized that not all judges rendered their decisions in accordance with Nazi law, except for the removal of Jewish judges, which was done on wholly other grounds, the Nazis made relatively few changes to the judiciary.

At the heart of Nazi family policy lay the distinction between the "worthy" and the "unworthy," a distinction that depended on the judgment of a number of professionals, including doctors and social workers. Even doctors who wholeheartedly supported the laws quickly became overwhelmed by requests from individuals who needed medical approval to participate in some aspect of Nazi life, and doctors were thus forced to rush their exams or to delay writing medical reports – both of which undermined the consistent implementation of Nazi family policy. Because of its need for doctors, the government hesitated to summarily dismiss those doctors who failed to join the party or demonstrate support for National Socialism and instead demoted them to small rural practices. Even so, in the privacy of their offices, doctors had ample opportunity to shield their patients from Nazi policy either by overlooking negative findings or by refusing to act on them. Disagreements among physicians about how to apply racial guidelines also made it possible for individuals to obtain a second opinion and overturn a negative medical assessment.

Social workers also exercised discretion in putting Nazi policy into practice. Although after 1933 all social work students were trained to follow Nazi racial guidelines, the fact that the population reserved special hatred for the Nazi-trained social workers suggests that many Weimar-trained social workers maintained a professional distance from Nazi racial and exclusionary policy. They frequently applied their own definitions of worthiness and nominated mothers for Nazi benefits even when they did not meet the strict selection criteria established by policymakers. Yet even those social workers who did not agree with Nazi aims also sometimes found that through their work they facilitated Nazi family policy's effectiveness, even as they spared individuals on a case-by-case basis.[5]

Mayors and other civil servants also played important roles in identifying and evaluating Germans, requisitioning space and resources, and running programs. Although Nazi leaders fired many civil servants, they lacked sufficient numbers of qualified people to fill all positions. Moreover, even those who were hand-selected did not necessarily implement uniform policy.

---

5 Schnurr, "Why Did Social Workers Accept the New Order?" 132. Bronwyn Rebekah McFarland-Icke drew a similar conclusion about psychiatric nurses who performed their duty even if they did not agree with Nazi policy. See *Nazi Nurses*.

In sum, this book reveals a far more discerning bureaucracy than the one swept up in the brutal and seemingly ubiquitous popular anti-Semitism unleashed by Nazi laws that Michael Wildt describes.[6] As Claudia Koonz has asserted, it was "not mindless obedience, but selective compliance that characterized Germans' collaboration with evil."[7] As a result, family policy was applied inconsistently, and despite the primacy of race in Nazi ideology, even racial policy was implemented unevenly.

Many Germans welcomed the idea of a *Volksgemeinschaft*. As historian Norbert Frei has argued, by the mid-1930s, the "large majority of Germans really believed in a 'national resurrection' and in a better life for themselves and future generations."[8] This did not mean, however, that on a personal level the majority of Germans supported Nazi family policy aims. Marriage loans, tax breaks for large families, and Mother Crosses all promoted domestic roles for women that had no part in many women's notions of a better life – or in their visions of a *Volksgemeinschaft*. On an individual basis, such incentives had to vie with ineluctable modern population trends.[9] Despite tremendous effort, the Nazis failed to reverse the decline of the birthrate between 1933 and 1945.[10] In fact, in 1939, 60 percent of couples who had married between 1933 and 1937 were either childless or had only one child.[11] Although Nazi propaganda consistently praised women who focused on their roles as wives and mothers, the number of women in the workforce did not decline after 1933. Instead, the number of officially registered employed women rose from 11.5 million in 1933 to 12.8 million in 1939 and, after the onset of the war, to 14.9 million in 1944. The percentage of the workforce that was female also rose correspondingly, from 36 percent 1933 to 47 percent in 1939 and to more than 50 percent in 1944.[12] Nor did women abide by Nazi definitions of what constituted women's work, consistently avoiding the two areas of employment deemed appropriate for women by the state: agriculture and domestic service.

6 Wildt, "Gewalt gegen Juden," 59–80.
7 Koonz, *The Nazi Conscience*, 12.
8 Frei, "People's Community and War," 64.
9 Nor, as David Schoenbaum and others have argued, did the Nazis succeed in uniting Germans into a *Volksgemeinschaft*. Schoenbaum, *Hitler's Social Revolution*; Günther Könke, " 'Modernisierungs-schub,' " Hans Mommsen, "Noch einmal," 391–402.
10 The average household in 1933 contained 3.6 people; by 1939, this figure had fallen to 3.27. Ute Frevert, *Women in German History*, 232.
11 Eighteen percent of couples had no children, while 42 percent had only one child. Bock, "Antinatalism, Maternity and Paternity" 127.
12 These numbers pertain to the German territories as of 1937. When annexed territory is included, the number of working women rises to 14.6 million. Bock, "Antinatalism, Maternity and Paternity," 121.

It was precisely in the area of women's employment that one of the rifts in the *Volksgemeinschaft* developed. Despite the claim that National Socialist policy would erase class divisions, Nazi labor policy had a markedly differential class-based effect on women. Where middle-class women were closed out of civil service and professional jobs and, at least initially, almost no women were allowed to study at university, working-class women continued to perform economically essential wage labor. By January 1943, women's work had become so critical to the war effort that the Nazis required all women between the ages of seventeen and forty-five who were not pregnant or caring for small children to register for work. Working-class women, long frustrated with middle-class women's exemption from work, celebrated the decree. When some middle-class women still succeeded in evading the decree, hostility among working-class women increased, and many of them denounced their middle-class neighbors as work dodgers (A*rbeitsscheue*).[13] Nazi officials neither succeeded in eliminating this tension nor solved the problem.

In the day-to-day application of family policy, though the state certainly tried, as Lisa Pine has asserted, to utilize "the family for its own aim," families consistently worked to keep the Nazis out.[14] Women regularly challenged the demands of Nazi family policy when it threatened them personally, and bureaucrats modified the implementation of policy in response. The private, individual nature of these challenges and responses can perhaps better be described as evasion and negotiation rather than overt resistance.[15] Couples failed to be examined before marriage, judges refused to adhere strictly to racial guidelines, and social workers overlooked national directives far more often than they directly or publicly contested policy itself. In addition, as they learned the risks associated with participating in Nazi programs, many women simply refused to apply or attend, much to the dismay and frustration of Nazi authorities at all levels. When alternative non-National Socialist programs existed, many women chose to participate in them. They kept their children at home or sent them to local church kindergartens rather than support Nazi kindergartens. They visited clinics staffed by churchwomen instead of the NSV clinics; they favored mother courses taught by local

13 Diewald-Kerlemann, "'Der große Lump'"; *Sopade Berichte.*
14 Pine, *Nazi Family Policy,* 181.
15 The Nazi attempt to make the private sphere public and to politicize family life, thus making many private life decisions into explicitly public acts, further muddies the definition of resistance. Michael Geyer and John Boyer have described the history of resistance as a "fragile history, that interwove both individual and collective choices and decisions." Detlev Peukert identified a continuum of behavior that stretches from private "non-conformist" behavior to public resistance. Geyer and Boyer, "Introduction," *Resistance against the Third Reich.*

women over those taught by Nazi instructors. They regularly challenged doctors, Nazi Party members, and social workers who refused to approve their applications for benefits or who nominated them for sterilization. Often grounding their protests in Nazi ideology, German women tried to arouse the sympathy of the Nazi officials who decided their cases. When this failed, they sought second opinions on health matters, called on priests to defend them, and rallied teachers and employers to support their cases. When they believed blame lay with local authorities' misguided judgments, they even appealed their cases directly to Hitler. But almost always such challenges were personal, not political; situational, not ideological. They were frequently directed at local officials' abuse of power rather than at National Socialism itself. There can be no debate that Jewish women were victims of Nazi policy, but the status of "Aryan" women is less clear.[16] Many women took part in and helped lead National Socialist activities, particularly in the BDM, NSV, and NSF. Certainly, some lost their children, were sterilized against their will, or otherwise suffered the malicious side of Nazi family policy. But many women found ample opportunities to challenge, negotiate, manipulate, or, most frequently, evade Nazi policy altogether. They maintained their families largely outside Nazi purview, leaning on their religion, families, and friends for support.

Although each of these acts diminished the impact of Nazi family policy, even taken together, they do not constitute resistance, nor did they significantly undermine the regime. Nevertheless, the fact that the state did not often lash out at those who protested or remove from their jobs those who demonstrated laxness in enforcement reveals a rather more flexible – or at least less powerful – state apparatus than has sometimes been suggested. Although the Nazi regime sought to be monolithic and squelched any Weimar-style debate about family policy, on a day-to-day basis at the local level, the Nazis never made it a priority to enforce the uniform implementation of family policy. Despite the rhetorical emphasis the Nazis placed on family policy and on building the *Volksgemeinschaft*, their financial and manpower resources were consistently devoted primarily to preparing for and waging the Second World War and the Holocaust. As a result, individuals continued to petition privately and effectively for personal consideration. In an effort to keep people appeased, to rectify mistakes quietly, and to bolster war morale, state agents felt the need to pay them at least some heed. Perhaps the most unsettling aspect of the Nazi regime's inability to implement

16 Koonz, *Mothers in the Fatherland*; Bock, *Zwangssterlisation im Nationalsozialismus*; Ebbinghaus, *Opfer und Täterinnen*.

its family policy uniformly – and of the level of obstruction it faced on the ground – is the contrast this provides to the Nazis' greater and less contested success in other, more horrific realms.

In the final analysis, Nazi family policy represented a radical departure from Weimar policy. Both regimes created policy that aimed to "strengthen" families, raise the birthrate, and reinforce proper social mores as, of course, did most other contemporaneous Western regimes. But when the Nazi state began to coordinate all family policy under an authoritarian regime with a racial ideology at its core, it broke from any historical precedent. But at no point during either regime – despite vigorous attempts by the Nazis – was national family policy implemented uniformly. Indeed, one might argue that the most continuous aspect of Weimar and Nazi family policy was the moderating effect that implementation had on policy. During both eras, local authorities and individuals interpreted state decrees and smoothed the otherwise distinct edges of a very discontinuous policy design. When social workers overlooked "flaws" in families and doctors rendered favorable second opinions, they caused Nazi policy to look more like Weimar policy than the Nazis had intended. German women were rarely passive targets of family policy. Rather, as they accommodated, negotiated, and evaded policy, the lines between collaboration and resistance often blurred. To understand family policy, even under a totalitarian regime, one must examine not only the state but also individuals and families.

Bibliography

ABBREVIATIONS

BaK	Bundesarchiv Koblenz
BaP	Bundesarchiv Potsdam
EVHA	Archiv Evangelische Frauenhilfe
LSVA	Landschaftsverbandarchiv, Münster
KaM	Kommunalarchiv Minden
SaM	Staatsarchiv Münster
StaB	Stadtarchiv Bielefeld
StaD	Staatsarchiv Detmold
StaM	Stadtarchiv Münster
StaP	Stadtarchiv Paderborn

MANUSCRIPT COLLECTIONS

Berlin

Landesarchiv Berlin
    Kinderrettungsverein

Bielefeld

Stadtarchiv Bielefeld
    Sozialamt
    Jugendamt

Detmold

Staatsarchiv Detmold
    D 23: Amtsgericht Alverdissen, Beverungen, Bielefeld, Blomberg, Detmold, Gütersloh, Herford, Hohenhausen, Horn, Lemgo, Petershagen, Vlotho,

and Warburg; Erbgesundheitsgericht; Landgericht Bielefeld, Paderborn Ehescheidung

D 20 A Zug 75/92

Dezernat 24 D 1: Dezernat Sozialhygiene

D 100 Detmold

D 102 Halle: Kreis Halle

D 102 Lemgo: Kreis Lemgo

D 102 Minden: Kreis Minden

D 102 Warburg: Kreis Warburg

D 106 Detmold

D 106 Detmold A

L 80 IA: Lippische Regierung, Abteilung des Innern

L 80 IC: Lippische Regierung Medizinalwesen

M1 I JU: Minden Jugendpflege M1 I JU

M1 IM: Minden Medizinalwesen

M1 IP: Minden Polizei

M1 IIB: Minden Schulabteilung/Jugendpflege

M1 IS: Minden Sozialwesen

M15: NSDAP Herford

L113: NSDAP und NS Organisationen in Lippe

M1 IE: Regierung Minden

Personal Akten Ärzte

Fond du Lac, Wisconsin

Author's private collection

Engels, Marie. "Meine Lebenserinnerungen." Unpublished. Borrowed from author's daughter. Ca. 1987–1994.

Fasse, Luise. "Erinnerungen an Kinder- und Jugendjahren Detmold." Unpublished. Borrowed from the author. 1986.

Lohse, Gisela. "Letters from the war." Unpublished. Borrowed from the author.

Stautmeister, Gertraud. "Mein Leben." Unpublished. Gift from the author. Ca. 1990 and 1995.

Welzenberg, Schwester Angelika. *Die Westfälische Provinz der Ordensgemeinschaft der Schwestern von der Göttlichen Vorsehung, 1842–1970* Bd 1. Privately published. Gift of Schwester O.

Hagen

Institut für Biographie und Gedächtnis Forschung

Koblenz

Bundesarchiv Koblenz
  NS: National Socialism
  R: Reichsministerium der Innern

Minden

Kommunalarchiv Minden
  Amt Dützen

Münster

Bistums's Archiv
  PfA Hiltrup St. Clemens
  PfA St. Christophorus Werne
  PfA St. Laurentius Warendorf
  PfA St. Maria Magdalena
  Landschaftsverbandarchiv
    B223: Fürsorgeerziehung
    CI: Kinderbeihilfe
      CI 762: Gesundheitspflege
      CI 765, 766: Zentralstelle für Volkswohlfahrt
    C 60: Familienpflege; Deutscher Gemeindetag; Zwangssterilisation
  Staatsarchiv Münster
    Amtsgerichte
    Erbgesundheitsgericht
    Kreis Siegen Kreis Wohlfahrtsamt
    Landgericht Arnsberg
    Landgericht Bochum
    Landgericht Dortmund
    Landgericht Hagen
    NS Frauenschaft
    NS Kreis- und Ortsgruppenleistungen
    NSDAP Volkswohlfahrt
    Oberlandesgericht Hamm
    Oberpräsidium Münster Medizinalwesen
    Personalakten des Landgericht Dortmund
    Regierung Arnsberg
    Regierung Münster
  Stadtarchiv Münster
    Amt 10

Amt Roxel A Fach 33, A Fach 36
Amt Wolbeck B 15
Armenkommission
Kreis C 1/76
Kreisarchiv B
Kreisausschuss Amt 43 E
Stadtverordneter
Zentralbüro

Paderborn

Erzbistumsarchiv Paderborn
  Stadtarchiv Paderborn
    Amt Neuhaus

Potsdam

Bundesarchiv Potsdam
  62 DAF 3: Deutsche Arbeiterfront Arbeitswissenschaft
  70 Re 2: Reichsgemeinschaft deutscher Hausfrauen
  BA R 41: Reichsarbeitsministerium
  BA R43 11: Arbeiter
  BA R 61: Akademie für Deutsches Recht
  NS 10: National Socialism
  R: Reichsminister des Innern
    R 15.01: Reichsministerium des Innern

Soest

Archiv Evangelische Frauenhilfe

INTERVIEWS

All names have been changed to preserve anonymity. Unless otherwise stated, interviews were conducted by the author and tape recorded. Interviews are in the author's private collection.

Frau Conradi, Münster, 18 January 1995
Frau Dewald, Detmold, 25 February 1995
Frau Frandsen, Detmold, 16 February 1995
Frau Gethmann, Münster, 16 January 1995
Frau Heubrock, Münster, 29 October 1994

Frau Kemper, Lemgo, 21 May 1995
Frau Klein, Münster, 11 January 1995
Frau Krämer, Detmold, 19 February 1995
Frau Kresing, Münster, 3 December 1994
Frau Kurscheid, Münster, 13 January 1995
Frau Kutsch, Münster, 24 November, 1994
Frau Linde, Münster, 14 December 1994
Frau Löhr, Münster, 7 January 1995
Frau Ludwig, Herford, 3 April 1995
Frau Mahne, Münster, 20 January 1995
Herr Meyer, Münster, 22 November 1994
Frau Mohr, Münster, 9 January 1995
Frau Müller, Detmold, 18 April 1995
Frau Neske, Detmold, 7 and 9 February 1995
Frau Otto, Münster, 8 November 1994
Frau Peters, Münster, 23 November 1994
Frau Roessner, Münster, 20 November 1994
Frau Rohde, Münster, 21 January 1995 and 15 March 1997
Frau Rott, Münster, 15 March 1997
Frau Schmitt, Detmold, 24 February 1995
Frau Schnabel, Detmold, 28 February 1995
Frau Schumacher, Münster, 28 January 1995
Schwester A., Münster, 17 November 1994
Schwester G., Münster, 17 January 1995
Schwester O., Münster, 20 January 1995
Frau Siebold, Münster, 5 November 1994
Herr Steinke, Münster, 8 December 1994
Herr Sträter, Münster, 8 December 1994
Frau Wolff, interview by Janice Mouton, München, 25 August 1996
Frau Zielert, Münster, 29 November 1994

PUBLISHED SOURCES

Abigail, Eva-Maria. "Eine ganz normale Geschichte." In *Eine Stumme Generation berichtet: Frauen der dreißiger und vierzieger Jahre*, ed. Gisela Dischner, 121–45. Frankfurt am Main: Fischer Taschenbuch, 1982.
Abrams, Lynn. "Restabilisierung der Geschlechterverhältnisse: Die Konstruktion und Repräsentation von Männlichkeit und Weiblichkeit in Scheidungsprozessen des 19. Jahrhunderts." *Westfälische Forschungen* 38 (1989): 9–25.
Adolphy, Erika. "Frauenalltag." In *Provinz unterm Hakenkreuz: Diktatur und Widerstand in Ostwestfalen-Lippe*, ed. Wolfgang Ermer, Uwe Horst, and Helga Schuler-Jung, 227–42. Bielefeld: AJZ Druck und Verlag, 1984.

Albertin, Lothar. "Deutschlands zerstörerische Größe 1933–1945: Stationen der Inhumanität." In *Nationalsozialismus in Detmold*, ed. Hermann Niebuhr and Andreas Ruppert, 21–41. Bielefeld: Aisthesis Verlag, 1998.

Allen, Ann Taylor. *Feminism and Motherhood in Germany, 1890–1914.* New Brunswick: Rutgers University Press, 1991.

———. "Children between Public and Private Worlds: The Kindergarten and Public Policy in Germany, 1840–Present." In *Kindergartens and Cultures: The Global Diffusion of an Idea*, ed. Roberta Wollons, 16–41. New Haven: Yale University Press, 2000.

———. "Feminism and Eugenics in Germany and Britain, 1900–1940: A Comparative Perspective." *German Studies Review* 23, no. 3 (October 2000): 477–505.

Allen, William Sheridan. *The Nazi Seizure of Power: The Experience of a Single German Town, 1922–1945.* New York: Orchard, 1984.

Aly, Götz. "Medicine against the Useless." In *Cleansing the Fatherland: Nazi Medicine and Racial Hygiene*, ed. Aly Götz, Peter Chroust, and Christian Pross, trans. Belinda Cooper, 22–98. Baltimore: John Hopkins University Press, 1994.

Aly, Götz, Peter Chroust, and Christian Pross. *Cleansing the Fatherland: Nazi Medicine and Racial Hygiene.* Trans. Belinda Cooper. Baltimore: John Hopkins University Press, 1994.

Aly, Gotz, and Florian Tennstedt. *Fürsorge und Wohlfahrtspflege, 1871–1929.* Vol. 2 of *Geschichte der Armenfürsorge in Deutschland*, ed. Christoph Sachsse and Florian Tennstedt. Stuttgart: Kohlhammer, 1988.

———. *Der Wohlfahrtsstaat im Nationalsozialismus.* Stuttgart: Kohlhammer, 1992.

Angermund, Ralph. *Deutsche Richterschaft, 1919–1945.* Frankfurt am Main: Fischer Taschenbuch, 1990.

Aschoff, Diethard. "Zum jüdischen Vereinswesen in Westfalen." *Westfälische Forschungen* 38 (1984): 127–57.

Augustin, Otto. *Die Ehescheidung im geltenden und im künftigen Recht unter Berücksichtigung der ausländischen Rechte.* Ph.D. diss., Friedrich-Alexander-Universität und Verlag Konrad Triltsche, Würzburg, 1936.

Bajohr, Stefan. "Illegitimacy and the Working Class: Illegitimate Mothers in Brunswick, 1900–1933." In *The German Working Class, 1888–1933: The Politics of Everyday Life*, ed. Richard J. Evans, 142–73. London: Croom Helm, 1982.

Bartov, Omer. "The Conduct of War: Soldiers and the Barbarization of Warfare." In *Resistance against the Third Reich, 1933–1990*, ed. Michael Geyer and John W. Boyer, 39–52. Chicago: University of Chicago Press, 1992.

Bender, Wolfgang. "Die 'NS-Machtergreifung' in Detmold." In *Nationalsozialismus in Detmold*, ed. Hermann Niebuhr and Andreas Ruppert, 233–57. Bielefeld: Aisthesis Verlag, 1998.

Bergen, Doris. *Twisted Cross: The German Christian Movement in the Third Reich.* Chapel Hill: University of North Carolina Press, 1996.

Berghahn, Volker R. *Modern Germany: Society, Economy, and Politics in the Twentieth Century*. Cambridge: Cambridge University Press, 1982.

Bessel, Richard. *Germany after the First World War*. Oxford: Clarendon Press, 1993.

Blank, Melanie. "'Die Schutzmittel wurden meistens unreifen Burschen und Mädels vorgeführt': Sexualaufklärung, Verhütung und §218 während der Weimarer Republik und in den ersten Jahren des Nationalsozialismus in Herford." *Historisches Jahrbuch für den Kreis Herford* (1995): 63–87.

Blasius, Dirk. *Ehescheidung in Deutschland im 19. und 20. Jahrhundert*. Frankfurt am Main: Fischer Taschenbuch Verlag, 1992.

Boberach, Heinz. ed. *Meldungen aus dem Reich*. Hersching: Pawlak Verlag, 1984.

Bock, Gisela. "Racism and Sexism in Nazi Germany: Motherhood, Compulsory Sterilization, and the State." In *When Biology Became Destiny: Women in Weimar and Nazi Germany*, ed. Renate Bridenthal, Atina Grossmann, and Marion Kaplan, 271–96. New York: Monthly Review Press, 1984.

———. *Zwangssterilisation im Nationalsozialismus: Studien zur Rassenpolitik und Frauenpolitik*. Opladen: Westdeutscher Verlag, 1986.

———. "Antinatalism, Maternity and Paternity in National Socialist Racism." In *Nazism and German Society, 1933–1945*, ed. David Crew, 110–40. London: Routledge Press, 1994.

Borscheid, Peter. "Vom Ersten zum Zweiten Weltkrieg (1914–1945)." In *Westfälische Geschichte*, ed. Wilhelm Kohl, 316–438. Düsseldorf: Pädagogischer Verlag Schwann-Bagel GmbH, 1984.

Brehmer, Ilse. "Frauen um 1945–Interpretationen von Biographien in Lippe: Eine lokalhistorische Studie an exemplarischen Beispielen." Unpublished Diplomarbeit, Univeristät Bielefeld, Fakultät für Padagogik, 1994.

Breyvogel, Wilfried, and Thomas Lohmann. "Schultag im Nationalsozialismus." In *Alltag im Nationalsozialismus: Vom Ende der Weimarer Republik bis zum Zweiten Weltkrieg*, ed. Detlev Peukert and Jürgen Reulecke, 199–221. Wupperthal: Peter Hammer Verlag, 1981.

Bridenthal, Renate, Atina Grossmann, and Marion Kaplan. *When Biology Became Destiny: Women in Weimar and Nazi Germany*. New York: Monthly Review Press, 1984.

Bridenthal, Renate, and Claudia Koonz. "Beyond *Kinder, Küche, Kirche*: Weimar Women in Politics and Work." In *When Biology Became Destiny: Women in Weimar and Nazi Germany*, ed. Renate Bridenthal, Atina Grossmann, and Marion Kaplan, 33–65. New York: Monthly Review Press, 1984.

Broszat, Martin. *The Hitler State: The Foundation and Development of the Internal Structure of the Third Reich*. Trans. John W. Hiden. London: Longman, 1981.

Brüggemeier, F. J. "Sounds of Silents: History, Narrative and Life-Recollections." *Poetics* 15 (1986): 5–24.

Bruha, Antonia. *Ich war keine Heldin*. Wien: Europa Verlag, 1984.

Burleigh, Michael, and Wolfgang Wippermann. *The Racial State, 1933–1945.* Cambridge: Cambridge University Press, 1991.

Caplan, Jane. "National Socialism and the Theory of the State." In *Reevaluating the Third Reich*, ed. Thomas Childers and Jane Caplan, 98–113. New York: Holmes and Meier, 1993.

Castell Rüdenhausen, Adelheid Gräfin zu. "'Nicht mitzuleiden, mitzukämpfen sind wir da!' Nationalsozialistische Volkswohlfahrt im Gau Westfalen-Nord." In *Alltag im Nationalsozialismus: Vom Ende der Weimarer Republik bis zum Zweiten Weltkrieg*, ed. Detlev Peukert and Jürgen Reulecke, 223–43. Wupperthal: Peter Hammer Verlag, 1981.

Crew, David. "German Socialism, the State and Family Policy, 1918–1933." *Continuity and Change* 1 (1986): 235–63.

———. "Bedürfnisse und Bedürftigkeit: Wohlfahrtsbürokratie und Wohlfahrtsempfänger in der Weimarer Republic, 1919–1933." *Sozialwissenschaftliche Information* 18, no. 1 (1989): 12–19.

———. "'Eine Elternschaft zu Dritt' – Staatliche Eltern? Jugendwohlfahrt und Kontrolle der Familie in der Weimarer Republik, 1919–1932." In *'Sicherheit' und 'Wohlfahrt,'* ed. Alf Lüdtke, 267–94. Frankfurt am Main: Suhrkamp, 1992.

———. "Ambiguities of Modernity: Welfare and the German State from Wilhelm to Hitler." In *Society, Culture, and the State in Germany, 1870–1930*, ed. Geoff Eley, 319–44. Ann Arbor: University of Michigan Press, 1996.

———. "A Social Republic? Social Democrats, Communists, and the Weimar Welfare State, 1919–1933." In *Between Reform and Revolution: Studies in German Socialism and Communism from 1840 to 1990*, ed. David E. Barclay and Eric D. Weitz, 223–49. Providence: Berghahn, 1996.

———. *Germans on Welfare from Weimar to Hitler.* New York: Oxford University Press, 1998.

Czarnowski, Gabriele. *Das kontrollierte Paar: Ehe- und Sexualpolitik im Nationalsozialismus.* Weinheim: Deutscher Studien Verlag, 1991.

Dammer, Susanna. "Kinder, Küche, Kriegsarbeit: Die Schulung der Frauen durch die NS-Frauenschaft." In *Mutterkreuz und Arbeitsbuch*, ed. Frauengruppe Faschismusforschung, 215–45. Frankfurt am Main: Fischer Taschenbuch Verlag, 1981.

Daniel, Ute. *The War Within: German Working-Class Women in the First World War.* Trans. Margaret Ries. Oxford: Berg, 1997.

Dickinson, Edward Ross. "State, Family and Society in Modern Germany: Child Welfare Policy from the Empire to the Federal Republic." Ph.D. diss., University of California, Berkeley, 1991.

———. *The Politics of German Child Welfare from the Empire to the Federal Republic.* Cambridge: Harvard University Press, 1996.

———. "Biopolitics, Fascism, Democracy: Some Reflections on Our Discourse about 'Modernity.'" *Central European History* 37 (2004): 1–48.

Dietrich, Otto. *Das Buch der deutschen Gaue: Fünf Jahre nationalsozialistische Aufbauleistung.* Bayerische Ostmark: Gauverlag Bayerische Ostmark GmbH, 1938.

Diewald-Kerkmann, Gisela. "'Der größte Lumpen im ganzen Land – das ist und bleibt die Denunziationen während der NS-Zeit': Politische Denunziationen während der NS-Zeit." In *Nationalsozialismus in Detmold*, ed. Hermann Niebuhr and Andreas Ruppert, 787–803. Bielefeld: Aisthesis Verlag, 1998.

Dischner, Gisela, ed. *Eine stumme Generation berichtet: Frauen der dreißiger und vierziger Jahre.* Frankfurt am Main: Fischer Taschenbuch Verlag, 1982.

Domansky, Elisabeth. "Militarization and Reproduction in World War One Germany." In *Society, Culture, and the State in Germany, 1870–1930*, ed. Geoff Eley, 427–63. Ann Arbor: University of Michigan Press, 1996.

Donzelot, Jacques. *The Policing of Families*. New York: Pantheon, 1979.

Dördelmann, Katrin. "'Private' Konflikte und staatliches Interesse: Denunziantinnen im nationalsozialistischen Deutschland." *Westfälische Forschungen* 45 (1995): 57–72.

Dreßler, Detlev, Hans Galen, and Spieker Christoph. *Greven, 1918–1950: Republik, NS-Diktatur und Ihre Folgen.* Greven: Verlag Stadt Greven, 1994.

Ebbinghaus, Angelika. *Opfer und Täterinnen.* Frankfurt am Main: Fischer Taschenbuch Verlag, 1996.

Eifert, Christiane. *Frauenpolitik und Wohlfahrtspflege: Zur Geschichte der sozialdemokratischen 'Arbeiterwohlfahrt.'* Frankfurt am Main: Campus Verlag, 1993.

Evans, Richard. *The Feminist Movement in Germany, 1894–1933.* London: Sage, 1976.

———. *Rethinking German History.* London: Unwin Hyman, 1987.

Feuchtwanger, E. J. *From Weimar to Hitler: Germany, 1918–1933.* 2nd ed. New York: St. Martin's Press, 1995.

Fischer, Otto, and Eugen Ebert, eds. *Bürgerliches Gesetzbuch.* München: Beck'sche Verlag, 1927.

Frei, Norbert. "Wie modern war der Nationalsozialismus?" *Geschichte und Gesellschaft* 19 (1993): 367–86.

———. "People's Community and War: Hitler's Popular Support." In *The Third Reich Between Vision and Reality: New Perspectives on German History, 1918–1945*, ed. Hans Mommsen, 59–77. Oxford: Berg, 2001.

Frevert, Ute. *Women in German History: From Bourgeois Emancipation to Sexual Liberation.* Trans. Stuart McKinnon-Evans. New York: Berg, 1989.

Fuchs, Rachel. *Poor and Pregnant in Paris: Strategies for Survival in the Nineteenth Century.* New Brunswick: Rutgers University Press, 1992.

Geary, Dick. "Unemployment and Working-Class Solidarity: The German Experience, 1929–1933." In *The German Unemployed: Experiences and Consequences of Mass Unemployment from the Weimar Republic to the Third Reich*, ed. Richard J. Evans and Dick Geary, 761–80. New York: St. Martin's Press, 1987.

Geiger, Susan. "What's So Feminist about Doing Women's Oral History?" In *Expanding the Boundaries of Women's History: Essays on Women in the Third World*, ed. Cheryl Johnson-Odin and Margaret Strobel, 305–18. Bloomington: Indiana University Press, 1992.

Gellately, Robert. *The Gestapo and German Society: Enforcing Racial Policy, 1933–1945*. Oxford: Clarendon Press, 1980.

———. *Backing Hitler: Consent and Coercion in Nazi Germany*. Oxford: Oxford University Press, 2001.

Gellately, Robert, and Nathan Stoltzfus. *Social Outsiders in Nazi Germany*. Princeton: Princeton University Press, 2001.

Geyer, Michael, and John W. Boyer, eds. *Resistance against the Third Reich, 1933–1990*. Chicago: University of Chicago Press, 1992.

Gluck, Sherna Berger, and Daphne Patai, eds. *Women's Words: The Feminist Practice of Oral History*. New York: Routledge, 1991.

Goldman, Wendy Z. *Women, The State and Revolution: Soviet Family Policy and Social Life, 1917–1936*. Cambridge: Cambridge University Press, 1993.

Gordon, Linda. *Heroes of Their Own Lives: The Politics and History of Family Violence, Boston, 1880–1920*. New York: Viking, 1988.

———. *Pitied but Not Entitled: Single Mothers and the History of Welfare*. New York: Free Press, 1994.

———. "Putting Children First: Women, Maternalism, and Welfare in the Early Twentieth Century." In *U.S. History as Women's History: New Feminist Essays*, ed. Linda Kerber, Alice Kessler-Harris, and Kathryn Kish Sklar, 63–86. Chapel Hill: University of North Carolina Press, 1995.

Grossmann, Atina. "The New Woman and the Rationalization of Sexuality in Weimar Germany." In *Powers of Desire: The Politics of Sexuality*, ed. Ann Snitow, Christine Stansell, and Sharon Thompson, 153–71. New York: Monthly Review Press, 1983.

———. "Abortion and Economic Crisis: The 1931 Campaign against Paragraph 218." In *When Biology Became Destiny: Women in Weimar and Nazi Germany*, ed. Renate Bridenthal, Atina Grossmann, and Marion Kaplan, 66–86. New York: Monthly Review Press, 1984.

———. *Reforming Sex: The German Movement for Birth Control and Abortion Reform, 1920–1950*. Oxford: Oxford University Press, 1995.

———. "German Communism and New Women: Dilemmas and Contradictions." In *Women and Socialism, Socialism and Women: Europe Between the Two World Wars*, ed. Helmut Gruber and Pamela Graves, 135–68. New York: Berghahn, 1998.

Gubar, Susan. "'This Is My Rifle, This Is My Gun': World War II and the Blitz on Women." In *Behind The Lines*, ed. Patrice Higonnet, Jane Jenson, and Sonya Michel, 227–59. New Haven: Yale University Press, 1989.

Guggemoos, Dr. Georg. "Schutz der Kinder aus zerrütteten Ehen." *Caritas*. Caritasverband, Caritasverlag, Freiburg im Br. Heft 10, 1927 (309).

Hachtmann, Rüdiger. "Industriearbeiterinnen in der deutschen Kriegswirtschaft 1936 bis 1944/45." *Geschichte und Gesellschaft* 19 (1993): 332–66.

Hagemann, Karen. *Frauenalltag und Männerpolitik: Alltagsleben und gesellschaftliches Handeln von Arbeiterfrauen in der Weimarer Republik.* Bonn: Verlag J. H. W. Dietz, 1990.

Hansen, Eckhart. *Wohlfahrtspolitik im NS-Staat: Motivationen, Konflikte und Machtstrukturen im 'Sozialismus der Tat' des Dritten Reiches.* Augsburg: Maro Verlag, 1991.

Hartmann, Jürgen. "Die KPD in Detmold." In *Nationalsozialismus in Detmold*, ed. Hermann Niebuhr and Andreas Ruppert, 773–86. Bielefeld: Aisthesis Verlag, 1998.

Harvey, Elizabeth. *Youth and the Welfare State in Weimar Germany.* Oxford: Clarendon Press, 1993.

Hausen, Karin. "Mother's Day in the Weimar Republic." In *When Biology Became Destiny: Women in Weimar and Nazi Germany*, ed. Renate Bridenthal, Atina Grossmann, and Marion Kaplan, 131–52. New York: Monthly Review Press, 1984.

———. "Mothers, Sons, and the Sale of Symbols and Goods: The 'German Mother's Day,' 1923–33." In *Interest and Emotion: Essays on the Study of Family and Kinship*, ed. Hans Medick and David Sabean, 371–413. Cambridge: Cambridge University Press, 1984.

———. "Unemployment Also Hits Women: The New and the Old Woman on the Dark Side of the Golden Twenties." In *Unemployment and the Great Depression in Weimar Germany*, ed. Peter Stachura, 78–111. New York: St. Martin's Press, 1986.

Heineman, Elizabeth. *What Difference Does a Husband Make? Women and Marital Status in Nazi and Postwar Germany.* Berkeley: University of California Press, 1999.

———. "Sexuality and Nazism: The Doubly Unspeakable?" *Journal of the History of Sexuality* 11 (2002): 22–66.

Herzog, Dagmar. "Hubris and Hypocrisy, Incitement and Disavowal: Sexuality and German Fascism." *Journal of the History of Sexuality* 11 (2002): 3–21.

Hitler, Adolf. *Mein Kampf.* Trans. Ralph Manheim. Boston: Houghton Mifflin, 1971.

Hockerts, Hans Guenter, ed. *Drei Wege deutscher Sozialstaatlichkeit: NS-Diktatur, Bundesrepublik und DDR im Vergleich.* München: R. Oldenbourg Verlag, 1998.

Holzhauer, Heinz. "Die Scheidungsgründe in der nationalsozialistischen Familienrechtsgesetzgebung." In *NS-Recht in Historischer Perspektiv*, 53–70. München: R. Oldenbourg Verlag, 1981.

Hong, Young-Sun. "The Contradictions of Modernization in the German Welfare State: Gender and the Politics of Welfare Reform in First World War Germany." *Social History* 17 (May 1992): 251–70.

———. "World War I and the German Welfare State: Gender, Religion, and the Paradoxes of Modernity." In *Society, Culture, and the State Germany, 1870–1930*, ed. Geoff Eley, 345–69. Ann Arbor: University of Michigan Press, 1996.

———. "Gender, Citizenship, and the Welfare State: Social Work and the Politics of Femininity in the Weimar Republic." *Central European History* 30, no. 1 (1997): 1–24.

———. *Welfare, Modernity, and the Weimar State, 1919–1933.* Princeton: Princeton University Press, 1998.

Huerkamp, Claudia. *Bildungsbürgerinnen: Frauen im Studium und in akademischen Berufen, 1900–1945.* Göttingen: Vandenhoeck and Ruprecht, 1996.

Hufschmidt, Anke. "Detmolder Sozialdemokraten zwischen Widerstand und Anpassung." In *Nationalsozialismus in Detmold,* ed. Hermann Niebuhr and Andreas Ruppert, 753–72. Bielefeld: Aisthesis Verlag, 1998.

Jarausch, Konrad. *The Unfree Professions: German Lawyers, Teachers, and Engineers, 1900–1950.* New York: Oxford University Press, 1990.

Johnson, Eric. *Nazi Terror: The Gestapo, Jews, and Ordinary Germans.* New York: Basic Books, 1999.

Kaplan, Marion. *Between Dignity and Despair: Jewish Life in Nazi Germany.* Oxford: Oxford University Press, 1998.

Kappelhoff, Hagen. "Organisation und Tätigkeit der Nationalsozialistischen Volkswohlfahrt (NSV) im Gau Westfalen-Nord, 1933–1939." Unpublished Magisterarbeit der Philosophischen Fakultät, Westfälische Wilhelms-Universität, Münster, 1986.

Kaufmann, Doris. *Katholisches Milieu im Münster, 1928–1933: Politische Aktions-formen und geschlechtspezifische Verhaltensräume.* Düsseldorf: Schwann Verlag, 1984.

———. "Die Begründung und Politik einer evangelischen Frauenbewegung in der Weimarer Republik." In *Frauenmacht in der Geschichte: Beiträge des Historikerin-nentreffens 1985 zur Frauengeschichtsforschung,* ed. Jutta Dalhoff, Uschi Frey, and Ingrid Scholl, 380–89. Düsseldorf: Schwann Verlag, 1986.

Kempowski, Walter. *Das Echolot: Ein kollektives Tagebuch.* 4 vols. München: Albrecht Knaus Verlag, 1993.

Kershaw, Ian. *Hitler 1889–1936: Hubris.* New York: Norton, 1998.

Kintner, Hallie. "Trends and Regional Differences in Breastfeeding in Germany, 1871–1937." *Journal of Family History* 10, no. 2 (Summer 1985): 163–82.

Kirkpatrick, Clifford. *Nazi Germany: Its Women and Family Life.* Indianapolis: Bobbs-Merrill, 1938.

Kjendsli, Veslemoy. *Kinder der Schande: Ein Lebensborn Mädchen auf der Suche nach ihrer Vergangenheit.* Trans. from Norwegian by Gabriele Haefs. Hamburg: Luchterhand Literaturverlag, 1992.

Klein, Herbert. "Der Weg zur Macht: Nationalsozialisten in Münster." In *"Wer seine Geschichte nicht kennt . . ." Nationalsozialismus und Münster,* ed. Iris Horstmann, Ulrike Junker, Katrin Klusmann, and Bernd Ostendorf, 13–25. Münster: Agenda Verlag, 1993.

Klinksiek, Dorothee. *Die Frau im NS-Staat.* Schriftenreihe der Vierteljahrshefte für Zeitgeschichte, no. 44. vol. 2. Stuttgart: Deutsch Verlags-Anstalt, 1982.

Knobelsdorf, Andreas. "Das Bielefelder Landgericht, 1933–1945." *Juristischer Zeitgeschichte* 1 (1993): 47–101.

Koch, H. W. *In the Name of the Volk: Political Justice in Hitler's Germany.* London: I. B. Tauris, 1989.

Könke, Günther. "'Modernisierungsschub' oder relative Stagnation? Einige Anmerkungen zum Verhältnis von Nationalsozialismus und Moderne." *Geschichte und Gesellschaft* 20 (1994): 384–608.

Koonz, Claudia. *Mothers in the Fatherland.* New York: St. Martin's Press, 1987.

———. "Ethical Dilemmas and Nazi Eugenics: Single-Issue Dissent in Religious Contexts." In *Resistance against the Third Reich, 1933–1990,* ed. Michael Geyer and John W. Boyer, 15–38. Chicago: University of Chicago Press, 1992.

———. *The Nazi Conscience.* Cambridge: Harvard University Press, 2003.

Koshar, Rudy. *Social Life, Local Politics, and Nazism: Marburg, 1880–1935.* Chapel Hill: University of North Carolina Press, 1986.

Kramer, Helgard. "Frankfurt's Working Women: Scapegoats or Winners of the Great Depression?" In *The German Unemployed: Experiences and Consequences of Mass Unemployment from the Weimar Republic to the Third Reich,* ed. Richard J. Evans and Dick Geary, 108–141. New York: St. Martin's Press, 1987.

Kühlmann, Carola. *Erbkrank oder erziehbar? Jugendhilfe als Vorsorge und Aussonderung in der Fürsorgeerziehung in Westfalen von 1933–1945.* Weinheim: Juventa Verlag, 1989.

Kundrus, Birthe. *Kriegerfrauen: Familienpolitik und Geschlechterverhältnisse im Ersten und Zweiten Weltkrieg.* Hamburg: Hans Christians Verlag, 1995.

———. "Forbidden Company: Romantic Relationships between Germans and Foreigners, 1939–1945." *Journal of the History of Sexuality* 11 (2002): 201–22.

Kunzel, Regina. *Fallen Women, Problem Girls: Unmarried Mothers and the Professionalization of Social Work.* New Haven: Yale University Press, 1993.

Kuropka, Joachim. *Meldungen aus Münster, 1924–1944.* Münster: Verlag Regensberg, 1992.

———. "Münster in der nationalsozialistischen Zeit." In *Geschichte der Stadt Münster,* ed. Franz-Josef Jakobi, 285–330. Münster: Aschendorff Verlag, 1993.

Lifton, Robert Jay. *The Nazi Doctors: Medical Killing and the Psychology of Genocide.* New York: Basic Books, 1986.

Lilienthal, Georg. *Der 'Lebensborn e. V.': Ein Instrument nationalsozialistischer Rassenpolitik.* Frankfurt am Main: Fischer Verlag, 1993.

Lüdtke, Alf. "Introduction: What Is the History of Everyday Life and Who Are Its Practitioners?" In *The History of Everyday Life: Reconstructing Historical Experiences and Ways of Life,* ed. Alf Lüdtke, 3–40. Princeton: Princeton University Press, 1995.

Mallmann, Klaus-Michael, and Gerhard Paul. "Omniscient, Omnipotent, Omnipresent? Gestapo, Society, and Resistance." In *Nazism and German Society, 1933–1945,* ed. David Crew, 166–96. London: Routledge, 1994.

Marx, Cordula. "Die Katholische Gemeinde in Detmold, 1933–1945." In *Nation-alsozialismus in Detmold*, ed. Hermann Niebuhr and Andreas Ruppert, 697–722. Bielefeld: Aisthesis Verlag, 1998.

May, Elaine Tyler. *Great Expectations: Marriage and Divorce in Post-Victorian America*. Chicago: University of Chicago Press, 1980.

McFarland-Icke, Bronwyn Rebekah. *Nurses in Nazi Germany: Moral Choice in History*. Princeton: Princeton University Press, 1999.

Mommsen, Hans. *From Weimar to Auschwitz: Essays on German History*. Trans. Philip O'Connor. Princeton: Princeton University Press, 1991.

———. "Generational Conflict and Youth Rebellion in the Weimar Republic." In *From Weimar to Auschwitz: Essays on German History*, trans. Philip O'Connor, 28–38. Princeton: Princeton University Press, 1991.

———. "Social Democracy on the Defensive: The Immobility of the SPD and the Rise of National Socialism." In *From Weimar to Auschwitz: Essays on German History*, trans. Philip O'Connor, 39–61. Princeton: Princeton University Press, 1991.

———. "Noch einmal: Nationalsozialismus und Modernisierung." *Geschichte und Gesellschaft* 21 (1995): 391–402.

———. *The Rise and Fall of Weimar Democracy*. Trans. Elborg Forster and Larry Eugene Jones. Chapel Hill: University of North Carolina Press, 1996.

Mommsen, Hans, and Manfred Grieger. *Das Volkswagenwerk und seine Arbeiter im Dritten Reich*. Düsseldorf: Econ Verlag, 1996.

Mosse, George. *Nationalism and Sexuality: Middle-Class Morality and Sexual Norms in Modern Europe*. Madison: University of Wisconsin Press, 1985.

Mouton, Michelle. "Sports, Song, and Socialization: Women's Memories of Youthful Activity and Political Indoctrination in the BDM." *Journal of Women's History* 17, no. 2 (2005): 62–86.

———. "Rescuing Children and Policing Families: Adoption Policy in Weimar and Nazi Germany." *Central European History* 38, no. 4 (December 2005): 545–71.

Mouton, Michelle, and Helena Pohlandt-McCormick. "Boundary Crossings: Oral History of Nazi Germany and Apartheid South Africa – A Comparative Perspective." *History Workshop Journal* 48 (1999): 41–63.

Müller, Ingo. *Hitler's Justice: The Courts of the Third Reich*. Trans. Deborah Lucas Schneider. Cambridge: Harvard University Press, 1991.

Niermann, Hans-Eckhard. "Die Durchsetzung politischer und politisierter Strafjustiz im Dritten Reich: Ihre Entwicklung aufgezeigt am Beispiel des OLG-Bezirks Hamm." *Juristische Zeitgeschichte* 3 (1995): 1–390.

Niethammer, Lutz ed. *Die Jahre weiß man nicht . . . Faschismuserfahrungen im Ruhrgebiet*. Berlin: Verlag J. H. W. Dietz, 1986.

Noakes, Jeremy, ed. *The German Home Front in World War II: A Documentary Reader*, vol. 4 of *Nazism, 1919–1945: A History in Documents and Eyewitness Accounts*, ed. Jeremy Noakes and Geoffrey Pridham. Exeter: University of Exeter Press, 1998.

Nolan, Mary. *Visions of Modernity: American Business and the Modernization of Germany*. Oxford: Oxford University Press, 1994.

————. "Rationalization, Racism, and *Resistenz*: Recent Studies of Work and the Working Class in Nazi Germany." *International Labor and Working-Class History* 48 (Fall 1995): 131–51.

Ortmayr, Norbert, ed. *Knechte: Autobiographische Dokumente und sozialhistorische Skizzen*. Wien: Böhlau Verlag, 1992.

Overy, Richard J. *War and the Economy in the Third Reich*. Oxford: Clarendon Press, 1994.

Passerini, Luisa. "Women's Personal Narratives: Myths, Experiences, and Emotions." In *Interpreting Women's Lives: Feminist Theory and Personal Narratives*, ed. Personal Narratives Group, 189–97. Bloomington: Indiana University Press, 1989.

————. "Introduction." In *Memory and Totalitarianism*, vol. 1 of the *International Yearbook of Oral History and Life Stories*. Oxford: Oxford University Press, 1992.

Pederson, Susan. *Family, Dependence, and the Origins of the Welfare State: Britain and France, 1914–1945*. Cambridge: Cambridge University Press, 1993.

Personal Narratives Group, ed. *Interpreting Women's Lives: Feminist Theory and Personal Narratives*. Bloomington: Indiana University Press, 1989.

Peterson, Johannes. " 'Systematische Arbeit muß anstelle der Zufallsarbeit treten': Historische und Analytische Aspekte der Entwicklung kommunaler Jugendbehörden." In *Waisenhäuser und Erziehungsanstalten in Westfalen*, ed. Christian Schrapper and Dieter Sengling, 187–211. Münster: LIT Verlag, 1985.

Peukert, Detlev. *Grenzen der Sozialdisziplinierung: Aufstieg und Krise der deutschen Jugendfürsorge, 1878–1932*. Köln: Bund-Verlag, 1986.

————. *Inside Nazi Germany: Conformity, Opposition, and Racism in Everyday Life*. Trans. Richard Deveson. New Haven: Yale University Press, 1987.

————. *The Weimar Republic: The Crisis of Classical Modernity*. Trans. Richard Deveson. New York: Hill and Wang, 1989.

————. "The Genesis of the 'Final Solution' from the Spirit of Science." In *Nazism and German Society, 1933–1945*, ed. David Crew, 274–99. London: Routledge, 1994.

Phayer, Michael. *Protestant and Catholic Women in Nazi Germany*. Detroit: Wayne State University Press, 1990.

Picker, Henry. "Das uneheliche Kind im deutschen Recht." *Zentralblatt für Jugendrecht und Jugendwohlfahrt* 27 (1935).

Pine, Lisa. *Nazi Family Policy, 1933–1945*. Oxford: Berg, 1997.

Pohl, Dieter. "The Murder of Jews in the General Government." In *National Socialist Extermination Policies: Contemporary German Perspectives and Controversies*, ed. Ulrich Herbert, 83–103. New York: Berghahn, 2000.

Pöppinghege, Rainer. " 'Keinerlei weltanschauliche Hemmungen': Zur Anpassungsbereitschaft der Justiz." In *"Wer seine Geschichte nicht kennt ... "*

Nationalsozialismus und Münster, ed. Iris Horstmann, Ulrike Junker, Katrin Klusmann, and Bernd Ostendorf, 172–92. Münster: Agenda Verlag, 1993.

Portelli, Alessandro. "The Peculiarities of Oral History." *History Workshop Journal* 12 (1981): 96–107.

———. *The Death of Luigi Trastulli and Other Stories: Form and Meaning in Oral History*. Albany: State University of New York Press, 1991.

Proctor, Robert. *Racial Hygiene: Medicine under the Nazis*. Cambridge: Harvard University Press, 1988.

Pross, Christopher. "Introduction." In *Cleansing the Fatherland: Nazi Medicine and Racial Hygiene*, ed. Götz Aly, Peter Chroust, and Christian Pross, 1–21. Trans. Belinda Cooper. Baltimore: John Hopkins University Press, 1994.

Ramm, Thilo. *Das nationalsozialistische Familien- und Jugendrecht*. Heidelberg: R. v. Decker and C. F. Müller, 1984.

Reagin, Nancy. *A German Woman's Movement: Class and Gender in Hanover, 1880–1933*. Chapel Hill: University of North Carolina Press, 1995.

Reese, Dagmar. "Bund Deutscher Mädel: Zur Geschichte der weiblichen deutschen Jugend im Dritten Reich." In *Mutterkreuz und Arbeitsbuch: Zur Geschichte der Frauen in der Weimarer Republik und im Nationalsozialismus*, ed. Frauengruppe Faschismusforschung. Frankfurt am Main: Fischer Taschenbuch, 1981.

———. *Straff, aber nicht stramm–herb, aber nicht derb: Zur Vergesellschaftung von Mädchen durch den Bund Deutscher Mädel im sozialkulturellen Vergleich zweier Milieus*. Weinheim: Beltz Verlag, 1989.

Renner, Hedwig, "Aus Unserer Adoptionsabteilung," *Helferde Härde: Blätter für freiwilligen Dienst in der Jugendfürsorge* 5, nos. 2–3 (June 1921): 30–1.

Reulecke, Jürgen. "Männerbund versus the Family: Middle-Class Youth Movements and the Family in Germany in the Period of the First World War." In *The Upheaval of War*, ed. Richard Wall and Jay Winter, 439–52. Cambridge: Cambridge University Press, 1991.

Rinderle, Walter, and Bernard Norling. *The Nazi Impact on a German Village*. Lexington: University of Kentucky Press, 1993.

Ritter, Gerhard. *Europa und die deutsche Frage: Betrachtungen über die geschichtliche Eigenart des deutschen Staatsdenkens*. München: Münchner Verlag, 1948.

Rosenberg, Alfred. *Der Mythos des 20. Jahrhundert: Eine Wertung der Seelisch-geistigen Gestaltenkämpfe unserer Zeit*. Munich, 1934.

Rouette, Susanne. *Sozialpolitik als Geschlechterpolitik: Die Regulierung der Frauenarbeit nach dem Ersten Weltkrieg*. Frankfurt am Main: Campus Verlag, 1993.

———. "Mothers and Citizens: Gender and Social Policy in Germany after the First World War." *Central European History* 30, no. 1 (1997): 48–65.

Ruppert, Andreas. "Die Ortsgruppe Detmold der NSDAP, 1925–1934." In *Nationalsozialismus in Detmold*, ed. Hermann Niebuhr and Andreas Ruppert, 203–32. Bielefeld: Aisthesis Verlag, 1998.

Sachse, Carola. "Hausarbeit im Betrieb: Betriebliche Sozialarbeit unter dem Nationalsozialismus." In *Angst, Belohnung, Zucht und Ordnung: Herrschaftsmechanismus im*

Nationalsozialismus, ed. Carola Sachße, Tilla Siegel, Hasso Spode, and Wolfgang Spohn, 209–74. Opladen: Westdeutscher Verlag, 1982.

———. *Siemens, der Nationalsozialismus und die moderne Familie: Eine Untersuchung zur sozialen Rationalisierung in Deutschland im 20. Jahrhundert.* Hamburg: Rasch und Röhring Verlag, 1990.

Sachße, Christoph. *Mütterlichkeit als Beruf: Sozialarbeit, Sozialreform und Frauenbewegung, 1871–1929.* Frankfurt am Main: Suhrkamp Verlag, 1986.

———. "Social Mothers: The Bourgeois Women's Movement and German Welfare State Formation, 1890–1929." In *Mothers of a New World: Maternalist Politics and the Origins of Welfare States*, ed. Seth Koven and Sonya Michel, 136–58. New York: Routledge, 1993.

Sachße, Christoph, and Florian Tennestedt. *Der Wohlfahrtsstaat im Nationalsozialismus.* Stuttgart: Kohlhammer, 1992.

Schäfer, Ingrid. "Verborgene Welten–Frauenleben in Vahlhausen: ein Beitrag zur regionalen Frauengeschichte von 1920–1950." In *Vahlhausen: Alltag in einem Lippischen Dorf, 1900–1950*, ed. Günther Hammer, Ingrid Schäfer, and Jürgen Scheffler, 107–59. Detmold: Lippischer Heimatbund e.V., 1987.

Schaumann, Remco. "Im permanenten Gleichschritt: Der 1. Mai 1933 als 'Tag der nationalen Arbeit' im Herford." In *Historisches Jahrbuch für den Kreis Herford* 1995: 123–36.

Schlögl, Rudolf, Michael Schwartz, and Hans-Ulrich Thamer. "Konsens, Konflikt und Repression: Zur Sozialgeschichte des politischen Verhaltens in der NS-Zeit." In *Zwischen Loyalität und Resistenz: Soziale Konflikte und politische Repression während der NS-Herrschaft in Westfalen*, ed. Rudolf Schlögl and Hans-Ulrich Thamer, 9–30. Münster: Achendorff Verlag, 1996.

Schnurr, Stefan. "Why Did Social Workers Accept the New Order?" In *Education and Fascism: Political Identity and Social Education in Nazi Germany*, ed. Heinz Sünker and Hans-Uwe Otto, 121–43. London: Falmer Press, 1997.

Schoenbaum, David. *Hitler's Social Revolution: Class and Status in Nazi Germany, 1933–1945.* New York: Norton, 1980.

Schröder, Hugo. *Das Problem der Unehelichen.* Leipzig: Kabitzsch, 1924.

Schücking, Ursula. "Annahme an Kindes Statt: Die Weiterentwicklung der gesetzlichen Grundlagen seit 1933." *Deutsches Recht* 49 (December 1941).

Schütte, Leopold. "Politisch zuverlässig? Eine Notarserkennung in Altena im Jahre 1935." *Der Märker: Landeskundliche Zeitschrift für den Bereich der ehemaligen Grafschaft Mark und den Märkischen Kreis* 39 (1990): 87–95.

Scott, Jutta K. "Governmental Laws and Family Matters: Elements of Continuity and Change in German Family Policy, 1871–1963." Ph.D. diss., Indiana University, 1992.

Shapiro, Raya Czerner, and Helga Cezerner Weinberg. *One Family's Letters from Prague, 1939–1941.* Chicago: Academy Chicago Publishers, 1991.

Siegel, Elisabeth. *Dafür und Dagegen: Ein Leben für die Sozialpädagogik.* Stuttgart: Radius Verlag, 1981.

Siegel, Mark A. "The National Socialist People's Welfare Organization, 1933–1939: The Political Manipulation of Welfare." Ph.D. diss., University of Cincinnati, 1976.

Sneeringer, Julia. *Winning Women's Votes: Propaganda and Politics in Weimar Germany.* Chapel Hill: University of North Carolina Press, 2001.

Soland, Birgitte. "Gender and the Social Order: Danish Women in the 1920s." Ph.D. diss., University of Minnesota, 1994.

Solinger, Rickie. *Wake Up Little Susie: Single Pregnancy and Race Before Roe vs. Wade.* New York: Routledge, 1992.

Southern, David B. "The Impact of the Inflation: Inflation, the Courts and Reevaluation." In *Social Change and Political Development in Weimar Germany*, ed. Richard Bessel and E. J. Feuchtwanger, 55–76. London: Croom Helm, 1981.

Stadt Museum Münster. *Bomben auf Münster.* Münster: Aschendorff Verlag, 1983.

Statistisches Jahrbuch für das Deutsche Reich. Vols. 46–59 (1927–1942). Berlin: Puttkammer und Mühlbrecht.

Statistisches Jahrbuch für den Freistaat Preussen. Vols. 27–29 (1931–1933). Berlin: Verlag des Preussischen Statistischen Landesamts.

Statistisches Jahrbuch für den Preussischen Staat. Vols. 17–26 (1921–1930). Berlin: Verlag des Königlichen Statistischen Landesamts.

Statistik des Deutschen Reiches. Vol. 554 (1943). Berlin: Verlag Sozialpolitik, Wirtschaft und Statistik.

Stephenson, Jill. "'Reichsbund der Kinderreichen': The League of Large Families in the Population Policy of Nazi Germany." *European Studies Review* 9 (1979): 351–75.

Sternheim-Peters, Eva. *Die Zeit der Grossen Täuschungen: Eine Jugend im Nationalsozialismus.* Bielefeld: Verlag Wissenschaft und Politik, 1992.

Stoehr, Irene. "Housework and Motherhood: Debates and Policies in the Women's Movement in Imperial Germany and the Weimar Republic." In *Maternity and Gender Policies: Women and the Rise of European Welfare States, 1880s–1950s*, ed. Gisela Bock and Pat Thane, 213–32. London: Routledge, 1991.

Sünker, Heinz, and Hans-Uwe Otto. "Social Work as Social Education." In *Education and Fascism: Political Identity and Social Education in Nazi Germany*, ed. Heinz Sünker and Hans-Uwe Otto, 144–60. London: Falmer, 1997.

Teichman, Jenny. *Illegitimacy: An Examination of Bastardy.* New York: Cornell University Press, 1982.

Teppe, Karl. *Provinz, Partei, Staat: Zur provinziellen Selbstverwaltung im Dritten Reich untersucht am Beispiel Westfalens.* Münster: Verlag Regensberg, 1992.

Trevor-Roper, Hugh, trans. *Hitler's Table Talk, 1941–1944: His Private Conversations.* New York: Enigma, 2000.

Trütken-Kirsch, Heinz-Jürgen. "Die Landgemeinde Schale und der Nationalsozialismus: Von der Allianz zum partiellen Dissens." *Jahrbuch für Westfälische Kirchengeschichte* 85 (1991): 347–61.

Turner, Shari. *The Myths of Motherhood: How Culture Reinvents the Good Mother.* New York: Penguin, 1994.

Usborne, Cornelia. "'Pregnancy Is the Woman's Active Service': Pronatalism in Germany during the First World War." In *The Upheaval of War: Family, Work, and Welfare*, ed. Richard Wall and Jay Winter, 389–416. Cambridge: Cambridge University Press, 1988.

———. *The Politics of the Body: Women's Reproductive Rights and Duties.* Ann Arbor: University of Michigan Press, 1992.

———. "The New Woman and Generational Conflict: Perceptions of Young Women's Sexual Mores in the Weimar Republic." In *Generations in Conflict: Youth Revolt and Generation Formation in Germany, 1770–1968*, ed. Mark Roseman, 137–63. Cambridge: Cambridge University Press, 1995.

Vedder-Schults, Nancy. "Motherhood for the Fatherland: The Portrayal of Women in Nazi Propaganda." Ph.D. diss., University of Wisconsin, 1982.

Vogelsang, Reinhard. *Im Zeichen des Hakenkreuzes: Bielefeld, 1933–1945.* Bielefeld: Stadarchiv Landesgeschichtliche Bibliothek, 1986.

Von Saldern, Adelheid. "Victims or Perpetrators? Controversies about the Role of Women in the Nazi State." In *Nazism and German Society, 1933–1945*, ed. David Crew, 141–65. London: Routledge, 1994.

Von Scanzoni, Gustav, commentator. *Das Großdeutsche Ehegesetz vom 6. Juli 1938.* Berlin: Verlag Franz Vahlen, 1943.

Von Soden, Kristine. *Die Sexualberatungsstellen der Weimarer Republik, 1919–1933.* Berlin: Druckhaus Hentrich Verlag, 1988.

Vossen, Johannes. "Gesundheitsämter im Kreis Herford während der NS-Zeit: Die Durchsetzung der 'Erb- und Rassenpflege.'" In *Historisches Jahrbuch für den Kreis Herford*, ed. Kreisheimatverein Herford, 89–118. Bielefeld: Verlag für Regionalgeschichte, 1992.

Wagner, 'Die Reformbestrebungen zur Neugestaltung des Nichtehelichenrechts,' Jur. D., Justus Liebig University, Giessen, 1971, 148.

Webler, Heinrich. "Einige Zahlen zur Kindesannahme." *Zentralblatt für Jugendrecht und Jugendwohlfahrt* 27 (1935): 277–316.

Wehrmann, Volker, ed. *Lippe im Dritten Reich: Die Erziehung zum Nationalsozialismus; Eine Dokumentation, 1933–1939.* Detmold: Topp und Müller, 1987.

Weindling, Paul. *Health, Race and German Politics between National Unification and Nazism, 1870–1945.* Cambridge: Cambridge University Press, 1989.

Weitz, Eric. *Creating German Communism, 1890–1990: From Popular Protests to Socialist State.* Princeton: Princeton University Press, 1997.

Weyrather, Irmgard. *Muttertag und Mutterkreuz.* Frankfurt: Fischer Taschenbuch Verlag, 1993.

Whalen, Robert Weldon. *Bitter Wounds: German Victims of the Great War, 1914–1939.* Ithaca: Cornell University Press, 1984.

Wildt, Michael. "Gewalt gegen Juden in Deutschland 1933 bis 1939." *Werkstatt Geschichte* 18 (1997): 59–80.

Winkler, Dörte. *Frauenarbeit im 'Dritten Reich.'* Hamburg: Hoffmann und Campe Verlag, 1977.

Winter, Gerd. *Sozialer Wandel durch Rechtsnormen erörtert an der sozialen Stellung unehelicher Kinder.* Berlin: Duncker und Humbolt, 1969.

Wisser, Eva Maria. *Kampfen und Glauben.* Berlin: Steuben Verlag, 1933.

Wittmann, Ingrid. "'Echte Weiblichkeit ist ein Dienen': Die Hausgehilfen in der Weimarer Republik und im Nationalsozialismus." In *Mutterkreuz und Arbeitsbuch: Zur Geschichte der Frauen in der Weimarer Republik und im Nationalsozialismus,* ed. Frauengruppe Faschismus Forschung, 15–34. Frankfurt am Main: Fischer Taschenbuch Verlag, 1981.

Wolff, Jörg. *Jugendliche vor Gericht im Dritten Reich: Nationalsozialistische Jugendstrafrechtspolitik und Justizalltag.* München: C. H. Beck'sche Verlag, 1992.

Wollasch, Andreas. "Von der Bewahrungsidee der Fürsorge zu den 'Jugendkonzentrationslagern' des NS-Staates: Die Debatte um ein Bewahrungsgesetz zwischen 1918 und 1945." In *Jahrbuch des Deutschen Caritasverbandes,* 381–94. Freiburg: Deutscher Caritasverband, 1993.

Woycke, James. *Birth Control in Germany, 1871–1933.* London: Routledge, 1988.

Zeller, Susanne. "Demobilmachung und Geschlechtsspezifische Arbeitsteilung im Fürsorgewesen nach dem Ersten Weltkrieg." In *Frauenmacht in der Geschichte: Beiträge des Historikerinnentreffens 1985 zur Frauengeschichtsforschung,* ed. Jutta Dalhoff, Uschi Frey, and Ingrid Scholl, 282–94. Düsseldorf: Schwann Verlag, 1986.

———. *Volksmütter – mit staatlicher Anerkennung – Frauen im Wohlfahrtswesen der zwanziger Jahre.* Düsseldorf: Schwann Verlag, 1987.

Index